CURRENTS OF ENCOUNTER

Studies on the Contact between Christianity and Other Religions, Beliefs, and Cultures

VOLUME 4

CURRENTS OF ENCOUNTER

GENERAL EDITORS: Rein Fernhout, Jerald D. Gort, Hendrik M. Vroom,
Anton Wessels

──────────── **VOLUMES PUBLISHED OR AT PRESS** ────────────

1   J. D. Gort, et al., eds.   *Dialogue and Syncretism: An Interdisciplinary
Approach* (copublished with Eerdmans)

2   Hendrik M. Vroom   *Religions and the Truth: Philosophical Reflections
and Perspectives* (with Eerdmans)

3   Sutarman S. Partonadi   *Sadradh's Community and its Contextual Roots:
A Nineteenth-Century Javanese Expression of
Christianity*

4   J. D. Gort, et al., eds.   *On Sharing Religious Experience: Possibilities of
Interfaith Mutuality* (with Eerdmans)

5   S. Wesley Ariarajah   *Hindus and Christians: A Century of Protestant
Ecumenical Thought* (with Eerdmans)

6   Makoto Ozaki   *Introduction to the Philosophy of Tanabe,
according to the English Translation of the Seventh
Chapter of the* Demonstratio *of Christianity*

──────────── **VOLUMES NEARING COMPLETION** ────────────

Julio de Santa Ana   *The Church and Human Rights in Latin America*
(with Eerdmans)

Rein Fernhout   *Word of Absolute Authority: A Phenomenological
Study of the Canonicity of the Veda, the Tipiṭaka,
the Bible, and the Koran*

──────────── **FURTHER VOLUMES ARE IN VARIOUS** ────────────
STAGES OF PREPARATION OR PLANNING

Volumes in this series unavailable from Eerdmans are available from Editions
Rodopi, Keizersgracht 302-304, 1016 EX Amsterdam, the Netherlands, or 233
Peachtree Street N.E., Suite 404, Atlanta, GA 30303-1504.

On Sharing Religious Experience

Possibilities of Interfaith Mutuality

edited by

Jerald D. Gort, Hendrik M. Vroom
Rein Fernhout, and Anton Wessels

EDITIONS RODOPI, AMSTERDAM

WILLIAM B. EERDMANS PUBLISHING COMPANY
GRAND RAPIDS, MICHIGAN

This edition first published 1992 jointly by
Wm. B. Eerdmans Publishing Co.
255 Jefferson Ave. S.E., Grand Rapids, MI 49503
and Editions Rodopi, B.V.
Keizersgracht 302-304, 1016 EX Amsterdam, the Netherlands,
and 233 Peachtree Street N.E., Suite 404, Atlanta, GA 30303-1504

Library of Congress Cataloging-in-Publication Data

On sharing religious experience: possibilities of interfaith mutuality /
edited by Jerald D. Gort . . . [et al.].
p.   cm.   — (Currents of encounter; vol.4)
"This volume . . . constitutes the end product of the second international workshop planned
by the Dutch interuniversity Encounter of Religions Research Group and held in April 1990
at the Free University (Vrije Universiteit) of Amsterdam" — Foreword.
Includes indexes.
Eerdmans ISBN 0-8028-0505-1
Rodopi ISBN 90-5183-207-9
1. Experience (Religion) — Congresses. 2. Dialogue — Religious aspects — Congresses.
3. Christianity and other religions — Congresses. 4. Religions — Relations — Congresses.
I. Gort, Jerald D.   II. Encounter of Religions Research Group.   III. Series.
BL53.05   1992
291.1'72 — dc20   91-41817
                                         CIP

Contents

Foreword   vii

Part I   *Can Religious Experiences Be Shared?*

1   Can Religious Experience Be Shared? Introduction to the Theme 'Sharing Religious Experience'   HENDRIK M. VROOM   3

2   Hermeneutics of Religious Experience   GERHARD OBERHAMMER   13

3   Transcendence and Wholeness   WILLEM DUPRÉ   25

4   Meaning, Power, and the Sharing of Religious Experience: An Anthropology of Religion Point of View   ANDRÉ DROOGERS   45

5   Can Believers Share the Qur'an and the Bible as Word of God?   WILFRED CANTWELL SMITH   55

6   Can Faith in the 'Inspiration' of Holy Scripture Be Shared   REIN FERNHOUT   64

7   Religious Experience: Autonomy and Mutuality   LAMIN SANNEH   76

8   Liberative Ecumenism: Gateway to the Sharing of Religious Experience Today   JERALD D. GORT   88

9   The Incomparability of God as Biblical Experience of Faith   WALTER STROLZ   106

10   From Sharing to Encounter   HASAN ASKARI   116

Part II   *Case Studies of Intra- and Interreligious Sharing*

11   What it is like to be a Banzie: On sharing the experience of an Equatorial Microcosm   JAMES W. FERNANDEZ   125

12 Sharing Religious Experience in Hindu–Christian Encounter
    MICHAEL von BRÜCK   136

13 Revelation and Experience in the Theosophic Tradition
    R. KRANENBORG   151

14 Religious Experience and Social Change: The Case of the
    Bangalore Madhvas   CORSTIAAN J. G. van der BURG   163

15 Father Hugo Makibi Enomiya-Lassalle and Zen
    TILMANN VETTER   178

16 Transmitting the Buddhist View of Experience
    HAN F. de WIT   189

17 Can Śūnyatā Be Shared? Religious Experience in Dialogue
    H. WALDENFELS   203

18 Sharing in Japan's *New* New Religions   JACQUES KAMSTRA   215

19 The Experience of the Prophet Mohammed
    ANTON WESSELS   228

20 Sharing Religious Experience as a Problem in Early Islamic
    Mysticism   HANS DAIBER   245

21 The Prayers for Peace at Assisi, October 27, 1986: What was
    Shared?   ARNULF CAMPS   255

Part III *Common Themes and Problems*

22 Sharing Religious Experience: Recapitulation, Comments, and
    Questions   HENDRIK M. VROOM   269

    Index of Names and Authors   285
    General Index of Subjects   291
    List of Contributors   305

Foreword

This volume, the fourth to appear in the series, CURRENTS OF ENCOUNTER: STUDIES ON THE CONTACT BETWEEN CHRISTIANITY AND OTHER RELIGIONS, BELIEFS, AND CULTURES, is devoted to the subject of SHARING RELIGIOUS EXPERIENCE. It constitutes the end product of the second international workshop planned by the Dutch interuniversity Encounter of Religions Research Group and held in April 1990 at the Free University (Vrije Universiteit) of Amsterdam.

As was the case with the previous symposium organized by this research group in 1988, the 1990 workshop was consciously designed to foster the further development and employment of a relatively new and, it is felt, promising methodological approach in and for the area of religious studies, namely, that of what perhaps might best be called *contextual correlation*. Those who took part in the workshop as well as the papers contributed to it and discussed there are representative of both so-called 'normative' as well as commonly termed 'descriptive' academic disciplines. This interdisciplinary arrangement was meant, on the one had, to discourage systematicians from shaping theoretical ideas without reference to a basis in reality and, on the other, to encourage empirically oriented scholars to articulate the philosophical and theological presuppositions and implications of their work.

One of the most important initial questions to be posed relative to the matter of interreligious encounter is that having to do with the very *possibility* of such sharing: Can people really share each other's religious experience? And lying at the heart of this query is the fundamental hermeneutical question as to whether —and if so, in what manner— adherents of differing religious traditions are capable of *understanding* each other. These and other, related questions are addressed in the first section of this symposium in terms of categories and insights derived from the fields of Philosophy of Religion, Anthropology, and Missiology. In the second section of the collection attention is turned to the possibilities and problems of interreligious sharing in the light of actual Hindu–Christian, Buddhist–Christian, and Muslim–Christian encounter.

PART ONE represents a composite of ten essays in which the workshop theme is explored in more or less general terms from a variety of disciplinary perspectives.

In the introductory paper, which was sent to the conference participants in advance for possible use as generative catalyst for their own thinking, **Hendrik M. Vroom** attempts to outline the broad parameters and elaborate the salient aspects of the notion 'sharing religious experience'.

Gerhard Oberhammer, who has delved deeply over the past years into the matter of the hermeneutics of religion, analyzes the nature of religious experience understood as encounter with transcendence and entertains the questions regarding the possibilities of sharing such experience.

Wilhelm Dupré provides a description of human self-awareness and takes into account the cultural embeddedness of human nature. Human beings experience moments of the divine mediated by religious traditions. Dupré argues for the encouragement of groups of people who, by virtue of their active engagement in encounter, form mediating communities within and among religious traditions.

André Droogers addresses the problem of understanding religious traditions from the perspective of cultural anthropology. He presents an in-depth analysis of the formation of meaning and the role of basic human experiences and deals in particular with the inevitable role power plays in all interhuman encounter.

Wilfred Cantwell Smith deals with the possibilities of understanding and sharing the beliefs of others. The specific question he raises and provides a very personal answer to is: Can a Christian experience the Qur'an as the Word of God?

Rein Fernhout compares the way in which holy scriptures have been ascribed divine origins in various religious traditions. Holy scriptures such as the Veda, the Tipiṭaka, the Bible, and the Koran have been received with reverence. Fernhout describes the role played in various traditions by the concept of *inspiration* and relates this to the question of the possibility of sharing faith in holy scriptures.

Lamin Sanneh describes the mystical experience that Shaykh 'Uthmān b. Fūdī or Shehu underwent, an experience which changed his own life and influenced that of many others. Religious experience is the affirmation of the Creator by the creature; through religious mediation life is both received by human beings and given back to God.

Jerald Gort considers in depth whether the attempt to achieve genuine sharing of religious experience might not better begin with shared action on behalf of the poor. Interreligious ecumenism can become more concrete and relevant by replacing any purely discursive content it has by one characterized equally or even primarily by deep concern for the needs of countless fellow human beings.

Walter Strolz deals with the difficult subject of the incomparability of the God of the bible. People should put their trust in God, not idols. Drawing on his long involvement in interreligious encounter, he offers a method for discovering areas of overlap and contrast between religious beliefs.

Hasan Askari is somewhat sceptical about the possibility of sharing religious experience. He opines that it is extremely difficult to gain a proper sense of the 'feel' of another person's 'clothes'. At points at which one's own tradition is weak, however, it should be possible to share in the experiences of those from another tradition. Such sharing presupposes real encounter.

PART TWO comprises a number of case-study examinations of the concept of interreligious sharing.

James Fernandez approaches the theme of the symposium in terms of his field experience with Bwiti, a syncretic religion in Gabon. He describes how, as an anthropologist, he came to an understanding of the customs, culture, and ideas of Bwiti.

Michael von Brück distinguishes between different levels of interreligious encounter: social, emotional, and personal, each of which presents varying possibilities for sharing. He underscores the social character of Hindu religious tradition and the implications this bears for sharing with that tradition.

Reender Kranenborg describes the tradition of unique religious experience within the theosophic movement. H. P. Blavatsky obviously had religious experiences that were not susceptible to sharing by others. On what basis, then, was she able to share her beliefs with other people?

Corstiaan van der Burg relates the story of a Madhva Brahman in South India who tried without success to reform his tradition. Although a measure of ideological change was realized, there were too many social factors operating in the background to effectuate anything like reformation.

Tilmann Vetter directs his attention to the work of Enomiya-Lassalle, who has employed Zen meditation to achieve more contemplative depth. Vetter shows how Lassalle combines his Christian beliefs with Buddhist meditative practice; he then applies this example to interreligious encounter in general.

Han F. de Wit, himself a Buddhist, relates that the Buddhist experience of reality is usually transmitted to others through the medium of a genuine teacher–pupil relationship. Because this experience of reality requires a transformation of one's consciousness, real sharing is no easy matter. If people wish to share on the religious plane, they should learn to meditate.

Hans Waldenfels is widely known for his penetrating and empathic studies of the Kyoto School. He addresses the question regarding the extent to which he himself was able, through this study, to come to understand and share the Buddhist experience.

Jacques H. Kamstra describes a case of encounter between Japanese Buddhism and some of the more recent syncretic neo-New Religions *(shin-shin shukyo)* of Japan.

Anton Wessels writes concerning Mohammed's conviction that he shared in the experiences of Jesus and the other prophets before him. The events experienced by earlier biblical and Arabic prophets are indeed strikingly similar to those encountered by Mohammed. Wessels also presents a proposal for reinterpreting the Koranic version of Jesus' death.

Hans Daiber describes the thinking of the early-Islamic mystic Djunayd with respect to the possibility of giving expression to his mystical experiences and the capability of others to share in it.

Arnulf Camps assesses the October 1986 meeting in Assisi at which representatives of the world religions prayed together for peace. What did they share? Camp argues the position that believers can have two loyalties: one to the religion to which they adhere and a second to the culture in which they stand, even if this culture has been shaped by another religious tradition.

PART THREE consists of an effort to recapitulate the common themes and problems articulated in the symposium papers and discussions.

Hendrik M. Vroom attempts, in the final essay of this volume, to take stock of the results of the workshop. He focuses particular attention on the nature and hermeneutics of religious experience and the complex of knotty questions attendant on the concept of interreligious sharing.

The translation of most of the articles written in Dutch and German is the work of John Medendorp. He, John Rebel, and Henry Jansen have revised the text of essays written in English by authors whose native tongue is another language. We thank them very much for their careful efforts. John Rebel prepared the camera-ready text. We are grateful to him for the care he has exercised in carrying out this exacting task.

The workshop itself as well as the translation/revision work and the preparation of this volume for publication have been made possible by very considerable grants from the Royal Dutch Academy of Sciences, the Mission Board of the Reformed Churches in the Netherlands, and the Special Committee set up to organize and facilitate the celebration of the 110th anniversary of the founding of the Free University of Amsterdam in 1880. We thank all three of these enabling agencies most warmly for their generous encouragement and support.

Finally, the editors wish to express their deep appreciation to the publishers of the series in which this volume appears, Wm. B. Eerdmans Publishing Company in Grand Rapids and Editions Rodopi in Amsterdam, for their unfailing cooperation and continuing confidence in the project in which we with them are jointly engaged.

The Editors

Jerald D. Gort
Hendrik M. Vroom
Rein Fernhout
Anton Wessels

Part 1

Can Religious Experiences
Be Shared?

CHAPTER 1

Can Religious Experience Be Shared?
Introduction to the Theme
"Sharing Religious Experience"

Hendrik M. Vroom

1 Introduction to the Subject

This volume is devoted to the subject 'On Sharing Religious Experience.'
In order to express the possibility that individuals from one religion may
not be able to share the religious experience of individuals from another
religion, the title of this short introduction to the subject has been
formulated as a question: Can we share the religious experience of
others?

This is one of the most important questions which can be posed with
regard to the Encounter of Religions. Religious encounter can take place
on various levels. Individuals with different beliefs sometimes encounter
one another in order to discuss social and moral questions. They can
also discuss their insights or the cognitive side of belief with each other.
It is often said that dialogue should actually deal with religious experience,
thus placing knowledge and insight more or less in contrast to experience.
We ought not address one another from a distance, it is then said, but
personally, in terms of our own experience. We must, in other words,
share our experiences. That sounds promising — if people 'understand'
each other, they are more likely to respect each other than if they argue
and contend with one another.

Furthermore, according to many religious currents, faith-experience is
the heart of religion. Religion has a social side and one can study the
social function of religion; religion has a cultural side and religion makes
up part of a cultural system; it is fascinating to analyze and describe the
customs, the rituals, and the teachings of the various religions, and it
produces many an interesting study. Yet the essence of religion is the
personal faith-experience, regardless of the different forms it takes in
various religious traditions (cf. Wilfred C. Smith's distinction between faith
and belief). Religion can be defined as involvement with transcendence.

3

The form which is given to this 'involvement' is subject to many different influences; it is socially and traditionally conditioned. In the world religions faith is ultimately a question of personal involvement and of personal religion. It must be emphasized at this juncture that this personal religion takes a different form in the faithful obedience of the Moslem than it does in the *bhakti* of South India or the Zen meditation of Japan. With respect to primitive religions one must ask which analogous phenomena can be considered as 'religious experience.'

2   Share Religious Experience?

Can one person 'share' a personal religious experience with another? The theme of this volume is the encounter between people from different religions. We will therefore concentrate on the question of whether it is possible to understand, sympathize with, or even 'share' the belief of others, to have one and the same experience, in other words. What is and what is not possible in this regard? The question regarding the extent to which one can share in the belief of others also comes into play in cultural anthropological research. Can a cultural anthropologist understand the religion of the peoples with whom he interacts? Is someone who practises 'comparative religion' really acquainted with the religion he describes? Does the philologist who translates and explains the classical texts of other religions really know what the author intended or 'what the text says'? These questions concern the contingent conditions for the study of religion and have therefore been much discussed. They are also related to our theme. While academic investigation attempts to maintain a certain distance, however, actual encounter between adherents of different religious traditions implies that one is personally involved. The theme of this volume bids us to consider explicitly the encounter of two individuals who stand within different religious traditions. The question is: Can they share in one another's religious experience?

With this we find ourselves in the middle of the hermeneutic problem: "das Verstehen anderer Personen und ihrer Lebensäuszerungen." Dilthey was thinking here primarily of thoughts and ideas. He maintained that 'thought-content' was transferred unchanged, "wie durch einen Transport," from the possession of the one person into the possession of the other — ideas have their own identity; if two persons understand an idea, then they have precisely the same thing in their minds (Dilthey, 253). Ever since Heidegger, Gadamer, Ricoeur, Wittgenstein, and the whole hermeneutical discussion of the past years, we are no longer quite as comfortable with a statement of this kind. And when such a statement concerns experiences rather than ideas, we are definitely unsure whether we actually understand what the other person is undergoing and whether we share that experience. 'Sharing' is not something disengaged, that much is certain. Whoever acquires new experiences, learns. New experiences always entail the question of whether what is old and familiar stands in need of correction. In that sense, new experiences are 'negative,' as Gadamer notes (p. 335f.). New experiences challenge one to consider reality 'anew.' A person is enriched through encounter and dialogue. When one 'shares' the experiences of others, one is challenged to see things as others experience them.

Discussing fundamental experiences thus requires real encounter with other people. Such encounters cannot be dispassionate. The situation of the other person must be taken into account. This was pointed expressed by an Indian woman on Christmas Eve 1988, in the cathedral of Coventry when she said, "the only things to share that are worthwhile are the things we need." She was speaking of the poor, who share their food with their guests even when they do not have enough for themselves. Furthermore, when we share religious experience, it cannot be a question of matters which do not demand involvement. Religion is 'ultimate concern' (Tillich, 10). If it is possible to comprehend what is 'ultimate' for another, it cannot be done by familiarization at a distance. It must be a question of encounter, community, and learning the intentions of the other, as the commission for dialogue of the World Council of Churches says concerning "dialogue in community" *(Guidelines)*. We know from both hermeneutics as well as on the basis of our own personal experience that we cannot completely understand another person with regard to the most profound things. Part of being human means always remaining 'the other'; understanding the other always escapes us, as Levinas says. Understanding what is going on in another person is not a question of 'all or nothing,' however. We can never understand each other completely, but we can still understand a great deal about each other. Is that also true with regard to religion? Is it possible to bridge the cleft between religious traditions? Can we understand something of what another person says about his or her belief? Can we share, to a certain degree, the religious experience of other people, from other parts of the world and from other religious traditions?

3 Religious Experience

The problem raised in this volume concerns the sharing of religious experience. But what should we understand by religious experiences? Are they special, intensive experiences, as William James has described them? Or is someone like Vergote right when he says that we often focus too much on such unique experiences? He has a much broader view of religious experience as being experiences which are interwoven into the fabric of day-to-day life. What is religious experience? How can we portray this experience? Does such a broad concept as 'experience' lend itself to scientific investigation? Vergote is of the opinion that it is impermissable for religious psychology to abandon the concept of religious experience; experience essentially belongs "to the psychic reality of those who bear witness to it." (Vergote, 111, cf. 112f.)

'Experience' concerns the subject's conscious perception of reality through which the subject makes sense of, actively responds to, and undergoes reality. In religious experience, concrete reality is experienced in relation to transcendence (regardless of how this might be further interpreted). The standard by which the veracity of religious experience is measured, according to the classical traditions, is that reality which is experienced as it really is in relationship to the transcendent. (Vroom, p. 357)

For philosophical theory as well, reference to the experiential basis of religion is fundamental, although the discussion is far from closed. The objective of this volume is (a) to further clarify the nature of religious experience, and (b) to inquire to what extent 'religious experience' can be 'shared.' In order to delimit the theme of the conference and the volume somewhat and to indicate how it can be further elaborated, we will first probe more deeply into the concept of religious experience itself.

Within the experiential basis of religion, there are different types of experience which can be distinguished. (We will not deal with the question of whether these experiences are based on something in reality; nor are these experiences necessarily present in every religion.) The following types of experience can be distinguished:

1. experiences of 'transcendence'
2. historical experiences
3. basic experiences.

4 Experiences of 'Transcendence'

Experiences of 'transcendence' are often taken to mean experiences of a more mystical nature. This is most easily understood if transcendence is identified with God — an identification which cannot be justified.[1] Then it is said that all people live under the all-seeing eye of God. Some

---

[1] E. g., the experience of śūnyatā is not to be identified with a 'mystical' experience of God. J. B. Cobb Jr., in *Beyond Dialogue: Towards a Mutual Transformation of Christianity and Buddhism* (Philadelphia, 1982), p. 110, comments: "For the more fully Emptiness is understood, the clearer it becomes that it does not mean what the Bible means by God."

people experience God's nearness very intensively. It is often said that in order to prepare themselves for this experience people should turn away from their worldly concerns and should focus on God. If they prepare themselves for this experience through spiritual exercises then they too can experience God. Such experience is ineffable, it is said. It can only be described metaphorically; the images employed cannot be taken literally. It is said, for example, that God is Light, but it is understood that God is not really 'light' (in the sense of sunlight or electrical light). And so it is said in *theologia negativa* that God cannot really be 'described.' Every term that is used for God must also be denied: God is Light, but not really; God is a spring, but not really a spring. The terms point to the Highest, but do not describe it literally.

This emphasis on the indescribability of God in intense religious experience is consistently found in the more mystical religious traditions. As a Christian, Karl Rahner relates the experience of the transcendent to God (Rahner, "Transzendenzerfahrung"). In one way or another, people experience that which is beyond them (transcendence). Rahner calls this experience the experience of transcendence *(Transzendenzerfahrung)*. That which is experienced as transcendence in this experience goes beyond words and comprehension. That is why each person expresses this experience in their own way, and why religious traditions differ from one another.

Since the modes of expression differ, there is no way of knowing for certain whether these transcendental experiences relate to the same transcendental reality. Two people who speak differently about their deepest experiences could in fact be having the same experience (Rahner, "Transzendenzerfahrung," 211). But it could also be the case that they have had different experiences and that these were not experiences of 'God'. One must carefully study which of these two possibilities is presenting itself in dialogue between mystical traditions. One cannot simply equate all mystical experiences. Such equivalence must be demonstrated through dialogue and further study in the area of comparative religion. By virtue of the universal salvific will of God, the possibility exists that people from outside the Christian church may also experience what Christians call God in their experience of transcendence. God has, after all, bound himself to all people, as Rahner states on the basis of Christian conviction.

It is widely known that the ineffable experience of union with transcendence is prominent in several religious traditions. In the Advaita Vedanta, one pursues the experience of the union of the human self with the Brahman; this experience is indescribable for such union cannot be described in words. One who speaks always distinguishes between the speaker and the object spoken of. For that reason, the transcendental experience is essentially ineffable. In Zen Buddhism, one pursues the experience of śūnyatā, an experience which is distinguished from the experience of 'normal' reality.[2] This experience of union is also ineffable. This experience of 'transcendence' (which in this case is taken to mean the present world experienced in a totally different way) has been seen as being equivalent to the experience of the divine by certain Christian mystics in the Middle Ages. It is very questionable, however, whether that is the case. Buddhists usually reject belief in God.

If all mystical experiences are identified with one another, it is assumed that there is but one transcendental experience which occurs in all religions. Ṣufis, Jewish mystics, and the like all experience the one transcendent, viz., God. In Rahner's opinion, this assumption should be regarded with caution. It is not possible to know whether all these experiences are the same. Although it may be possible that they are, it is also possible that they differ from one another.

Nor should the experience of God in monotheistic religions be too quickly identified with each another. If a Jew experiences the nearness of God in the celebration of the Passover, a Moslem in a pilgrimage to the Ka'ba, and a Christian in the Immanuel of Christmas, how can it be said that they all have the same experience? The means by which transcendence is experienced are different in each case. The experience of transcendence is thus a matter of continual discussion in comparative religion and in the philosophy of religion. (cf. Katz)

5 Historical Experiences

Some religions appeal, in part, to historical experiences. That is especially true of Judaism, Christianity, and Islam. The Jews received the Torah on Mount Sinai. Christians believe that God has revealed himself in a unique way in Jesus Christ, and that in his death and resurrection unique events have taken place which are decisive for the relation between God and man. Moslems believe that Mohammed received the revelation of God in its pure form, superseding the traditions of the Jews and Christians. These three historically related religions thus point to historical events in which God has revealed himself. The result is that they each claim exclusivity.

---

[2] T. E. Vetter, "Die Lehre Nāgārjunas in den Mūla Mādhyamikakārikās," in *Epiphanie des Heils: Zur Heilsgegenwart in Indischer und Christlicher Religion*, ed. G. Oberhammer (Vienna, 1982), p. 107. Cf. T. E. Vetter, *The Ideas and Meditative Practices in Early Buddhism* (Leiden, 1988), on the role of meditation and discriminating insight in early Buddhism.

Buddhism appeals to the Buddha's experience of enlightenment. The Buddha (the Enlightened), however, assumes a different position than Moses, Jesus, or Mohammed. He communicated no revelation, nor was he himself a revelation, but he achieved enlightenment and pointed out the path that others must take. Although Buddha assumes a different position than Jesus in this respect, here too it is possible to speak of a decisive historical experience which has serves as a 'signpost' for others.

When dealing with the historical religious experiences of such extraordinary individuals, we might well ask how other people have reached the point of attributing so much value to these experiences. The answer can only be that what Mohammed, the Buddha, and others have said and done has had a fundamental impact on people. They have experienced something sublime and special. The experience of these unique people has restructured the way in which other people experience reality. They have been offered a different interpretive framework for their lives, one which they consider correct. In cultural anthropology such an interpretive framework is described as a symbolical system, and as 'meaning making.' The philosophy of religion examines the conditions under which it is possible for such a 'search paradigm' to be adopted by people other than the one who first constructed it (Kuitert, 140). The basis for recognizing revelation and the religious experience of others lies, in my opinion, in the fixed structure of being-human. That brings us to a third category of religious experience.

6 Basic experiences

Religious traditions speak to people regarding experiences at the extremes of their existence. Inasmuch as these experiences lie at the basis of human existence as well as at the basis of religion, they can be called basic experiences. To these fundamental, universal human experiences belong intense joy and gratitude (for example, at a birth, or when all is going well with one's children), wonder (for example, at the beauty and complexity of nature), contingency (or, 'coincidence,' for example, when one reflects on how fragile life is after an accident, and how there is no reason why another dies 'but not you'), liberation from oppression and injustice, responsibility and guilt, experience of the finite and limited nature of existence (for example, when you 'realize your limits'), the experience of being granted insight (or of not attaining it), etc. These experiences are grounded in fixed features of human existence, which we therefore call *existentials*.[3] The examples which we give are in part

---

[3] This term was coined by Heidegger. Heidegger emphasized being conscious of existentials. My own use of the term is not especially linked to M. Heidegger, *Sein*

culturally determined; the experience referred to by them is not. Such anthropological constants to which we point (but which we cannot mention without interpretation) are *existentials*; they form the basis of 'existential experiences.' One can no more express and undergo these existential experiences without interpretation, than one can, according to Kant, know the *'Dinge an sich'* apart from the human faculties of perception and cognition.

This is in sum the theory of religion which the present author has formulated. The speakers at this conference are not required to share this theory. It can function as an investigative question; it may be referred to, endorsed, expanded, corrected, or contested. In what follows, this theory of religion will be further elucidated.

Religious traditions interpret these experiences. They do so through stories, practices, and doctrine. A classic example from the Christian tradition is the story of the Good Samaritan. This story and the point it makes are widely known. A man on his way from Jericho to Jerusalem was robbed and beaten by thieves. A priest came along; he had to go to the temple. What must he do? He passed by. Likewise a Levite. Finally he was helped by a Samaritan. At the end of this parable the question is posed: Who was his neighbour? The perspective shifts from that of the priest and Levite to that of the man who had been robbed. Such a change of perspective is typical for religion (H. de Wit, 45ff.). This parable has a certain interpretation of existential 'responsibility for others,' or, if one prefers, 'being-with-others.' Whoever grasps the parable gains a new perspective on human responsibility, the true scope and import of the command, and the full significance of love of neighbour.

Since religion offers an interpretation of reality, religion embraces all of life. Religions and world and life views interpret feelings of self-esteem, failure, joy, etc. Religion explains human existence within the context of the whole of reality. 'Allah knows' means 'God knows everything,' and at the same time, 'be careful what you do.' 'Allah is merciful' means 'God is good,' as well as 'you can always trust God.' This is the way in which doctrine functions in a religion. Meditation and rites also serve to engrave a certain experience of reality in one's mind. A religious view of reality consists of a configuration of such interpretations of the features of human existence. The *existentials* are the characteristics of the human condition which form the point of contact for human religion.

---

und Zeit (Tübingen, [11]1967); the connection between religion and human experience rests upon the fixed features of existence, of which one is conscious, and which (can) form the basis of penetrating experiences. Cf. my *Truth and the Religions,* Chapter 9.

These features of human existence play a role in the concrete experiences which people undergo. *Existentials* are actualized in concrete experiences. They can indeed only come to expression in concrete experiences. The interpretation of *existentials* therefore entails an interpretation of concrete experiences. A world and life view thus provides an interpretation of man and the world. Religious traditions are concerned with transcendence. They teach people to experience transcendence in and 'through' concrete experiences in the present world.

Concrete situations are interpreted in relation to transcendence. The Jewish tradition, for example, teaches us to see transcendence as God (and to experience) people as the image of God. Through the elaboration of the law, the Jewish tradition teaches us how to give expression to this belief in man as the image of God in everyday life. Life in accordance with the *halachah* (law, instruction) can thus have religious significance or 'everyday mysticism' ('normal mysticism,' as Kadushin (p. 257) has called it). Within Christianity, people sometimes distribute food to the poor and the homeless. They experience the Kingdom of God in this way. In Christian currents in which this type of faith experience is prominent, great significance is attributed to social life. One's relation with God is thus experienced in everyday life (see Jantzen). It is incorrect to connect religious experience only or even primarily with a specific transcendental experience, as Rahner correctly asserts. Religious experience is connected to concrete life in this world.

Religious experience is, in summary, sustained by three types of facts: (a) reference to transcendence, (b) the interpretive frameworks of religious traditions which have arisen in the course of history, (c) fundamental experiences (assimilated through experiences of concrete situations which have had a profound impact on people).

Access to such religious interpretation of basic experiences can be obtained through the symbols and doctrines of a religious tradition. Religious scriptures, and to an even greater extent, the means for transmitting the faith to new generations of believers and for initiating them into a religious tradition, as well as a tradition's rites and symbols, provide us with insight into the way in which human existence is understood.

7 Sharing religious experience?

Since religious traditions interpret experiences, and since there are no uninterpreted experiences, the question is whether one can understand and 'share' the 'religious experiences' of a religious world and life view different from one's own (or lack thereof). Can, for example, a Christian understand, or even 'share' the Buddhist experience of human finitude, or the Moslem experience of the greatness of God?

Understanding others, as we stated above, is always a matter of understanding in part. If that is true, then we must ask how far mutual understanding extends in a pluralistic culture. Since all religious traditions give an interpretation of the fundamental features of being-human, they can intersect at certain points or even overlap. It therefore seems obvious that 'sharing' can be spoken of particularly with regard to the third category of religious facts (see Vroom, Ch. 12). It will be evident from the contributions to this volume to what extent various authors agree with this sketch of a 'theory of religion' and to what extent it must be altered and nuances be introduced. The above text was discussed in the research group "Religious Encounter," and improvements have been introduced on a number of points (for which this writer is very grateful to his colleagues).

Bibliography

Dilthey, W. "Das Verstehen anderer Personen und ihrer Lebensäußerungen," in *Der Aufbau der geschichtlichen Welt in den Geisteswissenschaften,* ed. with introduction by M. Riedel. Stuttgart, 1970, p. 253.

Gadamer, H. G. *Wahrheit und Methode.* Tübingen, [2]1965, pp. 335f.

Guidlines on Dialogue with People of Other Faiths and Ideologies. Geneva, [2]1982, passim.

Jantzen, Grace. "Is There a Common Core of Mysticism?" *Rel. Stud.* March, 1990. –forthcoming.

Kadushin, M. *The Rabbinic Mind.* New York, [3]1972.

Katz, St. T. "Language, Epistemology and Mysticism," in *Mysticism and Philosophical Analysis,* ed. St. T. Katz. New York, 1978, pp. 22-74.

Kuitert, H. M. *Wat heet geloven?* Baarn, 1977.

Rahner, K. "Transzendenzerfahrung aus katholischer Sicht," *Schriften zur Theologie,* XIII. Einsiedeln, 1978, pp. 207-225; cf. "Anonymer und expliziter Glaube," *SzT,* XII. 1975, pp. 76-84.

Smith, Wilfred Cantwell. *Faith and Belief.* Princeton, 1978.

Tillich, P. *Dynamics of Faith.* New York, 1958.

Vergote, A. *Religie, geloof en ongeloof.* Kapellen/Kampen, [2]1987.

Vroom, H. M. *Truth and the Religions.* Amsterdam/Grand Rapids, 1989.

Wit, H. F. de. *Contemplatieve Psychologie.* Kampen, 1987.

CHAPTER 2

Hermeneutics of Religious Experience

Gerhard Oberhammer

This article seeks to elucidate the nature of the experience of transcendence by offering an anthropological analysis of such experience. The human subject is open to 'beyond-being'; when such beyond-being is present in an absolute encounter with the subject, then *Heil* ('salvation') is realized. Since the experience of *Heil* is mediated by a religious tradition, it cannot be shared with others outside of that tradition. In the immediacy of each person to transcendence, however, all people are alike. This rudimentary form of religious experience represents a form of community in which all human beings share, albeit by way of a hermeneutical inference rather than concretely.

In the context of a symposium on the theme of 'sharing' the religious experience of others —all others, including those of one's own tradition, for it makes no difference for the hermeneutics of religious experience whether we are dealing with a person of the same or with one of a different religious tradition, since the possibility and problem of 'sharing' must be answered on its own terms— the question concerning the hermeneutics of religious experience gains its decisive concreteness in reflection on the phenomenon of 'tradition' as the actualization-structure of historical-actual religion.

What exactly is the phenomenon of tradition, so understood? For the moment suffice it to say that tradition is the process of the 'mythologization' of 'transcendence,' a process which obtains supra-individual validity insofar as it comprises the adoption by others of the testimony of an actual personal experience of transcendence as 'mythical,' i. e., as an articulate pattern of one's own experience of transcendence.[1]

Understood thus, the phenomenon of tradition is the decisive principle of 'religious experience.' The question regarding the hermeneutics of such experience is particularly acute since the understanding of what 'religious experience' should be is itself prejudiced in a very specific way by the

---

[1] On this concept of 'tradition' see Oberhammer/Waldenfels, 31 f.; and Oberhammer 1987, pp. 38 ff.

very phenomenon of tradition. When the *communio* of tradition in the sense just described becomes the decisive determinant of religious experience, then 'religious experience' no longer allows for being misunderstood as an 'aesthetic-emotional experience' (i. e., as 'enjoyment') of religious forms of self-actualization. The aesthetic detachment characteristic of the one who enjoys or consumes such an experience excludes the *communio* of tradition along with the religious experience emergent within in it. At its most fundamental moment, religious experience is the subject-claiming experience of transcendence, of transcendence as the actuality of meaning of one's own existence, Any particular tradition attests to this experience, allowing its members to be confirmed in an unquestionable hope for *Heil*. Only such an experience of transcendence is, in the true sense, a religious experience, and only when experience is understood in this way, can 'sharing' the religious experience of others emerge as a problem.

We cannot, in the present context, take experience to mean the experience of an another's experience, or, more concretely, the reflective or aesthetically enjoyable becoming-aware of specific forms of expression and faith-content in which the experience of transcendence of a religious tradition is objectively manifested. We must take experience to be the realization of the experience itself that is expressed in the phenomenon of religious experience. The question which therefore arises for hermeneutics when prompted by a critically reflective desire to understand what religious experience actually is in order to be able to truly share it, is this: Under what conditions is such an experience possible, and in what way does this experience claim and condition a person.

1 Sharing and the actualization of existence

Such sharing seems possible only in free encounter with another person, which —in order to become real— presupposes the openness of 'self-presence' of the self to another subject.[2] Without such openness of self-presence, another person can never become a subject and therefore cannot be encountered either. The possibility of encounter therefore demands that the subject is permanently already open in a way that concerns neither a specific being nor simply being as such (although this openness is also the openness of self-presence toward the possibility of 'nothing,' even if this openness only becomes explicit in a real act of consciousness). The openness of self-presence and thus the 'reaching-out' of the subject cannot, therefore, be conditioned by the individual who is encountered. It can only arise by virtue of something which is itself not

---

[2] On encounter as an essential dimension of religious experience see Oberhammer 1984.

an individual being and which therefore cannot disguise the horizon of this reaching-out as being something objective. The possibility of an opening in the subject's horizon, where encounter becomes possible, can only be conceived if the horizon is opened through a self-mediating openness prior to any particular encounter. This encounter can be hermeneutically conceived as conditioning of the subject's reaching-out by the relationality of beyond-being. It is this relationality which opens to a person not only being as the openness of one who is self-present, but it is also precisely through this openness that the possibility of a fulfilment of meaning no longer relative is opened up, in other words, the possibility of *Heil*. This possibility opens up when this relationality becomes real as a freely desired relatedness to beyond-being in the human actualization of existence. As a mere a priori principle of transcendentality, *Heil* does not yet amount to a spiritual reality shaping existence.[3] 'Religion' therefore ultimately reveals itself only on the horizon of this hermeneutical framework as the phenomenon of opening oneself freely and unreservedly to transcendence (beyond-being) in the personal actualization of existence. This means that our framework constantly seeks to maintain an understanding of religious experience in the true sense — as the experience of transcendence as *Heil* constitutive for such an actualization of existence. The details of this hermeneutical framework cannot be elaborated in the present context.

In order to allow the hermeneutical approach to sharing the religious experience of others outlined above to bear fruit, it would be useful to briefly describe our understanding of *Heil* as a hermeneutical perspective for the understanding of religion conceived of as human actualization of existence. If it is correct that the a priori reaching-out by the transcendental subject to beyond-being has always already opened the 'self-presence' of the subject to this beyond-being, and, viewed from the other side, if it is true when this beyond-being is present in a categorical devotion of the subject in an absolute encounter, if it is true that this indicates lasting non-relative *Heil*, then it can also be said that every actualization of human existence which can be set within the perspective of unreserved surrender to this beyond-being as an historical, truly realized encounter of a person with transcendence is itself already a realization of *Heil* and fulfilment of meaning, one that is not to be expected only in the 'beyond.' Considered hermeneutically, being-in-the-world and non-relative *Heil* coincide in the actualization of existence. In every moment of existence understood thus, the self-presence of the human spirit extends itself into the infinite depth of the continually self-mediating openness of beyond-being and thus becomes immediate to its own *Heil*.

---

[3] For the basis of such an understanding of *Heil*, see Oberhammer 1987, 13ff.

It would seem important to pursue this in what follows, since a dimension of religious experience would then come into view which appears essential at a particular stage of the existential consciousness' development for the understanding of religion, as has become clear from the Indian example. Through the concept of emancipation as liberation from worldly existence, being-in-the-world (saṁsāra) and Heil (nirvāṇa, muktiḥ) were split into a duality, and the unity here demonstrated could only be attained through the 'ontological' devaluation of worldly existence, or by seeing world and liberation as successive moments. Religious experience, contrary to the dictates of the logical mind, seems nonetheless to have so altered the theory that 'World' and 'Heil' were conceived of together at a certain time. Cases in point are the equation of Saṁsāra with Nirvāṇa in Buddhism, or in the teaching of release during one's lifetime (jīvanmuktiḥ) in Advaitavedānta.

The exposition of the phenomenon of religion which we attempt here, that is, of religion as the realization of existence for Heil and the experience of existence as Heil which this enables, does not, of course, intend 'existence' in the sense of a trivial actualization of life. In order for the actualization of life to mean Heil, it must become the unreserved encounter with beyond-being in the responsibility for fellow-humanity and humanity's worldly existence, an encounter which encompasses the freedom of the subject. (This hermeneutical explanation of the actualization of existence as Heil and thus as religion is not intended to imply that such an identification of existence with Heil is somehow ontologically necessary. On the contrary, the identification can also be understood as a grace-event, to speak in the words of one tradition.) The phenomenon of concrete religious tradition only arises from the unreserved surrender to transcendence when the claiming presence of transcendence also becomes a theme as such in the actualization of one's fellow-human existence, when it is sought in the dynamic of encounter resulting in the infinite.

An important insight into the problem of sharing the religious experience of others already emerges at the present juncture. The understanding of religion we have outlined above lays the basis for the possibility of inter-human encounter on the common horizon of the continually-self-sharing-for-Heil openness of beyond-being, something which is required for sharing the religious experience of others. Moreover, one's own religious tradition can only become acceptable as religion on this horizon. For the 'learned' faith of the tradition into which one is born must also be received again in one's own transcendentality, so that a person, through and by means of the mythologizing of transcendence, can be made receptive to the reality of transcendence, and can transform faith into personal experience. The requirement of such regression into one's own being means that one will encounter the same self-mediating-as-openness-beyond-being and one will therefore undergo the same fundamental experience of transcendence enabling *Heil* as another. Receiving again one's own tradition in this way establishes in principle and predicates hermeneutically the possibility of sharing the religious experience of others.

2 *Communio* and the mediation of transcendence

In order to hermeneutically mediate the phenomenon of religious experience in its entirety, however, further reflection is required on the understanding of religion outlined here as the fundamental starting point of our enquiry. Beyond-being has been deduced up to this point as an a priori principle of human transcendentality, and an attempt has been made to define encounter with beyond-being for *Heil* as the inner essence of 'religion.' Nevertheless, it remains to be explained precisely how an a posteriori experience of this 'Wherefore' of human transcendental reaching-out is possible at all. After all, beyond-being never itself becomes the object of an experience; it always remains as the horizon of every experience, a *fellow-participant* in the experience of the 'objective.' A person has therefore been already opened to beyond-being *before* any particular experience, yet this already being opened can never itself be the object of experience, something which appears to be a demand of any actual encounter. How, then, is beyond-being mediated within encounter?

Insofar as a person expects the only possible meaningfulness of his existence from transcendence, which is permanently already open to him through the openness of the infinite horizon of his self-presence, he surpasses being-towards-openness by this expectation and adopts a stance of being unreservedly in need of this openness. The surrender to beyond-being which manifests itself in this need can only be obtained in an act of existence enalbing *Heil* if a person becomes immediate to the Wherefore of his transcendental reaching out a posteriori by opening himself through 'speaking' (i. e., by calling or speaking to). A person cannot experience relationality to another except through speech. Such becoming-immediate to transcendence through the mediation of 'speaking' (in the broadest sense of the word) permits a mythical pattern of experience to arise through which beyond-being becomes mythically present and which can thus lead to encounter. (Although it is not possible to locate and deduce the 'mythical present' here; see Oberhammer 1987, 19-37.) This process of mythical mediation by its very nature realizes itself in the context of 'fellow-humanity,' in the being-with relation to others.[4] It is through testimony by fellow-human beings to the continual reference

---

[4] On the function of 'fellow-humanity' in connection with revelation, see Oberhammer 1984.

beyond the individual being to an actually experienced meaningfulness and
Heil that a person acquires the confident trust which enables him to
adopt the mythical pattern of the experience of transcendence as *Heil* that
such testimony mediates as being the pattern of his own unreserved
surrender to transcendence.

A further implication of the social nature of such mythologization of
transcendence is that it can never be patterned on an individual case. A
subject must 'hear' the testimony from another person speaking in terms
of a supra-individual tradition. Otherwise the testimony of an actual
personal experience of transcendence, which permits the confident trust
constitutive for the pattern of an experience of transcendence to develop,
will not enter into the process of one's own mythologizing of transcendence. This is also borne out by the History of Religions, as demonstrated, for example, by the establishment of Christian dogma.[5]

When *communio* arises in this way as a continual sharing and granting a share in the mutual experience of transcendence, the 'religious
tradition' becomes reality, and 'religion' reveals itself as actualization of
existence which can by its nature only become an event within the *community*. Through hermeneutical mediation, therefore, religious experience
—the principle of tradition of which we spoke at the outset, manifest in
the concrete phenomenon of confident trust in the pattern of experience
of one's fellow man, enabling and demanding the adoption of that pattern
for one's own experience of transcendence— has become concrete and
reveals the conditions under which a person can share the religious
experience of another.

3 Encounter and patterns of experience

Confident trust in the pattern of another person and the adoption of that
pattern in one's own actualization of existence which such trust may
occasion serve to put the principle of tradition in a characteristic perspective. The mode of confident trust in which the *communio* of the tradition
becomes possible implies by its nature that other patterns are not adopted
and also cannot be adopted, thus establishing the exclusive validity of the
adopted pattern. This exclusivity lies in the nature of the pattern, insofar
as it mediates transcendence as present, non-relative *Heil* that conducts a
person to an encounter with transcendence through unreserved surrender.
The adoption of this pattern of experience of transcendence as one's own
no longer relative *Heil* raises the claim to exclusivity for this pattern by
definition.

---

[5] For an example of the Indian approach see the quotation from the *Paramasaṃhitā* on
page 20.

One cannot in the actualization of one's own existence wish to encounter transcendence in the guise of a mythologization which proves to be intended as not ultimate. The mythical mediation intended here is not a rhetorical stylistic-device for expressing spiritual aspirations. The 'mythologization' which takes place in such a pattern does not entail arbitrary labels in the exuberance of articulate encounter, as depicted by Rilke's Cornett in the encounter with the lover of his last night: "They will give themselves a hundred new names and remove them all from each other again, gently, like one removes an earring" (Rilke, 245). The mythical mediation of the pattern of experience which we wish to indicate here represents the only possibility for an a posteriori encounter with transcendence. Without such mediation, transcendence cannot become the 'partner' of human relationality. The presence of transcendence is not something that is objectively known through the autonomy of human knowledge and thus objectified in its 'whatness,' something which can then be secondarily labelled; it is rather something which is 'spoken to' a person through the meaning-mediating word alone, and therefore 'revealed' as a pattern of an experience. The fact that revelation is 'spoken to' a person in the word and is accessible in no other form of knowledge is of course only *one* of the aspects of revelation, but phenomenologically and hermeneutically an important one, since 'revelation' in this sense mediates the object which justifies the existence of faith and therefore also of theology. It is precisely in this that the decisive function of myth and mythologizing for religion appears to lie. (cf. Oberhammer 1988)

Nor can the experiences undergone in certain forms of mysticism be advanced as an argument against the mythical pattern's claim to exclusivity. Such objections come to expression in the appreciation for *'Name und Gestalt' (nāmarūpe)* in the Vedāntic tradition and in the Advaita, just to give an example. The mystical experience does not temper the *exclusive* validity of the mythical pattern by placing another pattern alongside of it as equally valid, but merely surpasses the mythical pattern time and again, aspiring the actual presence of transcendence mediated by the pattern. It is, furthermore, no indifferent matter to mystical experience which particular mythical pattern of the experience of transcendence is surpassed in the mystical experience of the 'encounter.' One may choose another 'mythologization' with a more comprehensive claim to validity and surrender the old one if this is demanded by one's own experience of meaning; one cannot, however, arbitrarily exchange patterns or regard them as equally valid.

4 The *Paramasaṃhitā* and mythical mediation

Perhaps it would be good to consider this phenomenon from yet another perspective, in order to clarify its religio-hermeneutical significance. The *Vaishnavic Paramasaṃhitā* (ca. 500 C. E.) expresses a notion which continues to be relevant:

> Hear, how this worship of the God of Gods is [to be carried out]. He can only be worshipped [insofar as] he has form. It is not [possible] to worship one without form. ... That is why people achieve perfection after they have depicted him, the unshakable, in human form and worshipped him [in this form] with highest devotion. If, however, the Lord of Gods has no form of appearance, then worship is not possible, nor meditation, nor even praise. That is why one may worship him in his form of appearance. ... Worship, praise, and meditation which are carried out in accordance with the recognized prescriptions regarding [his] form of appearance from the authoritative tradition *(śāstram)*. ... That is why one may only worship the God of Gods in this form. *(Paramasaṃhitā* 3, 4-10ab

This passage is primarily a justification of the temple image *(mūrtiḥ)* of God on the basis of its necessity for religious experience, as it is here understood (note the phenomenon by which religious existence is actualized that are mentioned in this text: "highest devotion," "worship," "praise," "meditation"). The "temple image" in this text represents, by way of example, what has in general been called the "mythologization of transcendence" (as elaborated in Oberhammer 1984).

From another perspective the justification of the 'temple image' presented in this text enables us to understand the phenomenon of mythologization and 'mythical presence' from a unique point of view. The form of God's appearance (i. e., mythologization) is not only a necessary mediation of God owing to its tangibility and articulation of the pattern of an experience. It is also necessary because the transcendent God continues to be mediated through the concreteness of an actual presence. The mediation of presence thus understood primarily demands the continuation of the mythical mediation in the tradition. "Only in this form may one worship the God of Gods," this text says:

> That is why the learned man may worship the highest God for the sake of emancipation or a [specific] fruit without giving up the imparted form of appearance. He may continually worship the characteristic form [of God] as it is given to You by me in this authoritative tradition, but he may not use one which has [simply] been devised. *(Paramasaṃhitā* 24, 5cd—7ad)

Why is this? From the perspective of a hermeneutic of religious experience one must reply: Because the mythical mediation must be such that the presence mediated by it is experienced as the very presence of transcendence which never becomes present except in mythical mediation; it therefore excludes the possibility that such presence remain generally indeterminate, since, as one actually present to which a person desires to open himself in the actualization of existence, it must be unique and definite.

This implies that the mythologization, as the pattern of an actual experience of transcendence, must contain an element of concreteness. The transcendence to which a person turns in opening himself, must be mythologized concretely enough so that it can be experienced in the definiteness of its 'identity' time and again. There must be a repeatable concreteness of the mythical presence of transcendence in the ongoing mythologization of transcendence by the tradition.

Moreover, in this respect, one cannot conceal the fact that transcendence, for example in the Christian tradition or the Advaita Vedānta are not mythologized using the same name, but with the words 'God' or 'Brahman,' or in Buddhism, with the word 'Nirvāṇa.' In these examples the respective word has become a concrete mythologization, in the sense of a personal name, by virtue of the fact that the terms can never refer to anything else. This means that the mythologization of transcendence —insofar as it refers to the 'Wherefore' of the transcendental reaching out by the individual subject to which the subject opens himself to *Heil* a posteriori in the actualization of life— must have the character of a distinctive 'individuality.' It is this individuality, to appeal to another Hindu example, which was ultimately the reason for a theological controversy during the flowering of Hinduism between the tenth and the fourteenth century: the question regarding who the absolute is, in other words, the question of whether the cause of the world's being is Viṣṇu, Brahmā, or Śiva (cf., for example, Vātsya Varadaguru's Tattvanirṇayaḥ). Christian belief in the incarnation of God, which is expressed using the familiar 'under Pontius Pilate,' ultimately fulfils the same religious-hermeneutical function. This is what forms the basis for the distinctive concreteness of the mythical mediation of transcendence preserved in the tradition even when this concreteness is the concreteness of an historical event.

5 *Communio* on the horizon of transcendence

We now return to our initial question. How can a hermeneutic of religious experience mediate the universal and, because it is universal, the exclusive claim of the personal experience of transcendence leading to *Heil*, how can this be mediated in such a way that a person can have community with his fellow man even with respect to his approach to transcendence, thus sharing his religious experience? If what has been said so far has any validity, then religious experience, fundamentally discloses itself only in community. This applies to the subject as well. But such disclosure presupposes a community which becomes concrete in the *communio* of tradition. This formulation of the matter is ambivalent and seems to point in two different directions.

Inasmuch as a person testifies to another concerning his experience of transcendence enabling *Heil*, he thereby discloses to his fellow man the radical exposure inherent in his own surrender to transcendence; an exposure through which another (and, to be sure, not just another person from one's own tradition, but from other traditions too) is led into the innermost core of this act at the very outset. By virtue of the fact that one's fellow man affirms and accepts the testimony as a pattern of his own experience of transcendence in the innermost core of the spontaneity of his own subjectivity, he opens himself to another by the very nature of this act: on the one hand he allows (abandoning his selfness) the pattern to be conveyed to him by another, and on the other hand, he can discover this pattern as his own experience only in unreserved surrender to transcendence — a surrender which in order to be possible at all, can only be conceived in terms of the complete exposure of the immediacy to transcendence which actualizes itself in this surrender, and which therefore also fundamentally presupposes the openness to one's fellow man of this act. In consequence of this brief analysis of the phenomenon of human *communio* in which the actualization of religious experience becomes possible, it appears for now that sharing the religious experience of others outside of one's own tradition does not occur inasmuch as this experience must be mediated through a foreign pattern — a pattern which one does not appropriate in its character as exclusivity.

An additional point remains to be discussed. Every belief which is initially accepted on the word of another and is thus merely 'learned,' must be received in the transcendentality of one's own existence in order for it to be transformed into religious experience. If this is correct, then it must also be said that man fundamentally possesses community with others in the experience of transcendence before any *communio* of tradition takes place; in fact, such experience conditions the very possibility of such *communio*. Another person is immediate to existence, death, and transcendence in the same way as I am. Just as other do, I experience the immediacy of my standing before Nothingness and its dissolution of every autonomous meaning of being, and like him, I am aware of transcendence as my own possible actualization of *Heil*, and I am initially independent of any particular pattern of the mythical presence of transcendence since the possibility for such awareness, and the actualization of existence emanating from it, is not cancelled or transformed by any specific mythical pattern. I am confronted by transcendence through the same affirmation of being-dependent as is another, and I accordingly possess community with him in this rudimentary form of religious experience.

A further dimension of sharing emerges in terms of this underlying sharing of the religious experience of others. Precisely because another person exists within a particular *communio* of tradition of surrender to transcendence, the other person becomes credible and thereby beloved and valuable to me in his unreserved and positive surrender to transcendence (to which I also want to be related in my most fundamental need). Inasmuch as he opens the innermost core of his subjectivity to the same transcendence to which I have opened myself as the centre of meaning for my own existence, he also becomes immediate to me in the actuality of the actualization of his religion.

It is not the sharing of the religious experience of another person, nor a philosophical tempering of one's theological position, which makes possible the acceptance of another into the community of standing before the Absolute. It is the actualization of human existence as encounter with another on the horizon of transcendence. The other person remains 'other,' claiming me in encounter, since he only experiences and can only experience transcendence in that mythologization which has been conveyed to him by another person from his own tradition and which he must therefore posit as universal and exclusively valid. Nevertheless, I share with him the experience of that which discloses itself to him in the discovery of the pattern he has made his own, namely, the mythical presence of transcendence leading to *Heil*. This is true even if the mythologization which mediates the experience it is not actualized for me in personal experience, but can only appropriated in a hermeneutical process of *intellectual* inference.

Bibliography

Oberhammer, G. "Transzendenzerfahrung im Hinduismus." *Acta Indologica* 4 (1984): 347-367.

———. "Der Mensch als Ort der Offenbarung." In *Sein als Offenbarung in Christentum und Hinduismus.* Ed. A. Bsteh. Beiträge zur Religionstheologie 4. Mödling, 1984, pp. 17-36

———. *Versuch einer transzendentalen Hermeneutik religiöser Tradition.* Publications of the de Nobili Research Library, Occasional Papers 3. Vienna, 1987.

———. "Mythos, woher und wozu? Zur Rationalität des Mythos." In *Mythos und Rationalität.* Ed. H. H. Schmid. Gütersloh: Gütersloh Verlag, 1988, pp. 15-26.

——— and H. Waldenfels. *Überlieferungsstruktur und Offenbarung: Aufriß einer Reflexion des Phänomens im Hinduismus mit theologischen Anmerkungen.* Publications of the de Nobili Research Library, Occasional Papers 1. Vienna, 1980.

Paramasaṃhitā [of the Pāñcharātra]. Ed. & Eng. tr. K. Aiyangar. Gaekwad's Oriental Series 86. Baroda, 1940.

Rilke, R. M. *Sämtliche Werke,* I. E. Zinn, ed., on behalf of the Rilke Archive with the collaboration of Ruth Sieber-Rilke. Frankfurt am Main, 1970.

CHAPTER 3

Transcendence and Wholeness

Willem Dupré

As religious traditions are constituted they form their own universes of meaning which are, in principle, open to all human beings, but are actually closed to those who do not dwell within that same universe. Therefore the answer to the question regarding the possibility of sharing the same religious experiences between people from different traditions must be an unmistakable 'no'. However, for precisely the same reasons that compel acceptance of this conclusion one could conceive of and promote the emergence of a community in which religious experiences are shared. Such a community might arise as people begin to understand themselves and their traditions anew through the dialogical experience of one another's otherness and sameness. Both conclusions are reached in this article by means of an analysis of the meaning of experiences and of religious traditions' constitutive core, as these focus on both the discernment as well as the fulfilment of the human task, a task inherent to man's very being by virtue of the transcendent character of personal and cultural existence.

1 The wanting paradigm

While pondering the possibility of sharing religious experiences with people from different traditions, I wondered what might have happened if Buddha, Jesus, and Mohammed would have had the opportunity to meet and develop personal relationships. Since the imagined meeting never took place, we must not look for a paradigm where there is none, nor try to construct an answer which could properly be given only by the people involved. On the other hand, although we have no paradigm, I do not think its absence is in itself sufficient reason to avoid the idea altogether, or to reject a similar opportunity if it is offered to us. In fact, I would like to make two points with this idea of an imagined meeting between the decisive persons of different religious traditions. First, I would like to emphasize that the question concerning the possibility of sharing religious experiences with people from other religious traditions is, above all, a matter of concrete encounters. If we (decide to) accept the challenge of such encounters, the deed itself will prove its meaning and truth. Secondly, I would like to argue that it is not only necessary to know why one should value and pursue personal relations with people from different religious traditions, but that it also makes sense to prepare oneself for the task that arises in and through the desired goal. When we realize that there is no substitute for actual experiences, it is in the anticipation of the event that we are asked to be responsible for the event and to recall whatever might be relevant to its effectuation.

Since conscience needs consciousness in order to comply with its own demands, the exploration of consciousness as it is indicated by philosophical and scientific interests is not just an option one might or might not try to realize, but a possibility that grows into an exigency of personal responsibilities, depending on historical conditions and cultural circumstances. Within this context it is important that we do not claim for philosophy and science what science and philosophy cannot give; that is, that we take them as efforts and deeds which are intended to serve (and not to replace) the meaning and truth of humanity. But for the same reason one must not forget that philosophy and science can be of service to the meaning and truth of being human only if, and to the extent that, they follow their own rules and accomplish what can be accomplished in terms of their specific conditions and tools.

In the following considerations I intend to focus on some of the philosophical aspects that pertain to the issue of personal religious experiences and the possibility of sharing them with people from different traditions. To comply with this intention I shall begin with a brief analysis of the role of experience in the process of communication and with regard to the constitution of religious traditions. In accordance with the idea that religious traditions are to be understood as the articulation and the fulfilment of a task that co-originates with the meaning of being human, the next steps will be a description of the structure of this idea, and the implications it has for the meaning of unity and diversity in religious traditions. Finally, since such an approach makes it possible to think of religious traditions in terms of ideal types, I will discuss this point and give an indication of the consequences it has for the question about the possible sharing of religious experiences with others.

2 Experience and the constitution of religious traditions

As the issue of the conference is presented, the questions that need to be asked and answered from a philosophical point of view concern, first of all, the human being and the meaning of experience. Who and what are human beings that they might, and even must, share experiences? In the second place, since we may assume that religious traditions have answered this question at least for the people who have come to form their communities of shared experiences, they are questions about the meaning of religious traditions. What are religious traditions as they appear (and disappear) within the horizon of cultural history; as they relate to the decisive aspects of being human and reality — and, more specifically, as they point to (if, indeed, they do) and delineate the conditions for the possibility of inter-religious dialogues?

The questions are by no means minor ones. And, as they are asked, I do not have the illusion of being able to give a sufficient answer. On the other hand, I do not believe that it is futile to ask them, or even possible to avoid answering them in one way or another. In fact, since there is no single instance that could prevent us from thinking once more about its meaning and from asking for more and better insights, the questions prove in their own actuality that the very experience of thought and speech is already guided by the idea of all and everything — both as this idea excludes nothing and includes everything. Hence, whatever else we might be, the moment we articulate a word and understand it as word, we know at least implicitly that we are beings who have already begun to place themselves and their intentions into a space of meaning that comprises everything and ends nowhere.

2.1 Experience in the thought of all and nothing

The reference to the idea of something and everything in the thought of all and nothing might seem to be trivial. However, if I bring it up at this point it is not only because I would like to justify the question I have asked, but also because I consider this idea a necessary element of the answer I would like to give with all the restrictions that befit such an answer. For what matters within this context is not just the fact that we have such an idea, but that the idea itself is essential to the word we speak, hear and understand, and thus, to ourselves as human beings, both as we live with the word and as it opens to the same horizon everyone who speaks and communicates. Whatever the differences between human beings, their cultures and traditions, might be, since there can be no doubt that language hinges upon the idea of totality, it is because of this idea as the common focus of all speaking beings that we find unity before we can and must think of diversity; that we may point to the one truth that covers everything before it appears in many expressions; and, finally, that there is the possibility of translation before one has to yield to the necessity of idiosyncrasies.

2.2 Necessity and contingency in sharing the same nature and experiences

Yet, if the idea of all and everything may be said to move and to connect human thoughts and words, one must not forget that its meaning is mediated by the particularities in which it becomes operative. For the moment we try to single out this idea and think of it as such, the very attempt to do so faces its own defeat: as we remove all thoughts and objects as they have been covered by the idea of all and everything, the idea itself becomes blank and empty. What remains is the distinct recollection of indefinite meanings, and the realization that we have to turn to the experiences in which we become aware of the particularities that impress themselves before we can think of them as these particularities. In contrast to the reflective distinctions which gain meaning in correlation with the notion of all and everything, we are referred to the events in which we distinguish all sorts of impression because they happen to take place and can be pointed out as such. What matters is not the indefinite idea of all things as it relates to, and becomes distinct in, the one truth of everyone's understanding, but the same nature of things and human beings even as, and to the extent that, it makes itself known in and to all of us. Whether we can understand one another is thus, above all, a question of whether we share the same nature, and if we do, whether it makes itself known to us in the same way; that is to say, whether we have the same experiences.

As we consider the possibility of communicating with one another, we are thus caught by and between (the assumption of) sharing the same nature and the experiences nature permits us to undergo, and the idea that we can think of all and everything and place it within the horizon of this thought. What seems to be a clear-cut case of universality becomes a question of contingent events. If we truly want to understand what others tell us, we have to have the same experiences. If we do not happen to have these experiences, we are lost.

2.3 Self-awareness and the experience of experiences

Since experiences are a necessary —though not necessarily a sufficient— condition for the awareness of things, and consequently, for the actual reference to the idea of all and everything, there is still another point that needs to be taken into consideration; namely, that the awareness we confirm in the articulation of signs and words is actually also a confirmation of self-awareness, and that the experiences we undergo as they happen to us are kept apart by the experience of these experiences as we relate to them. In both instances we are in a sense free to disregard the self and the experience that comes with experiences. But the moment we start to reflect upon the way we live in this world, we discover not only the fact that we have been involved in the development of the self and working with the experience of experiences, but also the possibility and —as the discovery evokes its own objectives— the necessity to turn to either one in order to become what we can and ought to be as human beings. What matters in this regard is the ability to rethink the experiences we have made, and to connect them with frames of reference (cf. Munson 1985, 9ff.) in which we recognize ourselves and our intentions as we have been responding to these experiences; and, more specifically, that we may confirm and revise them by turning the passivity of events into the activity of anticipating them in our own ways. Yet, important as this ability might be, because and inasmuch as it makes us realize that we live in a world of our own making, the point should not be lost that this world is actually present and anticipated in the self, as the self relates to what it becomes aware of, and is potentially included in the experience that stands out for itself, as it comes with the experiences we undergo, while it might also be developed through the experiences we search for.

The reference to self-awareness and the experience of experiences is significant in various ways. In a formal sense, one could argue that it draws attention to the idea of total mediation and unity prior to all differentiations of distinct experiences. For whatever the specifics might be, inasmuch as they are brought together in the figure of the self as it relates to, and joins in, the beginning actuality of all experiences indicated by the experience of this experience, there can be no doubt that this figure stands for itself and all that might possibly follow, no matter whether it actually does. Hence, even if the spectrum of natural impressions is not complete, since its possible meaning is already contained in "the soul that is in one way or another everything" *(anima est quodammodo omnia)*, and set apart in the deeds that come into being because of their own beginning in the experience of experiences, it is in the junction of these two moments that we may speak of a basic completion which, in principle, comprises everything and includes everyone who exists under such conditions. However, if one considers the same finding in a more material sense, the point that needs to be stressed is not the priority of unity and mediation as they precede all differentiations, but their immanence in the process of personal and cultural development. The idea that appears within this context is that of unity in the form of diversity. In contrast to the first observation where the possibility of communication is actually confirmed in the formal identity of total mediation and unity (and thus, where the understanding of each other might be expected because of the same conditions of being human), we are thus confronted with a second observation, where actual differences have to be acknowledged inasmuch as they conform with the unity and mediation that bring them together and prevail in them as shared and, if compared to one another, as excluding modes of differentiation: if people belong to the same form of diversity or difference, they know what they are talking about; if they do not, they are lost. Although the conflicts between the unities in the forms of diversity may vary in their intensity, I do not think that they consist only incidental matters. On the other hand, if it is true that the constraints imposed by the factuality of communicative situations are unavoidable, it is also true that the conditions which account for these constraints are such that they do not preclude new developments. In fact, as the formation of one's own world begins in, and is sustained by, the freedom in which we relate to the self and explore the possibilities of the experience of experiences, I would say that we must not only assume that the human person is, in principle, at home in every world or culture, but that there is also the continuous chance to begin anew and to start the same process all over again if situations change because other people become part of them; that is to say, that we continue the process that has already been initiated, both as it asks for a better understanding of all reality, and as it permits us to cope anew, and in different forms of unity, with changing situations, where they do occur.

2.4 Insufficiency of nature as basis for religious traditions

Since the reference to religion does not make sense if it does not include a reference to human beings who either are religious and have their religion or not, the three points I have indicated apply to the religious situation as well. In an elementary sense, this holds true for the idea of all and nothing. For the moment we start to think and to talk, we have already agreed on the conditions which are essential both to thought and talking; and thus, on this idea, inasmuch as it is indissolubly connected with them. As such it concerns religion not only as religion is, or is not, part of being human, but also the contents which are covered by religion if, and to the extent that, they can be known and referred to.

Of course, if it should be the case that the emergence of religion is entirely and exclusively due to the way nature makes itself known to us, then it is indeed thinkable that there are human beings who have something in common what others have not. We could thus project something like the community of those who share this same nature, and try to grasp the possible meaning of their experiences by the effects they have on the things we know and understand — as we might do, for instance, if we have no ear for music but enough senses to observe people who are engaged in 'strange' activities where the production of sounds seems to be central. But it would be beside the point if those who do not share the same experiences tried to connect them with the self and the experience of experiences; and it would be equally uncertain why those who actually share them should care to do so if the claim to understanding cannot be sustained by the universality of being human.

That such a thought has its heuristic value, I do not deny. In fact, if we look at the history of religious studies, we see that considerations of this kind play an important role in the methodology of these studies. However, since I do not think that they do justice to the demands of cultural reality, or to the fact that religious traditions do, indeed, understand themselves as traditions which, if they do not address all human beings expressly, at least offer themselves to anyone who is born into that tradition, I would say that we have to focus on the whole human situation as it relates to itself if we intend to come closer to the meaning of religious reality. (cf. Vroom, 321ff.)

On the other hand, if we accept the idea of an identical (human) nature, one could still argue that the experiences of this nature are the main issue, and that it is the recovery of these experiences in one and the same universe of meaning which provides the key to true understanding. Since nobody can ignore nature without destroying his own being, it is no more than reasonable that we pay the necessary attention to human nature as it presents itself in evolutionary and psychological terms. Under the assumption that one and the same nature has been, and continues to be, the basis of cultural reality, and that it provides the experiences which, as religious experiences, give rise to a particular —that is, to a religious— apperception of man and reality, one could thus try to trace the transformation of these experiences into their religious expressions; and conversely, by subjecting the religious expressions to the program of comparative hermeneutics (cf. Pye/Morgan), one could try to recover the experiences which are, and have been, at the root of these expressions. In either case we have to have some notions of the experiences and their correlates that are relevant in this context. But because the experiences we happen to be aware of do not necessarily concur with the phenomena we assume to be religious expressions, it is the difference between the two modes of knowing which permits us to search for their unity in and by the contrasts they generate in the circular opposition of two intentionalities.

I do not have to emphasize that such an approach evinces its own attraction. And, to the extent that it allows us to think of, in principle, one religion that is and continues to be realized in many religions, I do not see why we should reject the model it provides. However, and whatever the merits of an 'interpretatio Romana' may be (cf. Lanczkowski, 3-6), there are at least two objections which need to be taken into consideration. The first concerns the attitude of religious traditions toward each other; the second, the perception of religious phenomena. In the first instance, we have to account for the fact that religious traditions do not consider themselves as mutual 'translations' of the same 'message' that has come to be concretized in their ways of life. Perhaps, they are no more than that when taken as a matter of principle. But even then, we are still left with the actual differences. In the second instance, it is the question about the perception of religious phenomena which needs to be raised in this context. The point is that we do not just observe cultural phenomena, and especially other cultures and traditions, but that we do so with the 'eye' of the particular culture and tradition that has come to consist in and with us. Hence, even if it makes sense to listen to, and to rely on, the (one and same human) nature that makes itself known in us, we must not forget that this same nature has already been transformed in the mode of being in which self-awareness and the experience of experiences have come to form and frame their own beginning; that is to say, that the nature of all becoming has turned into the beginning of a new reality which is and is not the continuation of the old one.

2.5 Co-originality of religion with man and culture

What matters in these considerations is not that we abandon the questions and answers that might be asked and given in connection with the idea of all and everything on the one hand, and the experiences we are granted by human nature, but that we develop and thematize them together with the questions and answers that concern us as persons as well as cultural beings. If we accept this conclusion, we are still left with the question about the meaning and essence of religion. But as the question is asked, it allows for the hypothesis that human culture and being human are such that religion must be part of their being if it is of any importance at all. Or, to put it differently, we know that we must not begin with nature and thought, but with personal and cultural reality as they are given and realized in terms of their own (that is, freely accepted and responsibly enacted) syntheses. I come thus to the conclusion that we cannot think of religion in any substantial sense if we do not assume that religion is already an issue the moment we refer to the person and the forms in and with which humans come to exist in the initial completion of their being.

  That such an assumption fulfils what it promises becomes clear if we take into consideration that human existence is marked by the manner in which it relates to, and presents itself together with, elements which might be described as moments of the divine (cf. James, 42ff., 60, 346, 368). Without claiming to be exhaustive, I think in this context of the experiences of togetherness and acceptance, of goodness, trust, and solidarity, of justice, forgiveness, and peace, of meaning, grace, and happiness, of beauty, holiness, and truth. What is remarkable about these experiences is not just the fact that they do occur, but that they concur with the deeds in which they are realized; that they are part of the being that grows together with them, and, consequently, of the reality that comes to consist in them. And though we might wonder about the intensity of their meaning, we do not only notice that they extend into one another, but we realize also that they are —initially and ultimately— essential to any human situation; that there is no human being that could exist without them, and no culture with any chance of continuation that has not woven them into its fabric.

Moreover, if we ask how it is possible to distinguish between the human and the inhuman, between meaning and nonsense, between 'normality' and enormity, or why the absurdities we observe in and around us should be more than just events which happen to take place, I do not think that the question can be answered —or even more elementary, that it could even be raised— if the contradictions it confirms were not preceded by actual and potential syntheses which sustain the contradictions in the parts which lack them. Since the destructions that come with the deeds and experiences of inhumanity are real enough, we know that we can and ought to be different; or, even stronger still, that we have been different at least to the extent that we survive in some kind of decency and dignity. Yet, what is the 'other' that makes the difference, if not the divine that has come to be part of being human, and continues to do so as we surrender ourselves to its demands wherever they become obvious?

The understanding of religion that evolves from these considerations interlinks with the assumption that the idea of the divine is essential to the meaning of religion. However, to the extent that the divine is referred to as a set of moments which gain significance as they are synthesized with the meaning and unfolding of man's humanity, both as humanity subsists in the person and as it consists in interpersonal and cultural relations (or, negatively, as it is sustained in contradictions which, in the mode of absence, still give testimony to the divine in the form of actual deficiencies), it is obvious that the meaning of religion must not be sought apart from being and reality, but in qualities which confirm, disclose and preserve the divine character of the human being and the culture that responds to it. Religion is, or is not, given, depending on the intensity in which the divine is present or absent in the thoughts, deeds, and attitudes that cannot be realized apart from it, or should not be realized because of it.

On the other hand, if it is true that the human situation needs to be qualified in religious terms because it is marked by the divine, both in the sense that it contains moments of the divine as elements of its being, and that it asks for the preservation as well as the completion of this being in the recognition of the divine, we are not only confronted with ourselves as an existing task whose fulfilment concurs with the ways we are (and ought to be in the unfolding of our being), but we might also wonder whether it is not possible, and necessary, to distinguish this task and to cultivate it as such; that is to say, to speak of religion as the place where human beings articulate the original task of their existence, and the reality in which they try to grow together with the essence of this task. The question is a matter of recognition where the constitution of one's own situation serves as a (more or less) similar counter-image of other situations, and —since it presents itself as mediation of all reality— as principle of perception as well as of understanding. As such it binds the answer to the insights one has gained, and tries to gain, within the context of that situation. But at the same time, it offers in what appears to be similar and dissimilar an example that permits and compels us to assess and reassess this situation by focusing on the same essential conditions of being human as they are indicated by this and all other situations in which we discover the same presence of man. What counts is not only the plausibility that comes with the intuition in which one recognizes the same in different forms or images, but also the argument that demands that we deal reasonably with the differences.

3 Religion as fulfilment of an existing task

If we approach religion in terms of an existing task that generates its own reality inasmuch as the task is actually acknowledged and realized, several specifications begin to make sense:

1) In the first place, it is obvious that the transition from the existing to the realized task must be fluid. Since the task itself cannot be severed from the concrete mode of being human, the distinction between task and fulfilment is not a matter of two different things but of one and the same reality that continues to be attached to its origin, both as it unfolds this origin and as it enacts it again in the particular modes of fulfilment. Within this context the modes of fulfilment speak for themselves. But whether we emphasize their movements or their meanings, in either case it is necessary to correlate them to the inexhaustible meaning of being as being precedes all possible differentiations of its meaning. Hence, whatever the status of the task and its fulfilment might be, as they gain contours in the constellation of thoughts, deeds, and attitudes, there is always the possibility of 'more or less.'

2) In the second place, I would like to add that, for the same reason we must speak of fluid transitions, we must speak of an open-ended process as well. For as the distinction of the task and its fulfilment relates to their (in)distinct actuality, the acknowledgment of the task does not only influence this actuality because and as it becomes discernible as such, but changes also the conditions for the distinction and its possibilities. Moreover, since we cannot disregard the impact of freedom, understanding, and grace on this process, it is obvious that we have to include this point too. Hence, whatever our insights in the existing task and its fulfilment might be, in an elementary sense we have to accept the idea that the 'end' itself is always in the making; that we may think about the end as it comes forth in its beginning, but that the full extent of its meaning is to be left to the grace of the divine as it becomes manifest in the events of history.

3) In the third place, I would like to point out that the distinction of religion is thinkable only if the meaning of being human consists in actual as well as potential self-relations, and if cultural reality reveals this feature too. In a general sense, one could refer here to the observation that human beings present themselves together with their cultures as signs which become real inasmuch as they merge with the actuality of signification. More specifically, I think of the correlation between presence and representation, as it finds its expression in personal relations and symbolic indications; that is, as it becomes obvious when we relate to each other in the configuration of You, We, and I, and perceive the signs of cultural reality as occurrences which stand for themselves and the background that appears in them. In contrast to the idea of a mere presence, we have to conceive of the same presence as it recovers itself in its own actuality; and, thus, of the possibility to account for this presence by defining it in a representational sense. If we think of religion along these lines, its distinction denotes, in essence, the actualization of a possibility which is inherently given with the emergence of human beings and their cultures.

4) In the fourth place, I would like to contend that —in case it is true that religion concerns the essence of being human— we have to understand the development of religion as a process in which the enactment of humanity is mediated by the actual self-relations in which men and cultures have come to exist; and that it is the purpose of this process to recover the full meaning that is potentially given with the act of human existence and the

demands of cultural reality. Hence, whether we think of religious traditions as they appear together with cultural traditions, or of religions as they denote their own ways in —and in a sense— apart from the ways of the one or the other culture, in either case we cannot disregard the fact that there is an essential bond between religion and culture. As cultures and religions change, so do religions and cultures. And, if the one does, and the other does not, conflicts have to be expected.

5) Finally, I would like to draw attention to the idea that the distinction of religion gains the more significance the closer it comes to the original conditions of being human. Within this context the cultural mediation does not cease. But it becomes less important the more religious traditions succeed in the articulation of their task and the understanding of what it means to fulfil this task, inasmuch as the fulfilment is in tune both with the cultural potential and with the religious tradition itself as it creates its own distinct and unmitigated culture.

4   Unity and diversity in religious traditions

So far, I have tried to approach religion as it might be understood by the detached and reflective observer. Within this context it is important to note that the conditions for observing religion are such that they imply and depend upon the observer's participation in the constitution of the human situation. The achievement of detachment becomes thus a deed and a goal which need the acknowledgment and the understanding of their own mediatory character no less than the freedom of thought and reflection in which truth might —and must— be pursued, both as it is, and as it can be, understood. In the anticipation of the idea that all that is, and shall ever be, can be accounted for, we are referred to the initial syntheses of our own being. And, by distinguishing the elements of these syntheses as they become discernible in contrasting modes of unity, the idea begins to make sense to trace the possibilities of becoming both as they have been, and as they might be, realized under varying conditions; and, in consequence, to conceive of a convergence of the two ideas in which the difference of being and becoming has been overcome in the understanding of the truth that precedes either one. Since it is not possible under the present circumstances to develop this point any further, I have to leave it at that. However, I still have to answer the question about experiences shared with others.

If we approach religion along these lines, the point that matters in the dynamics of religious traditions is both their actual achievement and continuous responsibility in enacting, maintaining, and developing the wholeness, the integrality, and the integrity of the human being and his culture as they come into focus by the presence (as well as the absence) of the divine; that is, as they are marked by the Holy in all aspects of being and reality. How religious traditions do indeed fulfil their task is a question which cannot be answered beforehand. Since the fulfilment of the task extends into and concurs with the culture to which it belongs, we have to acknowledge the same idiosyncrasy that is typical for all cultures, and, in principle, for each human being who forms a world of his own. And since the distinction of the religious task cannot be realized apart from and without the means provided by tradition, the same holds true for religion as it defines itself in the distinction of its task and the actuality of the fulfilment of that task.

On the other hand, if wholeness and the Holy are the central issue of religious traditions, we must not assume that the realization of the religious task is only a matter of different developments and the unity that agrees with them. In a sense, one could point here to the universality of thought and thinking as an essential element in all communication, or to the similarities in the experiences of human nature as they are by and large discernible in the patterns of behaviour. And though the differences between human cultures are obvious enough, if we agree on similarities between them, we might as well expect that the constitution of cultural reality observes and follows at least in principle the same rules. However, what I consider even more important is the unity of the divine as it becomes manifest the moment one realizes that its meaning is not exhausted by any synthesis we may think of; or better, that it transcends all syntheses no matter how perfect and beautiful they might be. Hence, if it is true that the human person is the first synthesis of the divine, both in the sense that being human means to be actually called and attracted by the divine, and in the sense that the person is and remains free to surrender himself to the demands and the potential of the divine, we might as well turn to the person as the first and lasting sign that connects all religious traditions before they become different, and reconnects them again after they have been different, because the completion of personal being has always been the same goal. And conversely, if it is true that the divine carries us beyond all confinements, we might as well follow its indications as they comprise the various syntheses and try to recover the finite meaning of these syntheses as the infinite meaning of the divine precedes them all.

Since the idea of truth always means more than we know, if we are convinced that a statement is true or false, it is evident that this idea precedes and transcends all notions by which we try to grasp it. Whatever the meaning of truth might be, in accordance with its idea we know, thus, that it must be transcendent, and that it is necessary to think of transcendental truth if it should be meaningful to think at all. Hence, it is neither surprising, nor inconsistent with religious traditions, that they present themselves in terms of transcendental truth, or that philosophy has introduced the concept of 'the transcendent' as a symbol of religious intentions and the attempt to grasp and understand them.

To the extent that the concept of 'the transcendent' is indicative of the kind of thinking that is needed in order to cope with religious traditions, there is definitely no reason to abandon this symbol (cf. Vroom, 376ff.). But at the same time I would like to argue that this symbol alone is not sufficient if it is not complemented by another symbol, in and by which we relate to the person as the person grows into and together with the syntheses of the divine. Since the attachment to these syntheses and the symbols in and by which they are found and maintained is generally indicated by the term 'faith,' I think that it makes sense to retain this term — but, then, not in the sense of a possible or real opposition between knowing and believing, nor as a term which identifies only religious traditions, but as the symbol which stands for the person as the person becomes truly personal, and for cultural reality as cultural reality complies with the purpose of all being; that is, as the person and culture relate originally to themselves in accordance with the meaning of the divine, and to religion as 'their' religion draws them into the splendour of divine existence and holiness (cf. Cantwell Smith). Within this context it becomes obvious that faith cannot be separated from the beliefs one holds to be true, nor from the culture in which it is specified. But as the word 'faith' symbolizes the movement toward the completion of the human being in terms of particular traditions and cultures, it recalls also the conditions under which we become persons in the first place, and because of which it is possible to relate to ourselves and each other in the same medium of divine attraction and the continuous obligation of unrestricted holiness.

5 Toward a new community in the mediation of communities

Since personal experiences are not primarily a matter of shared feelings and identical thoughts, but of interpersonal relations that confirm the unity and priority of the person as they extend into, and connect themselves with, the realm of cultural reality, the test of whether it is possible to share personal religious experiences with another rests on the community that comes into being as a result of such experiences. To speak of religious traditions is, in this regard, equivalent to the conclusion that the task of religion cannot be fulfilled apart from the community that is formed in and because of its fulfilment. As such they invite, at least in principle, all human beings who are to become, and continue to be in need of becoming, true persons. But just because they are inviting and open to a culturally mediated realm of total meaning, they also close off those who do not live by the same symbols and sets of interpersonal relations.

Depending on what we would like to emphasize, we might either concentrate on religious traditions as they offer themselves to all human beings and attract the whole of cultural reality, or refer to them as they form their own universe; that is to say, as they are accessible to all, or out of reach for those who stay outside. Since both approaches are valid, they make it necessary to think of various situations and variable patterns of inclusivity and exclusivity. In terms of actual relations between human beings, we have therefore to expect different degrees of shared experiences and community formation. But at the same time we are also faced with the question of the possibility of sharing under the conditions of the 'ideal type.'

In accordance with their dynamics, religious traditions aim —ideally speaking— at a situation where everyone has found the completion of his being, and where the cultural milieu is such that it agrees with the divine character of all reality. In an essential sense, we are thus referred to a state of complete fulfilment in which the question of sharing has —as any other question— lost its urgency because the state that has been reached coincides with the answer that might and should be given.

Of course, as we realize that the envisaged fulfilment of the religious task is necessarily in the making, the goal assumes the character of a transcendental principle. But the fact that it assumes this significance does not imply that it ceases to be real, or that it should be less effective as far as its transforming impact on the constitution of the human situation is concerned. In either case, whether we think of the goal itself or the instances in which it is realized, if we accept religious traditions as they offer themselves in terms of their completion, we are confronted with both the fact and the idea that the same transcendental principle which necessitates us to stress the unity and universality of these traditions accounts also for an actual, and, because of this principle, lasting difference, and otherness among these traditions.

As there is no more than one totality of meaning, the immediate conclusion about the possibility of sharing personal experiences with people from other traditions must be —at least within the context of ideal types— an unmistakable 'no.' For with the same force that a religious tradition draws a person into its own realm of meaningful existence (cf. Munson 1975, 19), it conditions that person not only in the actuality and potential of his being, but presents itself also as the ultimate measure for the assessment and reassessment of all reality. And even if understanding and insight might suggest a different conclusion, since and as long as they are mediated by the same religious tradition, they do not really alter the exigencies of that tradition.

On the other hand, if it is necessary to stress the impossibility of sharing with others what is theirs and not ours, one might wonder whether the transformative force of religious traditions could not change these traditions from within and to such a degree that the obvious differences become secondary to their unity insofar as this unity is not a matter of fact but of principle. I do not know the answer to this question. But as it points to a community of people apart from, though essentially related to, and mediated in, the communities with which they identify themselves originally, one could at least try to find out whether the meaning of the divine is not only such that it invites us to think of and search for this community, but also of a kind that the place for this community is, in principle, a necessary constituent of any religious traditions; and, thus, that the formation and the development of this community is not just a discovery which cannot be refuted because a particular constellation of cultural history leaves no other choice, but an actual recovery of possibilities which should have been realized ever since human beings began to speak and to live with one another in adjacent traditions. In conjunction with the efforts to understand whatever is understandable, the option of a new, though structurally already asked for, community in the mediation of communities does not cancel the impacts of otherness. Yet, as this community begins to take shape because people join each other in the common —and at the same time new— search for their meaning and truth, the point that matters is not that they share experiences which cannot be shared, but that they enter a dimension in which it becomes possible to make old experiences anew, both as they relate to each other in personal ways, and as they do so, by recovering themselves and their traditions in the light of these relations.

6 Summary

(1) Since I have been asked to approach the issue of sharing religious experience with people from other traditions as a philosopher, a question that comes up almost immediately is one regarding the possible meaning of philosophy in this context; and, more specifically, of the kind of philosophy one stands for. The stance I take in this regard can, in a sense, be summed up by the idea that what is needed is actually a philosophy which is as much a matter of pure thought as it is a comprehensive account of the whole range of experience and fact. Moreover, as we know more than we realize and less than we think to know, I am convinced that traditional man is less ignorant that the expert tends to assume, and conversely, that both expert and traditional man are probably

more ignorant than either one is willing to concede; and thus, that it is possible for the expert to know more about traditional man (and less about himself) than is actually known, even if and as this knowledge is gained in the recognition of the primal truth of tradition. At any rate, what I consider most important is the realization that philosophy is definitely no substitute for the practical deed; that it is essential to recognize the priority of human existence and cultural reality if philosophy is to become truly philosophical; that it is not the task of philosophy to make and to provide the guidelines (or programs) for human attitudes and actions, but to understand them, to grasp their significance, their truth — and thus, to be of service (not to theology, but) to the development of humanity by taking care of the demands and possibilities of self-reflective consciousness in connection with, and in contrast to, the acknowledgment of man's conscience and cultural responsibility.

(2) As the question we have been asked concerns the relationship between human beings from different religious traditions, it is obvious that an adequate understanding of the character and meaning of these traditions is essential to a philosophical assessment of the possibilities (and impossibilities) connected with them. Hence, in one way or another we have to cope with questions about religious traditions: What are the conditions that enable us to speak of religious traditions and to study them? — What are, in the light of experience, fact, and understanding, the conditions and principles that account for the emergence, the successful development, the meaning, the distortion, and the failure of religious traditions? — What are the consequences of the constitution of religious traditions for the encounter between them; what are the possibilities, the limitations, and the options that are offered as a matter of principle and with regard to the people involved? — In the actuality of the event, the encounter is no doubt an issue that concerns primarily the people who are either free or forced to make their decision on this issue. But if we are to understand the process, I think that particular attention must be paid to the child that needs tradition before he can identify with it and be responsible as an adult person. Moreover, if it turns out that the child (and the convert as a symbol for the continuous and, in principle, identical significance of the relationship between person, tradition, and truth) is the true universal in all traditions, one can hardly overvalue the conclusion that a philosophy which is set on understanding religious traditions has to avoid the trap of unmediatated 'monism'; or, positively, that it has to begin with the principle of mutual equivalence in the assessment of religious traditions before it may turn to comparative differentiations, and to attempts at propounding criteriological evaluations.

(3) In focusing on experience within this context I consider it most important that we keep track of experience as experience correlates to the constitution of religious tradition, and finds its expression in the actuality of communal existence and speech. What matters in this regard is, on the one hand, the connections between thought and nature, or better, between human nature and the way we respond to it as it manifests itself to us, and on the other hand, that we give due credit to the fact that our attitude to experiences is a question of passivity as well as of activity; that we are not only capable of undergoing experiences, but are also capable of transforming them, and thus, of entering into a world where the space between people develops into the reality we actually live with and draw our energies from, to the extent that we are and become persons. Depending on the perspective, one can either emphasize the external or the internal character of this space. But whether one does either the one of the other, if religious traditions teach us anything, then they strongly indicate that the man's substance is not primarily the principle of life inasmuch as this principle defines the individual as a representative of the species within the continuity of the life-process, but is the event of humanity as it comes to consist in relations that define the whole of being human as an element apart from, and the elementary synthesis with the whole (in the self), as a part of, the human being; that is to say, that the (external) relation to the whole is in itself a particular element (an internal relation) of man's being which, inasmuch as and because it has come to exist as an elementary synthesis, is never complete but always, and necessarily so, open to additional intensive and extensive development.

(4) To the extent that the analysis of experiences culminates in the realization of what one might call the moments of the divine —both as they draw the human being into their own movement of meaning and reality, and as the refusal of their acknowledgment exposes the human situation to the threats of meaninglessness and absurdity— it makes sense to think of man's being in terms of an existing task (which one could also call the prototype of concrete universality), and of religious traditions as the place where this task and its fulfilment are actually and by means of the cultural environment distinguished and (in the figure of presence and re-presentation) formulated as such. The way the question is asked, it points to a specific net of relations which connects the expression of meaning and fact with the meaning of being and expression. And, as the question makes us ponder, and asks to remember, the infinite meaning of holiness and truth, it confirms the actuality of faith in the acceptance of, and the initial relation to, the divine. Moreover, as this notion refers to all possible situations and their particular make-up, but also to the moments of the divine as they give, and ask for, unity and coherence in these situations (that is, concrete wholeness and holiness), it permits and

necessitates us to consider different religious traditions and various attitudes within them. Besides, if it is true that it is the same faith in the divine which lends religious traditions their religious character and —as it merges with particular circumstances and symbols— their unity in the form of difference, the opposite holds true, too, namely, that it is the transcendent meaning of the divine which makes them similar and dissimilar inasmuch as it precedes, and merges with, the deeds, thoughts, and attitudes in which this meaning is concretized. In the common and structural convergence of wholeness and the task that symbolizes the achievement of holiness, they are thus similar and dissimilar for two reasons: because faith as faith enables the person to grow into the adulthood of the faithful believer, and due to the meaning of the divine as this meaning judges, and continues to do so, the symbolization of the existing task and its fulfilment. Hence, whether we emphasize the unity of the difference in religious traditions, in either case we have to remember that beginning and end are intertwined, and that it is impossible to reduce actual religions to immanence without transcendence or to transcendence without immanence.

(5) The model that appears as a result of these considerations is in itself a construction which might or might not be adequate. Since the model makes it possible to think of religious traditions in a certain way, however, it clearly indicates that our approach to them must be conditioned by the fact that they form their own universes of total meaning; that is to say, that their universality is a concrete and thus inverse universality which, by evoking its own kind of objectivity and reference, presents itself (not just as a fiction that is representative of meanings, but) as the very image which, in principle and essence, accounts for all of reality and truth. In spite of the fact that I have approached religious traditions on the assumption that they depend on the same constitutive principle, I thus reach the conclusion that they are, ideally speaking (and in disregard of their historical dynamics), different and exclusive because they are essentially universal and inclusive in their orientation and meaning; and, in consequence, that it is not possible to share in the religious experience of persons from another tradition. Yet, if this is one part of the story, it is not the end of it. For if we take into consideration that both the initial faith and the transcendent truth are such that no concretion and representation can ever exhaust them, and that the demands of actual wholeness and holiness already speak for themselves before they are subject to distinct interpretations, there is no reason why we should not appeal to them and let ourselves be guided by the perspectives they provide inasmuch as they tell us that there is no meaning in truth if it is not accompanied by peace, and no sense in faith if it rejects understanding. The realm that is opened up by such considerations is that of abstract univer-

sality, which might appear to mean little when compared with concrete life. But as this universality makes it possible to discern its enactment (in the sense of actual judgments), it may also be helpful (a) in understanding universality as it appears to be real and as it is rendered illusionary if the surrender to the divine turns into the usurpation of the divine; and (b) for the formation of a community which does not cancel the meaning of religious traditions, but grows in and with the encounter of human beings who truly care for their common task and are willing to accept themselves and each other in the light and mirror of mutual existence.

Bibliography

James, W. *The Varieties of Religious Experience: A Study in Human Nature.* New York: Mentor Books, 1958.

Lanczkowski, G. *Einführung in die Religionsphänomenologie.* Darmstadt, 1978.

Munson, T. *Religious Consciousness and Experience.* The Hague: Nijhoff, 1975.

——. *The Challenge of Religion: A Philosophical Appraisal.* Pittsburgh: Duquesne, 1985.

Pye, M. and R. Morgan, eds. *The Cardinal Meaning.* The Hague, 1973.

Smith, W. Cantwell. *Faith and Belief.* Princeton, 1979.

Vroom, H. M. *Religions and the Truth.* Amsterdam/Grand Rapids: Rodopi/ Eerdmans, 1989.

CHAPTER 4

Meaning, Power, and the Sharing of Religious Experience: An Anthropology of Religion Point of View

André Droogers

This article is on interreligious understanding. First, the possibilities and limits of an anthropological view of the theme of sharing religious experience are explored. A distinction is made between sharing as communication and as communion. It is then suggested that the general human capacity of meaning-making facilitates the sharing of religious experience, without necessarily guaranteeing successful communication, let alone communion. The fundamental human need of belonging and its fulfilment through the use of symbols in religion can facilitate the sharing of religious experience. Power should not be ignored as a fundamental aspect of situations in which people seek to share religious experience.

1 The anthropologist's role

In talking about sharing religious experience, we use the term 'sharing' in a double sense. First, it refers to transmitting experience, expressed in knowledge, from one person to the other, as an act of *communication*. Second, it refers to having a common experience, as an act of existential *communion*. Anthropologists have been active on the level of communication more often than on that of communion. And even at that they have rarely acted as direct participants in the concrete process of communication between religious persons who exchange experiences. Anthropologists have been more or less on the sidelines, as translators in the process of sharing as communication. Their contribution has been indirect, mainly through their publications. Anthropological monographs have provided the opportunity to learn about other religions; not all religions, but tribal religions, popular forms of world religions, forms of syncretism, and religious movements in particular. The focus has generally been on religion as a cultural and contextual phenomenon. Anthropology has offered a unique perspective on other religions.

45

Discussion on the possibilities of understanding other cultures has not been lacking in anthropology. Thus, monographs on religions (Evans-Pritchard 1937; 1956) led, in the sixties, to the so-called rationality debate. The central issue was whether 'scientific' empirical verification should be the criterion for an appraisal of, for example, witchcraft, or whether a culture's own logic and language should be the ultimate standard (Bernstein; Ulin; Wilson). In this article the emphasis is on meaning and signification as the universal basis of mutual understanding. This approach allows for difference and commonality, understanding and failed dialogue. Moreover, researcher and researched can be shown to belong to the same framework.

Though not participating directly in the sharing —in both senses— of religious experience, anthropologists have something to say on the encounter of religions. Anthropologists can reflect, in a general way, on the nature and contents of the religious encounter. They can also study specific situations in which adepts of different religions meet. This is not done entirely from an outsider's position. Even as a translator, the anthropologist cannot avoid influencing the contents of the communication. Moreover, the standard anthropological method, that of participant observation, suggests that the fieldworker seeks to share the experience of the people studied, if only as a research method during fieldwork. Because of this subjectivity in translation and in participation, communion is not totally absent from the anthropological work done at the level of communication.

Having thus defined the anthropologist's position in the process of sharing religious experience, the next step in this essay will be to describe the particular view this anthropologist would apply in analyzing this process. I will focus on meaning, on the basic human experience, and on power.

2 Meaning

Meaning, and the way it is produced, are essential elements of the encounter between people who share their religious experience. Sharing presupposes meaning. In order to speak of an encounter, a common form of expression is needed, especially when the participants in the encounter come from divergent cultural and religious backgrounds. The participants need some symbolic apparatus for their communication and for their communion: a language of words, of sounds, of gestures, of objects. Anthropologist have found this common ground in the concept of culture: human beings can be defined by their exclusive gift of culture, i. e., the capacity to produce and manipulate symbols, their meanings, and the patterns in which these are brought together (e. g., Crick). Symbols represent and evoke something else that is absent, abstract, opaque, or invisible. Among the symbols, metaphors play a predominant role. Metaphors, taken from one domain, have the useful characteristic of elucidating another —diffuse and unclear— domain, by comparing it with the supposedly similar but clearly patterned situation of the first domain. (Fernandez, *passim*)

Almost anything can serve as a symbol: sounds, colours, gestures, various of natural and artificial objects, etc. In the course of time, during the history of a society but also in the course of one's personal history, symbols can be given new meanings, meanings can be linked to new symbols, and symbols can be rearranged in new patterns. A particular culture represents the totality of symbols, meanings and patterns current at a certain moment. Participants in that culture make personal use of that stock, according to their needs and interests, reproducing their culture, but often also transforming it. Even in reproduction, change occurs, if we interpret re-production as reproduction. "Meaning is always *coming into being* through the 'happening' of understanding" (Bernstein, 139). Culture, both as a general human characteristic and in the sense of a particular culture, is therefore more a process than a static unity. The huge potential that symbols have for meaning necessarily leads to a dynamic situation.

Experience, as a phenomenon linked to time, cannot be understood outside of this dynamic cultural framework. It does not exist in an autonomous way, as if it were coming from the outside, imposing itself on the individual. Experience is in itself a process of interpretation, of imputing meaning. It is a way in which people account for what happens to them, in order to make sense of it. Their culture, and more specifically their religion, helps them to do so. As a consequence, anthropologists, and social scientists in general, are interpreters of an already interpreted reality, and work within a 'double hermeneutic' (Giddens, 284, 374). In describing experiences and communicating them, anthropologists are twice removed from the original situation. They share with others what was first shared with them. To the filter of the informant's interpretation, the anthropologist adds his own. Within the definition of culture just given, studying culture is in itself a cultural activity, a meaningful dealing with meaning.

If the element of encounter is added to this, not one, but at least two experiences, those of the two sides involved, must be taken into account, unless of course —as happens only exceptionally— the sharing of these experiences generates absolute communion. Normally, there is more misunderstanding than understanding. Even when people share the same symbols, they often impute different meanings to these symbols (Cohen). As long as they leave these meanings implicit, communication and even communion are realized, albeit as an illusion. But as soon as questions are raised, misunderstandings can crop up.

If the partners in the encounter belong to different cultures and religions, the chances that this will happen are greatly enhanced. Religions deal with an invisible, not empirically verifiable reality. This reality can be experienced as too rich for words, for music, for dance, or for any other expression. The mystery is always greater than the symbols used to express it. If extra-sensory perception is part of the religious experience, communication is hardly possible, communion virtually impossible. Even if one partner makes an effort to understand the central symbols from within the other partner's culture or religion, the result is not necessarily promising. Especially in the field of religion, where one deals with an inexpressible reality, different languages are spoken, even when the same concepts are shared (God, good, salvation, etc.). Anthropologists, though sometimes stereotyped as experts on foreign cultures, must also admit that their experience is partial.

Yet, the symbolic framework does not only produce confusion. In encounter, it not only leads to a chaos of varied symbols, double meanings, and differing patterns; it is also due to this same framework that communication and even communion are possible. When this happens, the participants experience the event as exceptional, and therefore as a landmark in their dialogue. People may hit on a common understanding of each other's symbols, or on a new symbol, serving as common ground. Even a structural resemblance between symbols or patterns can be sufficient. Some images are almost universal (e. g., road or path, birth, death, body, nature). The extra dimension religious experience contains also conceals promises for unexpected common experiences. Whatever the form of commonality and understanding, syncretism flourishes in this context (Gort et al.). It can be said that the symbolic framework is both the human being's weakness and its strength. Its potential combines both the limited and the unlimited.

One can see this at work in one and the same person when people convert from one religion to another. Old symbols, meanings, and patterns do not disappear immediately, not even when the conversion seems to be very dramatic. The convert faces the task of making sense of the new religion in contrast with the old one. In the process, symbols from one religion can be combined with meanings from the other. Patterns from one can be imposed on the other, rearranging symbols and transforming their meanings.

Not only can these processes of signification be observed among converts; they also occur when people from one religion seek inspiration from another religion, for example, from its meditation techniques. In a sense, it has also been present in at least part of the phenomenology of religion. Religious phenomena, assumed to be similar, have been given the same name and analogous interpretation. Phenomenologists thus imputed meaning within the framework of intercultural comparison.

3 A view of basic human experiences

A certain degree of commonality is reinforced by the fact that, despite the differences in meaning-making, human beings from different cultures and religions do not only share the human symbolizing capacity called culture, but also meet the same basic problems. These problems belong to the 'existentials,' 'the fixed features of human existence' (Vroom). Religious experience is marked by them. The solutions religions offer to the basic problems differ strikingly, yet the problems are largely the same. This reference to basic problems implies a particular view of 'the' human being. In the course of both cultural and philosophical anthropology, several of these views have been developed, especially in the context of the study of religion. The advantage of such views is that since they are not derived from one of the religions represented in an encounter, they can offer a common basis for understanding diverse experiences. In that sense, these views facilitate the sharing of religious experience.

The views in question cannot all be mentioned here. For the purpose of this essay, and in conjunction with the theme of sharing religious experience, a choice must be made. One view of the human being, developed in the anthropology of religion, is that of Van Baal (1972, 1981). Fernandez (pp. 25, 62, 188-213) offers remarkably similar insights. Characteristically, both these views are linked with the approach to symbols and meaning referred to in the preceding section.

In Van Baal's view, human beings live in a fundamental tension between being 'part' and being 'apart,' between belonging to a totality and being put at a distance. This totality can be society; it can also be nature. In any case, people have to deal with a double experience: on the one hand they feel part of that totality, on the other hand they sometimes experience it as a force and an intention directed against them, isolating them. One solution to this fundamental experience is offered by religion, through the use of symbols. Symbols enable communication, even when reality is experienced as hostile. Precisely because symbols are able to evoke an absent, invisible reality, they help to establish contact with that reality. It becomes possible to talk about it, and what is more, to communicate with it. If these religious symbols are shared by other people, it becomes possible at the same time to recover the experience of social belonging. Each and every religion produces its own forms and contents to express and solve the fundamental tension, but all share the basic experience of belonging as well as alienation. The sharing of religious experience is facilitated by this common tension.

Fernandez refers to the phenomenon that individuals are said to experience themselves as 'individuals.' The plurality of human experience frustrates the sensation of the whole. Essential to that sensation of the whole is the relatedness of things. It is this relatedness which is lacking in many of the new experiences with which people are confronted, especially in rapidly changing societies. In seeking to understand the new and the inchoate, "the dark at the bottom of the stairs" (Fernandez, xiii, 214), images are crucial because of their capacity to establish relatedness. Metaphoric predications are shown to have performative consequences: "it is the dynamic interplay of these metaphors that is most interesting and consequential and which gives the impression of coherence — of the return to the whole" (Fernandez, 200). Precisely because seemingly unconnected domains are linked through metaphors, the sensation of totality and wholeness can be restored.

The interesting thing about sharing is that it has the connotation of parts and a whole. The *partners* in the process of sharing, whether in communication or in communion, are *part*icipating in each other's experiences. The presupposition of sharing is commonality. Therefore, when talking about sharing religious experience, the reference to wholeness as the basic human problem is particularly relevant. The questions we raise in this book concerning the possibility of sharing religious experience are directly linked to what can be viewed as a basic religious problem and a paradigmatic experience: being part as well as being apart. The partners in dialogue seek to become part of a larger whole, a common context, although both are conscious of the fact that they are apart, separated by their differing religious traditions and experiences. In this instance too, metaphors make for wholeness.

The necessity for a focus on wholeness also stems from the present world situation. As we turn to the last decade of this century, there are signs of unexpected unity and commonality, especially between East and West. Yet, this should not close our eyes to the fact that humanity must urgently find a solution to acute crises like those of pollution and poverty. Here again the problem is one of belonging or falling apart. The world religions share a responsibility in this respect. Moreover, the process of secularization is often a common concern. The sharing of their religious experiences cannot be separated from that of sharing the experience of living in the same inchoate problematical world.

Summarizing what has been said up to this point, culture, as human dealing with symbols, makes for communication *and* for lack of communication. It corresponds with the basic human experience of being both part and apart. In religion, people use symbols to reduce the tension between belonging and alienation. Wholeness is emphasized. The encounter between persons from different religions and the present crises of humanity represent situations that fall within these same parameters of being part and apart.

4 Power

Anthropologists view religion as a cultural and social phenomenon. Signification is therefore not a process that is self-sufficient in its interpretation. Neither should it be reduced to the subject's individual creation. One way of taking the social and cultural context into account is by referring to power. When we discuss the sharing of religious experience, a reference to power can be particularly illuminating. This already becomes clear when the fundamental question on the possibility of sharing religious experience is reviewed in the light of the concept of power.

Power can be defined as the capacity to influence behaviour. The question about the possibility of sharing religious experience is also a question about the limits of power. Power is present in the process of signification, which is central to any religion, and therefore also when religious persons meet for dialogue. Room for sharing and for experiments in signification is reduced, or widened, by the exercise of power. On the other hand, power can be restricted by another way of signification, which may be the consequence of sharing religious experience. In other words, power relations themselves are subject to signification, since people attach meaning to the behaviour of certain people, who are in this way placed above others. In the end, none of the three —power, signification and sharing— can exist without the human cultural capacity to make symbols and to impute meaning to them.

With regard to religion, power is exercised at three levels: first, in the relations between human and supernatural beings; second, in the relations between people within a religious organization; and third, in the contacts between people in that organization and people in society. Power refers to a bilateral relationship, even if one side is dominant. Therefore, at each of the three levels, double relationships of power exist. Thus, people are under the impact of the power of God, gods, or spirits. They may feel overpowered. Yet, on the other hand, they seek to influence the behaviour of these supernatural beings. They strive for power over them. Within a religious organization, leaders or religious specialists exert influence over their adepts. At the same time, however, these adepts have a certain influence on the leaders and specialists. In contacts with wider society, the members of religious organizations often seek to influence the behaviour of people who do not belong to that organization. The social scientific study of religion has given much attention to the other side of the coin: the power that society can exercise on a religion.

All three levels influence the sharing of religious experience. The religious experience itself stems mainly from the first level, that of the relations between human beings and their God, gods, or spirits. It is largely this experience that is to be shared. The distinction we made between sharing religious experience as communication and as communion suggests two variations in the exercise of power at the two other levels, depending on the ultimate goal of the sharing. Communion is of course predominant on the level of the religious organization. With regard to the contacts with wider society, communication is more probable, but communion is not absent.

At the level of the religious organization, religious specialists often have a prominent role when the sharing of their personal religious experience is central to that religion. The very base of their power is the message of their experience. In a more general way, religious specialists can occupy a privileged and legitimized position with regard to the contacts with the supernatural. In that case, an effort is made to monopolize religious experience through them. This effort is never totally successful, since people have their own religious experiences, though these may be a faithful copy of that experienced by the religious specialists: followers can be *plus papiste que le pape*. Where the position of religious specialists is strong, the people's experiences have been relegated to the domain of popular religion, often judged negatively ('magic,' 'syncretism,' 'sect') by the specialists. Yet, in the context of the bilateral power relations between adepts and specialists, the give and take of negotiation is continuously occurring. The central questions are: What must be viewed as the central symbols; what do these mean; how do they relate to each other; and what are the consequences for the behaviour of people? The sharing itself seems more often a dynamic process of signification than a static exchange of taken positions. When communion takes the place of communication, this process is most productive. But even in the case of communication, reproduction of points of view can be reproduction and therefore transformation, if only on minor points. This also is typical of the third level, that of the relations between a religious organization and the rest of society, including other religious groups. When power is exercised, signification is at stake. This can imply the negation of a religion's truths, either by secular society, or by other religious groups. On the other hand, religions can be greatly enhanced by a society, as long as that religion serves the fundamental purposes of that society. In that case, the signification offered by the religion corresponds to expectations on the side of society.

Widening the horizon, the dialogue between religions belongs of course to this third level. Not much direct attention has been paid to power in dialogue situations, since reference to this aspect could hamper good contact. Yet, within the definition given above, dialogue too is a power situation. Western scholarship can be a source of power, notwithstanding the best of intentions. Leaders can stimulate dialogue, but also prevent it from occurring. People in dialogue seek to influence each other's behaviour, if only in the minimal sense of adopting an attitude of mutual respect and tolerance. But there can be more. It has been said that, as far as Christian theology is concerned, the interreligious dialogue dictates the agenda. In any case, the Christian theology of religions has to deal explicitly with power relations between religions. Power depends in large measure on the unique and specific qualities of a religion. It is therefore directly linked with the signification process. The definition of identity forms the basis of power. Here ideology can play a role. Construction of this power basis is a matter of negotiation, of taking in bargaining positions long before dialogue actually takes place. It is precisely for this reason that it is such a delicate job and rouses so much heated discussion. Explicit signification complicates dialogue.

It is, therefore, fitting to pay attention to informal dialogue between adepts, as being different from that of the formal dialogue among leaders or their representatives, and possessing a different power constellation. Signification seems to be much more implicit, metaphorical, practical, and problem-directed, and power is exercised in a more natural (i. e., cultural) way, as part of normal and on-going relations. Not all believers share their leaders' interest in maintaining orthodoxy and consistency. At the grass roots, the chances for communion in dialogue may therefore be much more promising than at the official level, where even mere communication can be problematic. Yet, utter failure of efforts at sharing religious experience is equally possible, both among leaders and common believers, as is clear from situations where religious differences contribute to the rise of armed conflicts.

There is one more aspect of power which shows links to dialogue. As we have mentioned before, religions form one of the forums where world problems can be discussed. The urge to find solutions serves as an extra means of pressure that dialogue must occur. The sharing of religious experience cannot be separated from the problematical context in which it takes place. World society thus influences the process of sharing at this level, but it can also be influenced by the results of dialogue. Here too signification is important: What kind of world do we live in; what is our task in it? Not only communication, but real communion is possible under the pressure of the world's problems.

5 Conclusion

The anthropology of religion can make an important contribution to the
debate on the possibilities of sharing religious experience. Sharing
religious experience, both as communication and as communion is shown
to be possible, but is a hazardous enterprise. The human capactiy for
meaning-making allows for extremes and vicissitudes, for heaven and hell.
The human fate of being part as well as apart, and the eternal longing
for wholeness can form a tragic basis for both commonality and separation. The fact that sharing experiences is a form of power may come as
a shock. Yet, it is realistic to be conscious of this aspect, especially when
it leads religions to the discovery of their common responsibility and
power in dealing with world problems.

Bibliography

Baal, J. van. *Symbols for Communication: An Introduction to the Anthropological Study of Religion.* Assen, 1971.

——. *Man's Quest for Partnership: The Anthropological Study of Religion.*
Assen, 1981.

Bernstein, Richard J. *Beyond Objectivism and Relativism: Science, Hermeneutics, and Praxis.* Oxford, 1983.

Crick, Malcom. *Explorations in Language and Meaning: Towards a Semantic Anthropology.* London, 1976.

Cohen, Anthony P. *The Symbolic Construction of Community.* Chichester/
London, 1985.

Evans-Pritchard, E. E. *Witchcraft, Oracles and Magic among the Azande.*
Oxford, 1937.

——. *Nuer Religion.* Oxford, 1956.

Fernandez, James W. *Persuasions and Performances: The Play of Tropes in
Culture.* Bloomington, 1986.

Giddens, Anthony. *The Constitution of Society: Outline of the Theory of
Structuration.* Oxford, 1984.

Gort, Jerald, Hendrik Vroom, Rein Fernhout, and Anton Wessels, eds.
Dialogue and Syncretism: An Interdisciplinary Approach. Grand Rapids/
Amsterdam, 1989.

Ulin, Robert C. *Understanding Cultures: Perspectives in Anthropology and
Social Theory.* Austin, 1984.

Wilson, Bryan R., ed. *Rationality.* Oxford, 1970.

CHAPTER 5

Can Believers Share the Qur'an and the Bible as Word of God?

Wilfred Cantwell Smith

The thrust of the argument set forth here is that we may perhaps best deal with the issue posed by considering two approaches to it, one more theological than usual, one more personalist. The two might be formulated a questions, one relating to God, one to the day-to-day life, behaviour, aspirations, and sensibilities of us as particular human persons:

(a) Does God use the Qur'an, and the Bible, to enter the lives of Muslims and Christians respectively, and speak to them, to them to Himself? More historically, has He in fact done so over the centuries, more or less effectively?

(b) Do human beings enter God's presence and become to some extent aware of His will for them, by treating one or other of these two books as scripture? Again, historically, have they done so?

If one's answer to these questions, or even to one of them, be, "To some extent, and in some cases, yes," then one is perhaps challenged to try theoretically to understand how this has been so, and practically to work out relations to one another in terms of it.

When I arrived in Harvard some twenty-five years ago to take up my post as professor of World Religions at the Divinity School, my duties included becoming Director of the then recently established Center for the Study of World Religions, and of the new building that had been erected for it, primarily a residence for the students and visiting scholars from diverse religious communities and various parts of the world who were —and in later years more and more were to be— participating in its programme. I found that this building included not only living quarters for my family and myself and for this group and their families, but also had, as a sort of appendage on the top, an 'inter-faith chapel,' a small and austere structure (the whole building was in the modern style of unrelieved concrete), quite undecorated except for one thing: namely, that the architect, on the view that the one symbol that 'the various religions of the world' had in common was light, had provided it with a skylight in the ceiling. Otherwise it was forbiddingly gloomy.

One of my first acts as Director was to turn this chapel into a colourful library, subsequently expanded and with picture-windows replacing walls on two sides to flood it with not symbolic but cheerfully helpful light (a project whose details were worked out by some of our enthusiastic students); and to turn what had been a small library, on the ground floor, into a Common Room, also after expansion: a social gathering place, and site for formal and informal discussion, parties, and community life. Throughout my time at that Center my wife and I took on as one of our prime tasks the building and nurturing of community. My idea with regard to the chapel was that Muslims should go to their mosques, Hindus to their temples, Christians to Church, and come back and still be friends — or better, should become friends, as we studied together (our foremost commitment), lived together, talked together.

From this rejection of a common chapel from our operation, you might infer that I did not believe in the possibility, or the advisability, of sharing religious experience. The proper inference, rather, was and is that I am not aiming at a sharing of religious practice. The Common Room that we established, and which became a central and very fruitful part of our academic enterprise, gave us who worshipped differently and separately an opportunity to learn, ever more deeply, that that need not separate us intellectually nor personally.

I have long contended that the interesting matter about religious practice, religious objects, all that I have called the differing cumulative traditions, is how they affect the persons who live in terms of them. Back in the days when I was still primarily an Islamicist, well before I had written *The Meaning and End of Religion,* I suggested that the Muslim experience of formally memorizing the Qur'an and the Christian experience of the Eucharist might fruitfully be compared.[1] ("The Qur'an is to Muslims what Christ is to Christians.") At least, this proposition seems worth pondering and discussing. What a comparativist compares is not objects so much as persons' experiences. Related to this point, for our purposes here, is that for Luther, Calvin, Zwingli the Bible was not itself the Word of God; rather, the Word of God comes to us *through* the Bible, if in reading it we are guided by the Holy Spirit. Of the four realities in interplay here —God, the Spirit, us, the Bible— the scripture itself is subordinate to the other three, just as we in turn are subordinate to the other two. Altogether, it has become increasingly evident to careful observation and to serious reflection that what matters in religious life is not the external visible forms through which the spiritual is medi-

---

[1] "Some Similarities and Some Differences between Christianity and Islam: An Essay in Comparative Religion," in James Kritzeck and R. Bayly, eds., *The World of Islam: Studies in Honour of Philip K. Hitti* (London: MacMillan, and New York: St. Martin's, 1959), pp. 47-59.

ated, so much as the role that these play —that these enable the Spirit to play— in the personalities, and living, of those affected.

Thus one could say that having turned away from the common chapel idea, we at the Harvard Center used our Common Room to 'share', in one sense of that word —to share with each other over a cup of coffee or over the critical analysis of an academic theory of interpreting religion— the experiences that we had had, or failed to have, in our diverse acts of worship, or our various understandings of our diverse theological or metaphysical heritages, or our understanding of a particular scriptural passage on which one of us was perhaps writing that week an academic paper.

You may therefore recognize that I had some difficulty with the title that was assigned to me for this conference: "Can you share the Qur'an and the Bible as Word of God?" Nonetheless, having been asked to speak on it, I dutifully accepted the topic, except for modifying "Can you share?" to "Can we share?", a change that I imagined would not be begrudged. Otherwise, I have attempted to address it as adequately as I am able. My own inclination, however, as you can see from the above, would be rather to think in terms of Muslims' and Christians' sharing their respective *experience* of the Qur'an and the Bible. I could even go so far as to suggest that although Christians, for instance, in some sense all share the Bible as Word of God, yet it is manifest that in historical fact and in actual living there is a serious —at times explosive— question as to how far we indeed converge, or diverge, in what it means to us; converge, or diverge, as to what it says, what it means, what it is. Moreover, both groups can learn something decisive and illuminating from the other's experience of one's own scripture. (Just last month I was entranced to learn of some 'native Canadians' —Canadian Indians, Amerinds— for whom the story of the Exodus elicited deep sympathy for the original inhabitants of the Palestine that those predatory foreigners from elsewhere came, conquered, and controlled.) I myself am more at ease with, feel more at home with, several of my Muslim friends (liberal intellectuals, like me) as we consider together the meaning of scripture in the modern world, or for us —or as we discuss the Qur'an, or some particular passage in it, or the Bible— than I do with certain fellow Christians, as we speak together about the Bible.

Nonetheless, I do not wish to set aside altogether the question posed to me, as to whether the Qur'an, as a specific objective text, can serve me personally as Word of God; or the counterpart question re Bible and Muslim. I may report that one of the handful of what some would call 'mystical experiences' that I happen to have had (though I agree with St. John of the Cross that all such experiences are negligible in comparison with the ability to love) was on an ocean liner one evening en route to India, with a magnificent sunset transforming the distant horizon. I chanced to be undergoing some grave personal difficulties at that time, when suddenly my spirit was quieted by a verse from the Qur'an coming to me, as it were audibly over the broad expanse of the calm waters, in Arabic: *huwa al-kāfī* — 'He is sufficient,' or more exactly, 'It is He who suffices.' Now quite obviously II Corinthians 12:9 might have served precisely the same purpose ("My grace is sufficient for thee"), and I am well aware that those words of St. Paul, and various other Biblical verses like it, have comforted many, many Christians in similar conditions over the centuries. The fact is, however, that in my case it was this verse from the Qur'an that arrived out of the blue, to my vast surprise (I was quite startled), and left me with a rather serene assurance of divine strengthening and support.

This was twenty-seven years ago, and neither before nor since has it nor anything like it recurred. Nevertheless at quite another level I have sometimes wondered whether perchance my strong theocentrism (which contrasts at times a whit starkly with some of my fellow Christians' Christocentrism, or fundamentalists' bibliocentrism) may have something to do —in part— with my having studied the Qur'an, and Muslim theological and moral thought based upon it, for some decades and with some sensitivity. There is a great deal in our Christian heritage, of course, especially in its pre-modern eras, on which such theocentrism could be and often has been grounded. Current Christocentrism is both modern and heretical, I think that one could (and should) contend; although it is strong.

My remarks just now on differing feasible ways of taking the phrase 'sharing experience' raises the issue of a certain potential ambiguity, not only in the notion of sharing but also in the notion of experience, and perhaps especially in that of religious experience. I am looking forward to the four presentations that will bear on this matter as the final sector of our conference. As some of you know, I have long been hesitant about the noun 'religion', especially its plural, and of late years I have become increasingly suspicious also of the adjective 'religious', recognizing more and more that the whole outlook involved in these terms is irremediably secularist. I would propose that our fundamental problem —both as academics seeking understanding, and as human beings seeking to address the problems of the modern world— is that of sharing, rather, *human* experience. To understand another person is in principle a challenge; not least, of course, when that other person is of another culture, or social class, or language, or civilization, or religious tradition, or lived in another century. (Nowadays, we are hearing some voices that would even assert: it is not possible for males to understand the experience of the other sex.) The challenge should never be under-estimated.

Neither (*pace* those feminists) should it frighten us off. My way of putting this point has been to say that human beings are inherently such that no two of them can understand each other 100%; yet any two of them can understand each other more than zero percent. And one may add: any can come to understand each other more this year than they did last year.

One result of considerations like this is that, left to myself, my particular inclination would be to write not on sharing each others' scriptures as Word of God, so much as something more like, "Qur'an and Bible — Words of God? Towards a Theology of Scripture, and the Sharing of Understanding." I mention this not in any fashion to complain about your conference or its programme; on the contrary, I am delighted to be here, and was quick to accept the invitation when it came. And as remarked, I have endeavoured to address myself directly to your question as formulated. I mention it, rather, simply in the course of that addressing, as I wrestle with the serious issues that your programme raises. Moreover, lest I seem evasive or to be splitting hairs, let me plead that as an historian, and in that vein empirical, I would modify also the original form in which the question was put to me, which itself related to a form that I myself had introduced some years earlier. In my book *Questions of Religious Truth,* one chapter was entitled "Is the Qur'an the Word of God?" Professors Vroom and Wessels accordingly wondered about my maybe carrying this forward by treating the further question as to whether the Qur'an, apart from being seen perhaps as the Word of God for Muslims, might also be that "to or for Christians and, if so, what the implications of this might be for the Christian's understanding of the Bible as the Word of God." This comes very close to my proposed formulation above, touching on theology; and indeed that proposed wording of mine might be regarded as a response to their query. As I have just said, I should like now, as historian, to modify both the title of my earlier chapter and our newer question, by introducing empirical differentiation. Both for the Muslim and for the Christian case I would wish to ask first: "Has it been?" (rather than "Is it?"). Presently I would move on to a little consideration of the present-day situation, for both groups; and finally, try to bring it all together by reflecting about possibilities, and opportunities, for the future — our common future.

The historian of religion faces the historical question, has the Qur'an been the Word of God for Muslims; or I would prefer, has it served God as His Word among them; better yet, has it served God as a channel for His word among them. My own answer would be, based on both my study of the historical scene and my observation of my Muslim friends over the past half-century since I first went to live in the Muslim world: in some cases yes, to varying degrees, in some cases no. (I would give the same answer, historically, for the Christian case, on the same two grounds, with that same important qualification, 'to varying degrees.') The only persons that could differ from this assessment, I feel, would be (a) those who are not familiar with Islamic history, and who do not have Muslim friends; (b) those whose prejudices dogmatically rule out any willingness or ability to consider transcendent dimensions of human life and history; (c) those who, although recognizing transcendence and our involvement in it (and its involvement in us), are not themselves theist but operate with some other conceptual framework to think and speak of it and yet are unwilling or unable to translate into that framework my theistic vocabulary. Perhaps I should include as a subclass of (b) those whose prejudices (I use the term in its literal sense, of a *pre*-judgement, formed before considering the particular data under assessment and not open to being modified in the light of new evidence) rule out any willingness or ability to consider those transcendent dimensions in human life and history outside their own particular community. I shall be interested to discover whether participants in our conference can point out to me a fourth group that I have overlooked. That the three that I have enumerated are validly proffered can be empirically demonstrated by citing clear instances of each.

I should also be interested to learn whether you find my same formulations applicable *mutatis mutandis* to Christian history and among Christian friends.

Turning now to the other aspects of our inquiry, we may ask whether in the past Christians have perceived the Qur'an as mediating the divine; or again, have discerned God as acting in the Muslim world through the Qur'an, as using it to communicate His presence and His will to Muslims. Also, whether Muslims have returned the compliment to us, *re* the Bible. Although I have not studied this closely, it is my impression that in the Christian case there have been relatively few exceptions before the twentieth century to a 'no' answer. Muslims in the contrary direction would score rather higher, because of their sense of having superseded the Christian dispensation, as Christians in turn can feel and have felt that they have superseded the Jewish. It is vastly more difficult to be sympathetic to a movement that comes later in time (as is illustrated by Muslim vehemence against still newer developments than their own.) Yet in our own day a mutual appreciation has begun to emerge, however inchoately, in scattered instances on both sides; although even where it has occurred, systematic theoretical formulations —to undergird or even to accompany appreciation— continue rare.

The contemporary phase of the internal impinging of our question is important. If we turn from what has been the case to what would appear to be happening now, the question gives one pause as to how successful

God is nowadays finding His task of getting into touch with Christians by means of the Bible. It would seem to me difficult to argue against the view that He is presumably finding that avenue less effective for His purposes that He did, say, a century ago — even though some of our fundamentalist friends would elatedly say that their movement is, on His behalf, ensuring an increasing return to that *status quo ante*. To what extent the bibliocentric, almost bibliolatrous, movement of (to cite U. S. instances) Falwell, TV evangelism, and general right-wing Christian activism, and the counterpart upsurge in the Muslim world of what many call Islamic fundamentalism, are the work of God and to what extent are that of none too wise or loving men and women and even of the Devil, I leave others to ponder. My own position, certainly, would be that scripture these days does not appear to be a way that is serving God very well, a way that is being used by Him very effectively, in His always agonizing endeavour to save humanity from its —from our— woes and follies.

Certainly Falwell not at all, and Khumayni only a little, has shown interest in the other side's sacred book. It is interesting to note, nonetheless, how remarkably parallel these two leaders have been in their renewed enthusiasm each for his own. An observer can hardly fail to perceive the similarities between their two positions in this respect, and may well feel then impelled to go on to speculate as to the apparently common bond by which they are inadvertently —and embarrassingly?— linked.

Leaving that, however, aside, let us turn rather to our own situation, with regard to the Bible. Has a century of powerful and sustained historical criticism not left us knowing far too much to be at ease with any sanguine conviction that its texts, composed by human authors addressing particular issues in remote situations in the past nowadays carefully reconstructed, do, or can, or were ever meant to, constitute primary divine guidance or spiritual illumination to-day for us as we confront the radically divergent problems of our strikingly new twentieth century, and soon those of the still newer and yet more different twenty-first? Is this the best that God can do for us, as He reaches out to help us on our way?

The question of scripture in our day is a serious one, needing profound wrestling, creativity, and grace. In this paper I do not aspire to answering it! My only contribution, tentatively, is to suggest that some help towards solving some at least of its problems may come from a sensitive appreciation of other communities' scriptures; or, more accurately, a sensitive understanding not of their scriptures as such, as texts, so much as of the role of those scriptures in their lives, over the centuries and to-day. For my sense is that present-day Christians' limitations in being able to have the Bible function as an authentic channel for God's voice to reach their lives, and their limitations in being able to perceive the Qur'an's functioning, or anyway having functioned, as such an authentic channel in Muslims' lives, are intertwined.

There is profit in understanding how it is that the Qur'an, the *Bhagavad Gītā*, the Buddhist *sūtra*s, and the rest —which we can see clearly were composed by human authors at specific times in specific situations for specific purposes— have nonetheless served God at later times in other situations for other purposes, including sometimes —grandly, or poignantly— His purposes. There is profit also in pondering what has been going on here as we observe that in every case there has been, in the human use of scripture, a human response to, on the one hand, the text and, on the other, to a transcendent dynamic at work through that text: a mixture of the human —sometimes all too human— and the divine (as in all human history?). In this mixture the relative proportion of the two factors has varied, not only from century to century, village to court, person to person, but from day to day even in a single person's life.

In the Christian case, none of the books of the Bible was scripture when it was written. They became scripture later, in an elaborate process that repays investigation. Once they had become scripture, some for Jews and in a substantially different fashion for Christians, others just for us, we have used them in various ways and God, it appears, has used them in various ways. The significant question about the Bible, and indeed about the Qur'an and all scriptures, is not whether they are inspired, but whether they are inspiring. At those times and in those places and for those people for whom they have been and are inspiring, the questions are how, and to what extent, and how authentically. The authenticity question only God can fully answer, on the Day of Judgement. To the others, we may and should put our minds.

I conclude, then, by just touching on the future phase of our question, of sharing Qur'an and Bible as Word of God. In addition to what has been the case, and how things stand now, we may ask whether we shall share them in future, which obviously no one of us can predict. Yet we may ask also whether we *shall* share them; and by that question each of us is at once engaged. It is up to us personally to decide how we will proceed. And to the question, *should* we in the future share, I hope that my presentation will nudge others to join me in answering 'yes.' Besides, there are considerations quite apart from those that I have raised pushing us to that sharing. In our increasingly unified world, with its increasingly shared problems, it seems unlikely that humankind can survive unless we all learn to share each other's problems, visions, hopes, and to understand each other's outlooks and experience, so as to turn our global society into a global community.

Finally, on the form, "*Can* we share," I personally have found that some of us can, and my hope would be that others will find this both possible and appealing.

CHAPTER 6

Can Faith in the 'Inspiration'
of Holy Scripture Be Shared?

Rein Fernhout

This article is of a phenomenological nature, that is to say, it attempts to answer the question raised in terms of the 'logic' of the phenomenon itself. The phenomenon examined is that of Holy Scripture, or more precisely, the canon as it appears in various religions. Pertinent canons from the great world religions have been included in the study, including that of Hinduism. Each of these canons is examined for what specifically constitutes their 'inspiration' —to what this canon owes its existence— according to its own testimony and that of the faithful concerned. A subsequent section examines whether and how such particular inspiration is regarded applicable to other canons beyond the confines of one's own peculiar faith. It appears that this has indeed often occurred, but at the same time, it could scarcely be said that such extension of the notion of inspiration has led to shared belief in inspiration. Finally we will examine the question regarding the manner in which such intercanonical extension could be extrapolated, and whether perhaps this might provide a basis for shared belief in the inspiration of the canons concerned. The outcome of the study is that such is simply not the case.

1 Introduction

This article refers primarily to the Bible (especially the New Testament), the Koran, the Veda (Hinduism/Brahmanism), and the Tipiṭaka (Theravāda Buddhism). The term 'Holy Scriptures' has been used in the title as a general designation, but they could more properly be termed 'canons,' in the sense of a collection of texts possessing absolute authority in the eyes of the believers. That such authority has been attributed to these texts is a matter of faith, which understands itself as obedience to this authority.

With the possible exception of the Koran, each of these canons is characterized by a great diversity of texts. The fact that they are, nevertheless, regarded as one corpus results from the belief that one and the same 'inspiration' lies behind this diversity. In this article we will examine whether this belief, whose primary reference is to the intra-canonical situation, can also be extended to the inter-canonical situation. In so doing we will pay particular attention to: (a) the notion of 'inspiration' as such, followed by (b) the inter-canonical application of this notion, and finally (c) the possibility of extrapolating such application. In the final segment of the article we hope at the same time to formulate an answer to the question posed in the title.

2 The notion of 'inspiration'

Inspiration can be operative without explicit reflection. For that reason we have spoken of the notion rather than the concept of inspiration. How can such a notion be discerned as an interreligious phenomenon? We have made use of the 'one specimen-centred' method.[1] This method entails first defining the phenomenon in terms of one specimen, in this case the inspiration of the New Testament, in order subsequently to seek analogies in other religions.

According to the New Testament, Jesus Christ himself designated those who were to proclaim his Gospel to the world. This proclamation bears the character of a witness concerning what people have seen and heard concerning Jesus (John 21:24; Acts 1:21-22), especially with respect to the crucifixion and resurrection (Luke 24:46-48; John 19:35). Although we must not define this circle of witnesses too narrowly —the apostle Paul was also considered one of them (Acts 22:15; 26:16-18; cf. Gal. 1:1)— a clear delimitation still exists. Only that which stems from the circle of witnesses can make the claim to absolute authority. It is this delimitation which provided the intrinsic need for the New Testament canon. (Kümmel, 82)

The Gospel cannot, however, simply be equated with a human witness. In order for it to speak with authority, the 'inspiration' of the Holy Spirit is needed. According to Luke, this inspiration is principally related to the effectiveness of the witness (Luke 24:49; Acts 1:8). In the Gospel of John, there is also mention of a transmission of knowledge: "He will take what is mine and declare it to you" (John 16:14). This Spirit is, of course, the Spirit of God, yet in such a unique relationship to the exalted Christ (John 14:26; 15:26; 16:7), that it can also be called the Spirit of Jesus. (Acts 16:7; cf. Rev. 19:10)

The New Testament scriptures tell us very little about the experience which accompanied this inspiration, with the exception of the book of Revelation, where it is directly related to apocalyptic (Rev. 1:10-11). In the Gospel of John we read that the Spirit would remind the witnesses of what Jesus had said (John 14:26) and would lead them in "all truth"

---

[1] I defended this method at the XVIth annual congress of the IAHR in September of 1990)

(John 16:13). In other words, inspiration consists of memories and insights occasioned by the Spirit of Christ. How these two were experienced remains unexpressed. It is not the nature of the experience which qualifies inspiration, but the fact that it mediates between A, the exalted Christ, and B, a limited circle of witnesses, resulting in C, a text with absolute authority. The letters have been added here in order to facilitate the detection and analysis of analogies. Part C of the analogy-formula is, in any case, already present in each of the cases under consideration — the respective canons. Parts A and B remain to be determined.

The analogy of B is already obvious with respect to the Koran. It consists of the one man, Mohammed. The technical term for the experience of inspiration is *wahy*. According to the tradition (*hadīth*) Mohammed himself explained that *wahy* came to him in two ways: "Sometimes it comes to me as the ringing of a bell —and this grips me the most— then it departs from me and I remembered what it said, and sometimes the angel appears to me as a man, and speaks to me, and I remember what he says" (al-Bukhārī I, *bad' al-wah*, 2-3). The first mode was accompanied, according to the tradition, by severe pains, numbness or a trance, and other phenomena which point to a type of ecstasy (Wensinck, 623). This reminds one of the possession which characterized the pre-Islamic tribal oracle, the *kāhin*. There are also stylistic similarities between passages from the Koran and oracles from the *kāhins* (Watt, 78). The similarities appear to be more than just a question of style, however. The *kāhin* was possessed by a spirit. Mohammed likewise attributed his revelation to "a trustworthy Spirit" (sūra 26:193-194), which was identified by the tradition as Djibrīl, Gabriel (cf. already sūra 2:97). It is no wonder that Mohammed's opponents reproached him for being a *kāhin*. (sūra 52:29)

There is, however, an important difference between Mohammed and the *kāhin*. In the case of the latter, the spirit manipulated the speech organs (Fischer, 207); Mohammed, however, received his revelation through recitation (*kur'ān*). He repeated what was recited to him (sūra 75:17-18). In the view of Muslims, the one whose recitation Mohammed heard was the angel Gabriel, who as 'angel of the *wahy*' repeated what he had heard from Allah himself (al-Ṣāliḥ, 24). Gabriel's relationship to Mohammed is, as it were, externalized in the second mode of *wahy*, whereby the revelation is imparted to Mohammed face to face.

The result is a text which derives, word for word, from Allah. This is the classical view which is still shared by the majority of Muslims: "[Mohammed] does not interfere in the inspiration, does not shape it by his own expression, does not express it in his own words, but only its recitation is granted to him; he is the reciter, not the speaker" (al-Ṣāliḥ, 30). In this the text of the Koran is distinguished, according to the same author, from the texts of the sayings of Mohammed preserved by the tradition. In the latter, the thoughts are those of Allah while the form is that of Mohammed himself. *(Ibid.,* 33-34)

Filling out the analogy-formula presents no problem in this case: *Waḥy* is the mediating experience between A, the one god Allah, and B, the prophet Mohammed, with the result C, a text which is, word for word, the word of Allah. Of course, A and C determine the nature of the inspiration. This can especially be seen in the role attributed by the Islamic tradition to Gabriel, the 'angel of the *waḥy,*' as mediator between the exalted Allah and the human Mohammed.

When referring to the Veda, we have in mind the most basic portion of this canon, that is, the collection of cultic formulas *(mantras)* and hymns, of which the Ṛgveda is the oldest. These collections are the work of the *ṛsis,* 'the seers.' The earliest commentator on the Ṛgveda, Yāska, has written: "The *ṛsis* were able to behold directly the transcendent reality *(dharma).* They passed on the texts to those who followed, who were unable to do so, through [oral] instruction" (Nirukta 1, 20). Yāska does not reveal why the ability of the *ṛsis* had disappeared. Their inspiration consisted of an experience which we could best briefly describe as enlightenment: " ... my ears are opened, my eyes [are] opened; this light which is placed in the heart, arises. The thinking of my mind is directed toward the distance" (Ṛgveda 6, 9, 6). The 'Hymn of Wisdom' (Ṛgveda 10, 71) depicts how inspiration is translated, via the traditional craft of the poets or seers, into the cultic word. The activity of the seers in this hymn establishes the truth of the Dutch saying that poetry is one percent inspiration and ninety-nine percent perspiration.

Worth noting is the role of the gods in inspiration. Agni (god of the sacrificial fire), Soma (god of the libation), Indra, Mitra, Varuṇa, and many other gods have been mentioned as givers of inspiration. The gods themselves, however, are also called *ṛsis.* The only difference between the human and divine seers, according to J. Gonda, is one of degree (1963, p. 141). Furthermore, there is an interesting cycle of inspiration: The inspired cultic word is supposed to motivate the gods to inspire cultic words. The gods even appear to depend on the cultic word not only for the ability to give inspiration, but also for their very existence. They live from them and become immortal through them. (Ṛgveda 10, 53, 10)

The *ṛsis* make up the B part of the analogy-formula. The texts of the Veda are the C part. A general designation for these texts is the term 'Vāc,' the Word, that is, pre-eminently the cultic word. How, should we conceive of A, however? The gods cannot be candidates since they themselves act as mediators. The ultimate origin of the Word lies in the *ṛta,* the vedic concept of the cosmic order. There is mention of "the song born of the *ṛta"* (Ṛgveda 10, 138, 2). By way of contrast, however,

Vāc gives rise to the cosmic order. We must, therefore, primarily regard the *ṛta* as the power inherent in Vāc (Renou, 1955–1969, I, 22). The dominant role of Vāc is especially evident in the well-known hymn in which Vāc, as goddess, sings her own praises (Ṛgveda 10, 125). There she says, among other things, that she makes *ṛsis* of those who she loves (Ṛgveda 10, 125, 5). The experience of the *ṛsis* is in essence the self-revelation of Vāc. The most orthodox current in Hinduism with respect to the cultus, Pūrvamīmāṃsā, has even done away with every idea of a human or divine author of the Veda. The Veda is eternal and *apauruṣeya*, that is, independent of any person.

The Tipiṭaka, the 'Three Baskets' (because it consists of three parts), of Theravāda Buddhism displays precisely the reverse (terms used here from the Tipiṭaka, including Buddha's former name, are given in Pāli, the language of this canon). This canon has its origin in the experience of enlightenment undergone by the recluse Gotama. We can distinguish two moments in this experience — that of ultimate liberation, and that of universal insight. The latter is the more important for our subject since it made Gotama into a *sammāsambuddha*, 'one perfectly awakened.' As such, he is distinguished from two other figures who have gained a share in the same liberation, i. e., the *paccekabuddha* and the *arahat*. The *paccekabuddha* achieves liberation completely independently of others, but is not in a position to instruct others in the path which leads to it. The *arahat* attains liberation only through the instruction of others. The *sammāsambuddha*, however, combines them both: He needs no one in order to achieve liberation, but obtains along with liberation the knowledge with which he is able to lead others to liberation. This knowledge is so comprehensive in nature that it entails omniscience, although there is some uncertainty as to the nature of this omniscience (Jayatilleke, 203; De Silva, 43-44). The *sammāsambuddha* is a unique figure, who only appears once in any given world period.

What is, then, the A part of the analogy-formula? One immediately thinks of *dhamma* (Sanskrit, *dharma*) as the 'teaching' of Buddha, although *dhamma* in Buddhism is a rather complicated concept (Vetter, p. 9). In any case, Buddha himself is intimately connected with *dhamma*. He himself stated: "Whoever sees *dhamma*, sees me; whoever sees me, sees *dhamma*" (Saṃyutta Nikāya iii, 120). Buddha is in a certain sense himself A. Inspiration is the experience which gave Gotama the quality of *sammāsambuddha*. Therefore, the Tipiṭaka, the C of the analogy-formula, is called *buddhavacana*, word of Buddha.

By way of summary, inspiration which leads to a canon, a text of absolute authority, consists of experiences which come to only a limited number of people, or sometimes just one person. The nature of these experiences appeared to vary greatly, oscillating between the virtually unspecified experiences of the witnesses of the New Testament and the *sammāsambodhi*, the 'perfect awakeness,' of Buddha. As a result, we speak of inspiration based not on the nature of the experience, but on the coordinates, the A's and C's, between which the experience takes place.

3 Inter-canonical application

Inter-canonical application can be observed in the case of all the canons dealt with. The basic model is to extend the inspiration specific to canon C to another canon, C^1. This means that such extension can be approached from two sides. From the perspective of canon C, we are dealing with attribution, that is, the inspiration specific to C is attributed to C^1. From the point of view of canon C^1, however, this is tantamount to annexation, for it is thereby subjected to the inspiration specific to C.

Already in the scriptures which were to form the New Testament, inspiration is attributed to the scriptures of what would later be called the Old Testament. In the epistle to the Hebrews, texts from the Psalms and the Prophets are ascribed to the pre-existent Christ (Heb. 2:11-13; 10:5-7). This same usage may perhaps also be found several times in the Gospels (Matt. 13:35; John 12:38-41). The first epistle of Peter furnishes a 'theory of inspiration' in terms of such attribution. The "Spirit of Christ" witnessed before to the prophets, that is, those of the Old Testament, "the sufferings of Christ and the subsequent glory" (I Peter 1:10-11). Not only the source of inspiration, but also its central theme —the witness regarding the crucifixion and resurrection— is thus found in the Old Testament. The prophets themselves, according to Peter, attempted to discover when the predicted saving events would take place. This same line can be traced through one of the Apostolic Fathers, Ignatius, who wrote with respect to the Old Testament prophets that they were, " ... inspired by His [i. e., Christ's] grace to bring full conviction to an unbelieving world that there is one God, who manifested Himself through Jesus Christ, His Son." *(Ad Magnesios* 8:2). In fact, such attribution, extended to the entire Old Testament, formed the basis for the way in which the early Church understood the Old Testament scriptures. We are, however, safe in assuming that to the Jews all this constituted unacceptable appropriation of their scriptures. The early history of the proclamation of the Gospel recorded in the book of Acts ends, significantly, with a dispute over the interpretation of the Old Testament. (Acts 28:25-27)

For the Muslim, it is beyond question that the *waḥy* granted to Mohammed is of the same nature as that given to the earlier prophets (al-Ṣāliḥ, 22). This is also confirmed by the Koran. Just as Allah inspired Mohammed, so He also inspired the Old Testament prophets and

'Īsā (Jesus; sūra 4:163-164). Attribution applies, therefore, both to the Old Testament and to the New, of which Jesus is called the prophet. The same Spirit of holiness, through whom the Koran was sent to earth (sūra 16:102) also strengthened 'Īsā (sūra 2:87; 253). Mohammed, however, assumes a unique position, according to Muslims, in that he, as the 'seal of the prophets' (sūra 33:40), was the last to be inspired. In other words, the Koran does employ attribution, but Islam itself discounts the possibility of any future appropriation of the Koran. Jews and Christians, who according to the Koran are both 'people of the Book,' have resolutely rejected the claims of Islam. In so doing, they also pointed to the contradictions between their own scriptures and the Koran. The Islamic reaction, based on the Koran itself (sūra 5:13), is that they have made themselves guilty of *taḥrīf*, distorting their own scriptures. (Fernhout, p. 70)

In the Veda itself, there can be no question of attribution, since no prior canon existed. Appropriation of the Veda, however, has occurred on a wide scale, among others, for the inspiration specific to the canons of Vaiṣṇavism and Śaivism, the *saṃhitās* and the *āgamas* respectively. The situation is very complex, however. 'Loyalty' to the Veda stands alongside its rejection (Renou 1960, 6-8). Here, of course, we are only concerned with examples of attribution to the Veda, which, as such, imply a certain kind of loyalty. With respect to Vaiṣṇavism, we have limited ourselves for practical reasons to the Pañcarātra. The inspiration specific to both the *saṃhitās* and the *āgamas* deviates from that of the Veda, since the content of these canons has been imparted by the highest god, Viṣṇu or Śiva, to a wise man in pre-historic times and has since then been faithfully passed on from teacher to student. (Gonda 1977, 118-121, 163)

Many of the *saṃhitās* and *āgamas* betray their affinity to the Veda. Vāsudeva (Viṣṇu), who revealed the teaching of the Pañcarātra, is "the root of the universe" and his teaching is "the root of the Veda-tree of which the Ṛgveda, etc., are trunk and branches" according to the Īśvara Saṃhitā (1:24ff., as cited in Gonda 1977, 50). This idea of one's own teaching as the root of the Veda *(mūlaveda)* is expressed elsewhere in the *saṃhitās* as well (Bhattacharya, 206). The Veda is encapsulated within a new view of inspiration. The Ajita Āgama teaches that all canonical revelation springs from the five faces of Sadāśiva, the 'eternal Śiva.' The Veda, along with the first ten *āgamas,* derive from the first face while the remaining *āgamas* derive from the other four (Gonda 1977, 195). How current the problem remains can be seen from a work by A. Shanmugha Mudaliar, published by the Śrī Kapaleeswarar Temple in Madras, under the title '*Śiva Āgamas*' *and Their Relationship to Vedas.* The writer argues in this book that the Veda and the *āgamas* have emanated from one and the same god, namely Śiva, who is the soul of the Veda. (Shanmugha Mudaliar, 14-15)

In spite of the flexibility which characterizes Indian religious thought, resistance has arisen against subjection of the Veda to the inspiration specific to the *saṃhitās* and the *āgamas*. The adherents of the Vedic orthodoxy of the Pūrvamīmāṃsā were of the opinion that Veda scholars could hold no esteem for these canons (Renou 1960, 7-8, n. 8). The Kūrma Purāṇa, which, like all the *purāṇas,* itself also displays a type of inspiration which deviates from that of the Veda, calls the *saṃhitās* and *āgamas* "deluding Scriptures" *(mohaśāstrāni)* intended for those who find themselves beyond "the pale of the Veda" (Kūrma Purāṇa 1, 16, 117-119). The well-known commentator on the law book of Manu, Medāthiti (ninth century), condemned the followers of these 'canons' as heretics who live in conflict with the Veda. (Dasgupta IV, 7-8)

It would have been possible for the Tipiṭaka to attribute its specific inspiration to the Veda, but this was not the case. On the contrary, the Tipiṭaka is generally critical of the Veda and is certainly not inclined to extend the inspiration of Buddha to this canon (Renou 1960, 43-45). The Tipiṭaka is itself the object of attribution in the canons of Mahāyāna Buddhism. One striking example is The Lotus of the True Law *(Saddharmapuṇḍarīka Sūtra),* or the Lotus Sūtra. This Sūtra shows us a change and radicalization of the model of inspiration in the Tipiṭaka. Indeed, according to this Sūtra, it is assumed that Buddha attained *samyaksambodhi* (Pāli, *sammāsambodhi*) after he left his family in Gayā, but "the truth is that many hundred thousand myriads of *koṭis* [*koṭi* 'ten millions'] of Aeons ago I have arrived at supreme, perfect enlightenment *(samyaksambodhi)*" (Ch. XV; trans. Kern, 299; ed. Kern, 316; ed. Vaidya, p. 189). Though he had himself formerly announced that he had received *samyaksambodhi* a short time before, this declaration was simply a question of tactics *(upāyakauśalya)*. If he had expressed it otherwise, he would not have been understood, since the full truth had not yet been attained. Buddha gave different *dharmaparyāyas* 'explanations of the dharma' in accordance with the ability of the public to which he was directing himself to comprehend (Ch. XV; trans. Kern, 300-301; ed. Kern, p. 317-318; ed. Vaidya, 190). Therefore, the Tipiṭaka is based on one of these *dharmaparyāyas*. The process offers, as a note from the translator, H. Kern, points out, rich possibilities for further attribution. According to Kern, Buddha here is "not only the Devātideva, the supreme god of gods, of Buddhism, but of all religions in the world; from him are all scriptures." (trans. Kern, 301, n. 2)

Within the Lotus Sūtra itself, however, opposition appears to arise from those who have little tolerance for such appropriation of the Tipiṭaka. When Buddha, after one of his disciples repeatedly insisted, decided to explain the true essence of his teaching, "five thousand proud monks, nuns, and lay devotees of both sexes" prepared to leave the meeting. They had no need for this explanation, since "they imagined having attained what they had not, and having understood what they had not" (Ch. II; trans. Kern, 38-39; ed. Kern, 38; ed. Vaidya, 26). When future preachers of the teaching of this Sūtra receive the warning that monks, nons, etc., will perhaps attack them with "clods, sticks, injurious words, threats, taunts" we are probably dealing with resistance from the same group (Ch. X, p. 28-29; trans. Kern, 225; ed. Kern, 237; ed. Vaidya, 248). The appropriation of the trusted canon caused an emotional reaction.

Attribution of individual inspiration appears to be the procedure by which means one's own canon is brought into relation with another canon. In each of the cases mentioned, this procedure is already present in the attributing canon itself. This attribution itself thus shares in the absolute authority of the canon which enacts the attribution. Appropriation evoked, as the obverse side of a coin, heavy resistance. It does not require a great deal of sensitivity to understand this. From the perspective of the appropriated canon, the A of the inspiration specific to the attributing canon is not its own A, but a more or less deviant variant, A^n. Acceptance of the attribution would mean 'conversion' to A^n. Although it is not within the scope of this article, it should be noted that attribution, of course, also has wider hermeneutical implications. In this sense as well, there are interesting interreligious parallels to point out. K. Bhattacharya, for example, has compared the allegorical interpretation of the Vedic rites in the Pañcarātra with the way in which Origen exegeted the rites of the Old Testament (Bhattacharya, 200-202). Besides, the Old Testament is the only instance in which the attribution has been used to such an extent that the two canons have merged.

4   Extrapolation

When we express the question from the title as follows, "Can you have faith in the 'inspiration' of another Holy Scripture?" then clear phenomenological verification becomes possible for answering the question positively. The attribution $C–C^1$ entails belief in the inspiration of C^1 by those who believe in the inspiration of C. The reverse, however, appeared not to be the case. Those who originally believed in the inspiration of C^1 experienced the attribution as inappropriate appropriation. There is, therefore, no shared belief. The only thing that is shared is the notion of 'inspiration,' but this notion cannot be the object of belief outside the coordinates, A and C, designating it as such.

This situation does not change when we extrapolate a given attribution $C–C^1$ to C^2, C^3, etc. If we again take the New Testament as example, extrapolation of the relation to the Old Testament would mean that canons C^2, C^3, etc., are considered to be inspired by the Spirit of Jesus Christ, and the 'authors' of these canons would be viewed as witnesses of his death and resurrection according to the analogy of the Old Testament prophets. One needs little imagination to understand how Muslims, Hindus, and Buddhists would react to such an extrapolation. The same is true, by way of analogy, when we take one of the other canons as our point of departure, rather than the New Testament.

There is, however, yet another problem. Only the attribution to C^1 is given in canon C.[2] A canon such as the Lotus Sūtra may suggest the possibility of further attributions, but that is where the process then ends. Extrapolation is the result of reasoning which we ourselves create. Although such reasoning may have a certain plausibility, it lacks the absolute authority of the canon itself. From the perspective of authority, there is, therefore, a radical difference between the attribution $C–C^1$ and the extrapolated attribution $C–C^2$, C^3, etc. The original attribution is a question of canonical authority, and thus of faith, whereas the extrapolated attribution is one of reasoning. If we allow that the appropriation involved creates no insurmountable objections, then one could only speak of shared reasoning, not of shared faith. Could the sting be taken out of this problem by assuming A^x, which transcends A, A^y as 'the divine,' or 'the transcendent'? A^x could then be the ultimate source of inspiration for various canons without one's having to be converted to the A^y of another canon (we will not here enter into the 'theological' implications of such an A^x). In this way extrapolation is radicalized, that is to say, it is rid of any intra-religious shackles. In this case too, however, it is true that one cannot speak of absolute authority in connection with such an extrapolation, since it is not confirmed by a canon. To put it more firmly, such confirmation is impossible in principle, since A^x is not intended to correspond to a specific canon, but to a number of, or even all, canons. There is no longer a C, but only C^1, C^2, C^3, etc. With radical extrapolation we forfeit the absolute authority of 'our own' canon, as well as the inspiration specific to it. In such a case, however, all questions concerning the sharing of faith in inspiration are rendered superfluous. There is nothing left to share.

The answer to the question "Can you share faith in the 'inspiration' of Holy Scriptures?" phenomenologically speaking, is quite simply, "No, you cannot."

---

[2] C^1 can represent more than one canon, as, for example, in the Koran.

Bibliography

Bhattacharya, K. "Le 'védisme' de certains Textes Hindouistes." *Journal Asiatique* 255 (1976): 199-222.

Bukhārī, Muḥammad b. Ismā'īl al-. *Al-Ṣaḥīḥ.* 9 vols. Cairo, [2]1927–1929.

Dasgupta, S. *A History of Indian Philosophy,* 5 vols. Cambridge, 1922–1955.

De Silva, Lily. "The Buddha and the *Arahant* Compared." In H. Jayasuriya, ed. *Pratidāna Mañjarī,* Festschrift for W. F. Gunawardhana. Dehiwala (Sri Lanka), 1987, pp.37-52.

Fernhout, R. "Syncretism and Intra-religious Normativity Illustrated by the Phenomenon of Sacred Scriptures." In J. D. Gort et al., eds. *Dialogue and Syncretism: An Interdisciplinary Approach.* Currents of Encounter 1. Grand Rapids/Amsterdam, 1989, pp.66-75.

Fischer, A. *"Kāhin." Shorter Encyclopedia of Islam.* Leiden, 1953, pp.206-208.

Gonda, J. *The Vision of the Vedic Poets.* The Hague, 1963.

——. *Medieval Religious Literature in Sanskrit.* Wiesbaden, 1977.

Ignace d'Antioche, Polycarpe de Smyrne. *Lettres: Martyre de Polycarpe.* P. Th. Camelot, O. P., ed. and trans. Paris, 1951.

Jayatilleke, K. N. *Early Buddhist Theory of Knowledge.* London, 1963.

Kümmel, W. G. "Notwendigkeit und Grenze des neutestamentlichen Kanons." In E. Käsemann, ed. *Das Neue Testament als Kanon.* Göttingen, 1970, pp.62-79.

Kūrma Purāṇa. G. Vasudeo Tagare, trans. Delhi, 1981.

Lotus Sūtra. See *Saddharmapuṇḍarīka.*

Renou, L. *Etudes Védiques et Paninéennes.* 17 vols. Paris, 1955–1969.

——. *Etudes Védiques et Paninéennes,* VI: *Le destin du Véda dans l'Inde.* Paris, 1960.

Saddharmapuṇḍarīka. H. Kern., trans. Sacred Books of the East 21. Oxford, 1884.

——. H. Kern and B. Nanjio, eds. St. Petersburg, 1912.

——. P. L. Vaidya, ed. Darbhanga, 1960.

Ṛgveda-Saṃhitā with the Commentary of Sāyaṇāchārya. 5 vols. Vedic Research Institute, eds. Poone (Pune), 1933–1951.

Ṣāliḥ, Subḥi al-. *Mubāḥith fī'ulūm al-Ḳur'ān.* Beirut, [2]1985.

Saṃyutta-Nikāya. 5 vols. M. Léon Freer, ed. London, 1884–1898.

Shanmugha Mudaliar, A. *Śiva Āgamas and Their Relationship to Vedas.* Madras (Sri Kapaleeswarar Temple), 1972.

Vetter, T. *The Ideas and Meditative Practices of Early Buddhism.* Leiden, 1988.

Watt, W. M. *Bell's Introduction to the Qur'an.* Edinburgh, 1970.

Wensinck, A. J. *"Waḥy." Shorter Encyclopædia of Islam.* Leiden, 1953, pp.622-624.

Yāska. *The Nighaṇṭu and the Nirukta*. Lakshman Sarup, ed. Lahore, 1927.

CHAPTER 7

Religious Experience: Autonomy and Mutuality

Lamin Sanneh

In this essay it is argued that religious experiences such as dreams and visions do not lead to deviation from the common forms of religious life in mainstream Islam. To the contrary, experiences of this kind reinforce the authority of the code, lead to the correction of dubious practices, and foster the replacement of inauthenticity by authenticity. Islamic religious experience consists, ultimately, in the 'affirmation' of the Creator by the creature. With respect to the matter of interreligious sharing it is necessary to avoid the extreme of an overly rigorous notion of the uniqueness of religious experience, which renders it strictly private and thus incapable of being shared, and that of a view of sharing so tolerant that it becomes superficial and merely 'user-friendly.'

1 The Theme

Recounting an experience about his calling to the religious life, the 19th century Fulani reformer of northern Nigeria, Shaykh 'Uthmān b. Fūdī (1754–1817), more commonly known as Shehu Usuman dan Fodio, or simply as the Shehu, describes how first God removed the veil from his sight and endowed him with spiritual gifts, more like *wāridāt*, of insight and understanding. This occurred when he was thirty-six (in ca. 1790).[1] The effect of what the Shehu himself describes as God's miraculous visitation was to confirm him in faith and intensify his sense of calling. Here are his own words:

> When I reached thirty-six years of age, God removed the veil from my sight, and the dullness from my hearing and my smell, and the thickness from my taste, and the cramp from my two hands, and the restraint from my two feet, and the heaviness from my body. ... That was a favour from God that He gives to whom He will. ... Then I found written upon my fifth rib, on the right side, by the Pen of Power, "Praise be to God, Lord of the Created Worlds" ten times; and "O

---

[1] An account is given by Mervyn Hiskett (1973).

God, bless our Lord Muḥammad, and the family of Muḥammad, and
give them peace" ten times; and "I beg forgiveness from the Glorious
God" ten times; and I marvelled greatly at that. (Hiskett 1973, 64f.)

In this particular experience we are introduced in fact to a general theme
of Muslim religious life, namely, the confession of faith in the *shahādah,*
now cast in a deep devotional setting. The Shehu cultivated a regime of
concentrated religious exercises, observing silence and withdrawing into the
desert for prayer for a whole year. He was rewarded with a vision of the
Prophet. On one occasion he undertook a fifteen-day retreat and received a miraculous transfiguration when he was taken to the throne of
God. Malam (Ar. *muʿallim)* Gidado, the contemporary biographer of the
Shehu, gives the following account:

> Then the Lord of Creation said to him: "I put you in the retreat of al-
> Ashʿarī, which is fifteen days, not the retreat of al-Junaid, which is forty
> days," and the Lord of creation gave him a *dhikr* and said to him: "Do
> not eat anything except what is required for bare sustenance during this
> period." He did this. When the period was complete the Lord of
> Creation led him to the Merciful and all the angels of the Merciful were
> present and the Shaikh, the pole of the Qādiriyya order, the Chosen
> One, was present — and the words that testify to the presence will come
> in due course— and the Shaikh ʿAbd al-Qādir took our Shehu by the
> hand and sat him in front of him and said: "This man belongs to me,"
> and for this reason the Shehu Usuman said in his *Qaṣīda al-sudāniyya*
> "Our intermediary to Muḥammad is the Shaikh ʿAbd al-Qādir." (His-
> kett 1973, 65)

Thus did the Shehu receive formal dedication for his historic work. His
religious experiences up to this point in his life act only to recognize and
strengthen his Muslim resolve: there is no departure from the standard
format, no change of direction, no new initiative to speak of. Rather, the
Shehu is drawn tighter into commitment he had earlier, and on less
dramatic ground, entered into, namely, teaching, devotion, and moral
guidance. For example, in speaking of his religious experiences at age
thirty-six he remarked on how those experiences enable him to observe
more scrupulously the code on dietary regulations, rather than circumvent-
ing the code altogether. This seems such a typical feature of religious
experience in mainstream Islam, the idea of supernatural experience
reinforcing and not weakening the authority of the code.

There are, of course, exceptions, such as among the Mourides of
Senegal where the peasant throngs surrender their religious obligations and
in turn vest all their faith in the *shuyūkh* of the brotherhood. For, they
contend, when you are travelling in a train you do not carry a heavy load
on your head: you set it down. The load is the religious code, the
locomotive is the presiding *khalīfah-general,* the carriages are the *shuyūkh,*

and the passengers are the Mouride followers (O'Brien, 152). Yet in this instance, it is not so much because of experience as because of trust in charismatic leadership that leads ordinary Mourides to lay down the demands of religion, an action that brings them within scandalous reach of reform-minded 'ulamā.

2 Experience and Structure

Thus, to get back to religious experience, it acts in the instances we have thus far considered as a facilitator, not the subverter of the canon. The intensely subjective character of the experience is counterbalanced by the objective criteria to which it conforms, not adding or taking away an iota of the law. There are, of course, numerous complex feature in religious experience, including the extreme outlandish type in which seeming delirium is embellished with pious titles, and its converse, where the mundane is taken out of context and made into an elaborate source of the fantastic. In a credulous atmosphere, events that might be striking in their external coarseness, including fables and other imaginative inventions, are dragged into reality and dogmatically predicated of the living present, with the eclectic appetite feeding the penchant. Fortunately, much of that, though heaven knows not all of it, dissolves from historical exposure.

Nevertheless, it would be a serious error, by which I mean a flagrant methodological intrusion, to dismiss all religious experience as tending to charlatanry. Counterfeits only exploit the original, and, furthermore, the requirement to share will expose a personal hoard to common currency. Clearly, then, religious experience, even when it has been obviously conditioned by practices conducive to it, may express enough of the sober nobility of spirit to command recognition to its common value.

Two elements in the Shehu's religious experiences may be relevant to the issue. One is that the religious experience may consecrate the person having it for the work of renewing the religion and securing greater adherence to religious teachings. In other words, there would be a convergence between experience and structure. The second is that religious experience at a deeper level may be sought to correct or confirm the doubtful import of another religious experience: the message one receives in a dream or vision is unclear or represents too radical a departure from the norm not to require a retake.

In the first case, the Shehu recounted what is essentially a vision of vocational service. He said at age forty "God drew me to him," precisely how is not clear, and brought him into the company of the Apostle, the aṣḥāb, the prophets and the saints who "welcomed me, and sat me down in their midst." Then 'Abd al-Qādir al-Jīlānī brought a green robe marked with the words of the kalimah, and a turban with the words, "He is God, the One,"[2] which he handed to the Apostle who clasped them to his bosom before handing them over to Abū Bakr al-Ṣiddīq, and so on down the line to 'Alī, to Yūsūf and finally back to 'Abd al-Qādir al-Jīlānī whom they appointed to act on their behalf. Then 'Abd al-Qādir

> sat me down, and clothed me, and enturbaned me. Then he addressed me as 'Imam of the saints' and commanded me to do what is approved of and forbade me to do what is disapproved of;[3] and he girded me with the Sword of Truth (sayf al-ḥaqq), to unsheathe it against the enemies of God. Then they commanded me with what they commanded me; and at the same time gave me leave to make this litany that is written upon my ribs widely known, and promised me that whoever adhered to it, God would intercede for every one of his disciples. (Hiskett 1973, 66)

That this experience is concerned with mobilizing the Qadiriyah ṭarīqah as a reforming and renewing vehicle in Muslim Africa is obvious. It is designed to bring to the surface tendencies and attitudes of Islamic identity that hitherto occurred in a vague or intermittent pattern. Reform and renewal would make public virtue of religious profession, and make the contrast with the alternative African heritage sharper. The experience is attached to the orthodox flagship.

The second element of religious experience as a corrective mechanism occurs also in the Shehu's biography, as it does widely in Muslim Africa. Religious experience might be compared, in the telling Shaker metaphor, to a tunnel: the deeper one gets into it the narrower it becomes, until finally one is out of range of recognizable landmarks and within range of the devil and wicked spirits. In that condition one is extremely vulnerable to straying. For Muslim religious masters the answer might be in other forms of experience that would contain corrective instruction. One of the most typical forms of such corrective experience is the lucid or perspicacious dream/vision (ru'yā al-ṣāliḥah), telling the subject what course of action to follow. In this regard, the Shehu decided shortly after his mystical installation to leave Gobir on what would be a hijrah. However, before he carried out his plans 'Abd al-Qādir al-Jīlānī appeared to him in a vision to forbid the action. Eventually in 1803 or 1804 he was instructed, again in a vision, to leave Gobir for Gudu, a move that opened the

---

[2] In all likelihood a reference to sūratu-l-ikhlāṣ (112).
[3] This is a reference to the verse in the Qur'ān, amal bi-ma'rūf wa nahy 'an al-munkar — "to enjoin good works and restrain from what is disapproved of" (13:21-22). In West African Islam it was first articulated as a reform principle by 'Abd al-Karīm al-Maghīlī al-Tilimsānī († 1506) who visited Songhay for the purpose. See Hunwick and also Mervyn Hiskett 1962.

formal stage of the Islamic revolution that left a permanent mark on all
Muslim West Africa.

If dreams and visions might restrain impulsive conduct, they might
also help jack up flagging resolve. The Shehu was once assured in a
vision that the Prophet would come to greet him, about which he remained doubtful. He agreed, nevertheless, to submit the message to the
test to prove its truthfulness, so he prayed for guidance. As a result, he
claimed the Prophet appeared to him "in circumstances that dispelled his
doubts." (Hiskett 1973, 67)

Many people enter the tunnel experience of dreams and visions by
using special religious exercises and devotions. *Khalwah* 'religious retreat'
is a standard device employed to bring on dreams and visions for a
special purpose, though an ill-prepared person might come out of it
confounded. Another highly popular practice is the *ṣalāt al-istikhārah*,
more technical than *khalwah*, but no less potent. Meaning literally 'prayer
of seeking guidance in a choice,' *al-istikhārah* became the classic dream
incubation method of Muslim reformers in Africa, the mid-night calm
before the day's storm. J. Spencer Trimingham (1959, 122f.; 1968, 84), a
pioneer scholar of Muslim Africa, claims that *al-istikhārah* was employed
by virtually all Muslim reformers in Africa. It occurs widely in Muslim
literature.[4] For example, Ibn Khaldūn (1332–1406) wrote extensively about
it and said he tried it to effect.[5] Ibn Baṭṭūṭa (p. 10), the veteran Arab
traveller who visited West Africa in 1325, also mentions the practice, saying
he employed it with benefit. What is crucial about *khalwah, al-istikhārah,*
and other forms of religious retreat is that the experience acquired
thereby should not become permanently peripheral, but instead should
leave things different from what and how they were. The tunnel should
bring what passes through it to the surface.

The special importance of dreams and visions as the culmination of
Muslim religious experience strikes a somewhat discordant note in our
own austere, sceptical age. Freud's impressive legacy about dreams as
pathological symptoms has sundered them from their roots in religion,
though dreams and visions occur in the Qur'ān, and, for that matter, in
the Bible, with embarrassing frequency. Even in Salman Rushdie's *Satanic
Verses,* dreams occur as a distortion of reality, a position Mr. Rushdie

---

[4] For a critical summary of the sources see Toufic Fahd.
[5] He writes: "A Man is said to have done this after he had eaten but little and done
dhikr exercises for several nights. A person appeared to him and said, 'I am your
perfect nature.' A question was put to that person, and he gave the man the
information he desired. With the help of these words, I have myself had remarkable
dream visions, through which I learned things about myself that I wanted to know."
Ibn Khaldūn then goes on to warn against thinking that we have in these techniques
a principle like *ex opere operate.* The work (I, 213) was written in 1377.

himself vehemently defends. For example, in an open letter to Rajiv Gandhi, then Prime Minister of India, Rushdie complains that Muslim critics of this book fail to recognize how the offending parts of the novel hang on the dreams of a sick person and how, therefore, the book is far removed from reality, a defence that amounts to self-incrimination.[6] It is instructive to reflect on how dreams may function for us as an instrument of unreality, of escape and fantasy, whereas in both Islam and the Bible dreams are the polished horn of the spirit's eloquence.

3 Autonomy and Mutuality

The central question we face about religious experience is whether, if it is too unique to share with other, it does not condemn us to silent isolation, and whether, if it is common enough, it may not flake into popular consumption, losing any uniquely experiential dimension at all. Furthermore, does no sharing itself open us to intrusion or even denial by others? The perils of the 'shareability' of religious experience, of making religious intimations 'user-friendly,' are thus obvious, for it opens the door to an indistinct mush as the common essence of all religions. And, in similar fashion, does not religious experience that is so unique that it cannot be shared lead ultimately to its demise? If religious experience is some sort of elegiac bourn from which no traveller returns, would that not leave the world to darkness and to us? Thus from the extreme flanks of religious experience we are led to the fringes. The closest we come to this is glossolalia, that species of strange utterances that remains sealed to understanding: in neat regular infusions glossolalia draws a shade over the light and leaves us in darkness. And it is to dispel such darkness that the Shehu and men of his ilk sought visions and received dreams.

We have, therefore, to ask whether sharing is possible as a middle course between extreme subjectivism and extreme legalism, and if so, what its import might be for religious experience. An important part of the answer has to do with preserving religious particularity, so that distinctive teachings do not get lost in superficial syncretism, or get sequestered by another tradition's particularity. This brings us to the anthropology of religious experience. While it is true that for Muslim reformers obedience

---

[6] Rushdie writes that the sections of the book causing the most offence occur "in a dream, the fictional dream of a fictional character, an Indian movie star, and one who is losing his mind at that. How much further from history could one get?" In the very next breath, however, Rushdie concedes that he is not unmindful of the reality of Islam. "In this dream sequence," he concludes, "I have tried to offer my view of the phenomenon of revelation and the birth of a great world religion ..." *The New York Times,* October 19, 1988.

and conformity to the codes was a paramount motivation, nevertheless they also appealed to the norms of *maṣlaḥah,* the welfare and well-being of the people. Thus a certain human spirit distinguished their religious work and experience, and they asked that their effort be judged in that light too.

4 Theoretical Formulations: Personal and Instrumental Religion

That human spirit is the uniting strand in the intricate mesh of religious experience, not just in terms of the psychology of overlapping feelings and emotional states, but in the quilted moral dispositions and attitudes that attach themselves to the whole design. Guilt, repentance, and release might occur as strong elements in experience, but truth, righteousness, and reconciliation might set the tone. Religious experience might be sought, not simply for what we might attain by it, but for what it enables us to be and to do. Certainly in Muslim experience, religion cannot completely be reduced to instrumental power, a mechanistic technique, the *efficient* principle of Aristotelian science. In the final analysis religious experience is the affirmation by the creature of the Creator, not giving or receiving anything that God does not already have, and thus receiving and giving only what God gives. And since ultimately what God gives is life, and the means for it, then through religious mediation we only receive and give that life, or the tokens for it. At it profoundest level, then, religious experience will bring us to the realization of self-giving as the only authentic form of giving, so that with regard to God as the source of life and being, we give nothing that is ours or that is not already God's. Hence self-abnegation constitutes the deepest level of personal religion, and through it the human spirit is refined into the precious thing God intends it to be. This sort of anthropology seems implicit in the religious basis of experience.

There is a second implicit factor that takes us beyond the purely private world of individual feelings and emotions, although in this matter, too, a certain theological tendency can be detected. We may approach it by asking whether language as such exhausts the meaning and content of religious experience of whether language, any language, is intrinsically inadequate to the truth of what it witnesses. The great Muslim mystics, such as Rūmī and Ibn al-ʿArabī, tended to the view that truth transcends all language, but it would be incautious to represent that as typical.

By drawing in other comparative materials, from the Christian tradition and primal religious traditions, the following position can be stated. Religious language —or symbols— may be defined on three levels. On the first level, religious language operates *elliptically* by representing religious experience in terms of instrumental effects rather than by calling attention to the nature and qualities of God. Almost in the Thomist sense, God is encountered at this level through the effects God produces in the material and phenomenal world. Religion at this level is *instrumental*, with the idea of a personal God somewhat faint in the background. Such instrumental ideas end up emphasizing results, consequences, and strategies towards religion, so that sharing any experience involves a certain degree of manipulation or bargain. This is the 'user-friendly' approach that media evangelists have refined into a booming industry in the United States.

The second level is in the new-Wittgenstinian sense of the primacy of context wherein religious language may be compared to a stream: it takes on the colour of the terrain over which it flows without completely merging with it. We might call this the *symbolic* use of language and understand it as the way language and symbols, while not representing God in themselves, become in certain specific contexts and to certain specific persons God, or the idea of God. For example, the sounds and tones of the Arabic Qur'ān represent to Muslim the very truth of God even though those characteristics of the language do not have that meaning for other native-born Arabs who are non-Muslim. Nor, in fact, do the characteristics of the language so considered carry the same weight even for Muslims outside the special context of the Arabic Qur'ān. Christians have taken this notion to its logical conclusion by denying to any one language the status of revealed truth, so that the truth of the *One* God is expressed in the *Many* forms of human speech. Religious experience at this level does not presuppose a uniform language or culture.

The Muslim attitude to the Arabic of the Qur'ān introduces the third level of the use of religious language, and that is as a *figure of identity*. At this level the proximity of language or symbol to the thing spoken about or thus represented is so exact that an equivalent relationship is said to exist. This is the position with regard to the Arabic Qur'ān in Islam and to Jesus Christ in orthodox Christianity. It is also the case in certain primal religious traditions. For example, in his classic description of the religion of the ancient Ainu of Hokkaido, Japan, John Batchelor (p. 479-496) tells how the bear is regarded as a divinity that is raised as a cub and sacrificed when full grown. Its worshippers then eat the flesh to effect the identity that they believe exists between them and their deity.[7] Yet the circularity of terms here, being quite obvious, set the Ainu apart: they sacrifice to the divinity what is in itself divine, and they themselves receive what they thus sacrifice. The paradox of this is that religious experience, completely lacking in any of the ingredients of piacular intention or self-abnegation, subsides, if it rises at all, in group projection,

[7] Joseph Kitagawa (p. 95-151) assesses Batchelor's unique materials.

not in the differentiation of consciousness. It takes *instrumental* elements from the elliptical domain and transposes them into figures of identity. Sharing experience at this stage is predicated on assimilating into the original medium itself.

Figures of identity, whether in their negative or positive effects, tend to rely on an absolutized conception of religious forms. Thus on the negative side they promote an exclusive view of the medium through which we experience religion, and, on the positive side, they support a normative inclusiveness such as might be expressed in monistic systems and other theosophic claims. On one level distinctions are reduced to a form that assumes a universal exclusive mode, and on the other they are invested all of them with a universal inclusive quality.

These three forms of religious language, the *elliptical*, the *symbolical*, and *figures of identity* combine to cut a deep channel for the different streams of religious experience. It is interesting to reflect that William James, in his classic work, *The Varieties of Religious Experience*, being his Gifford Lectures, was extremely critical of the tendency to absolutize the language and symbols of religious conversion, especially when the cases in question refer to stages of adolescent development (p. 164). Obviously biological changes and rhythms, when they also assume psychological forms, need not crystallize into spiritual types to recognize their role in religious experience. The very rule of relativity that James sought to rivet on so-called conversion experience exists in eloquent form with *elliptical* and *symbolical* kinds of religious experience. In their ideal conceptions, *elliptical* experience may bring individuals or groups to an existential awareness, while *symbolic* experience may call attention to the structures required to establish and nurture habits of conformity. With *figures of identity*, by contrast, we might produce an ideology consistent with it, namely, a prescriptive exclusiveness that perceives in the absolute equivalence of symbol and the thing thus symbolized a corresponding certitude of access, or even monopoly of truth and virtue.

Conclusions

I began with Muslim examples, and I should conclude with a Muslim reference that also draws upon some Christian parallels. My reference this time is to the Black nationalist militant, Malcolm X, who was assassinated in February, 1965, before he was forty, having earlier converted to Islam through the Black Muslims. In his autobiography Malcolm X describes his conversion in language that expresses a profound religious experience. He speaks of that experience as a dramatic change from guilt and moral twistedness to truth as person challenge. In terms of the theoretical formulations just considered, Malcolm X, making his first acquaintance with Islam through its dietary prohibitions against pork, comes finally to an existential experience of prescriptive religion. Of that experience he writes as follows:

> "Many a time," he confessed, "I have looked back, trying to assess, just for myself, my first reaction to all this. Every instinct of ghetto jungle streets, every hustling fox and criminal wolf instinct in me, which would have scoffed at and rejected anything else, was struck dumb. It was as though all of that life was back there without any remaining effect, or influence. I remember how, sometime later, reading the Bible in the Norfolk Prison Colony Library, I came upon, then I read, over and over, how Paul on the road to Damascus, upon hearing the voice of Christ, was so smitten that he was knocked off his horse, in a daze. I do not now, and I did not then, liken myself to Paul. But I do understand this experience. ... I have since learned — helping me to understand what then began to happen within me— that the truth can be quickly received, or received at all, only by the sinner who knows and admits that he is guilty of having sinned much. Stated another way: only guilt admitted accepts truth ... The very enormity of my previous life's guilt prepared me to accept the truth. Not for weeks yet would I deal with the direct, personal application to myself, as a black man, of the truth. It still was like a blinding light." (p. 257f.)

Elaborating on his experience, Malcolm X said he was compelled to revise fundamental ideas he had imbibed about the cultural and racial criteria of truth and virtue. This ethical transformation he also likens to a religious experience, thus identifying the sort of religious anthropology that shapes language and thought. For Malcolm X Islam's inclusive anthropology stood in profound conflict with his experience of the racial exclusiveness of Western Christianity, with the effect that what he deduced about God from Christian racism crippled him from being capable of any spontaneous gracious response. On a visit to Mecca on pilgrimage, and out of range of Western racial stereotypes, Malcolm X suffered a reversal of his long-held attitudes. Commenting on the generous hospitality of his Arab host in Jeddah, Malcolm came to this unsettling reckoning:

> I was speechless at the man's attitude, and at my own physical feelings of no difference between us as human beings. I had heard for years of Muslim hospitality, but no, one couldn't quite imagine such warmth ... There had before been in my emotions such an impulse to pray — and I did, prostrating myself on the living-room rug. Nothing in either of my two careers as a black man in America had served to give me any idealistic tendencies. My instincts automatically examined the reasons, the motives, of anyone who did anything they didn't have to do for me. Always in my life, if it was any white person, I could see a selfish motive. But there in that hotel that morning ... was one of the few times I had been so awed that I was totally without resistance. (p. 445f.)

Malcolm suggests that Islam had harmonized for him the *One* and the *Many* bringing together *One* God and the *Many* nations and races of the world who find in God a common humanity. He spoke of Islam having "Proved the power of the One God" (p. 452). At Mecca itself after he had complete the pilgrimage obligation and kissed the black stone of the Ka'ba, he testified:

> I understood it better now that I had before. In the Holy World, away from America's race problem, was the first time I ever had been able to think clearly about the basic divisions of white people in America, and how their attitudes and their motives related to, and affected Negroes. In my thirty-nine years on this earth, the Holy City of Mecca had been the first time I had ever stood before the Creator of All and felt like a complete human being. (p. 482)

It says something both for the autonomy and mutuality of religious experience that, in spite of bitter lessons to make individuals feel hemmed in in an impenetrable tunnel, Malcolm X should in that position go on to discover a basic underlying connectedness in genuine human encounter, finding that sharing helps to deepen religious experience, rather than sap it. It is equally instructive to reflect that racial injustice might, in addition to all the other facts of oppression, breed in its victims separatist instincts that sharing would overcome. Perhaps Malcolm may still serve the double purpose of encouraging a common mutuality and the suppressing of extreme impulses for separatist autonomy.

Bibliography

Batchelor, John. *The Ainu and their Folk-lore.* London: The Religious Tract Society, 1901.

Baṭṭūṭa, Ibn. *Travels in Asia and Africa.* H. A. R. Gibb, trans. London: Routledge & Kegan, 1929.

Fahd, Toufic. *La Divination Arabe: Études Religieuses, Sociologiques et Folklorique sur le Milieu Natif de l'Islam.* Leiden: E. J. Brill, 1966.

Hiskett, Mervyn. "An Islamic Tradition for Reform in the Western Sudan from the 16th to the 18th Centuries." *Bulletin of the School of Oriental & African Studies* 25, no. 3 (1962).

——. *The Sword of Truth: The Life and Times of the Shehu Usuman dan Fodio.* New York: Oxford University Press, 1973.

Hunwick, John. *Shari'a in Songhay: The Replies of al-Maghīlī to the Questions of Askia al-Ḥājj Muḥammad.* London: Oxford University Press for the British Academy, 1985.

James, William. *The Varieties of Religious Experience.* New York: New American Library, 1958.

Khaldun, Ibn. *The Muqaddimah: An Introduction to History.* 3 vols. Franz Rosenthal, trans. Princeton: Princeton University Press, 1968.

Kitagawa, Joseph. "Ainu Bear Festival (Iyomante)." *History of Religion,* I, no. 1 (Summer 1961).

Malcolm X. *The Autobiography.* With the assistance of Alex Haley. Rpt. 19-70. Harmondsworth, Middlesex, England: Penguin Books, 1968.

O'Brien, Donal Cruise. *The Mourides of Senegal.* Oxford: Clarendon Press, 1971.

Trimingham, J. Spencer. *Islam in West Africa.* Oxford: Clarendon Press, 1959.

——. *The Influence of Islam upon Africa.* Beirut: Librairie du Liban, and London: Longman, 1968.

CHAPTER 8

Liberative Ecumenism
Gateway to the Sharing of
Religious Experience Today

Jerald D. Gort

This essay represents an attempt to discover a promising *entrée* to interreligious sharing of experience. It is argued that within the present context
of global pluralization in the form of increasing religious division and ever
widening economic-political disparities such sharing is of vital importance.
Legitimate interreligious sharing, it is contended, must be understood in the
trilateral sense of mutual participation, mutual accountability, and potential
conversional movement. Moving vertically through the various levels of
articulated religious experience there is no prior reason to assume that true
sharing among people of differing faiths is impossible. Moving horizontally
from the general to the specific, however, the gap between religions widens
and interreligious sharing becomes relatively more difficult to achieve. An
eminently promising means of bridging this gap and of discovering possible
areas of overlap of religious experience is the practice of liberative
ecumenism, i.e., interreligious cooperation on behalf of and with the poor.

In reflecting on the notion of sharing religious experience one is confronted immediately with a number of interrelated questions. Why should
people want to share religious experience; what is it that makes such
sharing so important? What is religious experience? What does 'sharing'
mean in this context? Is it possible to share religious experience? If so,
how and by what means? Does sharing preclude witness, testimony?
These queries can, of course, be addressed from various disciplinary
viewpoints. In this essay the perspective will be that of missiology.

1 Today's World

In a recent essay J. van Raalte offers a lucid analysis of the condition of
the present world.[1] In the past societies led relatively, though of course

---

[1] Unless otherwise indicated the material in the first, third, and fourth paragraphs of
this section represents a free rendering of some of the main argumentation found on

never wholly, separate existences behind geographical borders. Now, however, due to the effects of an ever accelerating worldwide process of societal pluralization, we are coming to the discovery that we share life in the same large village called earth. Many, it is true, continue to find their well-being in tribal loyalties and atavistic bondings and hence resist the move to this new domicile. Nevertheless, people everywhere are being increasingly confronted in all dimensions and at all levels of society with the two principal aspects of pluralization, the two impinging realities of global-village life: *deep-seated human division* in the form of contending religious claims, dissonant cultural and ideological views; and *wide social bifurcation* in the form of huge economic and political disparities.

People throughout the world are beginning to come into more and more direct contact with a multiplicity of religious experiences and practices and confrontation with an increase of interreligious division and internecine strife in many areas of the globe, both East and West. Hindu revivalism, for example, and Muslim minority reaction to it are on the march in India today. According to a recent report in an Indian news magazine towns in that subcontinent that used to be Indian, in which there was interreligious harmony and even sharing, are today Hindu and Muslim ones, in which people live on either side of a communal divide in credal paranoia (Badhwar, 31). And in many towns and cities in Western Europe Christian majority groups have developed a minority complex in response to the influx of Hindu and Muslim minority groups into their communities.

Likewise, humans everywhere are starting to live in ever greater awareness of the nefarious structural forces of dependency and exploitation that bear some up to ever rising heights of wealth and power and vast numbers of others down to ever lowering depths of poverty and power-lessness. A "network of . . . institutions and relationships" beneficial to a few has been set up "at the cost of the suffering and death of millions" forced to live at the edges of human history and existence (Van Raalte, p. 16). U. Duchrow speaks in this connection of a "world structure of apartheid" which marginalizes the majority and stands athwart of justice and peace (p. 26). Today society is universally divided and broken.

Moreover, these two main facts of present planetary life are becoming ever more inextricably intertwined. The rich Northwestern side of the village is coming into steadily closer encounter with the poor Southeastern side, whereby the latter is questioning the former more and more pertina-ciously regarding the role it is playing in the present world disorder.[2]

especially pp. 7-23 of Van Raalte's composition.
[2] On this matter of the poor taking an ever more active role as subjects of history rather than suffering themselves to be the objects of a history made for them by

Furthermore, people of other faiths who live in 'first-world' cultures are for the most part immigrants from 'third-world' cultures, which means that in the Western Christian setting the religiously other is usually also poor. The modern world context makes it plainly evident that disunity and injustice occur conjunctively: the one exacerbates the other. That being the case, these two problems require to be tackled in tandem and their solutions, "deep-going and all-inclusive communication and transformation" (Van Raalte, 23), must be perceived to be symbiotically related: the one will vitalize the other. Separately these two problems —interreligious disesteem and economic dependency— are inexpugnable, just as singly their solutions —sharing and justice— are unsusceptible of realization.

In short: our world is too big for a divided humanity; our world is too small for a divided humanity. No contemporary search for a sharing of religious experience can validly or profitably ignore the implications of this new context of the pluralization of society. It is indeed clear that we are now living in an interdependent world in which there is growing evidence of an "interlocking of [human] concerns" (Balasuriya, iv); in which "the search for renewal is a common quest, a shared search for all people" (Samartha 1976, 243). If this is true, it is of vital importance that we come to an understanding of "what it is that separates us and what it is that unites us at the deepest level" *(ibid.),* namely, that of religious experience.

2 Religious Experience

According to Richard Drummond, Paul Tillich views "the universal religious basis ... to be the experience of the Holy within the finite" (p. 121). This very concise definition is pregnant with meaning and seems similar to William James' classic dictum: Religion is real because it has real effects, and to W. Cantwell Smith's well-known thesis that the Transcendent exists because throughout human history, both diachronically and synchronically, people have encountered and related to it as a reality beyond the subject (subjectivity) even though it can not be known or experienced outside the subject (subjectivity). All three of these conceptions imply or affirm, each in its own way, a number of principles: the existence of the Holy; the indispensability of the dimension of finitude for the mediation of the Infinite; the reality of human interior experience of the Divine; and the

others cf., e. g., Virginia Fabella and Sergio Torres (eds.), *Irruption of the Third World* (Maryknoll: Orbis, 1983); the various documents produced since 1976 by the Ecumenical Association of Third World Theologians (EATWOT) and published together in *Voices From the Third World,* XI: 1 (1988); and the excellent monograph by J. de Santa Ana, *Through the Third World Towards One World* (Amsterdam: Vrije Universiteit, 1990).

possibility of outward articulation of this experience of the Transcendent. Taken together these yield two important insights eminently germane to the notion of interreligious sharing of experience.

First, *the divine Other is susceptible of apprehension by human beings.* People come into contact with God through some form of revelation, which, according to *A Dictionary of Comparative Religion,* can be understood as a making known of that knowledge concerning God that can not be attained through normal human investigation and reasoning and as such is claimed by religious believers as the source of their religious experience (cf. Brandson, 538). Second, *human inward experience of the divine can be and usually is exteriorly articulated.* People have very nearly always given outward expression to their encounter with God since revealed knowledge about God always entails enlightenment in respect of the divine Will for the world (cf. *ibid.*). Religious people reflect on, celebrate and try to live out their reception and perception of revealed truth regarding the three basic human questions: How did we come into existence? Why are we here? Where are we going? That is to say, their response to God takes the form of articulated faith and order, life and work: it is expressed in different ways by divers means at various ideally linked levels. Moreover, this articulation occurs within two more or less closely related orbs.

In the domain of *fides quae,* the area of faith interpretation and explication, believers give conceptual (theological–confessional), organizational (ecclesiastical–sacramental), practical (pastoral–diaconal), and martyrological (missionary–witnessing) content to their religious experience. Through time the *fides quae* takes on the character of oral or written *depositum fidei* which is capable of being passed down and inherited. In the sphere of *fides qua,* the dimension of living and lived faith, the response of religious believers to the Holy takes concrete shape in forms such as *fiducia cordis*: intimate, knowing love of, basic trust in, and affective assent to God and the *fidelitas Dei,* which leads to religious surrender *(cor meum tibi Domine)*; *adhaesio intellectualis*: cognitive assent to the content of faith, the confessional act; *praxis cultus, pietatis* and *meditationis*: worship of God, celebration of and struggle to attain to God's truth; and *praxis caritatis*: normative assent to the divine Will.

Since most believers hold that supernatural disclosure forms the source of their religious experience and its various articulations and thus the justification for the special claims of their religions (cf. *ibid.*), it would be well at this point to look more closely at this notion of divine revelation. It is often contended that the various religions understand revelation in two basically contrasting and contradictory ways. Some view it deo-soteriologically as divine (self-)disclosure: 'I *am* the way'; others auto-soteriologically as human (self-) discovery: 'I will *show* you the way.' And indeed, these two modes of enlightenment as extremes are incompatible. But does the one or the other of them ever really exist *in statu puro*?

All the religions, including Christianity, contain or evidence more or less pronounced autosoteriological tendencies. But is it ever the deepest *intention* of any of the living religions to teach that the human person is ultimately the subject of her or his salvific religious experience? Even in the case of Zen ('abstract enlightenment') this does not appear to be so: " ... although [Zen] is said to be a purely human way, still the ultimate experience does not seem to depend on a person's effort" since "some may strive for years without having ... *satori* ('enlightenment') or *kensho* ('seeing one's nature')," while others "will come to it very quickly" (Raguin, 32). On the other hand, can there ever be divine revelation without active participation on the part of the human subject, without some form of spiritual discipline, instruction, preparation?

Certainly, one must take account of sudden divine revélatory interjections on the Saul–St. Paul model. Yet, even such conversion does not take place in a vacuum but within the framework and through the agency of the specific receptive capacities of the human subject. Moreover, just how sudden was Paul's conversion? According to Acts 9:3 it occurred as he approached Damascus, thus after a long journey on the road to that city. Anyone who has travelled that road —even in modern times— knows that it not only provides plenty of time for but also irresistibly leads one to contemplative reflection. And again, where was Paul during his three years of disappearance in the Arabian wilderness subsequent to his conversion (cf. Gal. 1:17), and what was he doing there? Was he perhaps near Peniel ('the face of God') reliving Jacob–Israel's ('he who strives with God' or 'God strives') long night of wrestling with the Angel of God?

Is the revelatory event, in other words, not always *bipolar,* involving divine disclosure *and* human searching discovery? And are the authentic religions of humankind ultimately not profoundly cognizant of that? Surely, the essence of revelation is most deeply expressed for all the living religions of the world by the following words of the great 19th century anonymous hymn:

> I sought the Lord and afterward I knew
> He moved my soul to seek Him, seeking me;
> It was not I that found, O Savior true;
> No, I was found, was found of Thee.
>
> Thou didst reach forth Thy hand and mine enfold;
> I walked and sank not on the storm-vexed sea;
> 'Twas not so much that I on thee took hold,
> As Thou, dear Lord, on me, on me. (ca. 1887)

The question to be put is whether any or all of the above-described articulations of religious experience belonging to believers from a given tradition, and claimed by them to be divinely inspired, can be shared by people of other faiths. But first we must examine the notion of sharing itself.

3   Modes and Dynamics of Sharing

In the field of religion the concept *sharing* has at least four distinct connotations. One can speak of sharing in the *confessional* sense of already existing commonly held views and common experiences and practices; in the *ecumenical* sense of mutual participation; in the *witnessing* sense of giving account and calling to accountability; and in the *conversional* sense of being won over to another position. It is the latter three of these senses that are of immediate significance for the concept of interreligious sharing of experience, even stronger, they are essential conditions for genuine sharing. This is by no means a self-evident matter, however. Whether these modes of sharing are applied *col*lectively or *se*lectively to the issue under discussion depends strongly on the theology of religion involved.

It is possible at one extreme to hold the *inclusivist* view that all religions are fundamentally the same. Religionists articulate their faith in different ways but this does not mean that they point to different realities. Religious experience, which is characterized by essential oneness and sameness, is equally expressible through the articulations of all religions. This view obviates sharing in the sense of witness and conversion. At the other extreme are those, including many Christians, who take the *exclusivist* position that the various religious experiences and traditions of humankind are diametrically opposed and wholly incompatible. This assessment precludes the possibility of sharing in the sense of mutual participation.

Both of these views seem to militate against common sense and good sense. More seriously, being of an aprioristic nature, they ignore any kind of empirical evidence. In addition, inclusivism is basically docetic in that it rules out the possibility of real revelational particularity, and imperialistic because it makes it impossible to assign any genuine significance to cultural specificity: in the end it is destructive of the principles of identity and identification. Exclusivism, on the other hand, fails to recognize the teaching of many religions, including that of Christianity, respecting the universal salvific will and saving presence and activity of God throughout the world. In the end this approach reduces God to the status of a tribalized deity or, expressed from another point of view, a universalized idol.

What is needed is a manner of theological thinking that allows for the employment of Kenneth Cragg's promising concept of "distinctiveness" as a substitute for "uniqueness," which latter disallows any "overlap of meaning and experience between faith-concerns" (cited in Forward). This idea leaves generous room for recognition of both similarities and differences between religious faiths and faith articulations and hence implies both the possibility and the need for all three of the above-mentioned applicable senses of religious sharing: participation, witness, and conversion. Interreligious mutual participation does not simply happen as a matter of course but must be fostered and cultivated. I should like to contend that witness and potential for conversion are essential to that process. In the course of the common pursuit of interreligious sharing, existing areas of greater or lesser overlap may well be discovered, which would obviously serve as bases for significant mutual participation. But if progress and growth in mutuality, a deepening and broadening of sharing is to take place, there must be sufficient room for open and honest mutual critical witness stemming from the remaining distinctives, as well as mutual freedom of movement to or towards the other's area of distinctiveness: each and all must be allowed the possibility of being led to utter Ruth's profession: "Thy God is my God."

The reasoning here is nicely expressed in terms recently applied by José Míguez Bonino to the Christian ecumenical movement (cited in Houtepen, 1). As Míguez wrote concerning relations among Christian denominations, so it can be said of those among religions that plurality may not be sacralized at the expense of coherence; on the other hand, coherence must not be sacralized at the expense of diversity. There will be areas of interreligious overlap to be discovered. Nevertheless, many genuine distinctives will also be found, which require mutual critical witness and freedom of religious movement. Without these latter two possibilities a form of sharing might be conceivable in the sense of *mutual seasoning*, whereby people of differing faiths add a little spice, a bit of zest to each other's religious life. But in the absence of mutual accountability and the potential for conversional movement there can be no sharing of religious experience in the sense of true mutual participation, i. e., a dynamic *mutual leavening* which is creative of new *theologoumena*, fresh insight, understanding and experience.

4 Extent and Range of Sharing

In practice there are both absolute and relative limits to interreligious sharing of experience this side of witness and horizontal conversion. Obviously it is not possible to share in the sense of mutual participation with those whose religious experience is clearly not genuine or lacks authenticity. Religious experience is genuine only when and if it is truly rooted in the Eternal and its authenticity is verified by the deepest intentions of its various articulations. Valid interreligious mutuality is impossible with those who show by what they say and do that their religious experience consists of encounter with Satan or some idol rather than with God. People of authentic religious faith cannot possibly share mutually with adherents of demonic movements or manipulative, totalitarian cults that teach pernicious doctrines, consciously foster human bondage, intentionally engage in evil or socially destructive practices.

Of course, even authentic religions are ambivalent in this regard. Particularly in their institutionalized forms they can be enslaving. Religions often impose on their followers "stultifying orthodoxies, restrictive patterns of behaviour, and authoritarian hierarchical elites, from which the people ... are rigidly excluded" (EATWOT 1987, 152). An egregious example of this is the uppercaste domination of the Dalits, the Black Untouchables, in India within both Hinduism and the Christian church, whose membership is fully 80% Dalit *(Dalit Voice,* Nov. 1–15, 1989, 15). Naturally, many additional cases of comparable religious oppression could be cited. Such degenerative tendencies, too, represent problems for but need not be interpreted as a hindrance to interreligious sharing. Since all living religions are involved here, these negative propensities could come to be understood as opportunities for mutual sharing of guilt, repentance, and transformation.

Aside from limitations of this nature, however, the quest for full sharing ought to be viewed as valid between and among religions whose beliefs and practices demonstrate that they "contain dreams of the new order and a new humankind, which are both a vision and motivating force" for the lives of their adherents (Dornberg, 112). The search for mutual sharing is eminently legitimate among religious people who have come face to face with God who is rich in mercy and causes salvation to dawn on earth; who show by their faith articulations that they understand that the final aim and purpose of revelation is to cause human recipients of light to reflect that light into the world in order that darkness may be held at bay. And indeed, moving *vertically* through the various levels and dimensions of articulated religious experience there is no prior reason to suspect that a true meeting of people of differing faiths is *absolutely* impossible. This is not to say, though, that sharing in the sense of mutual participation will be uniformly easy of attainment.

There are articulated religious experiences of a general, universal nature that are easily and fully shared soul to soul by all religious believers and probably all human beings. These include experiences of non-being and death such as awareness of finitude, ultimate helplessness, cosmic loneliness, fundamental vulnerability, contingency, fear of deprivation, feelings of ineptitude, of missing the mark and falling short of the purpose of life. All people feel the need, too, for some form of salvific help; yearn for transcendence, wisdom, safety and well-being; long for answers to their etiological, teleological and eschatological questionings. Such experience is well summed up by words from the text of a song by the pop singer Sting.

> Everyone I know is lonely
> And God's so far away
> And my heart belongs to no one.
> So now sometimes I pray:
> Please take the space between us
> And fill it up some way.[3]

And also salvific experiences, if generally articulated, are susceptible to ready and broad human sharing: experiences of infinity, oneness of the universe, awe of the Holy, the theonomous character of reality, bliss, joy, contentment, blessing, timely intervention and rescue.

But the question that immediately comes to mind is: What do these general, universally shared amorphous feelings and diffuse yearnings signify exactly? It is in the several religions and among religious believers that they are given specific meaning and content. And it is at this point that latent difficulties for sharing begin to appear. For moving *horizontally* through the range of generality toward specificity (diffusion toward concentration, extension toward intension, universality toward particularity, exteriority toward interiority) potential mutual interreligious sharing becomes relatively less easy to achieve. Specificity is creative of distinctiveness. The more rigorously religious meaning is *de*limited, the more limited the possibility for mutual participation among people of various religious faiths will be. Specification of articulated religious experience is conditioned by a number of particularizing determinants: historical and geographic place, cultural-religious tradition, language, confessional adherence, social condition, everyday experience, personality, and psychology. The farther and more extensively religious people are separated from each other by differences in these determinants, the narrower will be the initial overlap of articulation and thus the basis for mutual participatory sharing.

Finally, religious experience *an sich,* whether strictly confined to interiority or outwardly articulated, does not lend itself to transmission and accordingly is incapable of being shared. Joseph Spae has defined the "deepest meaning of salvation as an intimate event in which a loving God is perceived and accepted by an intuitive thrust of the heart" (p. 43). At this intensely personal level of religious experience there can only be a

---

[3] "O My God," The Police: Synchronicity, A & M, 1983.

sharing from spirit to Spirit between the believer and God. Not even believers from the same religion can ever really know whether their experiences of the Eternal are in exact harmony with each other. As the missiologist Marc Spindler points out, awareness of this fact has come to expression in recent Christian ecumenical-confessional statements such as the Madagascan Confession of Faith and the Constitution of the Church of South India, from the latter of which he quotes the following paragraph in German translation.

> Die unierenden Kirchen akzeptieren die Grundwahrheiten, die im aposto-
> lischen und nicaenischen Glaubensbekenntnis verkörpert sind. Mit dieser
> Akzeptierung wird aber dem einzelnen Christen nicht auferlegt, daß er
> jedem Wort und jedem Satz in den genannten Bekenntnissen zustimmt.
> Es wird auch nicht die Behauptung erwartet, daß jene Bekenntnisse ein
> vollständiger Ausdruck des christlichen Glaubens sind. (p. 24)

Indeed, in the consciousness of some, shared confessional terms and concepts and ecclesiastical practice can actually seem to point to different realities. There are Christians, for example, who wonder aloud whether they serve the same God as certain of their fellow Christians.

To sum up: At what points may religious believers expect, at least potentially, to achieve mutual participatory sharing? *Formally* there is room for sharing between religious people at all levels of outwardly articulated religious experience. Hence, the quest for greater understanding and mutuality among people of different faiths may range over the whole gamut of these areas. It would seem both legitimate to seek meaningful moments and possible to discover significant regions of inter-religious participatory sharing spirit to spirit, heart to heart, and mind to mind in the provinces of both theory and practice, both *fides quae* and *fides qua*. It is entirely reasonable to expect that the spoken, sung, acted, written, lived expressions of a believer's experience of the Divine could set off sympathetic vibrations of renewed or even new religious consciousness in the life of a person or persons of another faith. Faith articulations are both expressive and creative of religious experience.

Materially the search for mutual sharing of religious experience will be no light task. Notwithstanding the difficulties involved, however, and the continuing existence of many real distinctives and genuinely different truth-claims, this quest not only may and can be set upon but, being of vital importance, also requires to be undertaken. Why?

5 Motives and Aims of Sharing

According to the 17th century Dutch missiologist, Gijsbertus Voetius, the deepest source and final aim of Christian mission is God the Eternal One (Jongeneel, 147). This profound insight surely can and should be broadened to include all positive human actions. Everything good undertaken in this world can be said to redound to the glory of God. And certainly all religious endeavour, including the quest for interreligious sharing, ought consciously to have the increase of God's honour —however differently that may be understood— as its final purpose and inspiration. Subordinate to this ultimate goal and impetus, however, the possibility of a whole variety of important *pen*ultimate aims and motives exists.

Pursuit of sharing in the area of religion could be motivated by natural or academic curiosity; a yearning, born of the classic insight: *finitum non capax infiniti,* for complementary apprehensions of Truth; the felt need for fellowship with believers from other traditions in the face of impious secularism; the hope of achieving greater understanding by allowing the other's faith and religious life and work to act as a foil for one's own; the desire to clear away joint ignorance, reciprocal preconceptions, serious existing common deficiencies in the interpretation of the other; the wish on the part of many Westerners to breach the dense walls of no-nonsense pragmatism and run-amok rationalism that immure them to Heaven by seeking out the spirituality of others not so immured; the desire to honour and show respect for the other by taking the other's deepest feelings and experiences seriously.

But the most important penultimate aim and motive of religious sharing derive from the exigencies of our present world situation. For the honour of the Creator of humanity is most assuredly not served by the inhumanity of religious strife and political–economic injustice. All religions share responsibility for the dividedness of the human family, which forms one of the greatest and growing barriers to world peace, justice, and the integrity of creation. And it is clear in the new situation of globalized pluralization that all have a shared responsibility for defining these terms and for combatting injustice, division and enmity, and the shameless exploitation of nature. Religious groups are no longer alone and therefore may no longer act independently *in suo arbitrio* but must do so together *in concilio.* It is becoming increasingly evident that people of differing faiths, "sharing an endangered planet, also share an urgent global concern on which they have no alternative but to work together" (Van Elderen, 6). Justice, peace, and respect for creation "are not private matters ... that can be reserved for a certain people or a certain country; they can only be realized if all countries work for and profit from them together" (Zeid, 48). Religions owe it to God, to themselves and to the world to seek as much reconciliation of their diversity as possible; to attempt to arrive at mutual understanding regarding their various world-and-life views; to try to gain that unity in the truth to which they severally point that will make it possible to realize a greater measure of the righteousness for which the greatest share of humankind so yearns. How have the religions attempted to meet the needs of the contemporary world?

6 Dialogue, Mission?

Insofar as religious people or religions are presently concerned with the two great problems of our times, they far too often assign them differing degrees of urgency, thereby implying the assumption that these problems can be addressed separately. This is clearly illustrated by existing differences of opinion in this regard within Christianity. In recent decades growing numbers of Christians have come to see dividedness as the pre-eminent challenge and thus place heavy emphasis on dialogue, with its communicative thrust, as the most significant contribution that can be made to the solution of the problems mentioned. Barriers to unity and harmony must be broken down, the debris of rivalry and mutual fear and suspicion removed. Others, particularly those influenced by the discussions on the gospel for the poor which began in the late seventies and early eighties, view brokenness as the real problem and make a strong plea for mission, with its liberative thrust, as by far the most important task to be undertaken. Situations of oppression and exploitation must be addressed and redressed.

These divergent perceptions and approaches have led, as is well known, to no little disputatious discussion and wrangling in Christian circles. Those who stand for mission are often accused of basic disinterest in other religions and religiosities by the advocates of dialogue. Conversely, present mission advocacy frequently includes the accusation that those who plead the cause of dialogue evidence a serious lack of concern for the problems of poverty and injustice.[4] Nor can it be denied that there has been good and ample cause for this mutual recrimination. Broadly speaking, both dialogue and mission have been based on a faulty hermeneutic. Methodologically dialogue has failed to recognize that most religious people in the world are poor, whereas mission has been deficient in acknowledging the fact that the vast majority of the world's poor are deeply religious. Consequently, dialogue has indeed not given much attention to the poverty of the religious,[5] and mission has paid little heed

---

[4] Criticism from more conservative quarters often includes the contention that dialogue represents an inherent betrayal of the gospel: " ... there are those who continue to oppose dialogical encounter between people of differing faiths because they suppose it to be a 'new form of syncretism' or because they view it as a threat to mission and evangelism." (Gort, 48)

[5] It is possible to adduce a few notable exceptions to this general lack of interest in questions of poverty and justice on the part of dialogue; the Multi-Lateral Dialogue held in Colombo, Sri Lanka in April 1974, e. g., made a plea "for dedication to the

to the religiosity of the poor.[6] Of late, however, there is a growing
awareness within the spheres of both dialogue and mission that this state
of things is untenable.

It is coming to be understood that dialogue as often practised is an
inappropriate response to the problem of human dividedness precisely
because it does not take adequate account of human brokenness. Even
at the 'official' Genevan level there seems lately to be a certain degree of
recognition of this inadequacy. The report of the 1988 meeting of the
Working Group of the WCC Sub-Unit on Dialogue states that "those who
are committed to a dialogical approach to people of other faiths face the
criticism of not addressing the critical issues of poverty, justice, and the
relationship between power and powerlessness" *(Dialogue,* 14). And
indeed, even a casual review of the impressive number of publications
produced and gatherings held by the Sub-Unit throughout the years since
1969 can only yield the conclusion —which the *Report* just referred to
readily concedes (cf. p. 15)— that usually the chosen dialogue partners
have not been poor and justice has not been on the agenda. This
document asserts that "people of faith may wish to be understood as poor
or powerless. We must not insist on a religious or ideological definition
because we prefer it" (p. 14). But almost in the same breath it poses the
question: "How ... do we speak out against the evil of the caste system
and yet be seen to respect the faith of Hindus?" (p. 15)

This points up a fundamental problem, betrays a remaining weakness
in much of present dialogical theory and practice. The starting point is
wrong here. If dialogue takes 'respect' as its sole or main point of
departure, it will never be able to arrive at 'a speaking out against evil.'
This seems at first blush to have been understood by the 1988 Sub-Unit
meeting.

> The dialogical approach demands to be lived, not merely verbalized. ...
> The group felt that dialogue for Christians should serve justice and that
> no compromise ought to be made even for the sake of interreligious
> harmony or understanding. Dialogue as a way of life and witness is
> bigger than interreligious dialogue and in any discussion of dialogue in

---

promotion of peace and of social and economic justice, for a struggle against social,
economic, racial and religious discrimination" (Samartha 1975, 122); such exceptions,
however, do not disprove but rather support the validity of the thesis stated.

[6] Here, too, it must be pointed out that the perspective of this proposition is one of
generality; Yale University missiologist Lamin Sanneh has shown convincingly in various
publications, e. g., *Translating the Message: The Missionary Impact on Culture* (Maryknoll: Orbis, 1989), that the actual practice of many individual missionaries in Asia and
Africa was characterized by a dialogical concern and stance; nevertheless, taken as a
whole mission has by and large displayed little genuine interest in African and Asian
religions in and of themselves.

the context of mission it is as wrong to reduce it to what is admittedly the particular focus of our Working Group as it would be to reduce mission to just proclamation, or to just *diakonia.* *(ibid.)*

Though pointing in the right direction, on closer examination this argumentation does not go nearly far enough and even evinces a certain residual schizophrenia in the thinking of some regarding relations with people of other faiths. Distinguishing between two kinds of dialogue, the statement assumes that 'interreligious dialogue' can be divorced from 'mission,' from 'witness' or, in other words, can be authentically carried on bereft of liberative thrust after all. On the other hand, it fails to affirm unambiguously that mission can never be legitimately separated from dialogue. The insight that it is imperative to do away with the notion that mission can be properly exercised in the absence of dialogue is, however, on the increase, largely under the influence of the missiological reflection that has been emerging since about 1985 from the gatherings of the Ecumenical Association of Third World Theologians (EATWOT).

The idea is not that mission or witness and dialogue should be held together in some form of unresolved tension, as the 1989 WCC World Missionary Conference in San Antonio seemed to advocate (cf. Bosch, 133), but rather that they should stand together in a relationship of mutually beneficial interaction. These two entities need each other. Interreligious communication and human liberation go hand in hand. Dialogue must allow itself to be thoroughly informed by the liberative thrust of mission in the realization that justice is the ultimate aim and purpose of communication: interreligious understanding should be pursued with an eye to the discovery of "norms and values on the basis of which people from differing traditions can call each other to mutual responsibility" (Van Raalte, 20). Likewise, mission must let itself be shot through with the communicative thrust of dialogue in the awareness that religion lies at the basis of liberation: "No true liberation is possible unless people are 'religiously' motivated towards it" (Pieris, 19). Taken separately mission and dialogue are merely one-sided answers to a two-sided problem.

All this means that dialogue and mission will have to engage jointly in the search for a new common hermeneutic which takes full account of the religiosity of the poor and the actual living experience of people of other faiths, most of whom, as already indicated, are poor: "Jesus praxis, the life of solidarity with the poor and oppressed is the basis of this methodology" (Abraham, 2). The best means of achieving the successful development of a methodology of this nature, a "radical break in epistemology which makes commitment the first act of theology" (EAT-

WOT 1976, 16),[7] is orientation toward and cooperation with those religions or movements within the religions that have a liberative aim and force.[8] Such orientation and cooperation would yield the kind of hermeneutic needed, one that combines the two existing entities of dialogue and mission, each with its own *scopus,* transforming them into a new entity with a bipartite *focus,* which, to borrow a concept from a recent consultation of third-world theologians, could well be termed *liberative ecumenism.* (cf. EATWOT 1987, 168)[9]

7 Liberative Ecumenism

The methodological approach of liberative ecumenism is obviously fraught with significance in terms of interreligious sharing. Sharing in the full sense of participatory, witnessing, and conversional mutuality at all levels of articulated religious experience can best be entered through the gateway of joint interreligious praxis, cooperative solidarity on behalf of and with the poor, cooperative relations between people of various faiths and convictions who are involved in "movements of innovation, of renewal and of unfamiliar creativity." (Samartha 1976, 234)

> The liberational thrust helps us to enter into a dialogue and cooperation with people of other faiths and ideologies. The [1987 EATWOT] Delhi Consultation on Religion and Liberation clearly states that in the Third World countries, where all religions together face the challenges of oppressive social systems and the need to struggle for justice, religions should meet each other, exploring and sharing their liberative elements. It calls for the development of ... a form of interreligious dialogue which is concerned, not so much with doctrinal insights or the spiritual experience that different religions can offer to one another, as with the contribution to human liberation that each can make. The implications of this liberative ecumenism for relationships and concrete actions in the secular as well as religious areas of our life should be further explored. (Abraham, 2)

[7] Cf. here also the contention of the Oaxtepec gathering of third-world theologians: "Commitment to and practice of liberation comes first; praxis is pregnant with theory; theology articulates the truth of praxis." (EATWOT 1986, 125)

[8] There is a growing awareness that there are many such liberative elements and movements to be found within the living religions of the world, several of which have been identified in, e. g., EATWOT 1987, 159-166.

[9] The practical, organizational implication of this new hermeneutic for the Christian ecumenical movement, I would suggest, is that the Sub-Unit on Dialogue and the Commission on World Mission and Evangelism — now two separate departments within the WCC — should be merged into one new division of Liberative Ecumenism.

As has been demonstrated in the foregoing, this argumentation is applicable not only to countries in the Third World but to those in the whole world. Nowhere can we hope to achieve interreligious understanding or sharing by engaging in dialogue 'objectively' on 'neutral' ground or at the verbal level of theological–philosophical discourse alone. Fresh understanding and sharing, impulses for renewed dialogue will be realized as religious people live and work together in the increasingly unitary world of the present age.

This is not to suggest that religious believers could or should participate in all such innovative movements, for some of the latter, "including those within Christianity, can bring disintegration and new forms of bondage in the name of newness" (Samartha 1976, 242) For their part Christians must be concerned to discern "the points where God is at work" in the world (ibid., 241). Such perception of divine activity and participation in it requires the application of "certain criteria," the central one of which for Christians is Jesus Christ, who as the Christ "can not be restricted [biblically and theologically] to the historical figure of Jesus of Nazareth" (ibid., 242). Discernment of God's work by this criterion and participation in that work "might mean not only cooperating with our neighbours but also being in critical engagement with them in the total search for renewal" (ibid., 241). If a movement of innovation is in accord with the ministry and gospel of Jesus Christ, however, Christians may be assured that Christ through the Holy Spirit is at work in it. "Christ is at work wherever people are struggling for freedom and renewal, seeking for fullness of life, peace and joy" (ibid., 243). In other words, if a religious movement or praxis has a genuinely liberative thrust toward human justice and peace, Christians may feel free to align themselves with it and seek to relate to it in the form of cooperative participation, even though in doing so they will have to take "certain risks" and might "not know where [they] are being led." (ibid., 243)

Joint interreligious praxis among and on behalf of the poor will yield not only the enhancement of a greater measure of justice but also an increase of communication and understanding. It is in the crucible of praxis and solidarity that religious beliefs, perceptions, experiences are tested and can be given deeper and broader meaning and content. This is certainly true with respect to shared interreligious solidarity with the poor: they understand better than anyone what God's salvific will and intentions are and will be able to help their partners to correct any misapprehensions or misunderstandings. It is also in and through shared praxis among the poor that differing articulations of religious experience in the spheres of both fides quae and fides qua will be revealed to be compatible or not. Common praxis of this nature has a special capacity for bringing distinctives and areas of overlap to light.

Moreover, interreligious solidarity on behalf of and with the poor may also be seen as a form of common witness to the world of power and privilege. Further, liberative ecumenism may be said to have a sacramental character. It is a sign and seal, pointing to and verifying whatever shared articulations of religious experience there may be between believers from differing religious traditions. And finally, this mutual cooperation with the poor can itself become mediatory of shared religious experience of the *presentia realis Dei* in and among the poor, i. e., can lead to a shared vision of God *semper minor, semper maior,* the God who in becoming ever smaller becomes ever greater and who announces to all religious believers: *les amis de mes amis sont mes amis.*

Bibliography

Abraham, K. C. "Introduction." *Voices From the Third World* XI: 1 (1988): 1-2.

Badhwar, Inderjit. "Badaun: Anatomy of a Riot." *India Today* (Oct. 11, 1989): 30-31.

Balasuriya, Tissa. "Editorial." *Voices From the Third World* XI: 1 (1988): iii-iv.

Brandson, S. G. F., ed. *A Dictionary of Comparative Religion.* New York: Charles Scribner's Sons, 1970.

Bosch, David. "Your Will Be Done? Critical Reflections on San Antonio." *Missionalia* 17:2 (1989): 126-138.

Dialogue With People of Living Faiths: Minutes of the Eighth Meeting of the Working Group, Baar, Switzerland, May 1988. Geneva: WCC, 1988.

Dornberg, Ulrich. "Development and Interreligious Dialogue: Some Preliminary Remarks for Discussion." *Mission Studies: Journal of the IAMS* VI–2:12 (1989): 108-116.

Drummond, Richard H. *Toward a New Age in Christian Theology.* Maryknoll: Orbis, 1985.

Duchrow, Ulrich. *Global Economy: A Confessional Issue for the Churches.* Geneva: WCC, 1987.

EATWOT 1987. *Statement of the Consultation on Religion and Liberation.* New Delhi, India. In *Voices From the Third World* XI:1 (1988): 152-171.

—— 1976. *Final Statement.* Dar es Salaam, Tanzania. In *Voices From the Third World* XI:1 (1988): 3-29.

—— 1986. *Commonalities, Differences and Cross-Fertilization Among Third World Theologies.* Oaxtepec, Mexico. In *Voices From the Third World.* XI:1 (1988): 121-151.

Forward, Martin. "Ambiguous Terms." *Areopagus* 2:4 (1989): 51.

Gort, Jerald D. "Syncretism and Dialogue: Christian Historical and Earlier Ecumenical Perspectives." In Jerald D. Gort, Hendrik M. Vroom, *et al.*, eds. *Dialogue and Syncretism: An Interdisciplinary Approach.* Currents of Encounter Series Vol. 1. Grand Rapids/Amsterdam: Eerdmans/ Rodopi, 1989, pp. 36-51.

Houtepen, Anton. "Voorwoord." In Anton Houtepen, ed. *De Verscheidenheid Verzoend?* IIMO Research Publication No. 26. Voorburg: PSBBLN, 1989, pp. 1-3.

Jongeneel, J. A. B. "Voetius' Zendingstheologie, de Eerste Comprehensieve Protestantse Zendingstheologie." In J. van Oort, *et al.*, eds. *De Onbekende Voetius.* Kampen: Kok, 1989, pp. 117-147.

Pieris, Aloysius. "The Place of Non-Christian Religions and Cultures in the Evolution of a Third World Theology." *East Asian Pastoral Review* 19:2 (1982): 5-33.

Raguin, Yves. "Zen and Christian–Buddhist Encounter." *Areopagus* 2:4 (1989): 31-34.

Raalte, J. van. "Kerk en Plurale Samenleving op Weg naar de Toekomst." *Allerwegen* 20:1 (1989): 7-36.

Samartha, Stanley J., ed. *Towards World Community: Resources and Responsibilities for Living Together.* The Colombo Papers. Geneva: WCC, 1975.

——. "Mission and Movements of Innovation." In G. H. Anderson and T. F. Stransky, eds. *Third World Theologies.* Mission Trends No. 3. New York/Grand Rapids: Paulist Press/Eerdmans, 1976, pp. 233-244.

Spae, Joseph J. *East Challenges West: Towards a Convergence of Spiritualities.* Chicago: Chicago Institute of Theology and Culture, 1979.

Spindler, Marc. "De Fundamenten van de Eenheid." In A. Houtepen, ed. *De Verscheidenheid Verzoend?* IIMO Research Publication No. 26. Voorburg: PSBBLN, 1989, pp. 19-26.

Van Elderen, Marlin. "On Religious Plurality." *One World: A Monthly Magazine of the World Council of Churches* 153 (1990): 6-9.

Zeid, Hamzah. "Een Islamitische Bijdrage aan het Conciliaire Proces." *Allerwegen* 20:1 (1989): 48-53.

CHAPTER 9

The Incomparability of God as Biblical Experience of Faith

Walter Strolz

This contribution elucidates in three steps the incomparability of God as the biblical religious experience. This notion reaches its apex in the prophetic proclamation of deutero-Isaiah (5th century B. C.). First, the distinctive features of this radical monotheism are uncovered. These render a unity of creation and history which excludes any from of dualism between God and the world. It is ascertained that the problem of theodicy is subordinate to the mystery of creation, and that the evil which is still operative cannot be understood as an independent counter-force. Second, the question is raised regarding the extent to which Judaism, Christianity, and Islam agree in their confession of God's oneness and incomparability. Third, to examine, via schematic adumbration, whether the incomparability of God forms a point of contact with other religions, particularly in the dialogue with Zen Buddhism (*creatio ex nihilo*; negative theology; affirmation of the world through grace; spiritual peace).

The prophetic proclamation of biblical Israel reached its zenith in Deutero-Isaiah during the Babylonian exile. This already implies that the proclamation is time-bound, cannot be understood apart from the crisis of the exiled Jews, and only becomes a comforting word of salvation for the believer. The activity of this great unknown prophet falls in the period between the destruction of Jerusalem in the year 587 and the collapse of the Babylonian empire in the year 539. As a result of the fall of Jerusalem, Israelite faith in Yahweh fell into crisis. Its cultural centre no longer existed, the land had been torn from the Jews by a foreign power, and earlier promises of salvation seemed to be obliterated by the victorious Babylonians. In such a situation, Deutero-Isaiah proclaimed his prophetic word of salvation to the Jewish communities in exile after 550. (cf. Begrich)

The questions which now confront us are what such a contextually-determined message of salvation could mean for us today, thousands of years after its initial proclamation, and whether the biblical experience of faith in the incomparability of God can be *shared* with the adherents of another religious tradition. In this article we will demonstrate more specifically what it means to share religious experience, using the example of the prophetic word of salvation. Does sharing a religious experience mean understanding it, experiencing it oneself, without surrendering one's own religious affiliation? Or is the free recognition of *another,* alien religious experience, in its unavoidable otherness, in the first place an initial step in the approach to one's fellow humans (cf. Levinas)? Is it even possible to speak of sharing religious experience without the presupposed dimension of common engagement with the Transcendent?

As an initial attempt to answer such questions we will give precedence to the interpretation of the prophetic word of salvation. Only then can we consider whether the biblical testimony to the Unique finds any correspondence beyond the monotheistic religions in the traditions of the East. If there is only a partial correspondence, then the question becomes, what significance the irreconcilable, the unshareable in this biblical experience of faith can still have for the East–West dialogue.

1 The inseparability of creation and history

Deutero-Isaiah, called and empowered to prophecy during the Babylonian exile, addresses to the doubting and hopeless Israelites, in response to the crisis of faith in Yahweh, the message of the majestic uniqueness of Yahweh, the Creator and Lord of history. He is the Unique, to whom nothing can be compared, who reigns over the creation *without equal,* in whose stead nothing can stand. In the powerful, comforting opening verses of Isaiah 40, the prophetic word of God concerning the incomparability of Yahweh is three times proclaimed. It becomes, for the exiles, a word which distinguishes all creation from the transcendent God. This word of Yahweh, as the Unique, is factually concrete, that is to say, it is irreducible, it cannot be deduced from an already valid principle. As a prophetic word it is *historical-critical,* pointing to the *future.* It is for Deutero-Isaiah, from its inception on, a controversial, guiding, liberating word which provides courage and dissolves fear. What occurs in the world of the gods, in and through the earthly powers, is not ultimate; for all what is human stands under the unavoidable sign of vanity, all-questioning transitoriness (Isa. 40:7). Whether gods and idols remain historically effectual, will be demonstrated to Israel by whether they open the future. The claim of the God of Israel to exclusivity is formulated by Deutero-Isaiah with a question (Isa. 40:18):

> To whom, then, will you compare God?
> What image will you compare him to?

And it is answered with God's the creator and with praise of His Lordship over history. He, the Unique, is the creator of heaven and earth.

He is the one who called the visibly ordered creation into being, sustains and preserves it, and through it gives to man, first of all, the possibility of living from this natural gift. That God, according to biblical prophecy, can be compared to nothing that exists is a tremendous release for human thought and faith (cf. Thoma and Wyschogrod). The message of the incomparability of God enables man to discern the spirits, and the experience of history which derives from this faith has at the same time both a *critical* and *unifying* character.

It is critical in the sense that it unmasks the absolute regard for all things transitory as idol worship. That can be a totalitarian political ideology or the temporary predominance of a single leading principle for the interpretation of history. It can also, however, be a church's dogmatic claim to power, which turns against those who believe differently in order to subdue them. When the incomparability of God becomes a forgotten experience of faith, or a confession which is no longer realized, it undermines the dignity and freedom of man by obstructing the openness to non-scientific interpretations of existence through the pressure of the anonymous application of a system. And when the decisive insight into the *multivalence of being-human* is no longer effective, the artistic and religious room for self-determination in the battle against tyranny also disappears.

The prophetic word of salvation is unifying through its future-revealing reality for all people, whether they share this hope or not. Time, the world, history, and the creation as a whole were established by a beginning and are limited, according to the scriptures, by an end which is not subject to the powers of death but is intended to shatter the yoke of transitoriness (Isa. 25:8; Rev. 6:7, 17). Yahweh, the Unique, the Incomparable, is the first and at the last will be the same (43:13). *Elect Israel* is representative of this *experience of time* (Ex 3:14), which is completely incomprehensible within the leading concepts of Western metaphysics. As Yahweh spoke through the mouth of the prophet (43:10-11):

> "You are my witnesses," declares the Lord,
> "and my servant whom I have chosen,
> so that you may know and believe me
> and understand that I am he.
> Before me no god was formed,
> nor will there be one after me.
> I, even I, am the Lord,
> and apart from me there is no saviour."

It is of great significance for Christianity that this confession of the Unique, of God's creation and Lordship of history returns again in *Revelation,* the only prophetic book of the New Testament (Rev. 1:8; 4:8;

15:3). In this way the *ultimate unity of the biblical history of promise* is reflected. It inseparably fuses Judaism and Christianity (Rev. 5:5), in spite of the crucial differences in their understanding of redemption, in the *common* expectation of the total transfiguration of this transitory creation (Rom. 8:19-22; cf. Falaturi, Strolz, and Talmon). In the Babylonian exile, the prophetic message of the incomparability of God was intimately related to the confession of the creator God. Nowhere in the Old Testament is the interrelatedness of creation and history expressed so eloquently, nowhere does it provide such courage, nowhere does it grant such power of discernment, and nowhere does it so forcefully reject every dualistic conception of world and time as it does in Deutero-Isaiah. If Yahweh alone has created heaven and earth, the prophetic proof goes, then his sovereignty over creation excludes the recognition of the power of other gods. Then the Unique, who is also the Lord of History, rules over all earthly events, since they are at all times dependent on the creation; world history remains encapsulated within the mystery of the creation (Isa. 55:8-11). That Yahweh is the supreme ruler, who can just as easily call the Gentile King Cyrus to allow the return of the captive Jews from the Babylonian exile as he can plunge Pharaoh, the oppressor, into the depths of decay in order to stand in the breach for the liberation from Egypt, the house of bondage, is to be understood as the *historical* manifestation of the sublime transcendence of God. His creative power and the reality of the prophetic word of salvation in the historical situation of elect Israel are *inseparable*. This biblical experience of faith provides courage for living and hope for the future (Isa. 41:10; 51:7), leads to fearlessness in the face of threat (Isa. 44:2; 51:7-8), grants the bold freedom to stand in the service of the Incomparable, who can be measured by *nothing* created, by nothing mortal (Isa. 46:4-5). Israel is the *corporeal* bridge between revelation and history. It is the called mediator of God's word, a light unto the nations (Isa. 42:6), and an indestructible sign of renown for the Holy one of Israel. (Isa. 55:13; cf. Wyschogrod)

In the passage on the calling of the non-Israelite Cyrus, Deutero-Isaiah delivers the word of revelation concerning the all-encompassing uniqueness of Yahweh, which also embraces evil. Yahweh's uniqueness is not opposed by any self-sufficient, godless power which somehow evades his rule. Even evil remains *subject* to this radical monotheism, since the Holy One of Israel encircles it in his unfathomable embrace (Isa. 45:6c-7):

> I am the Lord, and there is no other.
> I form the light and create darkness,
> I bring prosperity and create disaster;
> I, the Lord, do all these things.

Does this prophetic self-disclosure of Yahweh offer the solution to the unresolvable human problem of theodicy? Who among contemporary theologians, after the genocide of the twentieth century, would be able to propose such a thing without shuddering (cf. Brocke/Jochum)? In the spirit of the prophetic proclamation, however, it is still no less valid to maintain that light and darkness, prosperity and disaster, derive from the creative, differentiating word of God *springing from his supra-antithetical, salvific will.* Good and evil, consequently, do not form an ultimate antithesis; they are neither primordial, equally valid, opposing world-principles, nor absolute, opposing powers. Mortal man, in spite of his *accountability* for the proper conduct of affairs, is thus *given relief,* since he is no longer forced to bear the entire burden of the puzzling question concerning the origin of evil. Isaiah 45:6-7 is and remains, without any effort on our part to heighten its jolting radicalism, a powerful word of hope from the Incomparable; for it does not allow the *opposition* between good and the evil which we suffer in history —constantly resisting, yet never overcoming— to triumph. Rather, the prophetic word of salvation posits the eternal destiny of man in the irrevocably *blessed unity* of creation and history. (Isa. 45:18; 51:6; Rev. 4:8)

2 Incomparability and the Eastern traditions

We now return to the question posed at the beginning of this essay, whether the biblical experience of faith in the incomparability of God expressed in the prophetic proclamation can be *shared* with adherents of other religions. The word 'share,' in the context of the theme of this symposium, does not refer simply to the exchange of information, or to comparisons made in the scientific study of religion, or to the pheno-menological distinction made between the basic types of meditative and messianic religion. What does it then mean to share religious experience with *another*? Can it legitimately be pressed to the point where my own religious experience meets *another* religious experience which is alien to me? What *common* foundation must be assumed in order for this sharing of religious experience to be possible?

Jews, Christians, and Muslims share a faith in the One, incomparable creator God. Belief in the creation and eschatology belong inseparably together for the monotheistic religions. Even though the Koran does not assume the prophetic tradition of Israel, although the prophets are considered bearers of revelation, the unity of belief in creation and resurrection still comes emphatically to the fore in its word of revelation. Thus it says in Sura 21:204, "On that day we will roll up the heavens as a scroll. As we brought forth the first creation, so we will bring it forth again. This promise is incumbent upon us. Behold, we are bringing it to pass." To those who doubt the possibility of the resurrection of the dead, with the question "Who will revive the bones once they have decayed?"

the Koran answers: "He who first created them will give them life, for he knows every creature" (Sura 36:78-79). For the Christian this text calls to mind the faith of Abraham, as it is extolled in the book of Romans; for he is, as the text says, "our father in the sight of God, in whom he believed — the God who gives life to the dead and calls things that are not as though they were" (Rom. 4:17). According to the Koran, Allah is, in absolute exclusivity, the Unique; beside Him there is no other god (Sura 42:11; 112:5). He rules without equal, according to the praise of Sura 57:1-6, as creator and sustainer, since He is, *as such,* the first and last of all being.

Although the Christian message of the Triune God distinguishes Christianity from Islam and Judaism, the unity of creation and eschatology witnessed in the Koran and the Torah remains an essential link between the monotheistic religions. Moreover, the biblical experience of faith in the incomparability of God is not annulled by the *saving mediation of Christ.* (Mt. 4:11; Eph. 4:6; II Cor. 4:14; John 1:18)

Is there anything in the Eastern religious traditions which corresponds to the belief in God, the Incomparable, expressed by Deutero-Isaiah, and also by several Psalms? According to the foregoing explanation, *this* belief is incomparably *time-bound,* since it is bound to elect Israel and its witness from generation to generation through the biblical word of revelation. There exists, for example, in *Zen Buddhism* no analogy for this type of *incarnational* character of Judaism and more particularly of Christianity (John 1:14). At the same time, it seems to us, at least part of the path to enlightenment through meditative contemplation can be *shared.* It is that part which has to do with the Buddhist experience of nothingness. If God, in accordance with the prophetic word, can be compared with *nothing* created, then there emerges in this experience of God that *fundamental distinction* which compels reflection on nothing. Ever since Plato, in his dialogues "the Sophist" and "Parmenides," posed the disturbing question concerning the being of non-being, it has remained an unavoidable question for philosophy. If, according to the message of Deutero-Isaiah, the God of Israel, as Creator and Lord of history, can be compared with *nothing* created, then the further definition of this 'nothing' demands the ability to accept by faith. Does the conceptual definition of the essence of God break up on the rock of this word of biblical prophecy (Isa. 26:4)?

Within the Christian tradition, *negative theology* points in this direction. Thus, when Dionysius the Areopagite says that the mystery of the Triune God demands "the affirmation of all things, the negation of all things, the transcending of every affirmation and every negation" (as cited by Von Balthasar, 28). Or when Meister Eckhart says in his mystic language exercise, "If he [God] is neither goodness, nor being, nor truth, nor one, then what is he?. Whatever you think he is, he is not" (as cited in Ueda, 40). Zen Buddhism speaks of awakening to the true selfless self in the field of emptiness, which K. Nishitani, the most important contemporary Japanese thinker, calls 'absolute Nothing' (Nishitani, 170ff.). The total dissolution of the subject-object relationship and the critique of substance-metaphysics is bound up with this meditative experience. Biblical faith can share this experience inasmuch as it does not attempt, on the basis of self-consciousness, to secure being-human before the *Unique* by means of logical justification. At its most acute, however, man is affected by Nothingness through his *destiny of death*. Human existence is transitory; death is comparable to *nothing* which has being and is thus the breach through which the Incomparable comes. This Incomparable, who is manifest in death before every specific revelation in history, *binds all people together in their mortality*. Yet the "God of all mortals" (Jer. 32:27) *cannot be compared* with the nothingness into which man enters at death. And that which one day awaits man, according to Revelation 21:1-5, is the free gift of the one who holds the keys of the world of the dead. (Rev. 1:18)

Perhaps the exchange of religious experience with Zen Buddhism and the Hindu teaching of emancipation should be begun again precisely at this point. Creation, transitoriness, the hope of the new creation of all things (Rom. 8:18-25) are highly charged themes of the Christian faith when brought into encounter with Eastern detachment, spiritual rest and the cessation of suffering. What *cannot be shared* with this religious experience, however, comes to flower in the *mystery of the creation*. The transitoriness of things is unable to supplant the primordial positiveness of the created (Gen. 1:31; II Tim. 4:4-5). The grandiose YES of the Creator, uttered once and for all to what his creative word, grounded in *nothing* Other, has called into being, continues to exist. The danger of the *gnostic* suspicion of creation is averted by the Jewish morning prayer with the words:

> Ruler of the world, maker of light and creator of darkness, founder of peace and creator of all things, who in mercy allowed the light to be enkindled for the earth and its inhabitants and who in his goodness renews the work of creation each day! Lord, how great are your works! With wisdom you created them all. The earth is full of your goodness.

If we now cast a glance at the *buddhahood of nature,* as experienced and described by the Japanese Zen master Dōgen in the first half of the thirteenth century, from the perspective of the Jewish-Christian creation belief, is there any correspondence between the *non-dual* spirit of this experience of the union of nature and the self and the biblical creation belief? If this belief excludes a dualistic understanding of the fundamental relationship of creator and creature, because God's faithfulness toward creation sustains and rules nature and history (Isa. 51:8, 15), and if man, on his own, originally possesses and can produce *nothing* absolutely, then the idea of the buddhahood of nature is at least comprehensible from the biblical perspective.

It is reported that Shakyamuni once silently raised an *udumbara* blossom during a sermon before a great gathering on mount Gei. Through this gesture, the 'true dharma' was communicated to his disciple Mahahasyapa, who smiled when he saw the blossom. With this *silent symbol,* everything had already silently been said. There is here no subject-object relationship, only selfless awareness. The indifferent and self-assured will never attain it, according to Dōgen. Human life is "destroyed by the three poisons — greed, anger, and ignorance." They seduce and weaken the mind, and make recognition of the Buddha paths realized through nature impossible. The truth appears in the things of nature, as they are in and of themselves, unintentionally. It is decisive for Dōgen's encounter with nature that one experiences the connection between self-recognition and nature as the *mystery of the self.* In "Shōbō-genzō," Dōgen's primary work, it says:

> The green needles of the pine tree in the spring or the beauty of a chrysanthemum in the fall is the true form of the truth. If a true master achieves this state of enlightenment, he is a teacher of people and gods; if you seek to lead people, however, without first having achieved enlightenment, nothing but strife will result. If you do not know the true form of the pine in the spring or the chrysanthemum in the fall, how can you know the true meaning of their existence? How can you perceive your own original being? (Dōgen, 121)

Encountering nature, therefore, is no harmless stroll, but presupposes a *radical transformation of the mind,* the Zen Buddhist 'great death.' Then from the emptiness, from what is neither substance nor ground, as the message goes, arises an all-encompassing world affirmation. There remains here no room for a transcending dynamic of the salvation-seeking subject in 'beyond being' (cf. Oberhammer, 25), since the reciprocal penetration of all things in the field of emptiness is unparalleled. Nevertheless, one must also remember that this religious experience of unity is also, in the strongest sense, *praxis-related;* it must be practised ever anew, and is not exempt from the polar consciousness of existence, as it is revealed in the opposites of ignorance and enlightenment, bondage and freedom, error and truth (Strolz). We thus stand once again (in the continuing dialogue among religions) before the great question concerning the mediation of being as human beings experience it in their nature- and language-conditioned essence. It is already a given in every form and content of religious experience and its symbolism. Considered from the perspective of Zen Buddhism, this problem of the mediation of being is contained in the relation of the historical world to absolute nothing. For the biblical experience of faith the problem is concentrated in the foundational relationship of *creatio ex nihilo* and *creatio continua*. It is God's faithfulness to creation, renewed each day (Gen. 8:22; Lam. 3:22-23), hovering over the abyss of the negativity of existence, which demands the language appropriate to this saving experience. (cf. Schmidt; Bloch)

This brief allusion to the common and distinctive in the comparison of biblical-prophetic proclamation with the religious experience of Zen Buddhism reveals the particular within the universal and vice versa. The word of salvation from the incomparable God, who is active in the history of Israel, is addressed only to this people, and yet in its meaning is dedicated to the salvation of all humanity and the entire creation. At the time of the fall of Israel it becomes an indispensable witness to the Unique within world history, which bestows a future-consciousness (Jer. 29:11) in their situation of doubt (Isa. 53:1). The incomparable God confronts the thinker and the believer with the question concerning the *essence of the human*, who is able to *understand* this message. In fragmentary language (I Cor. 13:12), it makes known along the *several* paths of the nations (Mi. 4:5), in word and in silence, in East and in West, the appearance of deliverance.

Bibliography

Balthasar, H. U. von. "Bibel und negative Theologie." In *Sein und Nichts in der abendländischen Mystik.* Ed. W. Strolz. Schriften zur Großen Ökumene 11. Freiburg, 1984.

Begrich, J. *Studien zu Deuterojesaja.* Ed. Walter Zimmerli. Theologische Bücherei 20. Munich, 1963.

Bloch, L. *Das Prinzip Hoffnung,* II. Frankfurt am Main, 1957.

Brocke, M., and H. Jochum, eds. *Wolkensäule und Feuerschein: Jüdische Theologie nach Auschwitz.* Munich, 1982.

Dogen Zenji. *Shobogenzo: Die Schatzkammer der Erkenntnis des wahren Dharma,* I. Zurich, 1975.

Falaturi, A., W. Strolz, and S. Talmon, eds. *Zukunftshoffnung und Heilserwartung in den monotheistischen Religionen.* Schriftenreihe zur Großen Ökumene 9. Freiburg, 1983.

Levinas, E. *Die Spur des Anderen: Untersuchungen zur Phänomenologie und Sozialphilosophie.* Freiburg/Munich, 1983.

Nishitani, K. *Was ist Religion?* Frankfurt am Main, 1982.

Oberhammer, G. *"Begegnung" als Kategorie der Religionshermeneutik.* Vienna, 1989.

Schmidt, W. H. *Zukunftsgewißheit und Gegenwartskritik: Grundzüge prophetischer Verkündigung.* Neukirchen–Vluyn, 1973.

Strolz, W. *Heilswege der Weltreligionen,* II: Christliche Begegnung mit Hinduismus, Buddhismus und Taoismus. Freiburg, 1986.

Thoma, C. and M. Wyschogrod, eds. *Das Reden vom Einen Gott bei Juden und Christen.* Bern, 1984.

Ueda, S. "Eckhart und Zen am Problem Freiheit und Sprache." In *Luther und Shinran: Eckhart und Zen.* Beihefte der Zeitschrift für Religions- und Geistesgeschichte 31. Cologne, 1989.

Wyschogrod, M. *The Body of Faith: Judaism as Corporeal Election.* New York, 1983.

CHAPTER 10

From Sharing to Encounter

Hasan Askari

Religious sharing varies from one religious discourse to another depending on the extent of our recognition of the other as a person. What we share with the other is the state of exile in this world and of being clothed by body and belief.

Those who stay at the level of the outward are the kin of the outward. The inward are kin to the inward. Recognition precedes sharing.

We share the transcendent dimension with the other inasmuch as we perceive the transcendent within ourselves, the other in us, our own soul. Unless we postulate such a principle and revive the classical discourse on soul, we cannot rise beyond divisions of body, belief, and consciousness to attain to a spiritual and non-discursive reality. First Soul, then God.

Can we share our religious experiences? Who are 'we'? Either we are those who belong to the same tradition or to different traditions, or to no religious tradition at all. The issues common to all three possibilities involve the experience of the transcendent, its preservation in the memory of the experiencing subject (self-communication), and its communication with the other (by making an attempt through an intelligible concept, image, or act). The most important among the specific issues is the combination of the personal and the collective modes of self-awareness. It appears that the sharing of religious experience in general may increase in experience and depth with the growing recognition of the other as a person rather than as a collective representation. But can one be a person and a representation at one and the same time? Can these two identities be co-present within each individual and between individuals without cancelling each other out? Let us first refer to another set of preliminary questions.

Can we share the religious experience of the other? It seems that 'the other' is usually taken to refer to anybody outside one's denomination or tradition. If it can be allowed that there are, among others, four major religious discourses (namely, theistic, monistic, Buddhist, and animistic), the shared ground within one religious discourse is so constant and real that it not only provides for deep and extensive sharing but also for acute and persisting conflict. The degree of intelligibility of ideas and values, however conflicting, is far greater within one religious discourse (say, between Judaism, Christianity, and Islam which constitute a single theistic discourse) than between Buddhism and Islam (which represent two disparate discourses).

This brings us to the idea of sharing. It seems that all the emphasis lies on what is similar and common between religious traditions, whereas there is another area of 'sharing' which involves matters wherein people differ, even those matters wherein they differ absolutely. For example, when a Muslim meets a Christian in deep faith and testimony, they not only share their common theistic faith (for they belong to a shared religious discourse and a shared prophetic dimension of history), but also encounter one another in where they differ. When a Muslim shares the Qur'ānic critique of the Christian belief in the divinity of Jesus, he is asking the Christian: *What dare ye say of God?* The way the Muslim raises this tremendous question should rest primarily upon his own immediate experience of the very question he is asking. Without undergoing a tremor within himself, he cannot raise this question for the other. It was Muḥammad's experience of the transcendence *(subhaniyya)* of God that first led to the experience within himself of the question which he asked his Christian contemporaries. Similarly when a Christian shares 'his' story of Christ with a Muslim in a manner that expresses his own immediate experience of the Divine love, he thereby confronts the Muslim with the grave moment of his encounter with Christian witness. *Now sharing is encounter of immediacy with immediacy.* Such encounters presuppose a shared religious discourse.

One more preliminary question remains, concerning the inquiring principle itself. Can we share our religious experiences? Are the inquiring principle and the sharing principle one and the same thing? Furthermore, who is asking the question? If the question is raised within the encounter between two religious persons itself, the inquiring principle is an integral part of the encounter itself. Can the question ever be asked independently? Can a student of religion who does not subscribe to any religious faith or spiritual dimension ask this question? Is it not true that in this case the other is an alien? He has no kinship whatsoever with that other. If we accept identity with the object of knowledge as one of the principles by which knowledge is possible, he would have no way of knowing about the religious other. He cannot properly understand his own question. The question therefore cannot be meaningfully located outside the context of sharing and encounter. The question is of itself a religious question and must be thus asked religiously.

The inquiring principle says something about the inquirer, namely, that he carries the key to his inquiry right within himself. Before starting to answer the question, one should pause to reflect on the question itself.

Both of us, you and I, should be holding up the meaningful-ness of the question between ourselves. Our first unspoken testimony is that the question is meaningful. On both sides, the question's meaningful-ness is linked to our religious being. The question thus answers itself. The inquiring principle is the shared principle.

Although the inquiring principle is involved in the sharing principle, it cannot be wholly identified with it. Otherwise the sharing principle would suffice, and there would be no need then to maintain two distinct principles. Even though the inquiring principle's meaning is shared and its reality as a principle is linked to the shared ground of our religious being, it ought to be something separate and transcendent. It forms a triangle between the two parties, me and my other. Its status as such spreads a canopy over our encounter with one another in our diverse and even conflicting experiences. It leads us to the awareness that somewhere —beyond all of us— contraries meet.

Taken in and of itself, it can be an interesting exercise of thought to present the diversity and conflict of religious beliefs and practices as evidence, which suggests that the sharing of religious experiences between people of such vastly different and divergent traditions is an uncertain prospect, if not an outright impossibility. Such a line of inquiry, however, destroys the question we are pursuing at the very outset, for in this manner the question has already been answered negatively. The question then ceases to exist, whereas it is the question itself in its claiming urgency which holds the key to its answer.

How long are we going to repeat such doubts as: How could a Zen Buddhist share the Christian belief in the death and resurrection of Christ? How could a Jew or a Muslim share the Hindu or the Christian idea of God as incarnate, in many forms or in one embodiment respectively? It is like asking: How can one experience the clothes on somebody else's body? *What is shared with the other is the fact of being clothed and covered,* not the very clothes themselves. "Cover me! Cover me!" urged the Prophet, calling upon his wife, Khadija, on the morning of his first revelation as he was shivering with a strange shivering. On that morning when the Prophet was wrapped in a mantle and comforted, his experience of the nakedness of his being before God was covered and protected. On that morning the entire body of Islamic beliefs and practices came into being as a covering over the immediacy of and the tremor at the first experience.

One Sunday morning in London's Hyde Park while I was walking along one of the paths, I saw a variety of people lying on the grass. Most were foreigners. They seemed to belong to those thousands of people in the West who are jobless, who have left their homes in far-off countries, and who now have no means of either improving their circumstances here or of going back home. Each of them was culturally and religiously different and yet between them there was a community of homesickness, a feeling of being in a state of exile. It enabled me to understand that all those who remember their true home would feel as though they were in exile here in this world.

Before proceeding further, let us clarify another issue which has become a platitude through sheer repetition: How can one have the idea of the one transcendent ('entity') while we have so many varied experiences and expressions? This amounts to seeing a difficulty where no such difficulty in fact exists. We ourselves sometimes first place an obstacle in our path and then worry about how to overcome it. The transcendent is by definition both one and above all variety and change, without divisibility or interval. Its presence is one and whole, unattached and free. The transcendent as Source cannot be the same as the idea of the transcendent as its manifestation in one expression or another. How dare we equate the transcendent with one or another form of our experience of it? To experience the transcendent is to experience something within ourselves which possesses a kinship with it, something which is transcendent in us. What is at issue is not the unity and the transcendence of the transcendent but its apprehension by a subject who is bound by body and belief, by space and time, by culture and history. This binding is not a limitation but rather a clothing and a covering over the ineffable.

Can I share the religious experience of another? In the light of what we have said so far, the answer must be affirmative *insofar as it pertains to sharing the state of exile in this world and of being clothed by body and belief.* With regard to the transcendent, we share it with the other *inasmuch as we perceive the transcendent within ourselves, discerning the human principle to be of the same stock as ultimate reality.* Such awareness demands of us a different kind of reflection.

Let us return to the question regarding the other. Is the other really one who believes and practises differently, or who is even opposed to one's own belief and practice? To allow ourselves to be contented with such a definition, however, would be tantamount to ignoring the differences present within each religious tradition, irrespective of whether the religious discourse is shared or not shared. In fact, each religion contains 'three' religions, or modes of awareness (with corresponding modes of being).

First there are those who are consider only the outward forms of their belief and practice. They divide the human community over mutually exclusive identities. They uphold their beliefs as completely true and unique, final and binding for all. They face those with different beliefs either with tolerance and discussion, or with subordination and even elimination. No matter how much they use words such as 'understanding' and 'dialogue,' they do not regard the other as a religious equal or even as superior. They nevertheless form a single breed, no matter how intense is the rejection of the one by the other. They 'share' a negative brotherhood. There are also those who look beyond the outward forms to the inward dimension. They are present in each community and culture. Though scattered, they still constitute a single fellowship. Finally there are those who have surpassed both outward and inward. To them all things are one. They are both known and hidden; they are both present and absent; the moment of encounter with them is akin to that of death or resurrection; they are the elect and are mirrors of one another; they do not bear any name as a group, nor do they assemble under one banner. Lacking any visible marks, they are distinguished only by their state, by what they give and what they take. Each religious type is separated by a veil from the other, but there is also a connecting bridge between them.

The people of the inward are scattered throughout the world like seeds; mobile like the wind, silent as the skies; they are our true neighbours though their actual abode is unknown to us; they are real friends without suffering our acquaintance; they are the meek, through absence to themselves; they are the salt of the earth; they are the peacemakers.

As soon as we admit the reality of these three types within each religion, we are enabled to discern their universality as communities which transcend all religious and cultural boundaries. The same principle, let us stress, operates even on the outward level. The people of the outward dimension constitute one community whether they be Jews, Christians, or Muslims. The other is therefore no longer an alien: *The outward man is kin to the outward man; the inward is kin to the inward.* The question at hand is thus no longer primarily one of sharing but of recognition. The question can thus be reformulated: *Do I recognize the other as my hermeneutic kin, as an associate in awareness and being?* When meeting a so-called fellow believer, I may not recognize in him my inward kin. On the other hand, in meeting a so-called other, though he belongs to a different religious tradition, it is possible to recognize in him my inward companion. *Encounter now is a prelude to lasting friendship and union.*

These three types (outward, inward, and beyond outward/inward) are not only objective realities but also levels of awareness within each one of us. We are a plurality within ourselves. We are all continually ascending and descending this inner hierarchy. Once stability is attained at one level, we know who we are, and can see what our future will be. Self-recognition precedes recognition of the other.

To reach out to the other requires of us not only awareness of the other's differentiation as outward-looking or inward-looking, but it also demands a firm conviction regarding a twofold necessity — (1) the theological necessity for more than a single religious form, since ultimate reality in all its infinity and transcendence cannot be equated to only one form; and (2) the spiritual necessity to move from the outward forms to the inward dimension, since the unity of the ultimate truth will otherwise run afoul of the multiplicity and conflict of the outward forms.

The first step towards realizing inwardness seems almost synonymous with reaching out to the other as a person. It requires a self-emptying, an emptying oneself from one's collective history and tradition, whereby one touches an emptiness resembling a mirror which reflects all the fullness and eternity of being. Only then may one turn —as though a visitor— to the contents and constructs of one's religious consciousness, now both empty and full. Only then can one reach the centre of one's general and specific humanity, and only then is one able to be at one and the same time this or that individual as well as all mankind. One is then enabled to face an other from a different culture or tradition as both a portrait of one's own religion and culture as well as an empty mirror whose reflection discloses both oneself and the other. We then become neighbours, first in one other, and then, to each other. This is a communion of soul unto soul.

Without the unifying reality of the Soul we shall run aground on the multiplicity and conflict of the forms of life and culture. The Soul is one: multiple being, one, and divided at the same time, fully one with itself, in possession of a vision of what is above. Unless we postulate such a principle and revive the classical discourse on Soul, we cannot rise beyond divisions of body, belief, and consciousness to attain to a spiritual and non-discursive reality.

Before posing questions regarding the *other out there,* we should ask about the *other in us,* our nobler and loftier neighbour and companion —our own Soul— which clasps with one hand our body and mind here on earth and with the other, holds fast the reality which surpasses itself. Only then can we hope to pass from one hand to the other, from the many to the One. Hence, to experience the truth about oneself and about the other is to experience the reality of the Soul, which at once individualizes and universalizes all of us. *First Soul, then God!*

Part 2

Case Studies of Intra-
and
Interreligious Sharing

What it is like to be a Banzie: On sharing the experience of an Equatorial Microcosm

James W. Fernandez

The anthropological project is one of 'sharing-in' through long-term field research and participant-observation in another culture and, subsequently 'sharing-out' in the ethnographic writing. This paper considers the ethnographer's challenge to 'share-out' with his or her reader the complex sensorimotor, enactive, and cognitive aspects of the field experience. The focus is upon conveying the sensorium in which the alien religion is enmeshed; the reservoir of 'likenesses' by which that religion conveys to its members what the experience of their membership should be actually like; and the narrative within which these likenesses are embedded and which are intended to capture the religious imagination of the adepts. The challenge to make the ethnography itself a convincing narrative is also considered. The conclusion avers that we cannot share what a religion *is* only what it is *like!*

The 'what-is-it-like-to-be-a' (WIILTBA) question is particularly and perennially anthropological. Insofar as the anthropologist conceives of his project as being that of 'understanding' rather than 'explanation;' of 'taking the native's point of view' and not using things native as a way of advancing one or another western tradition of theorizing about society and culture. My own view, to be sure, is that the anthropologist has a foot in both camps and is constantly negotiating a hermeneutic circle between understanding and explanations, ethnography and ethnology. In this paper, however, I am glad to take up the challenge of our theme, "On Sharing Religious Experience," to reflect upon my efforts at ethnographic understanding of an African Religious Movement, Bwiti, which I studied in the late fifties and early sixties (Fernandez). I made a major effort in a long ethnography to share wit the reader my understanding of what life in the equatorial forest and in this religious microcosm was like. I would like to reflect upon that effort as a method of sharing.

The 'what-it-is-like-to-be' question is particularly tested cross-culturally but its pertinence for humans is not limited to cross-cultural situations. It is a recurrent and an intriguing question that arises frequently within cultures, across classes or racial divisions, across the sexes. There is now

a whole genre of books —call it the Prince and the Pauper genre—
written by members of one class, race or sex who have been able to 'pass'
from that class, race or sex to another: a white man who has passed as
a black in an American ghetto, an Israeli who passed as a Palestinian, a
President of an American College who spent his summer vacations
working at various menial lower-class occupations. And, of course, a
driving theme in recent feminist literature, in the face of the dominant
male or patriarchal definition of what human experience is like, is the
attempt to 'share-out' women's experience to a patriarchal world; to see
things, that is, in feminist terms and from a woman's perspective.

But this interest in 'what-it-is-like-to-be' is not limited to trying to be
like other people of distinct sex, class or culture. Humans are and have
been, since paleolithic times, fascinated with imagining 'what-it-like-to-be'
members of another species. Paleolithic cave art gives us plenty of
evidence of that. In modern times we recognize that there is a whole
genre here — one that we particularly, though not exclusively, associate
with children's literature. In English one can name one's own favourite.
Presently in the United States the World Wildlife Fund, in cooperation
with local wildlife groups, is seeking to enhance children's empathy with
wild animals. For example, in an effort at 'sharing experience' with
wolves, those unfortunately denigrated animals of folklore, children are
blindfolded and allowed to wander in a garden full of diverse and various
strong scents noticeable to humans. In this way they are encouraged to
share the experience of possessing a 'sensory apparatus' primarily focused
on olfactory cues.

So our 'thematic preoccupation' at this conference is by no means
unique. The 'empathetic impulse,' to 'be like' or to 'share with' (if we
can equate these for the moment), whatever its fruits, is old and widespread in human societies. Indeed we might argue that this kind of
experiential ('that is to say cognitive and emotive') 'sharing' has gone hand
in hand with that ancient sharing out of material resources that paleo-
anthropologists identify as a distinctly human characteristic. So we have
long had the capacity, and, thus, a concomitant desire to share. To be
sure the sharing of material resources, on the one hand, and the sharing
of experience, on the other, are two different things. It is one thing to
share with others and thus know them through the exchange of material
objects. It is quite another thing to share with others in the sense of
'knowing other minds.' That is a more problematic achievement and,
indeed, that is why we are preoccupied with it here in this symposium.

Moving from the third to the first persons:
On sharing the Sensorium

Recalling the effort of The World Wildlife Fund to have children experience the particular sense (scents) of the world experienced by wolves puts us in mind of a relevant article in philosophy by Thomas Nagel titled "What is it like to be a Bat." Nagel writes about the problem of knowing other minds without knowing other mind's experiences of their own bodies. He evokes the implications for empathetic understanding of the mind-body problem.

Now the point about bats is that their sonar equipment is so unlike anything we possess that it is unlikely that we could ever know what it is like to be a bat.

> Even without the benefit of philosophical reflection, anyone who has spent some time in an enclosed space with an excited bat knows what it is to encounter a fundamentally *alien* form of life ... To the extent that I could look and behave like a wasp or a bat without changing my fundamental structure, my experiences would not be anything like the experiences of these animals. On the other hand, it is doubtful that any meaning can be attached to the supposition that I should possess the internal neurophysiological constitution of a bat. Even if I could by gradual degrees be transformed into a bat, nothing in my present constitution enables me to imagine what the experiences of such a future stage of myself thus metamorphosed would be like. The best evidence would come from the experiences of bats, if we only knew what they were like. (Nagel, 438-439)

Now Nagel goes on to argue that though we might describe in objective terms the auditory apparatus the bat possesses we cannot begin to conceptualize his or any other being's world unless we can take his 'point of view,' and taking his point of view involves apprehending what his sensory equipment is telling him where he is. For it is a particular sensory apparatus operating from a particular point of view which gives him the basis of his conceptions. An anthropologist would heartily agree with this emphasis on 'phenomenological subjectivity' and, indeed, it should be our main object, I would argue, to give as adequate an account as we can of the sense world in which our subjects act and think but which, and this is most important, is being processed from their 'point of view.'

> There is a sense in which phenomenological facts are perfectly objective: one person can know or say of another what the quality of the other's experience is. They are subjective, however, in the sense that even this objective ascription of experience is possible only for someone sufficiently similar to the object of ascription to be able to adopt his point of view — to understand the ascription in the first person as well as in the third, so to speak. (Nagel, 442)

So the problem remains of representing another point of view. Of course portraying what it is like to be a member of another religious culture, challenging as it may be, does not require such degrees of metamorphosis as in trying to be a member of another species: a dog, a bat, a cockroach, because we assume that all humans have the same sense apparatus although cultures both differentially emphasize and differentially constitute the senses. There is some talk in the literature, for example, about visual cultures, tactile cultures, auditory cultures etc.

But without getting into the 'national character' or 'national sensorium' argument what I want to argue is that when we set about to represent what it is like to share another's being in the world we must first focus, more or less, objectively, on what senses are being stimulated and deployed —the particular sensorium that is being activated and brought into being in that culture— and second we must try to register just how that particular sensorium is being represented and registered. For this second effort can bring us close to the point of view of those experiencing the sensorium. This second effort demands, moreover, that we pay attention not only to how the sense modalities are being evoked but how they brought into relation with each other ... the particular synthesis that is taking place from a particular synthesizing point of view. This second effort we might say is *synesthetic:* it is the study of the way that sense modalities are excited by being brought into relation with one another. Most often this synesthetic approach involves being attentive to the analogies by which the adepts grasp the import of their experiences in other terms and thus conceptualize the meaning of their sensed world. It involves being attentive to the phrase and the word 'what it is *like.'* Nagel, who is sceptical about this method and hopes for something more objective puts it this way:

> At present we are completely unequipped to think about the subjective character of experience without relying on the imagination — without taking up the point of view of the experiential subject. This should be regarded as a challenge to form new concepts and devise a new method — an objective phenomenology not dependent on empathy or the imagination. Though presumably it would not capture everything, its goal would be to describe, at least in part, the subjective character of experiences in a form comprehensible to beings incapable of having those experiences.
>
> We would have to develop such a phenomenology to describe the sonar experiences of bats; but it would also be possible to begin with humans. One might try, for example, to develop concepts that could be used to explain to a person blind from birth what it was like to see. One would reach a blank wall eventually, but it should be possible to devise a method of expressing in objective terms much more than we

can at present and with much greater precision. The *loose internodal analogies* [emphasis mine] —for example 'red is like the sound of a trumpet'— which crop up in discussions of this subject are of little use. (Nagel, 449)

While we await this millenarian phenomenology, this quantum jump in objective understanding it is precisely these 'internodal analogies' —these statements of *likeness*— that should be a main object of our study for in them we see the synesthesia to which we refer ... the way, that is, that the selected sense modalities are brought into relation to each other and thus come to share in the construction of —in our case— religious experience.

In any event let me now proceed to examine the ways in which I tried, by a variety of approaches, to enable 'readers,' 'listeners,' 'viewers,' (even 'tasters' and 'smellers') to share the religious experience of the members of Bwiti, the Banzie, by first registering the specifics of the Bwiti sensorium and, second, by seeking to grasp the Bwiti point of view towards that sensorium primarily as that has been coded in 'internodal analogies.' In the old colonialist phrase how did I go about trying to bring Bwiti back alive. This effort took place on a number of levels.

LEVEL I Auditory, Gustatory, and Visual Recording

1. *The Sharing of Things Heard:* In a very literal sense I 'registered' the Bwiti sensorium by making an effort to record all aspects of the all-night ceremony from the solo harp music at nightfall in which the chapel was 'prepared' for worship to the songs at midnight to the final farewell songs at dawn. Some thirty hours of tape were eventually edited and published as a record by Folkways Records.[1]

2. *The sharing of things seen:* I also attempted to register by photography all aspects of the rituals in both black and white photographs and colour slides. An extensive selection of these black and white photographs is bound into the ethnography while exhibitions from the much more extensive collection of photographs have been mounted in various museums and university exhibition halls a half a dozen times over the years. Very frequently, in giving talks and lectures on Bwiti I accompany the verbal with both the visual of the

---

[1] *Music From An Equatorial Microcosm: Fang Bwiti Music from Gabon,* Ethnic Folkways Records No. 4214.

colour slides and the auditory of selections from the Folkways record.

3. *The sharing of substances tasted, smelled, and reacted to:* The
sharing of the gustatory and olfactory experiences of Bwiti or
of any distant religious experience is more difficult for both
logistic and technological reasons and because sight and
sound, and not the gustatory and olfactory, are dominant
modalities in our western cultures. I brought back the
psychoreactive alkaloid 'eboga' with me in small amounts to
share with those who might wish to taste or smell or experience the mind-altering effects of this substance. For obvious
reasons this 'sharing' soon became problematic in the developing drug culture of our own in America. I also returned
with *okoume* wands —used as incense in Bwiti —but have
never burned them and they have been deposited in a
museum collection.

But clearly these substances give one increased power to share
the experience of Bwiti to those sensibly and mentally inclined to
do so in a more complete way. Moreover it is hard to imagine
sharing of the sensorium without acquainting one's interlocutor
with the smell, and taste and subsequent effect upon the body of
these substances.

LEVEL II Being There

1. *Revelatory incidents:* An ethnographer whose life in the field
is usually full of events and incidents whose possible meaning
in respect to his problems he must constantly ponder will be
quickly convinced by the 'case method' of presenting his
materials. This is a method whose intent is to share with
the reader the dynamic in respect to persons and places of
these events. I sought this sharing in Bwiti through the
device of beginning every one of the 20 chapters with a
'Revelatory Incident' whose dynamic in respect to personages
and 'points of view' I, then, sought to explain (I had framed
the book in the Introduction with a long 'genealogy' of
significant persons involved in village and religious life with
whom I had lived in the field and something of whose personalities and problems I wished to convey to the reader).
This method of seeking to involve the reader with the revelatory incidents of the field and, to that extent, share with him
or her the field experience itself also applied to religious
experience. In Part III of the book I selected various inci-

dents related to Bwiti ceremonial in which the reader might share some feeling for the ceremonial process and its problems. These revelatory incidents were designed, in short, to enable the reader as much as possible to 'be there' in the ongoing ethnographic task and to share in the ethnographer's efforts to, himself, more closely share the problematic world of the Banzie.

2. *Figures of understanding:* Perhaps the most important way (as far as my particular (tropological) theoretical perspective is concerned) by which I sought to share the experience of the Bwiti religion was through close attention to the various devices by which the Banzie 'figured' their religion: that is to say the various tropes that they employed in their sermons, songs, mythology, theology and religious casuistry. It is true to say about human understanding that 'by indirections we find directions out.' We often understand something best by bringing something else analogous —something else we understand better— to bear upon it. This involves the use of the various tropes. In an oral culture particularly and even more in religion, surely, where we are dealing with the 'ineffable' we must take these figures of understanding very seriously indeed. For in the face of so many things that the Banzie themselves do not understand very well it is their way of telling themselves 'what-it-is-*like*-to-be-a-member of Bwiti.' And we take note, once again, that it is 'what it is *like*' not what it *is* to be a member that, by focusing on figurative devices, we are sharing with our readers and auditors.

This distinction between 'what it is *like*' and 'what it *is*' to be, built into the very title of our argument here, raises the questions of 'knowing other minds' in any objective way. It is the question treated by Nagel with the hopeful expectation of a phase change in that capacity of knowing. But those of us engaged in fieldwork among 'others' and obliged to (and desirous of) sharing that fieldwork cannot put aside that obligation to await such a phase change. What we can do now is be attentive to how others share with themselves an understanding of the meaning of their experiences by trying to say what their experiences are *like* rather than what they *are*. That is to say, we can attend to their experience by showing how they bring, synesthetically, experiences, very often, from other sense modalities to bear upon lacunae in their understanding.

Let me give just a few examples from Bwiti of the way the Banzie use various images to argue to themselves what it is like to be a Banzie.[2]

> Images of the earth and undergrowth abound in Bwiti 'evangiles.' Clay and swamp and fens appear, and men are lost in the leaves of the underbrush and wander unable to see each other, let alone their tutelary supernatural. In such a context, it is apt that the speaker compares the Bwiti chapel to the hunter's bower of leaves in the deep forest. For within this spiritual 'bower' men can become, as he suggests, like crossbows, tensed to 'shoot' their souls to the above. (Fernandez, 499)

> Two {images} must be further explained: the reference to tobacco and to the light of the mirror. The smoking of tobacco (sometimes hemp) is employed in chapels of Bwiti to represent the distillation of the spirit out of its corporeal substance and its rising to the 'above.' Often the reference to tobacco occurs, though not in the sermon, in relation to the forging of the body in the ritual activity of the chapel — its reinvestiture with spirit upon its rebirth in Bwiti. But smoking is an image with opposite implications here, for its implies the destruction or burning down of the body and the divestiture of spirit. (Fernandez, 515)

LEVEL III Sharing through the Narration of Experience

1. *Bwiti narratives:* If it is true that it is characteristically human to tend to understand and share the meaning of difficult things by bringing other things they understand better to bear upon them —by understanding something else as it were— it is also true to say that humans often best understand who they are and what they are about by telling stories to themselves and to each other about themselves. Story telling, often enough, is simply a more extended way of trying to understand one thing by telling about something else: 'thereby hangs a tale' as it is said. Religion, particularly, because it treats of the ineffable —the non-empirical, on the

---

[2] The ethnography, Bwiti, makes extensive reference throughout to 'the argument of images' going on among Fang involved in this religion. For a more focused argument see, however, J. W. Fernandez, "The Argument of Images and the Experience of Returning to the Whole," in *The Anthropology of Experience,* V. Turner and E. Bruner, eds., Urbana: University of Illinois Press, 1986, pp. 159-17.

one hand, and subtle moral casuistry on the other —is full of the sharing of narration.

Fang and Banzie, thus, share experience with each other not only by the use of analogies but also by means of stories they tell each other about themselves. We can share in their experience by carefully transcribing these narratives. Thus in Bwiti we took special care to transcribe and comment upon these narratives: The narratives of family and village migration attached to the genealogies (Chapter 3); the narratives of first contact with the European (Chapter 4); the narratives of culture defining myths and legends, the stories, that is, they tell themselves about themselves before the arrival of the Europeans (Chapter 2); the narratives of initiatory narcotic excursions and dreams that confirm one's identity as a Banzie. (Chapter 18)

These latter narratives involving the sharing of recondite religious experience are of particular interest to our topic here. These narcotic excursions are thought to be such private and mysterious matters —although, in fact, they tend to be stereotyped in the act of narration— that it is felt to be necessary for the initiate to recount the specifics of his drug-induced experiences to the leadership in order to confirm their propitiousness for the interests of the group. 'Sharing' is crucial here not only because the drugged excursion is otherwise a wholly private matter but also because it is likely to be coopted by any of the multitudinous malevolent forces in the universe against which Bwiti is struggling. The narration of these narcotic dreams of initiation is a way of assuring against ego-centric malevolence and confirming group purpose. If the Banzie were to be asked why they so desire to share this particular religious experience, they would reply that it was to prevent ego-centric forces from appropriating their religion and to assure themselves that theirs is a shared religion and not a private ego-centric relation between an adept and supernatural power.

2. *Bwiti as a narrative:* Here I want to treat briefly the entire set of rituals in Bwiti as a narrative, on the one hand, and the ethnographer's task to provide for his reader a convincing narrative ethnography, on the other. For clearly any representation of another religion, even a representation of its narratives, must be more than a compilation of facts or of narratives. It must be a narrative itself. If one is to effectively share one must work to narrate in an interesting way the revelatory incidents, or the translations of myth, legend and genealogical narratives one wishes to present. But if the

reader is to really share what is achieved in a culture, and
particularly a religious culture, one must also give the entire
ethnographic presentation convincing narrative form. And it
is also a narrative that must in some way relate to local
religious narrative.

My view of the overall narrative of the Bwiti religion was that
the Banzie in the succession of rituals, songs and dances that
they call *The Road of Birth and Death,* were seeking to overcome
or transcend the malaise of Life which is Death in its various
forms and obtain to permanent ancestral status. In the ethnography I sought to offer, relating to this overarching narrative in
Bwiti, a resurrection narrative in three parts: a narrative of
cultural decline (Part I), a narrative of liminal meditation about
culture (Part II), and a narrative of cultural revitalization or
resurrection (Part III). It was a narrative, in other words, of
margination–separation, transition and reintegration.

This ethnographic narrative involved numerous images but two dominant images were fundamental: from the Western perspective, *The Road
to Xanadu,* the Coleridgian path image based on the poem by the same
name, and from the Fang perspective, *The Path of Birth and Death,* a
fundamental organizing image, as we have said, in the Banzie experience.
Part of the task of enabling those foreign to a religious culture to share
its experiences is to endeavour to present the images that are present in
that culture and its members' minds and which are present during ritual
action or which act to guide these activities. But sharing also involves
finding cognate images in our own culture which can serve as a guide to
the understanding of these 'other' images. The Road to Xanadu is an
instance of one of these cognate images which can, in its similarity and its
differences, enable us to bridge over and thus share in that 'other image.'

Conclusion

If we are to believe the paleo-anthropologists sharing is an ancient human
capacity ... and humans are characteristically interested in sharing not
only materially but spiritually as well. That is to say we are interested
not only in the exchange of objects but also in the exchange of experiences. But the problems of fully sharing in the latter mode are very
great indeed, particularly if we envision it as a process of coming to know
other minds in any objective way that does not involve substituting our
subjective experience for theirs. For the ethnographer the strategy must
be a modest one of seeking to approximate to the knowing of other
minds by trying to carefully register: (1) the sensorium in which these

other minds are enmeshed; (2) the revelatory incidents in their lives in which their identities and the problematics of their lives are at play; (3) the analogies by which they 'figure out' for themselves what their experiences are *like;* and (4) the narratives that they recount to each other in an effort to compose their experiences and capture each others imaginations. In the end the most we can probably hope for from this strategy of ethnographic sharing is being able to understand what it is *like* not what it *is* to be a member of another religious culture. Perhaps, finally, this is only to recognize the meaning of the word *share:* that is, to be able to have some part but never the whole of another's stake in things material or mental.

Bibliography

Fernandez, James W. *Bwiti: An Ethnography of the Religious Imagination in Africa.* Princeton: Princeton University Press, 1982.

Nagel, Thomas. "What is it like to be a Bat." *The Journal of Philosophy* XXXIV (1974): 435-450.

CHAPTER 12

Sharing Religious Experience
in Hindu–Christian Encounter

Michael von Brück

Experience is participation in an event and as such is culturally conditioned.
In the process of maturing everybody encounters his/her tradition, shaping
and changing it in the process. The process of adapting to other traditions
forms part of the cultural development of every culture. Assimilation, contrast, drawing borders, or synthesis are different types of development within
this process. Different fields of identity should be distinguished in this
process, and these are significant for the question of sharing in the respective
identity of any 'other' person, be it social, emotional, or personal identity.
This article analyzes different areas of identity and sharing in Hindu–Christian
encounter and on the theoretical basis of such types concludes that there are
singular cases of sharing in the emotional, personal, and even the social
identity of an other person. This is not, however, tantamount to a *communicatio in sacris* between Hindus and Christians due to the persisting differences
in social identity between the two groups. This circumstance can change,
however, particularly in social action groups who share a common task, albeit
on the basis of different religious backgrounds, thereby creating a common
social and emotional identity as a basis for genuine religious sharing.

It is quite likely that in every paper at this conference the question of the
definition and meaning of the term 'religious experience' will be raised.
That is the reason that I shall indicate in the first section of this article
the sense in which the term religious experience will be used. Second, I
will identify certain areas of religious experience in Hinduism. The third
section deals with the problem of sharing religious experiences within
Hindu–Christian encounter. Observations and clarifications in this field
may eventually contribute to the general question raised at this symposium.

1   Religious Experience

Experience is participation in an event and as such is not necessarily
accompanied by conscious observation. Hence, observation and experience
are to be distinguished. This distinction prompts us to ask how we can
determine what a religious event capable of producing religious experience
actually is. There is obviously no universally acknowledged scheme of

classification which could indicate the significance of all phenomena studied under the term 'religion.' It is obviously "not something one can see" (Smart, 3). Rather, one can take note only of its manifestations or interpretations. Geographical, historical, sociological, and linguistic systems provide different sets of parameters which enable us to observe certain selected phenomena. The very complex and ever changing situations of encounter and participation, however, cannot be adequately understood within such parameters. This raises a basic epistemological problem not limited to phenomena which are termed religious.

What we call religion is dependent on our cultural conditioning. As is well known, the term 'religion' is itself not a universal one. What the Hindu tradition calls *dharma* is by no means identical with the object of study called religion in the Latin epistemological tradition. Comparing these structures of language and systems of thought enables us to discern the limitations of any system of thought. In addition, we can become aware of the assumptions on which any possible structuring system depends, even though these do not form part of the system itself. Any system is thus an open one. Such openness is precisely what we could call the methodological point of intersection in comparative religious studies. The consequence is that religious —and for that matter any linguistic or cultural— encounter is always creating both new religious forms as well as new structures of religious meaning and interpretation. There is no way to write a 'history of religious experience,' as Ninian Smart attempts (Smart, Preface), but only a history of its ever changing interpretations. There can never be a hermeneutic framework providing us with unequivocal data that we can share in a hermeneutic community of scholars or of religious practitioners; what does exist, however, is the hermeneutical process that moulds and changes that which is shared as well as those who are sharing it in the very process. In fact those who share and what is shared are inseparable.

We could perhaps make the following distinction:

1) Encounter *with* a religious event within a rather stable framework of tradition, such as when a Hindu or Christian is confronted by his/her own tradition. The language, symbols, and non-verbal and verbal forms of interaction are pre-shaped by the community in which this encounter takes place. In early childhood religious or national stereotypes already provide a frame of reference which exists prior to the formation of any concepts as well as prior to any experiences of our own that might alter such stereotypes. The possibility that an individual find order in a complex world seems predicated on the presence of such an ordering structure (Adler). In other words, preconceptions and predispositions as well as prejudices are basic and inescapable epistemological factors which need to be further studied by social psychology. (Tajfel)

Still, any confrontation with a religious event is itself a religious event which not only accrues to the tradition, but which, in some sense and to some degree, changes the very framework of perceiving a tradition. Since there is no tradition outside the event(s) of participating in this tradition, the tradition itself will be altered by the event of participating in it. The degree of alteration is dependent on various circumstances that account for relative differences in a tradition's stability, and in rethinking, reforming, revolutionizing, etc., the tradition.

2) Encounter *between* religious events from different sets of meaning (expressed in different languages, cultural patterns, hermeneutical approaches to meaning, etc.), for instance, encounter between Christian and Hindu individuals or groups. It is obvious that this is a secondary event of participation, since such an event creates an experience that is unprecedented in any of the traditions concerned considered alone. Such encounter thus creates a new experience influenced by far more complex symbols, religious content, and structures of meaning.

The difficulty which is thus introduced is that the religious subject forms part of a network of cultural relations which is not shared universally, as Geertz and others have shown. Interreligious encounter also establishes a different basis for the structures of experience. It alters such pre-established notions as the person, group, individual time, social time, etc.

Since the formation of group mentality and stereotypes ('we' as opposed to 'they') occurs in early childhood at the age of six or seven, religious experience and social identity form a close-knit unity. Taking a discovery by social psychology into consideration makes the situation even more complex. Humans tend to perceive their own group in a differentiated way, whereas strangers are perceived as 'they' and tend not to be perceived as individuals with their individual experiences (Tajfel, 175 ff.). Prejudices can be intensified by actual encounter, since perceptions might seem to accord with preconceived ideas, and this in turn influences the experience of sharing the religion of a different social group.

The question of this symposium is whether such encounter, participation, and experience belong to the second type of encounter, or, put differently, whether sharing the religious experience of other groups is possible. The simple answer is that such sharing has always been going on where different cultures have met and have translated one set of meanings into an other language, etc. The history of humankind, as far as we know, is largely an interplay between what we have just termed the first and second levels of encounter and human experience. An inevitable conflict between the two, however, ensues due to the problems posed by *identity.* The question today seems rather to be whether we can become somewhat more conscious of what actually happens during such encounter. Can we outline such factors as the anthropological, psychological, epistemological, and hermeneutical implications of encounter in a way that would diminish the potential for conflict to a minimum and would optimally increase the potential for creative new religious configurations, mutual enrichment, and intensification of purpose and meaning?

Present day experimental studies (Bochner, 5-44) teach that there are at least four different patterns for types of behaviour in a cross-cultural situation, changing one's own cultural/religious identity built by social conditioning: assimilation, contrast, drawing borders, and synthesis. Not all the factors are adequately understood, nor the complex configurations that determine which type of behaviour ensues. The observations I shall present in § 2 and 3 are, consequently, not yet sufficiently comprehensive to construct a theoretical framework.

A 'religious group' is here called a religious group because a group of people feel they are a religious group. I would like to suggest characterizing religious experience as participation in any event in which a wholeness is realized that gives identity and orientation in the search for meaning by an individual and/or a group. Since the whole integrates all aspects of individual, social, and transcendental relations, it is always beyond any actual empirical realization inasmuch as it encompasses all *possibilities* and not just actualities. Since all the possibilities are not known, however, religious experience is not closed, limited, or fixed. According to our definition, the experience of wholeness is participation in wholeness. If this participation is intensified and leads to a transformation of one's identity such that one's individual identity becomes at least partially identical with the identity of the whole, then we can speak of *mystical experience:* It is the experience of unification based on unifying awareness. (von Brück 1987a, 251ff.)

This would imply that we can speak of collective religious experiences when, for instance, a tribe participates collectively in an act of meaning that embraces the whole (such as sacrifice). In contrast, mystical experience is always the experience of an individual who *overcomes* his/her socially conditioned individual identity through an act of participation in ultimate integration. In this respect mystical experiences may be *structurally* very similar across different cultures and different periods, but psychologically the experiences differ inasmuch as they depend on what there is to overcome through such integration, viz., the multiformity of individuals and circumstances as reflected by a tradition.

Participating in another's mystical experience is therefore impossible, just as it is impossible to participate in the experience of someone eating an apple. I may eat the other half of the same apple if given a chance, but my experience will probably be different. In fact, there is no way of knowing whether I taste the same 'flavour' as someone else or not — it depends on my sensory apparatus and on incidental circumstances. In the case of the apple, however, as well as in the case of religious experiences, one can share one's interpretation or personalization of this experience, expressing joy, discomfort, or whatever. The result of different experiences may be similar among different individuals but the experience is never identical. This holds true for any relatively stable religious identity (though it is also subject to modification in the end) possessed by differing individual subjects.

2 Hindu Religious Experience

I shall now proceed to identify areas or levels of religious experience within Hinduism which constitute events of sharing religious experience within that culture and which might be relevant to Hindu–Christian encounter. Since experience as an act of participation in an event involves the entire life-long process of forming a person's identity, I will outline these areas according to three aspects of identity: *social identity, emotional identity,* and *personal identity.* I will advance an argument for adopting this sequence shortly.

The background paper to this conference states that "the essence of religion is the personal faith-experience" (Vroom, 1). This assertion is, however, very much the question. It might be true for highly personalized cultures and religions such as Buddhism and Christianity, but is questionable with regard to tribal religions and many forms of Hinduism. In Advaita Vedānta and other self-conscious *darśanas,* of course, as well as in *bhakti-*movements that occur, for instance, within Śaivism and Vaiṣṇavism, a personal experience of a form of consciousness which is pervaded by God-consciousness or which has been totally transformed by the experience of identity with the One occupies a central position. Yet the village religion of tribal and lower caste Hindus as well as many 'higher' forms of Hinduism consist rather more in a collective integration into the harmony of the universe, as expressed in the term *dharma.* This harmony consists in the appropriate interplay of different forces, qualities *(guṇas),* and hierarchical structures on the cosmic, social, and personal levels. What is distinct remains nonetheless distinct, but the equilibrium of all is *dharma.* (Manusmṛti XII, 24-51; I, 102, *et al.*; Mahadevan, 54ff.) It is not so much the individual experience or the experience of the individual as such that counts but rather the collective awareness of being in tune with the specific pattern of cosmic and social events which is experienced by this specific tribe, clan, or village. This is often overlooked when highly individualized specialists with Hindu or Christian backgrounds meet in a neutral location detached from the actual live background to the experiences discussed. Our point of departure must, therefore, be closer to this more basic area of encounter.

1) The cultic community centred around sacrifice *(yajña)* has always been the central religious and social framework for Vedic religion (Ṛgveda I, 164, 35). This group constitutes a more or less coherent basis for a *social identity* that distinguishes those who participate from others who do not. Since performing these rituals means sharing in the cosmic order, such a group is imbued with a cosmic dimension, realizing and enhancing the universal *dharma* throughout the whole of reality, including, of course, the caste-order, which is the very representation of the creational order (Ṛgveda X, 90; Manusmṛti I, 31), and certainly not a mere social contrivance to which religion confers legitimacy. In this context, religious experience *is* to *live* the *dharma* according to the cosmic order as specified by the Vedas and the *dharmaśāstras*. Sacrifice as participation in the universal act of God's creation most certainly represents a universal symbol. Yet in actual Hindu history, sacrifice always has the specific meaning of fulfilling *this dharma* for *these* people, and this applies equally to other traditions. As a salvific act, it is concrete, mediated by a particular group sharing in a specific tradition. (Chethimattam, 175 ff.)

To share this experience would imply sharing their life, becoming a caste-Hindu, offspring of ancestors who have also been participants in the village's community. It is obvious that this is impossible, and that a Christian cannot, by definition, share this aspect or level of religious experience. One could perhaps share in the ritual but once cannot share in the experience which is the social identity of a particular group. For the sojourning Christian who participates in such ritual the experience would be a different one than for the villager. On the other hand, there may well be a longing on the part of Hinduism to communicate by means of the (Christian) Eucharist (Panikkar 1964, 211). But in what sense? In so far as the Eucharist signifies the universal sacrifice that allows human beings to resonate to the cosmotheandric reality (Panikkar), no problem arises. But what if the scope of such sharing also encompasses a different religion with other value systems, social structures, and political ambitions? This is hardly conceivable. Yet the notion of sharing religious experience cannot simply treat the two aspects as separate lest such sharing remain an academic enterprise.

It bears repeating that the level of the sacrificing community is a basic level of religious experience for religion rooted in the Vedas, despite the fact that it was somewhat transformed at a later time. In later times, it is true, it was not *yajña* but *pūjā* that was central. *Pūjā* is much more personalized than *yajña*, in many cases amounting to exclusive meditation, especially in such elements as concentration, invitation of the Godhead, and participation in God which approaches a certain measure of deification, all in a community that seeks its identity in this transformative way (Rao, 582ff.; Vandana, 106ff.). Nevertheless, the rhythm of *pūjā*, the festive calendar of processions, pilgrimages, etc., still retain their original function of exemplifying and reenacting the basic *dharma* of a specific community.

2) The ascent of *bhakti*-movements and the personalization of religion, however, represents a counter tendency which displays relativity of the former pattern. The Bhagavadgītā (BG) is a case in point in connection with this transition. The story running through the Gītā —Kṛṣṇa's admonition to Arjuna who refuses to fight— suggests the narrative operates substantially on the level of the *dharma* and *svadharma* ideology which establishes social identity, whereas the teaching of *karma-yoga*, explained in the later chapters as being a complement to the central path of *bhakti*, focuses on an individualized *emotional identity*. All cultic action has both a cosmic as well as an emotional aspect, but the shift from *karman* as cultic act to *karman* as fulfilling one's *svadharma* diminishes the emphasis on the community and increases that placed on the individual. The social identity of the caste-person is no longer merely belonging to a particular caste by birth, but in *bhakti* proper thought and action according to *svadharma* confers perfection *(siddhi)* and oneness with God (BG XVIII, 41-45); the individual is asked here to express his love and oneness with God by dedicating everything to Him. *Emotional identity* is the main focus, summoning the individual's response rather than the tribe's. Various individuals may thus share a common *karma-yoga* and *bhakti* effort. This can give them a certain common social identity, even though their individual experience of *emotional identity* may differ. It is a striking phenomenon that such personalization as we encounter in *bhakti* at the same time produces a shift in emphasis away from the exclusive relation between a single teacher and his student toward a new group which accommodates people with dissimilar social identities. The *bhakti*-movements thus tend to transform secret transmission of religious experience to mutual sharing among groups which had formerly been separated by their cultic and social-religious identity. (Carman, 216ff.)

3) Actual God-realization, direct experience *(anubhāva)*, *brahmavidyā* or *jñāna* is the climax of religious experience for many Hindus, not just for those who follow the Vedāntic teachings. This form of contemplation has been compared to a *cosmic sabbath*, which is the crown of creation, something also to be found in biblical tradition, wherein all particular forms of experience and symbols come to abide in the completely unbroken light of a 'beyond.' (Sahi, 615)

On the basis of the concepts of *adhikāra* or *upāya* in Hinduism and Buddhism respectively, different philosophical tenets, concepts of reality, and forms of worship are accepted as preliminary stages which ultimately reach full maturity in contemplation. A famous passage in the Gītā states: Which particular form such and such a devotee with faith wishes to worship, each to his own faith I confirm (BG VII, 21). This can be interpreted as referring to different images of God as well as to different stages in the personal assimilation of worship. Hinduism has what might be called a pedagogical tolerance. It is accepting with regard to all possible forms of worship, but *ātmajñāna* or *brahmavidyā* alone represent true sacrifice and the ultimate goal (Chethimattam, 182). *Personal identity* is attained in the actual experience of *mokṣa* or liberation, which is a liberation from ego, including the ego's fabric of consciousness which creates its identity in particular symbols, experiences, and interpretations, and such liberation could be termed *transpersonal realization*. The relationship between the personal and the transpersonal will not be elaborated in this context. (von Brück 1987a, 287ff.)

It is clear that aspects of social and emotional identity at this level play a much less important role, and this is the reason that the mystics from all religions can more easily share and understand each other than can religious people who have not attained this level of experience. This is not, however, tantamount to claiming that all mystical experiences are the same. It has been convincingly demonstrated that there is no way of knowing and comparing experiences apart from their respective interpretations (Katz 1978). Yet —and this point must not be ignored— mystics are aware of the permanent need to move beyond concepts and interpretations, including, of course, their own. This fosters an openness and readiness that is more accepting and receptive to sharing religious experience with others. At the same time, however, this is also the reason that mystics often encounter difficulties in explaining themselves to people from their own religious group who are not mystics. The boundaries in this case run not so much between different religions as between various types of religious people such as mystics and non-mystics across religious lines.

3 Sharing Religious Experience in Hindu—Christian Encounter

The above analysis holds a number of consequences for the question of sharing religious experience in Hindu—Christian encounter.

1) It has been suggested that sharing religious experience between Hindus and Christians might be most easily accomplished at the level of mystical experience, as historical evidence seems to suggest. Nanak, a mystic, succeeded to some extent in unifying Muslims and Hindus, whereas Akbar, a politician, failed (John, 203ff.). As we can infer from the existence of the different levels of identity outlined above, however, the problem is much more complex.

Mystical experiences are shaped by interpretation, i. e., a distinctive religious tradition of language and meaning. Thus, many Christian mystics experience the union with the Divine in a specific way, co-suffering in the wounds and pains of Christ (Katz 1983, 14-16). The distinctive character of the experience cannot be shared by those who do not share the frame of meaning provided by the Christian story of the suffering Christ. Although one can ponder a general abstraction of mystical experience such as 'union with the Divine,' the flavour and emotional texture of such experience remains particular unless the partner in dialogue from a different religion crosses over to the comprehensive framework of meaning presupposed by the other religion. This usually happens only in the course of an extensive and protracted process of syncretism and integration. An example would be the integration of Neo-Platonism into Christianity, which is not just the work of Dionysius the Areopagite, but forms a whole chapter of history.

The mystic, furthermore, is the exception, and in most cases even the mystic belongs to a group that seeks social identity by differentiating itself from other groups. It has, nonetheless, been an undeniable experience in many Hindu–Christian encounters that silence and meditation and/or the contemplative reading of Holy Scriptures from various traditions enhances the *communio* of those assembled (von Brück 1987b). Though the mystical experience as such cannot be shared, those engaged in its interpretation and in expressing its repercussions in their lives and language tend to be tolerant, flexible, and open, realizing from their own experience that words and symbols cannot convey the full meaning of this experience. They are aware of the fact that language here is not descriptive but evocative. Those who see God in everything and are totally immersed in God-consciousness are free to disregard the differentiating symbols which portray a stratified social-religious order. It is far more important to a mystic to lead others to the actual experience than is agreement on interpretation.

That which distinguishes sharing between mystics from that between theologians is their basically different approach to religious epistemology. The mystic flourishes and remains within an experiential attitude. His experience as well as his sharing of that experience is an ongoing, never ending process. Certainty *(certitudo)* is an experiential aspect of the experience itself, and does not stand in need of support from security *(securitas)* which is purportedly founded on formulating conceptual or social limits.

The quest for experience is the common bond that shapes such encounters between mystics from Hindu or Christian or other backgrounds. They understand because they do not speak. They also tend, however, to live by themselves and do not try to form an interreligious social community based solely on mystical experience. This is the reason that considerations regarding social and emotional identity are less important for this kind of encounter and sharing.

2) It is much more difficult to engage in sharing religious experiences which in some way involve the level of *emotional identity*. There is a difference in attitude between Hindus and Christians in this regard. Hindu society is accustomed to religious pluralism, Hinduism itself being a pluriformity of types of religious and ethical observances, philosophies, symbols, and rituals. As long as no violation of his/her *svadharma* is implied, a Hindu has no difficulty in participating in the religious rites of other communities, at least, not insofar as the four classic forms of religious life according to the *āgamas* are concerned, i. e., recitation of the names of God *(japa)*, sacrifice *(yajña* or *homa)*, meditation *(dhyāna)*, and devotion to God who is worshipped in the form of an icon both at the temple and at home *(arcana)*. Matters lie differently with respect to the rites of initiation *(samskāras)*, since here a special form or manifestation of the Godhead is celebrated which requires celebrants to respond with specific duties which cannot be shared outside those who are initiated. Such groups are determined by caste and religious denomination (Manusmṛti II, 62; II, 65-66, *et al.*). Even though an individual has a particular affiliation with Vaiṣṇavism or Śaivism and perhaps with an even more specific *iṣṭadevatā*, for instance, there is general respect for other rituals, images, and forms of devotion that can be easily shared. The rituals and liturgies, with the exception of the initiation rites, are specific but not exclusive. Holy places may be visited by people who have a different religious affiliation, and Hindus are even permitted to visit Muslim and Christian sacred sites for the sake of receiving spiritual blessings. Thus, the tomb of the Ṣufī saint Muʿīn al-Dīn Chishtī in Ajmer/Rajastan is visited by Hindus as well as Muslims. In Southern India Christian festivals such as Good Friday processions, prayer meetings, etc., are visited by Christians as well as Hindus. Depending on the local political and religious atmosphere, such sharing can be rather uninhibited. Thus, it is reported that for lack of a Hindu priest in the village, a Christian priest was asked to celebrate a Hindu *pūjā*. The status of priest as a sacred person may well be more distinctive than the difference in religion (Puthanangady, 71). Hindus frequently request to participate in the Eucharist, and more recently even (Catholic) Christians have argued for admitting Hindus to the Eucharist, provided that they have truly long for it. The ensuing fellowship among participants has already developed into a kind of *communio*. (Puthanangady, 800)

Generally speaking, however, Christians encounter more difficulties in sharing religious experience with Hindus, especially rituals. This is partly due to the exclusivity of the traditional understanding of Christ, the history of Christianity in India, etc., but there are additional obstacles as well. As a minority, Christians seems in need of justifying their existence and of establishing their identity by preserving and emphasizing a distinctive behaviour in cult as well as in ritual. 'Christian' symbols such as using candles, certain songs, the cross, etc., have often been adopted and absorbed by Hindus. What marks a Christian and establishes his/her identity is no longer simply a matter of one's own symbol but of deliberate non-participation in the world of Hindu symbols and rituals. A positive social identity is created through a negative emotional identity, such as not being a vegetarian or avoiding the vicinity of a temple, etc.

In the Christian Ashram movement, deliberate efforts have been made to integrate Hindu rituals into Christian liturgies. Not just readings from Hindu sacred scriptures, recitation of the names of God *(japa)*, mantras for inviting the deity into the *mūrti*, fire symbolism *(ārati)*, and observation of Hindu festivals (such as Onam in Kerala, Pongal all over Southern India, etc.), but the whole life style of the Hindu *sannyāsin* has been integrated. Yet this enculturation is not really an exchange of religious experience. Mantras may be used, but rarely will a Christian chant *Oṁ namaḥ Śivāya,* preferring *Jesu namo,* just as a Hindu chants the names of the Hindu gods and not *La ilāha illā' llāh.* Mystics in all religions, though transcending rituals and formalized concepts, nevertheless practise on the basis of the specific symbolism of their own tradition (Katz 1983, pp. 20ff.). Although general Hindu symbols such as *Oṁ* or the *Gāyatrī* are being used by these Christians, the very names of God that give these symbols an emotional flavour and which serve to identify them with a particular history are not shared. It is difficult to predict whether Indian Christians may eventually create a synthesis of Yahweh and Śiva just as Rudra and Śiva were synthesized hundreds of years ago.

Even in contemplative communities (as for instance in Shantivanam Ashram near Tiruchirapalli) Christians remain largely among themselves. Even after decades of indigenous Christian worship no real sharing of ritual between Hindus and Christians has been achieved, due to the enduring difference in social identity between the two groups. Where, on the other hand, such social identities do merge in common action for the improvement of social-economic conditions in India, new social groups emerge who show hardly any desire to share specific religious experiences from their respective backgrounds. For them the *communio* in social action itself is the symbol for the trans-religious dignity of every human being. Further pursuit of this would lead us prematurely to the third aspect.

Before elaborating the third aspect, it seems helpful to generalize the problem of sharing rituals on the basis of a very personal experience. While living in India to study Hinduism I developed a great interest in participating in Christian liturgies that had become indigenous and had been saturated with traditional Hindu symbolism. This was all very meaningful, and the backdrop of Vedāntic symbols and language had contributed to a deeper Christian understanding of sacrifice in the Eucharist and to a more profound realization of the gradual divinization which takes place in a Christian life. Some Hindu friends, however, remained reluctant to rejoice in such rediscovery of Hindu rituals within a Christian environment precisely because the social identity of such a Christian group remained separate from the Hindu one. Although symbols do refer to a universal reality, they are also a means of identification and as such create group boundaries. Though we ought to distinguish between specific and archetypical symbols, it remains true even of universal symbols that they can create a relatively closed social-religious group within the intersubjective process of symbolization.

Some time later I had the opportunity to share a Zen-Buddhist Vesak ritual at Shasta Abbey in Northern California. Rather to my surprise, I felt uncomfortable when some of the well-known English Christmas carols were sung by the (excellent!) Buddhist choir — the text had been changed. The texts now narrated the story of the Buddha's birth and life. Although I have no major intellectual difficulty relating the Buddha and Buddhist experience to Christ and the Christian experience as being complementary, *emotionally* I felt discomfort precisely because my early childhood religious socialization was connected to those Christmas carols. This was a unique experience, drawing out a social-religious identity which is prior to any conceptualization and possible comparison to other religious experiences. Since cult, liturgies, and the whole ritualistic aspect of religion is normally learnt by the child in a more or less exclusive socialization process which is dependent on a specific family situation, the values thus created obtain a unique importance to each individual. Such values may be so basic that they may present difficulties in translating them into a different social-religious context. This probably constitutes the reason that religious people all over the world are hesitant about effortlessly sharing their rituals and liturgies with outsiders — they represent the very intimate tokens of emotional identity for a specific social context. Unless there is a genuine modification in *social identity,* the sharing of rituals between Hindus and Christians may be unacceptable to major portions of these religious groups.

3) Despite a strong tendency towards separation and antagonism between different religious groups in India, there is also growing communication, due to urbanization, migration, and other economic-political factors. Poverty and social misery provide one of the main sources for social conflicts and communal violence. The question of social identity cannot, therefore, be raised only in the context of the past, i. e., traditional

religious identities such as Hindu or Christian, but ought to be raised in terms of the present and future, i. e., the crisis of India's social reality and the survival of all human beings in the face of economic and environmental crisis as well as the general crisis of values. Motivation for creating an awareness of a new humankind is by all means to be nurtured, and in that context, Hinduism, with its rich cosmic symbolism and its dedication to harmony with mother earth, and the Christian sense for social justice certainly form good candidates for meaningful dialogue.

Mere repetition of sacred symbolism is insufficient, however. A cardinal ritual such as pilgrimage forms a fitting example. First, many of the Hindu *yatras* possess cosmic symbolism, culminating in the participation in the divine power at a special place which is consecrated as *axis mundi* during a particular rite. Second, pilgrimages are often non-sectarian in design, including both Śaivaits, Vaiṣṇavas, as well as others (Vaidyanathan, 72). Third, they help in surpassing social boundaries, since caste discriminations are often overcome. A case in point is the famous pilgrimage to Lord Ayyapan at Sabarimala which attracts millions of devotees every year. Even Christians have been known to participate in this pilgrimage, as well as in others. To the extent that such dynamics are at play, pilgrimage serves as an example of a ritual that does not seem bound by religious borderlines. Social limits are eliminated only temporarily, however. It can be shown that pilgrimage depend on a specific static social structure and even serve to stabilize social organization precisely through such merely temporal transgression of the social order (Arockiadoss, 655f.). What is more, such pilgrimages tend to underscore and reinforce existing group identities. Even such examples of ritual remain particular and exclusive. This is not remarkable, since all religious symbols serve to unify and differentiate society at one and the same time, creating social group identities.

Communication in the actual everyday social praxis of various people is required if *communicatio in sacris* is taken seriously. All ways of sharing ritual or of intellectual dialogue are secondary and can do no more than interpret the actual sharing occurring between social-religious groups. Otherwise sharing religious experience remains an isolated matter. On the other hand, it has been correctly observed that there can be no common *social identity* on the part of a cooperating social unity (such as the Indian nation) without sharing each other's sacred traditions lest the *communio* be reduced to mere intellectual communication (Panikkar 1973, pp. 65). Unless the urgent need for human solidarity is truly felt as a common concern, any participation in the other's rituals will not be very meaningful and perhaps even disturbing. A real 'mutation' in human consciousness needs to occur (Panikkar 1988, 230), but such mutations are successful only under circumstances of extreme environmental pressure.

In other words, unless the urgency, danger, and fragility of the human situation is felt by major portions of the various religious groups, any sharing in the well-springs of other religions can take place only among a few selected and mostly intellectual participants engaged in dialogue in artificial situations. Such dialogue is occasioned by countless conferences in India, and it is certainly enriching and perhaps forms a testing ground. Nevertheless, such dialogue does not yet amount to *communicatio in sacris* between Hinduism and Christianity.

Bibliography

Adler, P. S. "Beyond Cultural Identity: Reflection on Cultural and Multi-cultural Man." In R. W. Brislin, ed. *Culture and Learning: Concepts, Applications, and Research.* Honolulu: University of Hawaii Press, 1977.

Arockiadoss, P. "The Hindu and Christian Pilgrim Traditions and the Practice of Common Worship." In Puthanangady, *Communicatio,* pp. 647-658.

Bochner, S. "The Social Psychology of Cross-cultural Relations." In S. Bochner, ed. *Cultures in Contact.* Oxford: Pergamon, 1982, pp. 5-44.

Brück, M. von. *Einheit der Wirklichkeit: Gott, Gotteserfahrung und Meditation im hinduistisch-christlichen Dialog.* München: Chr. Kaiser, 1987a.

———, ed. *Dialog der Religionen, Bewußtseinswandel der Menschheit.* Goldmann: München, 1987b.

Carman, J. B. "Conceiving Hindu 'Bhakti' as Theistic Mysticism." In S. T. Katz, ed. *Mysticism and Religious Traditions.* Oxford: University Press, 1983, pp. 191-225.

Chethimattam, J. B. "The Universal Sacrificial Ethos and *Communicatio in Sacris.*" In Puthanangady, *Communicatio,* pp. 173-191.

Geertz, C. "Person, Time, and Conduct in Bali." In C. Geertz. *The Interpretation of Cultures.* New York: Basic Books, 1973.

John, T. K. "Religious Experience." In Puthanangady, *Communicatio,* pp. 192-216.

Katz, S. T. "Language, Epistemology, and Mysticism." In S. T. Katz, ed. *Mysticism and Philosophical Analysis.* London/New York, 1978, pp. 22-74.

———. "The 'Conservative' Character of Mysticism." In S. T. Katz, ed. *Mysticism and Religious Traditions.* Oxford: Oxford University Press, 1983, pp. 3-60.

Mahadevan, T. M. P. *Outlines of Hinduism.* Bombay: Chetana, 1954.

Panikkar, R. *Kultmysterium in Hinduismus und Christentum.* München: Alber, 1964.

———. *Worship and Secular Man.* Orbis: Maryknoll, 1973.

——. "Chosenness and Universality." In Puthanangady, *Communicatio*, pp. 229-250.

Puthanangady, P., ed. *Sharing Worship: Communicatio in Sacris*. Bangalore: NBCLC, 1988.

Rao, S. N. *"Communicatio in Sacris* Seen from the Perspective of Hindus." In Puthanangady, *Communicatio*, pp. 580-596.

Sahi, J. "An Artist's Understanding of *Communicatio in Sacris."* In Puthanangady, *Communicatio*, pp. 614-623.

Smart, N. *The Religious Experience of Mankind*. New York: Charles Scribner's Sons, 1969.

Tajfel, H. *Human Groups & Social Categories: Studies in Social Psychology*. Cambridge: University Press, 1981.

Vaidyanathan, K. R. *Pilgrimage to Sabari*. Bombay: Bharatiya Vidya Bhavan, 1978.

Vandana, Mataji. "Worship beyond 'Worship'." In Puthanangady, *Communicatio*, pp. 88-115.

Vroom, H. M. "Can we Share the Religious Experience of Others?" Background Paper. Amsterdam (unpbl.).

CHAPTER 13

Revelation and Experience
in the Theosophic Tradition

R. Kranenborg

In certain esoteric groups we encounter the phenomena of the 'Ascended Masters.' This term refers to super-natural creatures which manifest themselves to people while they are in a state of trance. During such manifestations, the Masters pass on their messages and teaching to and via the medium. The onset of the phenomenon extends back to 1875 when Helena P. Blavatsky, the founder of the Theosophical Foundation, made her appearance. Many people have since declared that they too have had experiences with these Masters, e. g., Leadbeater, Krishnamurti, Steiner, Bailey, Zohra.

It thus appears that the religious experience that Blavatsky underwent with regard to the Masters is capable of being transmitted. This gives rise to the following question: How is this experience of the 'Ascended Masters,' still current since its inception in Blavatsky's time, transmitted? We could say that the origins of a tradition emerged with the advent of such trances and the revelation that occurred in them. As an increasing number of people became familiar with such trance experiences and the revelations associated with them, this material grew into a cumulative tradition. When people now enter trance and meet the Masters, the occurrence implies that by means of this trance, they will be brought into contact with this cumulative tradition and the values incorporated in it. They thus experience what Blavatsky too experienced (and others after her). It further appears that the content of such trance experiences remain congruous with Blavatsky's (and others) experiences on the one hand, but, on the other, also charts new waters; the doctrine revealed to Blavatsky (and others) is subject to marked elaboration by people who have undergone such experiences (making it cumulative). Those unfamiliar with such trance experiences either adhere strictly to the existing revelation or break with it.

In short, the trance experience contains the possibility of sharing in the religious experiences which others have had of the Ascended Masters.

A central concern in religious experiences is experience of another reality or of the world beyond. This world beyond is home not only to God (or Being, or the divine force) but also to other 'inhabitants.' There are, accordingly, angels, spirits, saints, blessed ones, etc. Experiences of such creatures from the world beyond properly belong to the category of religious experience. Among the creatures inhabiting the World Beyond 'according to the esoteric tradition,' are the Masters, beings who, according to this conviction, have attained a high spiritual level, are arranged according to a hierarchy, and are quite intent on guiding the people on earth. We could characterize experiences with these beings or masters as religious experiences.

The first to have had such an experience of the Masters is Helena Blavatsky. She identified many of the details associated with such experiences. We can ascertain that a substantial number of religious experiences with the Masters have occurred within the esoteric tradition since then; by means of such experiences others thus share in the religious experiences of Blavatsky. Since Blavatsky had her first experiences, the Masters have constituted an integral component of all subsequent religious experiences attained within the esoteric tradition. The question which arises is: How are these religious experiences with the masters transmitted and how do people share in them? This contribution to the present volume would like to show how trance plays a central role here.

1 The Appearance of the Master

At the end of 1974 Mrs. E. W. Bertrand-Noach fell into a trance, during which, according to her account, a male person appeared to her, dressed in glittering clothes and enveloped by an iridescent green light. He introduced himself as Hazrat Inayat Khan and passed messages on to her from the spheres. She was to be called Zohra and was to be the mediator between the other world and this world. In 1977 another person, Master Morya, appeared to her and passed knowledge of occult teachings on to her. In 1979 the third —and last— voice, that of Master Jesus, came to her in a trance. He appeared to be the leader of a hierarchy of 'Masters of love and wisdom' and had selected her to relay the messages of this 'heavenly brotherhood.' Master Jesus, in turn, was the mouthpiece of a higher being: Christ. According to Zohra, this Christ had manifested himself in Gautama the Buddha, had united later with Jesus of Nazareth, and would return to earth as Maitreya the Christ.

Zohra (born in 1928 in Dutch Indonesia to Dutch-Jewish/Indonesian parents) grew up a convinced Catholic. Although she had paranormal gifts she did not exercise them, nor was she affiliated with any kind of esoteric movement. After returning to the Netherlands in 1950 she remained a convinced Catholic until 1974. Up until that time, she knew nothing of the esoteric or occult tradition nor of the Masters associated with it; the 'revelation' thus came as a complete surprise. The teaching of the three Masters was unknown to her and yet she was the recipient of messages about matters of which she knew nothing. She did, however, report that from her youth onwards she had had "special gifts (clairvoyance, magnetism)."

Zohra attracted attention when she made her revelations and experiences public. Many saw her as a medium mediating between this and the other world and considered her religious experiences to be of great importance. The question that arose after she and her group became known was: What was the origin of Zohra's experiences and how did she acquire this religious knowledge? What was the source of the concept of the Masters (especially that of Jesus as Master)?

2 The Cumulative Esoteric Tradition and the Masters

2.1 H. P. Blavatsky

The esoteric tradition in Europe is centuries old, though it often operated underground (cf. the alchemist, Boehme, 1575–1624). At the beginning of the eighteenth century many non-Christian groups arose which appealed to a clandestine occult tradition. Of important in this regard are the Freemasons (since 1717) and the Swedenborg cult (1688–1772). The nineteenth century witnessed the rise of spiritualism, which displayed great interest in trances and hypnotism, alongside of Romanticism. Since those involved in spiritualism seek contact with the other world through such extraordinary experiences, trances and the like became an important component of the Western esoteric tradition.

Madame H. P. Blavatsky played a prominent role in this tradition in the last century (1831–1891). Much remains obscure about the period of her life preceding her appearance in New York in 1874. She appears to have been paranormally gifted; she was able to fall into trances and had spiritualistic abilities (such as apport, telekinesis, etc.). She related first having met a Master in 1843, after a fall off a runaway horse in Asiatic Russia. There she was cared for by an extraordinary man who suddenly appeared and who disappeared just as suddenly. She afterwards saw him sporadically in visions. In 1851 she saw Master Morya in the company of some Hindu princes and from that time he maintained contact with her. In 1860 she met Master Hilarion. In 1868 Morya directed her to go to Tibet and she reports actually having gone, receiving instruction in Morya's teaching in Shigatse for two years while living in the house of Master Kuthumi, along with Djwal Khul, a fellow pupil. While in Egypt she met Master Serapis Bey and his brother Tituït Bey in 1870. She also encountered Master P., or the Venetian. According to her account, these Masters not only appeared to her in trance, but they actually materialized in her presence. In 1874 she met H. S. Olcott (1832–1907) and together they founded the Theosophic Society. In 1875 she wrote *Isis Unveiled*, most of it while in trance, aided therein by persons from the other world such as Master Narayan and Master Rakoczi (also known as the Count of Saint

Germain). In 1879 she left for India, meeting A. P. Sinnett in 1880. After some time Sinnett started to receive letters from the Masters, later published as the *Mahatma-letters*. Several other figures, such as W. Q. Judge (1851–1896) and W. Hube-Schleiden (1846–1916), received similarly paranormal letters from the Masters. Others (H. S. Olcott, C. W. Leadbeater, K. Damodar, S. R. Iyer, W. T. Brown, and A. Besant) were even granted the privilege to meet a Master in material form. A scandal erupted in 1884 in connection with Blavatsky's contacts with the Masters and the letters. A report by Hodgson of the Society for Psychic Research proved to be devastating. Whatever the case may have been, no further letters were received from the Masters after 1884. But Blavatsky remained in contact with the two most important Masters, Morya and Kuthumi. In 1888 she wrote *The Secret Doctrine*, ordered and inspired to do so by the Masters.

A great quantity of occult material which surfaced in Blavatsky's books derives not from the Western occult tradition, but from Eastern sources which she labelled "esoteric Hinduism and Buddhism." This Eastern tradition is actually the same as the ancient Western esoteric tradition, according to Madame Blavatsky. The two were allegedly still united at the time of ancient Egypt, the mystery cults, and Atlantis. The present world religions are actually distortions of this primal esoteric religion.

It is not possible for us to examine Blavatsky's teaching here. For our present purpose the only element that bears fuller explication is the notion of the Masters. These, according to Blavatsky, are adepts who once lived on earth and could have chosen to retire to eternal bliss upon attaining the highest level of enlightenment and degree of perfection, but who instead remained in this world, directing their concern towards humanity. The Masters attempt to guide human beings on the evolutionary path, spurring them forward on the road towards unity. They live on the astral plane and are capable of doing extraordinary things, such as materializing in the form of earthly bodies. Ever since the time that Blavatsky encountered them in trance and spoke out about them they have been a central element in the esoteric tradition. The masters mentioned above are the ones with whom Blavatsky was acquainted. It is worth noting that Jesus is not among them. Although Jesus plays an important role in occult thought, he is not a Master like the others, according to Blavatsky. With Blavatsky there is not yet mention of an organized hierarchy of higher beings in the spheres or of Christ as one of these personalities. Nonetheless, her discussion of the Masters furnished the fundamental basis for all further reflections about these beings. She thereby amply augmented the esoteric tradition.

2.2   C. W. Leadbeater

C. W. Leadbeater (1847–1934), originally an Anglican priest, became a
member of the Theosophic Society in 1883, obtaining a prominent place in
the movement after meeting Blavatsky in 1884. He possessed paranormal
abilities such as clairvoyance. Although he did encounter the Masters
from time to time, insofar as we are able to establish, he did so virtually
exclusively in the company of Blavatsky herself. He was of the opinion
that any person would be able to view the Masters on the astral plane by
developing his/her latent possibilities. His importance stems mainly from
his efforts in systematizing theosophical thought concerning the Masters
and from his insertion of Jesus among them. Leadbeater viewed all of
the higher beings as belonging to a hierarchical structure, in which "The
Lord of the World" was at the Ninth —the highest— level of Initiation,
the Buddha at the Eighth, and the Bodhisattva, Manu, and the Mahachohan at the Seventh. The Bodhisattva was identified as Christ or Maitreya.
The Masters were situated at the level of the Sixth Initiation. In support
of this scheme, Leadbeater cited Kuthumi, the Count, Jesus, Hilarion,
Serapis, Morya, and the Venetian (p. 201). In his *The Christian Creed*
(1899) he assigned Jesus a position as a Master and articulated the view
of Christ as a higher being. He stated that Master Jesus was born in
105 B.C. and, after receiving training in Egypt and among the Essenes,
made his appearance when he was age thirty. Then the Maitreya
descended upon him and he started to propound esoteric teachings, but
after three years he was stoned in the temple. He subsequently preached
for forty years in the astral world. According to Leadbeater, Jesus was
born again some time after having been stoned, to wit, in the year 1 in
the person of Apollonius of Tyanawas. It is this Apollonius who the
Bible designates as Jesus of Nazareth, Leadbeater continues. This reincar-
nated Jesus taught a secret esoteric doctrine; for the uninitiated, however,
he provided the teachings which are recorded in the bible we know.

It is quite certain that Leadbeater had no personal experiences of the
Masters except for a several in the company of Blavatsky. However, he
accepted what Blavatsky had said in regard to them, not revealing any
fundamentally new information about them by means of his paranormal
gifts. He did claim actually having seen the hierarchical scheme of the
Masters on the astral plane. This lent his statements a high degree of
authority. Yet his view of Jesus does not seem to arise so much from
paranormal visions as from his knowledge as an ex-theologian and from
his need to give Jesus a greater place within the system. In any case,
Leadbeater's elaboration of the cumulative esoteric tradition included
elements whose absence from that tradition would now be inconceivable.

2.3 Krishnamurti

Leadbeater was convinced that the Maitreya (or Christ, or the World Teacher) would reveal himself within a foreseeable period of time. In 1909 Leadbeater discovered Krishna, later known as Krishnamurti (1895–1986) and foresaw Maitreya in him. Educated by Leadbeater, Krishnamurti was brought into contact with the Masters. This contact virtually always took place during sleep when Leadbeater would lead him to the astral plane. Krishnamurti thus encountered Kuthumi (1909), Maitreya-Buddha, the Venetian, Jesus, Serapis, Hilarion, and Rakoczi. During this time Leadbeater received messages from the Masters directed to Krishnamurti. In 1911 Krishnamurti produced the booklet *At the Feet of the Master* under the name of Alcyone. Although he does not cite the Master by name, it is generally accepted that this book is about Kuthumi who, by the same token, supposedly dictated the book to him. It is almost certain that Krishnamurti did not write this text himself; the English style is much too accomplished for an Indian boy of his age. Leadbeater is seen as the author, yet, according to him, Alcyone was an earlier incarnation of Krishnamurti. Krishnamurti had no actual meetings with the Masters though he sometimes was granted a glimpse of them (as in 1922 and 1924). In 1922 Krishnamurti underwent a radical physical and spiritual experience after which he became critical of theosophy. In 1927 he declared that he had not, in fact, had any contact with the Masters. He said nothing explicitly in regard to their actual existence, although he did confirm that he believed in them and that he needed the conception of the Masters to achieve supreme unity with the truly 'Beloved,' just as in his youth the image of the deity Krishna had helped him to learn to play the flute. We know that from that time onwards he no longer spoke of the Masters. Krishnamurti never experienced trance and thus had no capacity for direct contact with the Masters. He did, however, undergo another religious experience: that of unity of consciousness. The notion of the Masters paled in the light of this experience. Krishnamurti made no contribution to expanding of cumulative esoteric tradition. The theosophic experience proved to be incompatible with his own experiences.

2.4 R. Steiner

Another important figure with regard to the conception of the Masters is Rudolf Steiner (1861–1925). He apparently already had paranormal gifts during his boyhood, and was particularly clairvoyant. He was able to see beyond mundane reality, discerning beings 'behind' the elements of Nature such as the trees and the plants. These natural beings were to play an important role in the anthroposophical movement later established by him. There are additional strands of esoteric tradition unique to him. He did not come into contact with esoteric thought until later, and then largely through his studies of Goethe and his contact with Edouard Schuré (1841–1929). It was in 1888/1889 that he first encountered theosophy. He agreed with the prevailing thoughts regarding reincarnation, spiritual development, the unity of religion and science, the union of the material and spiritual, etc. His *Philosophie der Freiheit* appeared in 1894 and provided an exposition of his thought. He became a member of the Berlin Theosophical Chapter in 1900 and was its secretary from 1902 onwards. Initially, one might assume, he experienced no disparity between his own views and the theosophical position. It is striking, nonetheless, that he never discussed the Masters. He does mention them a few times, however, and it is due to this that much of his work has been labelled uncertain and abstruse (Miers, 277). In any case, the Masters do not play a role of any significance in his thought, and although he did go into trance on occasion, he reports no encounters with the Masters. His disagreement with Theosophy reached the breaking point when Leadbeater announced that the Maitreya would appear in Krishnamurti. This was not commensurate with Steiner's experience. For him Jesus Christ was much more central, and in this he had certainly been inspired by Leadbeater's own notion concerning the division between Jesus and the Christ. Steiner himself spoke of two Jesuses, one of whom died young and then united with the other, who was still alive.

Steiner was thus acquainted, as was Blavatsky, with the trance or half-trance experience, through which he was able to see 'beyond reality,' perceiving many of the same things Blavatsky had perceived. Although he rejected much in the revelations she had received he also enlarged upon some matters (Atlantis, for example). Steiner remained true to his own experience and he allowed nothing with which he was not personally familiar to impose itself upon him — a principle which he always tried to impress upon his followers. In his trances (or 'perception,' for which anyone, according to him, has the potential) he sometimes adopted elements from the cumulative esoteric tradition, but he also generated his own school of thought, thereby enriching the tradition in a wholly unique way.

2.5 A. A. Bailey

Alice Bailey (1880–1949) presents us with a different development. She claimed that she had been in contact with Master Kuthumi in 1895 already, when she as yet knew nothing of theosophy. It was not until 1915 that she joined the Adyar Theosophic Society in California and 1918 that she became a member of the Esoteric School that existed within the Society.

Through a trance in 1919 she came into contact with Djwal Khul ("the Tibetan"), who passed some new matters on to her. This contact and the revelations she had gave rise to conflicts within the Society, leading to a rupture. In 1921 Bailey founded the Theosophical Association and within this association she established the Arcane School in 1923, which was a continuation of the above-mentioned Esoteric School. The Masters play a central role in her teachings. These contain a hierarchical scheme of Masters and beings similar to Leadbeater's, although differently arranged. Her scheme also places the Bodhisattva, the Mani, and the Mahachohan, at the same high level, and she too identifies the Bodhisattva with Christ or the World Teacher. At a lower level there are three groups of Masters: (a) Morya and Master Jupiter; (b) an unknown European Master, Kuthumi, and Djwal Khul; and (c) Serapis, Hilarion, Jesus, Rakoczi (Bailey, 54). Of interest is the fact that Bailey was familiar with the trance experience and was thereby able to come into contact with the cumulative esoteric tradition. Inspired by her own trances, however, she developed a different approach and diverged from the path pioneered by Blavatsky and her successors. Her trances show that she too was working with material from the tradition, yet she conferred personal colour and signficance on this material. She also enlarged upon this material in a number of respects, revealing hitherto unknown things about the Masters, and adding members to their company. The Masters, however, remained pivotal to her teaching, placing her squarely within the tradition. It is noteworthy that like Blavatsky and Leadbeater, Bailey too expected the imminent coming of Maitreya the Christ (in about 1975, according to Bailey). She passed the torch on to her own acolyte, the Scottish theosophist, Benjamin Creme.

3 Trance Experiences and the Cumulative Tradition

In view of the above it is clear that the trance or 'half-trance' plays an essential role in transmitting the religious experiences involving the Masters. During trance one's personality is changed; one 'loses' one's own consciousness and 'another consciousness' comes into play. Often the voice, language, and expressions of the medium change. Other physical reactions can also occur. While entranced, one is (a) highly susceptible and (b) very open to suggestion. One might speak here of 'clairvoyance,' by which is meant that one feels, sees, or articulates the thoughts, wishes, and desires of others present. Also, (c) the creativity of the medium is greatly enhanced. In many cases the medium has no conscious memory of what he has said while in trance.

In most trances a certain amount of information surfaces and some substantial knowledge is passed on. The trance experience is always a full one; 'empty' trance experiences are very rare. The content of the trance experience is old as well as new. It is, on the one hand, old insofar as the medium and his followers stand in a particular cultural tradition or a movement within that tradition. The content of the trance owes its specificity to this background. In other words, knowledge is already present in the medium and in the people around him. The medium and his followers are not blank slates.

On the other hand, the knowledge that is passed on is also new. No medium exclusively reproduces something that was already known, but rather shapes the available material in his own fashion, changing, reorganizing, or merging it with new elements, thus gradually expanding it.

Revelation received by the medium thus represents elaboration of the knowledge that already exists within the tradition concerned, allowing us to speak of a 'cumulative tradition.' This cumulative tradition forms the foundational material from which a subsequent medium can begin. During the trance experience the medium can be said to seek —unconsciously— for answers (or messages) based on the expectations of his environment. Through the agency of the aforementioned susceptibility, suggestibility, and creativity he 'discovers' material that can be used. This material can only be an extension of what is at hand, that is, the knowledge present in himself or in those around him. This is due to the fact that the medium comes into intensive contact with the cumulative tradition while in trance. From this cumulative tradition the medium derives the elements which he seeks; these are passed on to those in the medium's circle. The latter consider such communications received via trance as originating in the other world and, accordingly, as 'new revelations.' As already intimated, the medium draws upon cumulative tradition selectively. The medium cannot, after all, grasp everything; his knowledge and that of those around him is limited.

The medium's knowledge derives from the past. If items of current knowledge are revealed, its source is experienced as lying in the existing stock of cumulative knowledge. Revelations concerning the future are not found in trance experiences. Cumulative esoteric tradition does not originate exclusively through nor is it limited to what occurs in trance. It is the whole of that knowledge which comes into existence within a specific movement by means of discourse, written works, novels, preaching, etc.

What is experienced in trance is seen as authoritative. It is felt that in the trance experience something or someone other than the medium is the source of the message and that this agent provides information with which those present are unacquainted. Such information is seen as 'new revelation.'

Trance experiences are of a religious nature because a transcendent reality is perceived in them which is allegedly indiscernible to others in the same way. Although other people do, to be sure, experience transcendent reality, the experience of those in trance is of a different order: it is more intensive and authoritative. Many of those in the medium's presence never experience trances themselves. For them there are two possibilities: either they accept what the medium has said as authoritative, believing the messages and embracing these as a guideline for their lives, or they reject such communications for any of variety of reasons.

Sometimes there are people in the medium's circle who themselves undergo the psychic experience of trance. For them it is also possible to come into contact with the transcendent world in this specific manner and to have someone from the spheres 'speak' through them. They will, consequently, no longer simply take the medium's experiences for granted. At the very least they will view their own experiences as equally valid. Since experiences are never wholly the same, differences are bound to arise between one medium and the other. In that event one of the following things can happen: (a) a split may occur. (b) The previous experiences and messages of other mediums are placed on a hierarchically lower level, one's own revelation being portrayed as encompassing the preceding ones. Differences arise, it is then said, because the first medium did not fully understand the message, or because the knowledge given earlier can now be seen in terms of a greater whole. (c) The concepts of temporality or locality may be applied: experiences of other mediums are said to have been intended for a specific time period or group. It may on occasion even be said of one's own experience that it is 'local.'

4 Conclusions

When we consider the experiences of the people described in § 2 in the light of the remarks made in the previous section, we can reach the following conclusions:

(a) Ever since Blavatsky first encountered the Masters, they have formed a central element of the esoteric tradition. Time and again there are people who have experiences which feature these figures.

(b) When people who are familiar with this tradition fall into trance they will, we may assume on the basis of what has been stated above, encounter the Masters.

The following question remains to be considered: Is 'sharing' in these specific religious experiences possible? The answers which people give diverge widely:

1. People who do not have the gift of trance will be unable to share in the experiences of Blavatsky and others with regard to their visions of the Masters. They can either (a) accept what Blavatsky and the others state concerning these higher beings, or, (b) train themselves according to the precepts of anthroposophy, developing their senses and thus enabling them too, to experience such an encounters.

2. People capable of going into trance who stand in the same tradition are indeed capable of sharing the experiences of Blavatsky and others. At the same time, however, these new experiences are so individually coloured that the differences between them and the older ones will dominate. This can have a variety of consequences. Depending upon their earlier knowledge and experiences these people will either land up being closer to or further from the experiences of Blavatsky. Steiner, who had already had undergone a long process of development and who had has his own experiences, appeared to come into conflict with her. Krishnamurti, who did not in fact have any such experiences but underwent something entirely different, drew the obvious conclusion and broke with her. There are others who developed their trance experiences within the theosophic tradition but who later went their own way when they were bold enough to attribute more authority to their own experiences than to the experiences of others. For this group of people their own experience with the Masters was so authoritative that they were willing to risk a break with the others or did in fact go their separate way. In short, their own experience had priority over that of others.

There are still many questions that remain unanswered, but two must in any event be addressed. First of all: How did Ms. Zohra arrive at her experiences with the Masters? Her experience with Inayat Khan is unique, so far as I can trace it. Nevertheless, her encounters with Master Morya and Master Jesus and the Christ show that she was familiar with the esoteric tradition (or that someone in her circle was). In connection with these Masters she took her the schemes of Leadbeater and Bailey as her point of departure, rounded them out, and interpreted them in her own manner.

In the second place: What is the origin of Blavatsky's experience of the Masters? No answer to this question is available at the present time. Webb states that the concept of the Masters is not derived from Eastern religion, since such Masters are unknown to adherents of Hinduism and Buddhism, in spite of their (pseudo-)Eastern names. Also, the stories familiar to people in India concerning holy men are entirely different from those of Blavatsky regarding the Masters. Webb states that the idea of the Masters stems from Western occultism and refers in this connection to the Order of Freemasons of Martinez de Pasqually (Order of Martinists, and later the "Improved Scottish Rite") and of Karl Gotthelf von Hund (the "Strict Observance") that arose in the eighteenth century. This material is nonetheless scanty. Von Hund did speak of a mysterious knight who helped him and sometimes mentions "mysterious leaders," and "unknown superior beings," but these ultimately prove to be no more than vague allusions and do not seem to be in any way linked to Blavatsky's teachings. Blavatsky knew of the Martinists and her commentary on them is expressed in very negative terms. All in all there seems to be no reason to suppose that this movement was her source for the discovery of the idea of the Masters; Martinez' world and life view differs too much from that of Blavatsky to make any such debt plausible. She supposedly conceived it herself during the unknown period in her spiritual past. She did indeed fundamentally expand the cumulative esoteric tradition with her experiences.

Bibliography

Alcyone. *At the Feet of the Master.* 1911.
Bailey, A. A. *Initiation, Human and Solar.* 1932.
Blavatsky, H. P. *Isis Unveiled.* 1877.
——. *The Secret Doctrine.* 1888.
——. *The Key to Theosophy.* 1889.
Congar, M. *Combined Chronology.* Pasadena, 1979.
Hanegraff, W. *Uit de Schaduw der Tempels.* 1988. (manuscript)
Kranenborg, R. "Wie is Maitreya de Christus?" *Religieuze Bewegingen in Nederland* 5 (1983): 3-17.
Leadbeater, C. W. *The Masters and the Path.* Madras, 1983.
Levi, E. *Transcendental Magic.* London, 1984.
Lutyens, M. *Krishnamurti: The Years of Awakening.* London, 1976.
Miers, H. *Lexikon des Geheimwissens.* Freiburg, 1970.
Overton Fuller, J. *Blavatsky and Her Teachers.* London, 1988.
Schuré, E. *Les Grandes Initiés.* Paris, 1889.
Singelenberg, R., et al. "Het orakel van Uncle Sam." *Religieuze Bewegingen in Nederland* 16 (1988): 82-120.
Sinnett, A. P. *The Mahatma Letters to A. P. Sinnett.* Pasadena, 1979.
Slavenburg, J. *De geheime woorden.* Deventer, 1989.
Tillett, G. *The Elder Brother.* London, 1982.
Webb, J. *The Occult Underground.* La Salle, Illinois, 1974.
Wilson, C. *Rudolf Steiner.* London, 1985.

CHAPTER 14

Religious Experience and Social Change: The Case of the Bangalore Madhvas

Corstiaan J. G. v. d. Burg

Although it might be possible in theory for the Madhva laity of southern India to currently share in the religious experience of Madhva, the 13th century founder of this Brahman community, there appear to be situations which interfere with this process of sharing to such an extent that it almost appears that the gap in time is superseded by that in culture. In the case which we will consider, the community's cohesion was endangered by differences concerning the ideological legitimation for relations between the Madhvas and the Harijans which had been changed by the force of economic circumstances. Even an appeal on the part of the community's spiritual authority to the traditionally shared egalitarian religious experience *(bhakti)* could not prevent the orthodox believers from shielding their religion against Harijan interference, even though they were not opposed to *social* equality as such. In contrast to comparable cases, *bhakti* does not play the egalitarianizing role we would expect. This is all the more remarkable since it is a general assumption that devotionalism and a tendency towards *religious* egalitarianism go hand in hand.

1 Introduction

Early in the seventies the community of Madhva Brahmans in Bangalore, South India, drew public attention by two rather painful incidents. The first incident concerned the showing of the prize-winning film "Samskara," produced by Girish Karnad and based on U. R. Anantha Murthy's novel which came out in 1965. The film deals with the head of a Brahmanic community's loss of identity and takes place in a village in the state of Karnataka. The Madhvas saw the film as an obvious criticism of the Brahmans in general, and particularly of themselves. Most Brahmans in Anantha Murthy's novel belonged to their own community (Anantha Murthy, 149). This was reason enough for them to take the matter to court in order to prevent it from being shown. They were unsuccessful in their bid, although they did manage to keep the film off the screen for a year.

The second incident was more or less a consequence of the first. It revolved around an internal conflict which gave rise to no less a commotion within the community. Some time after the film incident, the most important religious leader of the Madhvas at that time, Svami V., paid a visit to one of Bangalore's 'colonies' (residential quarters) for the *Harijans,* the lowest caste in Indian society, where he was received with due homage. He invited them to learn the universal philosophy of Madhva, the founder of the Madhva community, after which other forms of religious and social contact would follow in due time.

Part of Svami's Madhva following did not take very well to this initiative. A serious controversy followed and there was imminent danger of a split within the community. In the end, certain prestigious members of the community managed to reconcile the contesting parties to prevent the situation from getting any worse. They managed to keep the Svami in office by pointing to the latitude for personal freedom of action which a world renouncing figure such as Svami V. is allowed. (Dumont, 46)

Without further comment on the film incident, we will now concentrate on the second incident, which virtually seems to prove what the film was trying to expose: the struggle of an elite community with its own social identity and religious values in a society in transition. The conflict offers an excellent opportunity to see differences of opinion within the community which would otherwise have been concealed. It may enable us to ascertain whether certain elements in the cultural and social background of the conflicting parties could be seen as important factors for change in the traditional attitudes towards other (lower) status groups. For such change in attitude is what the controversy was all about. At first blush it is surprising that the conflict came to a head over a matter such as 'a more updated approach (specifically in the religious sphere) to these social categories.' Since time immemorial, the Madhva community has been known for its distinguished devotional *(bhakti)* religiosity, while in (Western) scholarly circles it is generally assumed that devotionalism and a tendency towards religious egalitarianism go hand in hand. It remains to be seen whether this holds true in the present case (cf. Van der Veer). In order to judge, we must know more about the position and the function of the *bhakti* tradition in Madhva religiosity and about its role in processes of religious change.

The purpose of this case study is to show that even though it might theoretically be possible to share today the religious experience of someone who lived so many centuries ago, there are, even within the same religious tradition, situations which interfere in the process of sharing. Such situations alter the system of meaning to such an extent that the distance in time appears almost to be superseded by the gap in culture.

More particularly we wish to refer in this connection is to ideological aspects of change in the relations between high-caste and low- or outcaste Indians, and especially to the inherent religious obstacles impeding such change. First we will outline Dumont's and Holmström's theories of religious change and its social implications, which will serve as general orientation. Then we will analyze the (accompanying) process of ideological legitimation for such change in social relations in terms of an inquiry into the prerequisites for successful ideological transformation of a group's religious identity without endangering its cohesion.

Although our point of departure is the presupposition that processes of historical change will likely have an impact on value orientation since they alter the way in which people live, we will include the theoretical arguments of Dumont and Holmström in our analysis, even though these seem to be based on presuppositions which differ from our own. Our conclusion is —contrary to what might have been expected on the basis of the theories mentioned— that it was not the marginal position of devotionalism within the Madhva religion which prevented Svami V's initiative from succeeding. Rather, it was the attitude of organised Brahmanical orthodoxy (sangha) which very nearly brought down Svami V. This is not due to the fact that sangha members were against certain forms of social equality or integration, but owed to their opposition to religious equality in attempting to safeguard their religion —which they saw as the essence of their identity— from Harijan interference, even in the face of renewed appeals to their own tradition's legacy of egalitarian inspiration.

2 Religious Change and Egalitarianism: a Theoretical Approach

In an article on the relation between Hindu religion and morality, Mark Holmström states that existing Hindu societies and Hindu history can only be understood by paying attention to the interplay of two radically different kinds of religion, associated with two kinds of morality and social relations (Holmström 1971, 28-40). On the one hand, he discerns a religion which consecrates the existing social order, values of submission and hierarchy, and a particularist morality of closed groups. On the other hand he finds a devotional religion with values of choice and equality, and a tendency towards a universalist 'open' morality. In his opinion these two types of religion exist in an unstable combination within every Hindu community, traditional as well as modern. They correspond to values of heteronomy and autonomy which coexist in every social morality. He argues, then, that innovation in the field of morality, influenced, but not directly determined by [changing] circumstances, upsets the equilibrium between the two types of religion, which in turn implies change in the nature of social relations.

Holmström refers to the broad contours of Louis Dumont's views, who distinguishes between two types of religion in a famous article on world renunciation in Indian religions (Dumont, 33-62): 'group religion' and 'religion of choice.' The latter is, according to Dumont, associated with —and on the whole even derived from— the religious experience of the *sannyasin*, the renouncer who has broken bonds with society in an attempt to reach *mokṣa*, liberation from rebirth. Dumont sees in Hinduism the polarity of 'social religion' and 'religion of choice' as an elaboration of the polarity in the experiences of the heteronomous 'man-in-the-world' as opposed to that of the autonomous world renouncer.

Both Dumont and Holmström see devotional religion as a very specific combination of elements from these structurally opposed forms of religious experience. Dumont calls this combination an "invention of the renouncer" (Dumont, 57), for it is a way of applying the world renouncer's views to life in the social world. It is the coexistence of the idea of *mokṣa* —or, alternatively, of the idea of continual communion with a personal God— with life in a society which is shaped according to the values of the caste ideology. Such devotional religious experience thus contains a set of heterogeneous religious values which exist in an unstable mixture.

Dumont's approach to religious change is problematical. He states, as we have seen, that innovation comes from the religious experience of the world renouncer who is seen as the "agent of change" and as the "creator of values" (Dumont, 46). In his view, such innovations would be absorbed by group religion. The result would then be an ideology which renews and adjusts itself again and again. However, according to Dumont, when innovation is attended by change, it is an autonomous process. In his analysis, he seems to exclude the possibility that other factors —socio-economic or political— could influence this change.

Some of Dumont's critical followers, among them Holmstöm, see a weakness here in Dumont's model. He regards other than religious factors not so much as direct causes but as reasons for change which should be taken into account. In our analysis of the Madhva conflict, we will refer to these divergent theoretical points of departure and their implications.

3   Change: the Determinants and the Actors

Before we turn to the analysis itself, we shall give an overall picture of the urban setting in which the Madhvas live, of the various groupings and their roles, and of power relations within the community, in order to obtain a better understanding of the conflict's background.[1]

The Svamis

In terms of Dumont's typology, the Madhvas in Bangalore, the capital of the state of Karnataka, represent both types of religion in combination: a composite of a caste-bound Brahmanical or 'group religion' and a 'religion of choice' which was not originally caste-bound. Since they are followers of the thirteenth century philosopher Madhva (Glasenapp), practically all of them are Brahmans. Originally, it was a group of followers of one of the traditional *sampradayas,* philosophical schools. They, together with, for example, the Shri Vaishnavas and the Vaikhanasas, belong to South Indian Vishnuitic orthodoxy. Their Brahmanical religion is inspired by the exponents of the 'religion of choice,' i. e., the Svamis, who belong to the *Vyasakuta,* the class of scholars who are traditionally concerned with the doctrine and philosophy of Madhva, and with the Brahmanical rituals and texts which have been transmitted in Sanskrit. Next to them, we find exponents of the *bhakti* tradition, which is not disproved of by the Brahmanical religion, although it represents a later addition. They are called *Dasakuta,* the community of *Dasas* (devotional servants) of the God Vishnu. They will be discussed later.

Svami V. is a representative of the *Vyasakuta.* As pontiff of one of the eight Madhva monastic orders, he stands thirty-second in the apostolic succession of his *math* (monastery). He stands in the tradition of the spiritual men who embody the ascetic values of renunciation, devotion, and knowledge, as laid down in the philosophy of *Dvaita,* 'realistic dualism,' developed by Madhva (Glasenapp; Sharma). As one of the spiritual leaders of the Madhva community, he is bound to live according to these values as an example to his followers.

Through such pontiffs, the monasteries which were founded by Madhva and his successors are in close touch with the Madhva community. However, as is apparent from our research, the pontiffs and their monasteries are no longer the centres of congregational religiosity that they formerly were. Much of their power, prestige, and wealth has been lost. The one-time petty 'princes of the church' have become the humble servants of the faithful. They are dependent on the generosity and loyalty of the faithful now that the monasteries have been deprived by the state of most of their landed property.

---

[1] These and the following findings are the results of a survey in 1975 on Madhva religiosity in the mid-seventies. A sample of 300 Madhvas was put together according to the male–female ratio in the then not yet fully published 1971 census data which were made available to me at the Census Office in Bangalore.

Svami V. seems to have been an exception to this rule right from his accession to office. In 1953, he founded the *'Akhila Bharata Madhva Maha Mandal,'* the 'All India General Madhva Association' (Yuvaka, 5). He established several Sanskrit schools and hostels, and he took the initiative in founding a seminary for priests, the *'Purna Prajna Vidyapitha,'* the 'Seminary for Full Wisdom,' in Bangalore, where he is said to train even outcaste youths for the priesthood. That is why he is regarded by some as a progressive clergyman, committed to the interest of the community. His visit to the Harijan colony should be seen in line with these activities.

The Sangha

In spite of the fact that only 45% of the males and 38% of the females in our sample turned out to be members of the *sangha* (the congregation) this very *sangha,* which comprises ten branches in various locations in Bangalore, is the real centre of power in the Madhva community. The monastic pontiffs deal with this organisation of the faithful more than with any other group. It is this institution which determines, to a considerable extent, the image of the Madhvas. Consequently, it was mainly these very *sangha* members who united against the showing of the disputed film.

The *sangha* represents the traditional social religion "which," in Holmström's words, "consecrates the existing social order, values of submission and hierarchy, and a particularist morality of closed groups" (Holmström 1971, 28). Members of the *sangha* are therefore characterized by the fact that they value certain groups, events, and roles by associating them with the *dharma,* the eternal order in the universe, in which everyone has a particular part to play. In this understanding of reality, the individual only has value as bearer of his role in the total order. Personal responsibility is, as a rule, reduced to that role, and moral relations exist only on the level of one's own caste. This category of Madhvas embodies these values, most notably in a notorious preoccupation with *madi* (ritual purity) and impurity. This is carried to such an extent that they are mockingly called *madivalas,* (literally 'washermen'), 'those who are always occupied with ritual purity'.

It is clear that such a value-system leaves little room for a positive attitude towards the 'impure', that is, the lower castes and the Harijans, by its very nature. This is confirmed by the fact that, although a surprising 95% of the sample agreed with the statement that "acting according to the *dharma* should never mean that human rights should be denied to Harijans," 51% of the Madhvas do not wish to see Harijans treated as their equals. The *sangha* does not violate doctrine in this latter respect because Madhva's teachings are rather strict in these matters.

In everyday reality, however, other factors seem to tip the scale in social relations, among them such things as social legislation, industrialization, and egalitarian ethics originating from sources other than one's own social ideology, such as Western education, for example. It is obvious, for instance, that an egalitarian attitude towards the Harijans, also implies a departure from the ideological foundations of the greater part of traditional social religion. Realizing this, many Madhvas have dissociated themselves from the *sangha* in the past, though without abandoning their Madhva-hood. This new development continually suggests the possibility of polarization within the community. It is therefore not surprising that subcutaneous polarization of this sort was exposed by an incident such as the one surrounding Svami V., which then proceeded to escalate into an overt controversy.

The Dasas

One group actually remained outside of the conflict, namely, the Dasas, members of the Dasakuta group. Yet they play a central part in it, not as a party, but as a reason, in Holmström's sense of the word (Holmström 1971, 31). Ever since their appearance, the position of these Dasas has been ambivalent with regard to their relation to orthodox Brahmanism. Although they have always been the preachers of the message of religious and social equality for God and men, their social activities have never resulted in a full-fledged popular movement, with equality as a central theme, as was the case, for example, with the movements surrounding the Virashaivas and the Alvars (Sharma, 173). The reasons for this lie in their history.

The great movement of Vishnuitic devotionalism had its medieval roots in the Dasakuta, the order of Vaishnava psalmists and holy men. This order originated in what is now Karnataka as a result of the spread of Madhva's philosophy in that state. The Dasa order initially consisted of holy men who dedicated their lives to God by wandering the countryside as itinerant preachers, sounding the praises of Vitthala of Pandharpur, the order's divine patron. Even when Pandharpur gradually came into the Maharashtrian sphere of influence, and the town was seen as the centre of Maharashtra mysticism, Vitthala remained the group's favourite divinity. In due course these devotees transformed their cult into a living faith and into an instrument for religious inspiration of the masses who were easily reached by their inspiring devotional songs in the vernacular languages. Over the years their association with the philosophy of Madhva generated a number of Dasas who ranked as authorities in the field of the Sanskrit tradition of Dvaita Vedānta. Moreover, they were able to make the common people understand the central themes of that philosophy. Thus, for example, they connected the concept of *taratamya*, the gradation of souls, and that of *pancabheda*, the five fold classification of reality, with a mysticism which stressed egalitarianism and held out the prospect of liberation, irrespective of caste barriers.

With time the Brahmanical exponents of the philosophical tradition and its non-Brahmanical devotional preachers became increasingly distinct. This eventually resulted in the incorporation of a part —the Brahmanical part, of course— of the Dasas into the Madhva community. Their ethical message of social equality lost its import because these Dasas were by then socially bound to the heteronomous ethics of caste society. The rest of the Dasas continued to exist as an independent group under the old name.

This complete absorption of the Brahmanical Dasas into the Madhva community gave *bhakti* religiosity a firm foothold within Brahmanism, so that devotional association with God as an end in itself came to be seen as being at least equal to living in accordance to the *dharma*. However, it also prevented any significant egalitarian social movement from arising among the Madhvas. Even the saints of the high days of Dasa mysticism have been silenced as far as their egalitarian message is concerned. Although the veneration of these holy men may still be in vogue and even enjoy a remarkable new popularity (Rao), from the point of view of the *sangha* they currently play only a marginal role in the religious configuration.

The Dasas continue to display some peculiar differences with their orthodox surrounding in their opinions and behaviour. They have a surprisingly rigid attitude towards low-castes and Harijans, but otherwise exhibit extremely 'orthodox' behaviour (v. d. Burg, 110ff.). Consequently, they offer no argument whatsoever for equating religious and moral universalism. In this respect, hardly anything remains of their initial religious and social egalitarian outlook. This is very much in line with the findings of Van der Veer, who in a study of North Indian ascetics and bhaktas concluded that there is a close affinity between ascetics becoming sedentary, the devotional worship of images in temples, and caste inequality. (Van der Veer, 693)

In search of the initial egalitarian attitude, we find ourselves back at the other group of Dasas (the 'independent' group). Groups of hereditary devotees, such as the one surrounding *Guru Govinda Vitthala Dasaru*, a Mysore mystic (Panduranga, 17ff.), still adhere to the traditional egalitarian themes. They are, however, too isolated and marginal —as well as being at a safe distance from the Brahmanical sphere of influence— to innovatively influence Madhva orthodoxy.

4 Ideological change

That the Madhvas could not have been unaware of Bangalore's industrial growth can be deduced from the migration figures for the sample (v. d. Burg, 101-111). While 40% witnessed this development from childhood onward as native Bangaloreans, nearly 42% of the males settled in the city between 1942 and 1974.   It might therefore have been expected that Bangalore's industrial climate and metropolitan activity would have an impact on the social attitudes and behaviour, and even on the value-orientations and religious outlook of these urbanised Madhvas.

From our 1981 study we can indeed conclude, that there are circumstances in the urban setting which favour egalitarian ideas, or at least specific attitudes and behaviour in which egalitarianism plays a part. There are forms of situational, social, and legal pressure which promote such behaviour or even enforce it.   An example would be occupational situations where caste distinctions are officially nonexistent.   Living as a Madhva in a 'westernised' industrial city such as Bangalore gives ample occasion for such a trend.

Svami V. and his advisers assumed with good reason that the time was ripe for the total Madhva community in Bangalore to reconsider its social position in view of recent developments, one of which —the film incident— we have mentioned.   In fact, the Svami was attempting —for reasons we will explain later— to prompt the Madhvas into moving in the direction of the Harijans, and he intended to support such a *rapprochement* by updating the old egalitarian devotionalism into a renewed ideology proceeding from the religious centre itself.   That his assumptions about the community's outlook were perhaps too optimistic is borne out by our statistical data.

One of the most remarkable findings of our 1981 survey is that in some cases a great disparity appears to exist between a certain form of social conduct and the related traditional Brahmanical doctrine.   Such disparity becomes visible in changing practice, while the doctrine itself retains an unjustifiable esteem.   This is well illustrated by the practice of the concept of *dharma* and the value ascribed to it.[2]   We have seen above (p. 168) that, although 95% of the total sample was in agreement with the principle that "acting according to one's *dharma* can never mean withholding from those lower than oneself (in particular Harijans) their human rights," only

---

[2] In the traditional Brahmanical view *dharma* is the norm, and conduct according to that norm, to which every individual is obliged to adhere, and which varies according to sex, age, class, and occupation.   This holds true for everyone who wants to preserve his or her place in the religious social system.   By acting in accordance with one's *dharma* one can favourably influence one's present and future existence, it is believed.

44% of the sample were of the opinion that treating Harijans "as equals" was not contrary to one's *dharma,* while 51% thought it was. Next, 70% of the total sample blamed man's suffering on his own bad *karma* while 27% did not believe in such a causal relationship.[3] More specifically, "Being an Untouchable is due to one's own bad *karma*" was the opinion of 57% of the total sample, while 41% disagreed with this statement.

In addition to *dharma* and *karma,* other 'social symbols' based on the concept of *harper* (purity), such as *madi* (ritual purity), *mailige* (ritual impurity), and *acara* (proper ritual behaviour) have also been exposed to the constraints of the urban environment. Only 50% of the total sample still performed the purification rites connected with *madi,* 33% did not perform them strictly, and 17% had abandoned them completely.

Our statistical figures thus far do not bear out any trace of a coherent correlation between certain categories of respondents, their religion-based behaviour, and the value they ascribe to the related doctrines. This means that we were not able to validate Svami V.'s impression of his congregation's mentality, since the total sample shows no general trend towards egalitarianism in attitude and conduct. In order to prevent jumping to conclusions we also had to be sure that both supporters and opponents of Svami V. in the conflict did not show egalitarian characteristics which would confirm his impressions after the fact.

We therefore looked more closely into the Madhva community and tried to characterise the conflicting parties (in broad outline, the members of the *sangha* who denounced Svami V.'s inclination towards the Harijans, as opposed to the rest of the Madhva community) according to the independent variables of sex, age, education, occupation, income, duration of being in Bangalore, being *vaidika* or *laukika,*[4] and, in addition, according to the dependent variables of attitude towards the Harijans and towards the Svami's action. The figures we obtained lead us to infer that on certain points such as education, income, and religious background, the *sangha* are vaguely distinguishable from the non-*sangha* sample in our survey. This demanded further inquiry on our part into the social outlook of the conflicting parties.

Comparison of *sangha* members and non-*sangha* members in terms of status consciousness, their sense of belonging to the Madhva community, their attitude and behaviour towards the Harijans and towards the Svami's

---

[3] *Karma,* the credit or deficit of one's past deeds, is believed to determine the quality of one's present existence.

[4] Traditionally each *Vyasakuta* group includes *Vaidika* families, who hereditarily used to engage in religious studies (*Veda* and *Shastra*) and who lived from donations, and *Laukika* families, who nowadays have secular occupations, e. g., in the civil service and in business. Today the *Vaidikas* are mostly landowners and small merchants.

activities, showed that there was apparently no coherent pattern of marked differences between *sangha* members and non-*sangha* members, apart from the fact that the former group eventually voted against Svami V. The data reflected a broad range of personal choices in attitudes and behaviour which could indicate that a generally received form of individual behaviour which codefined —or was tied to— the identity and social status of the Madhvas as a group no longer existed.

5   The Conflict

Having described the parties in the controversy, we now return to the conflict itself, and how it was settled. We will recapitulate a little. Some time after the film incident Svami V. deemed it necessary to show that the Madhvas had learned something from the incident. He wanted to make a friendly gesture towards the Harijans. Although it had been, in general, Harijans who were badly treated by the Madhvas in the film at issue, it is hard to imagine that an authority such as Svami V., who is seen as the personification of the ideal of Brahmanic purity, should deliberately overlook the severe caste distinctions which are an essential condition for his office for this reason alone (Van der Veer, p. 694). It is likely that mutually related aims motivated his initiative. The most decisive of these was probably the prospect of an 'alliance' between Brahmans and Harijans similar to the kind Holmström hints at (Holmström 1976, 88). Such patterns of alliance between top and bottom castes do seem to have emerged in economics and politics at that time. Because both groups are marginal in comparison to the powerful middle-caste bloc in South Indian society, a *rapprochement* could be politically and socially beneficial to both, while it would also serve alleviate the burden of guilt for certain Brahmans for the way in which Harijans have been treated until recently. By inviting the Harijans to take cognizance of Madhva religion, Svami V. also wanted to rehabilitate the Madhva community after the grotesque demonstrations against the showing of the film. Last, he wished the Madhvas to be exonerated from the blame which had long been publicly attributed to them, namely, that the Madhva religion contained discriminatory elements. Here, Madhva's doctrine of *taratamya* becomes pertinent. It is said to classify the human race into three groups, according to their inherent nature, the lowermost of which —comprising the Harijans— is believed to be excluded from liberation from the cycle of rebirth because it is unworthy of such liberation. (Prabhushankara/Puttamma)

Upon his visit to the Harijans the *sangha* members of the community demanded that the Svami openly admit his *faux pas* and resign. In their eyes his behaviour was in every respect inconsistent with his office as spiritual leader of the community. Another part of the community, who had long hoped for some *aggiornamento,* defended the Svami by pointing to the fact that he paid the visit on his own prerogative and that he was not bound to account for it to his congregation.

On the surface it seems as if the conflict would never have arisen had Svami V. assured the *sangha* that he had approached the Harijans only as an autonomous *sannyasin.* This would have been nonsense, however, because the whole undertaking was based upon his acting officially on behalf of the total Madhva community. In doing so he manoeuvred the *sangha* into an impossible position, and not without political motives, as we have seen. We know how the conflict ended. Eventually Svami V. had to disavow his *démarché* and he had to state that he did not go to the Harijans on behalf of the Madhvas as a whole. The Svami was forced into complying, and so the incident was finally closed.

6 Conclusions

When we consider the explanatory value of Dumont's and Holmström's typologies in the light of our empirical findings we cannot help but conclude that they elucidate the matter only to a certain extent. Both models, which complement each other, proved extremely useful as points of departure, not only for the structure they provided, but also for their explanatory potential in our case.

At first sight, Dumont's model seems too structuralist to provide the explanations we need. It seems quite clearly to be an ideal typical model of a closed world-view in which all change is reduced to tiny ripples in an untroubled sea of eternal values. Besides, he sees religious change too much as an autonomous process which takes place outside of an historical context, in a 'void', so to speak. In spite of this drawback his typology will prove its worth in our final analysis.

Holmström's model certainly has many advantages over Dumont's, if only for the fact that he starts from the idea that religious change need not be an autonomous process. The problem with the Madhvas to our mind is not in the first place that they have an institutionalised devotionalism which has long been incorporated into their Brahmanical tradition, for that also holds for Holmström's *Shrivaishnavas.* The difficulty is that although we can analytically distinguish within the Madhva tradition "on the one hand a religion which consecrates the existing social order, values of submission and hierarchy, and a relativist morality of closed groups," and on the other hand, devotional religion, this devotionalism appears to acknowledge —even more strongly— exactly the same values.[5] This

---

[5] This assumption bears out Van der Veer's conclusions in his article on the *Ramanandis,* namely that devotionalism can easily associate itself with any value-orientation,

implies, in contrast to Holmström's case, that the Madhvas apparently lack
not only a tradition of social egalitarianism, but of religious egalitarianism
as well. As a consequence, we cannot assign to the *bhakti* tradition the
key role in our argumentation which Holmström was able to give to it in
his, precisely because in the case of the Madhvas it proves completely
irrelevant to distinguish between caste-religion and devotional religion in
order to account for a possible tendency towards religious change in the
direction of social egalitarianism. We are therefore inclined to conclude,
at least in our case, that such a tendency seems to have little to do with
the presence of devotionalism as such, but rather with favourable historical
circumstances which promote the proper conditions for a particular form
of religious organisation and outlook.

When we test the theories of Dumont and Holmström by comparing
them to our research we are led to the following observations. Besides
the fact (as appears from the historical development of their religion and
from the data we collected) that the Madhvas had never had an organisation which gave rise to a popular devotional movement advocating moral
universalism by incorporating the Dasa tradition, even the traditional
Madhva *bhakti* (being the institutionalised form of Dasa devotionalism)
stressing religious universalism was too encapsulated by the Madhva
Brahmanical religious system to contain viable egalitarian elements. We
noticed how rigid even today's Dasakutas still are, not only towards social
equality but even with respect to religious equality. This means that in
our case we fail to perceive a tendency by traditional *bhakti* to overflow
into moral universalism, or rather, we are unable to validate Holmström's
hypothesis on this point (Holmström 1971, 30) since Madhva devotionalism
met with an untimely silencing.

Although Dumont's and Holmström's models provide some structure
and clarity, they still leave us with the problem of how to account for the
fact that we found hardly any evidence of Holmström's "modern *bhakti*"
among the Madhvas. By "modern *bhakti*" Holmström means moral
universalism, or, alternatively, at least a general consensus about a collective positive attitude towards the Harijans, in accordance with Svami V.'s
views. Holmström's reply would be that Svami V. failed because the
sangha was never involved in a permanent dialogue of ideas which,
according to him (Holmström 1971, 30), was a condition for promoting and
warranting Svami V.'s initiative, viz., the *rapprochement* with the Harijans.
Our interpretation, on the contrary, would be that because the Svami's
visit implied more than a personal act of compassion —he had made the
entire community party to it— the most Brahmanical faction, the *sangha,*

---

whether hierarchical or egalitarian, depending on the historical situation (Van der Veer,
p. 682).

refused to be held accountable for the consequences this act could have for the total community.

What exactly were the consequences for which the *sangha* refused to be held accountable? It was in our opinion not the social consequences of Svami V.'s *rapprochement* with the Harijans but rather the religious consequences which they rejected. Our survey indicates a tendency towards social egalitarianism on the part of half of the community, but in the area of religion there is a tendency towards distinctions on the basis of caste and status. Most *sangha* members have learned to take practical circumstances into account. They have been induced into practising a kind of general, secular, and 'civil' egalitarianism. They were in fact the pioneers of a 'morality' which was individually expressed towards other low or outcaste individuals or towards collectivities for that matter, as a kind of concession to the concept of the secular state. They refused however to accept an imposed form of group-egalitarianism, a communal or collective equality which implied further consequences, social as well as religious, for the Madhva community as a whole. This was the kind of equality on which Svami V. had set his sights for whatever moral or political reasons he may have had, and which provoked the *sangha's* anger.

Contrary to what might be inferred from Holmström's study, it was not a rigid and uninspired traditional devotionalism which was at the bottom of the controversy, by not allowing an opening towards social egalitarianism. It was rather the attitude of Dumont's 'man-in-the-world' which clashed with the mentality of religious and social openness of his other ideal type, that of the 'renouncer'. To gain the advantage in the conflict, the Madhva 'man-in-the-world' used an equally stereotypical but no less effective weapon, that of purity connected to status. The greatest grudge the Madhvas were said to bear against Svami V. was not that he had appealed to the old *bhakti* egalitarianism which Madhva and his followers had espoused in his overture to the Harijans, but rather that he had defiled the Madhva community by allowing the Harijans to touch his feet and to decorate him with garlands, he who was seen as the very embodiment of Madhva purity and the symbol of the Madhva collective identity. Svami V. thereby set to nought the essence of Madhvahood, which qualified the Madhvas as a status group. He had not thereby transgressed the boundaries of his personal position as *sannyasin* but in the *sangha's* eyes he certainly had transgressed the established borders of his office as spiritual leader of the Madhva community.

Seen in this light we are inclined to view the whole conflict and the way it was settled —or rather side-stepped— as a device to confirm the new order of things, while at the same time every attempt was made to preserve the group's cohesion, in spite of an honest endeavour —however biassed— to level the caste barriers by resuscitating the old egalitarian message and referring to the experiences of the Dasas.

Bibliography

Anantha Murthy, U. R. *Samskara: A Rite for a Dead Man, A translation of U. R. Anantha Murthy's Kannada Novel,* by A. K. Ramanujan. Delhi: Oxford University Press, 1976.

Burg, C. J. G. v. d. "South Indian Urban Brahmins and Religious Adjustment." In D. C. Mulder, ed., *Secularization in Global Perspective.* Amsterdam: VU Boekhandel/Uitgeverij, 1981, pp. 67-111.

Dumont, L. "World Renunciation in Indian Religions." *Contributions to Indian Sociology* 4 (1960): 33-62.

Glasenapp, H von. *Madhva's Philosophie des Vishnu-Glaubens.* Bonn: Kurt Schroeder Verlag, 1923.

Harper, Edward B. "Ritual Pollution as an Integrator of Caste and Religion." In Edward B. Harper, ed., *Religion in South Asia.* Seattle: University of Washington Press, 1964.

Holmström, M. N. "Religious Change in an Industrial City of South India." *Journal of the Royal Asiatic Society* (1971): 28-40.

——. *South Indian Factory Workers: Their Life and their World.* Cambridge: Cambridge University Press, 1976.

Panduranga. *Shri Panduranga Vittala and Mukhya Prana Devara Sannidhi Souvenir.* Mysore, 1974.

Prabhushankara, S. and K. V. Putamma. "Letters to the Editor." *Madhvavijaya.* Bangalore and Mysore, 1975.

Rao, C. R. *Pujya Raghavendra Swamiji: His Life; A Brief Outline.* New Delhi, 1972, rpt. 1974.

Sharma, B. N. K. *Shri Madhva's Teachings in His Own Words.* Bombay: Bharatiya Vidya Bhavan, 1969.

Veer, Peter van der. "Taming the Ascetic: Devotionalism in a Hindu Monastic Order," *Man* (N. S.) 22 (1987) no. 4, 680-695.

Yuvaka. *Shri Madhva Yuvaka Sangha Silver Jubilee Souvenir.* Bangalore, 1970.

CHAPTER 15

Father Hugo Makibi Enomiya-Lassalle and Zen

Tilmann Vetter

In central Europe, Father Enomiya-Lassalle, s. j., is renowned for his books and training courses on Zen-meditation. He is a Christian of the monastic type, striving for perfection as prescribed by the great Fathers and Doctors of the Catholic church. Zen-meditation is commended by him as one of the best means to achieve this goal. He justifies this commendation by pointing to a long, but now nearly forgotten tradition of non-objective Christian meditation. However, he only adopts such Zen methods as do not cast doubts on the medievally static world-view sustaining this goal, i. e., a kind of Zen-meditation which, although it has no object, does presuppose a world of fixed structures in which one can strive for the elimination of moral faults and weaknesses through (a) meditation, (b) attainment of *satori* through meditation, and (c) repetition and intensification of *satori*. He disregards such Zen 'thought' as is represented by Zen-master Hui-neng and the tradition to which he belongs, in which meditation as a means to attaining *satori* and character building through repetition of *satori* has little place. This is in contrast to the attitude of most theologians who are engaged in theoretical dialogue with Japanese Buddhism and who see eminent possibilities for mutual understanding by (partially) adopting Zen dialectics (Hui-neng's tradition) and sharing the experiences which stem from this. Father Lassalle, though he apparently shares in some Zen experiences in a much more impressive way than such theologians, seems nevertheless to be prevented from fully understanding and experiencing other currents within Zen by his theoretical presuppositions.

This symposium is part of a research program devoted to interreligious encounter. The theme of sharing religious experience is limited, therefore, to the possibility of an adherent of one religious community (under these circumstances, we think primarily of a Christian) sharing an experience which is characteristic of another religious community.

That I, as a Buddhologist, was in a position to contribute to the symposium initially seemed obvious. An example also immediately came to mind, one which seemed most appropriate for illustrating the possibilities for expanding the horizon of Christian experience, that is, Father Lassalle's contact with Zen meditation.

Upon further consideration of this material, however, I began to have grave reservations as to whether I was indeed qualified to make a judgment on such a matter. After all, questions such as whether an actual sharing of the experience of another has been achieved, or whether one's own experience has been thereby enriched or endangered, would be better answered by those who are directly implicated. I can at best come to a conclusion by analyzing and comparing the statements of others.

It would have been lamentable, however, had Lassalle not been represented in some way at this symposium. It could never be altogether superfluous to again raise his experiment for review and discussion. I cannot, therefore, altogether avoid comment. Such is, after all, in part already entailed by the choice of material.

The following three points will be touched on: (1) the most important dates from the life of Father Lassalle, (2) his own justification for his attempt to integrate Zen meditation into Christian practise, and (3) a sampling of the discussion surrounding him.

1   Important dates from the life of Father Lassalle

For the following, I have relied on the curriculum vitae found in the *Festschrift* for Father Lassalle edited by Günter Stachel, and on the two contributions to it by Pedro Arrupe and Douglas V. Steere, as well as on the curriculum vitae found in Lassalle's own *Zen und christliche Mystik*.

Hugo Lassalle was born in 1898 in a village in Westphalia. In 1919 he entered the Jesuit order and was ordained as priest in 1927. He began work in Japan in 1929 and served as Superior of the local Jesuit mission. On August 6, 1945, he was injured at Hiroshima as a result of the dropping of the atomic bomb. In 1947, he began soliciting support in Japan and other countries for the building of a Peace Church in Hiroshima; on August 6, 1954, the church was consecrated. He received Japanese citizenship and took the name of Makibi Enomiya. In 1962 he accompanied the bishop of Hiroshima as a secretary to the Second Vatican Council.

He had his first contact with Zen meditation in 1943, which he renewed and intensified in 1956. He built a Zen exercise house in the environs of Hiroshima in 1960 and in the same year wrote his first book on the subject: *Zen — Weg zu Erleuchtung*. The book was initially charged with displaying heretical tendencies, but was cleared of these accusations during Vatican II. In 1968 Lassalle gave, for the first time in Europe, and primarily in monasteries, a course in Zen which lasted several days. Since then, every year or two he returns to Europe to hold Zen courses.

In his personal reminiscences, Pedro Arrupe refers first to the frustration of the Christian mission in Japan and then describes with great admiration how Lassalle strove "with all his strength and with the highest commitment to penetrate Japanese culture and to Christianize it from within" (Arrupe, 13). According to Arrupe, enculturation must not remain superficial: "It means learning and adopting the values of a specific culture in order to preserve their true value and absorb them into the Gospel, since all truly positive human values of a culture can merge with the Gospel without a loss of its unique beauty or its relation to transcendence" (Arrupe, 13). This must have been Arrupe's primary motive in permitting Lassalle —he was Lassalle's superior at the time— "to devote himself first and foremost to the study of Zen, regardless of the other classical and traditional apostolic work of the society, and subsequently to the broader task of relating Zen methods and their influence to the personal life and prayer of the Christian" (Arrupe, 17). This account evidences the notion that the Christian too might well benefit from such enculturation.

That notion, then, formed a second motive, and may even have been the primary motive for Lassalle. A comment made by Douglas V. Steere points in that direction (p. 29):

> Lassalle related how his Ignatian meditation, which he had conscientiously practised over a long period of time, had become routine and had proved no longer capable of reviving, renewing, and liberating his inner self, and how he had achieved a refreshing breakthrough in his prayer through practising Zen meditation.

Considering these two motives together poses no problem. Only a Christian who had undergone experiences equal to those of Zen and had been shaped by them would make any impact among the Japanese who are sympathetic to Zen. Only such a person would also be in a position to address those people (whether Japanese, European, or whatever) who are no longer satisfied with mere words and rituals. He was helped by the practice of Zen, and thus he is now able to help others through it.

2   Father Lassalle's own justification for the attempt to integrate Zen meditation and Christian practice

I have based the following section on two of Lassalle's books: *Zen und christliche Mystik* (1986), and *Zen-Meditation für Christen* (1987). For his statements on Zen, Lassalle appealed primarily to Sogaku Harada, the Zen master of the Hosshin Temple in Obama, with whom Lassalle had practised Zen for many years before Harada died in 1961. Master Harada belonged to the Soto sect but had first found enlightenment under a Zen master of the Rinzai sect, and subsequently combined the two streams. (1986, 36)

According to Harada, Zen meditation consists of three elements: the position of the body, breathing, and mental disposition (1986, 27; 1987, pp. 12-15). All those who participated in the Zen course had to assume the lotus or half-lotus position for a prescribed period of time and to focus on breathing. We will not pursue this matter further within the current context.

The mental disposition is designated as *munen muso* (without words and without thoughts). It is no nap, but rather a mental activity which is experienced as intrinsically worthwhile and which is at the same time the foundation for enlightenment *(satori)*, a form of intuition not sought by all practitioners.

To those who sought enlightenment, Master Harada gave a kōan (a paradoxical story from the tradition) as a means of concentration, which in each case was the same, the kōan of the nothing-character *(muji)*. We could relate this kōan as follows. When a monk once approached Chao-chou and asked him whether a dog possessed the Buddha nature, he bellowed a powerful *mu*, which means, 'nothing.' The practitioners were counselled not to concentrate on the Chinese character for 'nothing,' by which the call of Chao-chou was conveyed, nor to speculate on its content. Rather, they were advised powerfully to drive this *mu*, which was neither a 'yes' nor a 'no', deep into the lower abdomen by means of the rhythm of the breathing, and sometimes, as long as it did not disturb anyone, to say it aloud. (1986, 36-37)

This will suffice as a description of the Zen training undergone by Lassalle. We now turn to the question how he attempted to justify to the Christian reading-public the *Satori* which he sought and apparently also achieved by means of Zen, and which meant so much to his personal faith-life. The argumentation concerned takes two directions. First, he enlisted the many points of comparison from the history of Christian mysticism, and second, he gave a division of the various Zen methods, which had apparently been provided him by Master Harada.

Only very few of the many references to Christian mysticism provided by Lassalle will be considered here, namely, in abbreviated form, references to Clement of Alexandria, the Victorines, and *The Cloud of Unknowing*.

Clement held to the teaching that faith had to be supplemented by sight already in this life; one had to pass from heathenism to faith and then from faith to insight *(gnosis)*. Clement did not intend to imply that no one, not even those who had faith, could be saved without gnosis. In his view, however, no one could be a complete Christian without gnosis, since it was this insight which bestowed the strength to bear all manner of suffering and abuse. (1986, 268-269)

After a description of the teaching of the Victorines, Lassalle drew the following conclusion:

If one reflects on what has been said, one is amazed that some of the
Eastern methods of meditation are disapproved of by Christians because
they lack an object of contemplation. Even those who have only a
limited theoretical knowledge of Christian spirituality know that there is
a prayer of composure and rest, during which no object is reflected on.
There certainly is no Christian meditation in which God is not present,
or even excluded. But God can be there as object, or in union; consciously as the wholly Other, or unconsciously and 'undescribed.'
(1987, 46; cf. 1986, 287-300)

From *The Cloud of Unknowing*, which was probably written by an English
Carthusian, in the fourteenth century, Lassalle cited, among other things,
the following statements in order to show that his practice of Zen meditation was not fundamentally new or, as he expresses it in what immediately
precedes, a phenomenon specially restricted to the East, but something
rooted in human nature, which recurs in Western Christianity again and
again, and could without further ado be assigned a place within the
system of Saint Thomas Aquinas.

The *Cloud of Unknowing* recommends first meditating objectively.
"Nevertheless, it is proper for the man or woman who has practised this
type of meditation for a long time to relinquish it, pressing it deep down
into the cloud of forgetting and to keep it there if they are to penetrate
the cloud of unknowing which stands between them and their God" (1986,
pp. 314). And, "One gains little or no benefit in such endeavour by
meditating on the goodness and greatness of God, Our Lady, or the
angels and saints in Heaven" (1986, 315). A comparison with the use of
the *mu* recommended by Master Harada comes to mind at the *'Cloud's'*
following counsel: "If you are inclined to affectionately condense this
striving to a single word so that you might gain a better grasp, choose a
short word, with one syllable; that is better than one with two syllables,
for the shorter it is, the better it accords with the work of the Spirit."
(1986, 317)

We now turn to the second argument, an arrangement of the various Zen
methods which seems to make it possible to avoid the question concerning
the consistency of Zen and Christianity. This division (1986, 47-48, 229)
recognizes five Zen methods: (1) Bompu-Zen — the Zen of the common
people, of the 'child of the world;' (2) Gedō-Zen — the Zen of adherents
of non-Buddhist religions; (3) Shōjō-Zen — Zen of the Lesser Vehicle, for
those who have not yet come to believe that everyone is by nature a
Buddha, but have seen suffering and wish to overcome it; (4) Daijō-
Zen — Zen of the Great Vehicle, for those who practise Zen with the
firm conviction that they will find happiness in suffering; and (5) Saijōjō-
Zen — Zen of the Highest Vehicle, the Zen of the true tradition in
which it becomes clear that the All is the one Buddha-nature.

Christians who practise Zen belong to the second group. They may believe in a small, medium, or large 'I', in the human soul, the state, or God. Zen is only a psychological method which does not affect one's world view. It does, however, build character, and the more it is practised, the more character it builds. According to Master Harada, all five groups practise proper body position, proper breathing, and the proper 'non-thinking.' That sounds reassuring to Christians, who must take for granted that this scheme relegates them to an ancillary position with respect to the possible truth content of their world view. Christians themselves have long wielded the weapon of inclusivism, and reciprocation in kind poses little difficulty, accomplishing this in respect of Zen by maintaining that even the highest enlightenment still demands an even more eminent sequel in an experience of the personal God.

Although Father Lassalle also thinks that the enlightenment of Zen demands a sequel, he does not appear to feel downgraded by this scheme, making no attempt at a rejoinder, nor referring to the scheme again. It remains valid, however, in the sense that Zen as a psychological method can be practised by everyone. He is certain that 'non-thinking' does not essentially affect one's point of departure, but rather leads to its heightening through the experience of enlightenment (satori), achieved after a period of time. By repetition of such experiences, a person is transformed and made capable of great deeds.

If one considers the self-interpretations of Zen available elsewhere (especially in the Kyoto school), this appears to be an altogether too simple description of Zen. One must accordingly concede that when Zen is applied with a certain consistency, it considerably transforms, if not altogether destroys, concepts such as that of the person of God which are indispensable for the Christian. Generally speaking, however, Lassalle only takes from Zen what he can use, and which does not endanger his own faith. He thinks it possible to adopt just about everything from Zen as a spiritual method and he attributes that which is incompatible to Buddhist dogmas. We would like to follow him in this for the time being, and to consider what type of problems arise as a result.

For Lassalle, Zen, regardless of the fundamental beliefs which accompany its practice, leads all those who seriously practise it to enlightenment (satori) sooner or later. Characteristic of this experience is that it cannot be expressed. Nevertheless, it is susceptible to specific interpretations. For the Christian, according to Lassalle's own experience, it is the greatest conceivable heightening and strengthening of faith. Could it then be viewed as an experience of God, inasmuch as that is possible in this life? Lassalle feels that such a premise is not only justified, but indeed required (1987, 84). Since he recognizes degrees of satori, but no actual distinctions, he is inclined to attribute an experience of God even to the

Zen master. To be sure, the Zen master would refuse, on the basis of his dogmatic presuppositions, to conceive of *satori* 'dualistically;' nevertheless, *satori* per se would not be insusceptible to such an explanation.

'Experience of God,' however, is certainly the most extreme description permissible for *satori*. Such a predicate seems to confirm that God appears as the ultimate and absolute Truth in this experience, but not that God is a person, and certainly not that God is three persons (1987, 86). It must also be conceded that the experience of enlightenment is such that the Buddhist can describe it as impersonal. The indisputable fact remains, however, that Christians can feel greatly confirmed in their faith in God through this 'encounter with God.' (1987, 87)[1]

Lassalle's view could lead one to the conclusion that such confirmation also extends to the dogmatic constructions connected with faith in God. Then the impression created by the scheme of the five Zen methods would be borne out: the practice of Zen does not affect the presuppositions of one's world view, nor does it add anything to them; it simply improves character and perhaps strengthens the influence of those presuppositions.

In the pertinent pages of his book (1987) this issue appears to be less simple. Zen does not lead to a fundamentally different relation to reality than the one with which one began. It does, however, make this relation more profound, eliminating conceptions which are too anthropomorphic. The concept of person, therefore, cannot be so easily applied to *satori* interpreted as experience of God. Nevertheless, Lassalle is convinced that Christians are not in any way hindered by this experience from praying to God as a Father in Heaven (1987, 87). They only lose many of the naive conceptions which are usually associated with Him and gain the feeling that this experience has brought them somewhat closer to the Truth. "God is not a 'You' in the same way that a person is an 'I'. Conceptually speaking, His 'You' is infinitely removed from the human 'I', being boundless and beyond comprehension." (1987, 87)

Finally, it should also be mentioned that Lassalle sees no contradiction between this conception and the interpretation of *satori* current in Zen circles, i. e., that it is an immediate perception of the self (1987, 88). According to him, this does not inhibit the experience of God since the actual self is so rooted in the ground of all existence, which is God, that it cannot be perceived immediately and without reflection except in its relation to absolute being. One could add here that the followers of Zen are simply not completely aware of this. Here would lie an opportunity to recast their concept of *satori,* by means of the radical positions of Meister Eckhart, whom Lassalle esteemed highly. Zen adepts cannot,

---

1 See also "Erfahrungsberichte," in Stachel, 438-452.

however, be portrayed in this way as practising the imitation of Jesus Christ in the literal sense of the word.

3 A Sampling of the Discussion on Father Lassalle

The impression gained from reports on the work of Father Lassalle and from reading his writings is that his case is an instance of sharing the experience of another tradition which has been achieved to a considerable degree and which has proven itself fruitful for one's own faith life. Here we find a fruitful, albeit partial, dialogue at a practical level which does not bear the signs of futility which all too often adhere to the theoretical dialogue between Christian theologians and Zen 'theologians.'

It is, moreover, the Christian specialists in this dialogue who point out how partial is the sharing achieved by Lassalle. At the same time, they caution him not to endanger what is distinctly Christian and certainly not to surrender so naively to such experiences without at least having reflected on their legitimacy within the framework of a theoretical dialogue carried out at a high level and leading in the direction of a theology of religion.

Hans Waldenfels has offered an accurate assessment, in my opinion, when he implies in his contribution to the Festschrift (p. 409) for Lassalle that Lassalle did not represent the Zen school of Hui-neng (I would also add that of Dōgen). Hui-neng had refused to separate meditation as means from enlightenment as goal. Lassalle, however, does separate them (apparently in imitation of his Zen master). The means–goal thinking on the part of Lassalle is even more extensive than can be gathered from Waldenfels' comment. According to Lassalle, non-objective meditation should lead to enlightenment. There are, however, degrees of enlightenment. Through the repeated practice of meditation one must repeat and intensify enlightenment. In this way one's character is transformed. For the Buddhist scholar, Indian patterns of release and Sanskrit terms would spring to mind at this point. A method is implicitly present here by means of which one attempts to achieve and then to repeat (*bhāvanā*) a thorough apprehension (*abhisamaya*). In this way, all faults are eradicated and one's character is completely transformed.

Lassalle's is a less imposing mysticism than that of Hui-neng. Yet, when one considers the importance of character building, it is a sensible alternative. In any case, no one has yet overcome the tension between extreme mysticism and character building. Lassalle has climbed one mountain, and Waldenfels is pointing to another.

Waldenfels is also concerned about the possible loss of what is distinctively Christian in this undertaking. If one views this distinctiveness as a focusing on an historical event, something which has not always and everywhere been true of Christianity in the extreme measure that is the case today, then one might indeed have reservations. Yet without some form of compromise the undertaking is without promise. Waldenfels himself suggests such a compromise when he echoes an expression of W. Kaspers which describes faith as trusting and building on the power of God active in Jesus, and establishing a ground for existence in God. (p. 411)

For Waldenfels, this statement by Kaspers, along with a few others, forms the point of departure for ascending a mountain which to his mind rivals that of Hui-neng in its impressive beauty and yet remains distinct as a Christian asset. Furthermore, the connection with the historical event of God's revelation in Jesus is not overemphasized, yet it is here represented more adequately (Jesus' surrender is the paradigm for all surrender) than in Lassalle, who, whenever he actually does elaborate his Christian belief in connection with Zen, generally prefers to work with a cosmologically based portrayal of Christ.

Lassalle's theological background, when seen from this perspective, appears medievally static. Lassalle does not undertake an attempt at theoretical dialogue, but confines himself to using what he finds profitable in others. In this sense, he seems to linger far behind theologians who attempt to understand Zen, at least as this is presented by the representatives of the Kyoto school, and who by attempting to understand Zen as well to defend their own position have come upon a remarkable dialectic stimulated by their Zen counterparts. This seems to me to be the quintessence of what Jan van Bragt says at the end of his contribution to the Lassalle Festschrift. I will return to this briefly below.

It should first, however, be mentioned that Lassalle not only adhered to the traditional practice of Christianity in an uncomplicated manner, but also left intact its accompanying conceptuality. One can suspect his orthodoxy just as little or as much as that of the Fathers and Doctors of the Church, who adopted from the heathens what seemed profitable to them and posed no threat to their system. Moreover, Lassalle restricted himself to authorities on Zen who viewed Zen primarily as a method.

Many Christian theologians, however, have now progressed to the stage that they consider it unsatisfactory if they do not understand the other as he wants to see himself understood, and also if they do not endeavour to include what is most eminent in a movement (in the case of Zen, without a doubt, Hui-neng and what can be associated with his name). Difficulties in understanding are not simply eliminated by ascribing them to deficiencies in the other. One's own system can also be adjusted; if not for the sake of the other, then for the sake of the advantage which thereby accrues to one's own teaching.

What was mentioned above with regard to Waldenfels can be considered such an attempt, as can that which was said by Jan van Bragt in the Lassalle Festschrift (pp. 378-396), which I would now like to briefly consider.

Van Bragt presents for reflection in connection with a truly in-depth dialogue with Zen the hypothesis that religious reality is dialectically structured on three levels: (1) the level of the empirical self, the sphere of immediate affirmation of the world and of a God who stands in a too direct continuity with man; (2) the level of transcendence, of the true self and of the mystical intuition of the Whole, to which denial of the world and negative theology correspond; (3) the level of super-transcendence as return to the marketplace — the sphere of the Trinity, of the cross as unity of death and resurrection, and of the actual secularization of the true eccentric self.

According to Van Bragt, the Christian dynamic, which appears spread over (1) and (2), only finds its point of convergence in such a third level. And only at such a level can a convergence between Christianity and Zen be considered with full recognition of their respective distinctiveness. For Van Bragt it is evident that Christians can learn a great deal from Zen with respect to the second level. Christian religiosity too often remains at the first level. At the same time, he points out that Zen religiosity appears to him to be too narrowly reduced to the second level. The maxim 'Return to the Marketplace' often does not sound very convincing. That could be because Zen religiosity pays too little attention to the first level.

Dialectical structures are probably only convincing when they reflect a spiritual process in which one experiences as not unsalvageably lost something which formed an inevitable point of departure but had to be denied in the course of that process. That is, in general, not akin to Lassalle's manner of speaking. As we saw above (at the end of the second section), he does make statements justifying the expectation that he would not fundamentally oppose such a representation of matters, and that he would accept the hypothesis put forward by Van Bragt as a general framework. What we cannot expect of him, however, is complete participation in the mental processes which lie at the basis of Van Bragt's proposal and which must inevitably cast doubt on the logically unequivocal edifice in which his thought thrives. Such doubt, however, will be impossible to avoid if the dialogue continues to develop in this way. Yet up till now experience teaches us that one ought not fear for the essence of one's own tradition in the process, unless one attributes to certain words an absolute value. Those so fixated on the word, however, have invariably been confronted by quandaries.

Bibliography

Arrupe, Pedro. "Hugo Makibi Enomiya-Lassalle: Persönliche Erinnerungen." In Stachel, pp. 11-17.

Bragt, Jan van. "Tangenten an einem volkommenen Kreis?" In Stachel, pp. 378-398.

Enomiya-Lassalle, Hugo M. *Zen und Christliche Mystik.* 3rd edn. Freiburg im Breisgau: 1986 (1st edn., Zen-Buddhismus. Cologne: Bachem Verlag, 1966).

——. *Zen-Meditation für Christen.* 6th edn. Otto Wilhelm Barth Verlag, 1987. (1st edn. Bern: Scherz Verlag, 1968).

Stachel, Günter, ed. *Munen muso: Ungegenständliche Meditation. Festschrift für Pater Hugo M. Enomiya-Lassalle SJ zum 80. Geburtstag.* Mainz: Matthias-Grünewald Verlag, 1978.

Steere, Douglas V. "Enomiya Lassalle zum achtzigsten Geburtstag." In Stachel, pp. 29-33.

Waldenfels, Hans. "Christlicher Glaube und Zen." In Stachel, pp. 405-418.

** Michael von Brück has kindly contributed the following additional remark: Lassalle's thought and theological reflection on his own Zen experience shows significant development. In earlier works (1960–ca. 1975) he interprets Zen as a method to enhance religious experience which is presumed to be correctly understood in classical Christian theological tenets. A form of Christian personalism excluding any monistic interpretation of the Zen experience is seen as the highest standpoint (cf. *Zen-Buddhismus,* Köln, [2]1972, p. 398). Whereas he misconstrues the Buddhist concept of śūnyatā as a nihilistic view of reality in 1966, by 1975 he has modified his interpretation, clarifying the issue as follows: emptiness is liberation from conditioning with regard to the ego and its desires. The mental transformation achieved by *zazen* is explicated in his books, *Wohin geht der Mensch?* (1981) and *Leben im neuen Bewußtsein* (1986), as the advent of a new form of consciousness that all but transcends the dualistic structures of the traditional religions, including Christianity. It seems apparent that in the sixties Lassalle was eager to defend his practices towards watchful ecclesiastical authorities, whereas in the eighties he advocates a global change of paradigm, presented as a transrational form of consciousness, as an alternative to the rational reductionism marking recent human development (Jean Gebser).

For a more detailed discussion of Lassalle, cf. M. von Brück, "Christliche Mystik und Zen-Buddhismus: Synkretistisch Zugänge," in *Neu glauben? Religionsvielfalt und neue religioöse Strömungen als Herausforderung an das Christentum,* eds. W. Greive and R. Niemann, (Gütersloh: Gütersloh Verlagshaus, 1990), pp. 146-66.

CHAPTER 16

Transmitting the Buddhist View of Experience

Han F. de Wit

In this paper the concept of 'sharing religious experience' is discussed in terms of the Buddhist notion of transmission and in terms of two modes of experiencing reality. 'Transmission' does not refer to the act of sharing (an) experience but to the transmission of a way of being and experiencing. In Buddhist psychology 'experience' refers to the private product of our mental and sensory faculties. As a result of our lack of discriminating awareness we do not see to what extent our experience is the product of and relative to our own mental fabrications. The experience of this relative reality —the world as we think it to be— is therefore fundamentally the result of ignorance, which manifests itself in a solipsistic and egocentric reality distortion. The experience of absolute reality —things as they are— is based on clarity, which sees the emptiness of one's self-conceived experience. The traditional emphasis on the inseparability of these two contrasting modes of experiencing —experiencing absolute reality is seeing the emptiness (illusory or imaginary) of one's experience of relative reality— prevents us from misunderstanding absolute reality/truth to refer to a transcendental dimension. Some implications for interreligious dialogue are discussed.

1 Introduction

The question whether we can 'share' religious experience among practitioners of different creeds is an interesting one from a Buddhist perspective. Within the Buddhist tradition we would rather not use the once fashionable yet vague concept of 'sharing.' We would rather use terms like 'the meeting of minds' or 'transmission.' Transmission refers to pointing out certain qualities and modes of experience. Therefore, we will first address the issue of transmission.

Buddhists claim that their contemplative path provides a gradual way to clarify our conventional experience of life. The implication is that our moment to moment experience of life is somehow systematically distorted. This distortion results from a particular mental activity, which is referred to in terms of ignorance and confusion. Therefore, in Buddhism, the clarification of *experience* involves a clarification of the *nature of mind*.

This two-fold clarification leads to an enlightened way of experiencing and to the concurrent realization of the enlightened mind. We will therefore secondly need to discuss briefly the Buddhist view of mind and confusion.

Within the Buddhist traditions, the concept of 'experience' is used in a more specific way than we use the term. The Buddhist concept of experience is bound to a first person context; the experience that my sense faculties provide cannot be shared by your sense faculties and vice versa. However, creating a situation that affects the mind of the student in such a way that its concurrent mode of experience changes in the direction of the enlightened mode has been used by the lineage holders of many schools as an effective means of transmission. In order to refine our understanding of the term 'experience' in the context of transmission we will thirdly need to look into the 'contemplative psychology' of Buddhism.

In general, our approach to the topics mentioned above will not so much consist of a scholarly analysis of a particular choice of ancient Buddhist texts. Rather, we will draw upon the psychological understanding that we find among the living contemplative traditions of Buddhism, since this seems to be more fruitful for interreligious dialogue. In particular we will draw upon the contemplative tradition of Tibetan Buddhism. This contemplative tradition also calls itself 'three *yana* Buddhism,' which refers to the fact that it contains a coherent blend of the key notions from the three main schools of Buddhism — Theravāda (or Hīnayāna), Mahāyāna, and Vajrayāna.

2 Transmission

The Buddhist tradition is an ancient one. For over twenty-five hundred years its adepts have practised its contemplative disciplines and studied its particular view on human existence. In various ways they have transmitted what they themselves have understood and realized as well as the methods that are supposed to lead one to complete and perfect enlightenment. This transmission, however, always takes place within the context of a genuine teacher-student relationship. Buddhism is thus a living tradition with a great variety of schools in many different cultural settings. What binds this variety together is not so much a similarity of outer forms of religious practice, or study of the same texts —be it *sūtras* or *śastras*— but rather the inner understanding of the nature of one's experience and mind. Consequently the great variety of schools and traditions does not cause a 'problem' for most Buddhists regarding the nature of 'true Buddhism.' Rather it is viewed as an expression of the richness of the Buddhist teachings themselves and as an expression of the Buddha's skilful means or compassion.

Ultimately Buddhists do not trust in conceptual truth, but they care for the spiritual effectiveness of their concepts. The development of a multitude of Buddhist schools —which was also foreseen by the Buddha— in fact accommodates the different outlooks and lifestyles of human beings who enter upon the Buddhist path. Although there is a body of theories and texts common to almost all schools, it is seen as a means of transmitting a way of being and experiencing which is to be cultivated among its students. The texts do not possess an absolute status. They do not present the Truth. They are neither the word of God nor dogma, as is the case in the Western religions. They do not even have to be Buddha's words or *sūtras*. They might be —and often are— *śastras,* i. e., commentaries written by people who have realized and manifested Buddhist enlightenment at later times. This non-dogmatic approach to texts is somewhat similar to the Jewish tradition that views its religion as something unfolding through time, according to the circumstances and needs of its practitioners. We also find the same approach to certain texts in some of the contemplative traditions of Christianity (e. g., the unfolding through time of the Rules of the monastic orders).

Buddhists therefore can live peacefully with the fact that no clear-cut, overarching conceptual definition of their religion can be given. The Western mind is much more preoccupied with the concept of truth. We worry, and in the past have even physically fought, about the Truth and about who holds the Truth. Buddhists do not fight about the Truth. They worry about what can help sentient beings to see through their blindness and confusion which bring so much unnecessary suffering, and they ponder what would help human beings to discover and cultivate their own wisdom and compassion. Obviously, the study of texts and theories can be, and always has been, helpful as a means of transmission. One of the leading Tibetan Buddhist meditation masters, Chögyam Trungpa, remarks, "It is often mentioned in the Scriptures that without theories, without concepts, one cannot even start. So start with concepts and then build up theory. And then you use up the theory and it gradually gives way to wisdom, to intuitive knowledge, and that knowledge finally links with reality." (Trungpa, 22)

There is a well-known Buddhist metaphor, that of baking bread, which clarifies the Buddhist view on how transmission, or 'sharing,' of experience takes place. In order to bake a good loaf of bread one needs a recipe. The instruction in the contemplative disciplines and theories of Buddhism are like a recipe. The recipe can be very old, handed down from (or shared by) one generation to the next. However, in order to actually bake this bread one needs real, fresh flour, which comes from grain that has been grown recently in the fields. This grain might have developed slightly different qualities than the grain of the past. Some interplay between the use of the ancient recipe and the use of the fresh flour needs to take place. The flour refers to our personal life experience and way of being. Baking the bread is like travelling on the Buddhist path. In this process the actual transmission takes place. Then, finally tasting the bread is like realizing that one's way of experiencing has in fact become closer to, or the same as, that of the Buddha. One shares the mind of the Buddha.

This metaphor also shows in what sense the Buddhist path is both new and old; the recipe is old, but the baking of the bread has to be done with our experience, as it has ripened up to the present. The metaphor also indicates the personal quality of the process. We have to bake our own experience, so to speak, if we want to actually share the Buddhist way of experiencing reality. The only way to really share, little by little, the enlightened way of experiencing is by cultivating one's own mind through the practice of meditation, thus working through one's own blindness and harshness. To the extent that we have done so, we develop a personal realization of how an enlightened attitude tastes. This personal involvement also appears to be necessary for any genuine sharing of religious experience between people of different creeds. The recipe can readily be shared , but the bread —the experience— cannot be shared so readily or directly. One needs to practice the contemplative disciplines of the (other) tradition to some extent in order to make a connection with the experience to which it refers. Then some recognition can take place. This recognition is not just conceptual, not just a purely intellectual act, but rather a contemplative one, a tasting of each other's way of being. On that basis, a meaningful dialogue can develop about the recipes that different traditions offer (e. g., Walker).

3 A general Buddhist view on experience

The Buddhist concept of experience is closely related to the idea of a path. In fact, the Buddhist notion of a contemplative path refers to the gradual development of one's way of being and experiencing. This development has stages. Each stage has its own view and mode of experiencing one's life. Through travelling on this path, the mode of experience of ordinary beings is gradually transformed into the mode of experience of the enlightened ones.

The fundamental characteristic of all stages on the path towards enlightenment is that they are permeated in various degrees by ignorance or confusion and by an egocentric psychology based on that ignorance. There are many sophisticated theories about how ignorance and confusion come about (e. g., Vasubandhu). However, I will only discuss the basis of ignorance and confusion here. The basis is a mode of experience that is fragmented in some way. This mode is called '*vijñāna*' in Sanskrit which is often translated as 'consciousness,' that is the consciousness of ordinary human beings. Within *vijñāna* we conceptualize our experience dualistically in terms of 'me' and 'other.' Not being aware of this dualistic mode of experience, we mistake our self-conception and our world-conception for realities. When we begin to direct our actions on behalf of and towards these self-conceived 'realities.' This obviously leads to suffering, against which we in turn attempt to protect our self-conceived self in our self-conceived world. The confused mode of experience leads to the ordinary experience of life that unenlightened beings share with each other. In order to discuss the enlightened mode of experience, we need to make the meaning of terms like 'mode of experience' and 'ignorance' more precise. The contemplative psychology of Buddhism provides a helpful context for that.

4 Buddhist psychology of experience

According to the *abhidharma*, i. e., the contemplative psychology of Buddhism, the field of experience that human beings live in results from the interplay of six sense faculties. These sense faculties are the five external sense faculties of sight, sound, smell, taste, and touch, plus the sixth, internal sense faculty of mentation. In much the same way that our faculty of sight has form and colour as its field (or object, if you like), so this sixth faculty has as its field most of our mental activities; our thoughts with their particular emotional colour and intensity, our memories, expectations, dreams, ideas, fantasies; in short, whatever can be thought of, whatever plays in the mind. William James called this internal field, 'the stream of thought,' because it is in a constant state of flux.

As the fields of the external sense faculties are in a state of flux as well, we could also speak of the 'stream of external experience.' These streams merge together into one's moment to moment experience of reality. We could call this experience '*personal reality*,' since its content is dependent on our own internal and external sense faculties. For instance, someone might be walking towards us. You might see your good friend John approaching whereas I might see a stranger. The contribution of our internal faculty merges unnoticed with the contributions of our external faculty. Your good friend and my stranger are a reality to you and me respectively; you see John and I see a stranger. We are not lying; our experience is simply different. This indicates that our overall experience of reality, our personal reality, is somehow relative. It is relative to you and to me, and at the same time true to you and to me.

This 'relative reality' or 'relative truth' is called *'saṃvṛti-satya'* in Sanskrit, which literally means 'all dressed up reality/truth.' Dressed or covered up by what? By the products of our sixth sense faculty. Our mental faculty has the capacity to fill up any experience with whatever our mind has in store. The stream of thoughts that our mental sense faculty produces is a kind of running commentary on our experience, which at the same time fuses *with* our experience. This running commentary does not just consist of discursive thoughts, but also of images, emotional qualities, and whatever can be thought of. From a practical or psychological point of view, the confluence of the products of our six faculties *is* our reality, even though it is made up or dressed up by us, because it is *all we have*. There is nothing to be experienced outside of this overall experience.

5 The nature of ignorance and confused experience

Within our overall experience there is usually no awareness of the individual contribution of each sense faculty. That is why the noise of a car passing by can give us the experience of a car passing by. The same type of non-awareness usually happens when the contribution of our internal faculty merges with the contributions of our external faculty. Not being aware of the contribution of our internal mental faculty, you and I both experience the approach of your good friend and of a stranger as a reality, and we are unable to see to what extent our reality is relative; we tend to see things and events in the external world around us that actually originate from our mental activity. The dressing that is internally produced is experienced by us as qualities of the external world. Herein lies, according to the Buddhist analysis of experience, the origin of our ignorance and confusion.

Let me give another example to show how deeply this confusion permeates our experience. Imagine or visualize a red dot in your mind. Now imagine this red dot moving and settling down on the top of the page you are reading. Does this imaginary dot exist on the page or in your mind? Is it outside or inside your mind, or both, or neither? If it is inside of your mind, what is the difference then between imagining a red dot inside of your mind and imagining a red dot on top of the page you are reading? If it is on the paper why can only you see it? And how much more that you assume to experience outside of your mind is in fact as much or as little outside as this red dot? If this dot is both inside and outside your mind there are two red dots, but you imagined only one. If it is neither, where else can this imagined red dot be? The difficulty in answering these questions shows the depth of our ignorance. It shows how hard it is to discern the dressed-up quality (our mental contribution) in our experience. In particular, when your six sense faculties and mine produce more or less the same stream of experience, which seemingly makes us share the same relative reality, it becomes even more difficult for us to discern the relative aspect of our experience and the extent of our confusion. When you see this delightful person, your good friend John, does he exist in your mind or outside of it, in the external world? Can we answer these questions univocally or do they actually point to our confusion? Let us have another look into the nature of confusion, from a slightly different perspective.

The English phrase, 'the world as we know it,' referring to the world as we think it to be, is an interesting way to refer to what we have called our self-conceived relative reality. The opposite could then, in Buddhist terms, be called 'absolute reality' or 'the world as it is,' which we will explore in more detail below. Obviously, the world as we know it need not be the same as the world as it is. According to various Buddhist schools, the nature of our confusion is that we confuse the world as we know it with the world as it is. In other words, the nature of our confusion is that we mistake our relative reality for absolute reality.

We have to be careful here, for how is the Buddhist concept of absolute reality to be understood? The Sanskrit name for absolute reality or truth, *paramārtha-satya,* literally means something like 'reality/truth *(satya)* in the highest *(parama)* sense *(artha).*' This evaluative definition is not very helpful. Another somewhat more descriptive contemplative term to refer to absolute reality is tathata, which is the Sanskrit term for 'thusness,' or 'things as they are,' or, in our phraseology, 'the world as it is.' Clearly, if we mistake our relative reality for something that is not, we do not see our relative reality as it is. That gives us an indication of how we should understand absolute reality. If we see our self-conceived reality as it is —to wit, as self-conceived— then we see it as it is is and no longer confuse it; then we can see things as they are, i. e., absolute reality. Absolute reality and relative reality are thus inseparable, as it is traditionally said. 'Seeing one (thing as it is) is seeing all' is a Buddhist saying which refers to the fact that our self-conceived relative reality, when seen as it is, has the same quality as absolute reality. As we shall discuss below, absolute reality is also called 'emptiness' *(śūnyatā)* in Mahāyāna Buddhism because it is empty of our fixation on, and belief in, the reality of our self-conceived world.

6 The content of confused experience

In what way does the world as we know it differ from the world as it is? In the world as we know it there are, roughly speaking, things we believe to be there which are not, and things we believe are not there which are in the world as it is. This lack of realism leads to the suffering and anxiety that are inherent to relative reality. When we react to suffering and anxiety with further mental fabrications in an attempt to mentally reshape our self-conceived reality in a less painful direction, we in fact increase our confusion and pain. We move in self-perpetuating circles. This is why our relative reality is also called 'saṁsāra' in Sanskrit, which literally means 'going round.' It is said that saṁsāra is endless; when we try to escape it by attempting to go in a less painful direction, we actually extend saṁsāra into that direction. Why is this so? It is because our attempts are performed in and against our world as we believe it to be.

According to all living Buddhist schools, the crucial difference in content between absolute and relative reality is this: the experience of relative reality, or saṁsāra, is permeated by a particular concept — the concept of 'I' or 'ego' (ātman). Our attempts to maintain this concept in our mental stream and to hold on to it as if it were a reality, permeates each and every aspect of our ordinary experience. The concept of 'I' blends almost incessantly with our stream of experience.

The experience of absolute reality, however, is free from the influence of this concept, for in it the concept of ego has been exposed as having no substance or reality at all. In the enlightened mode of experience there is no 'I' as the beholder or subject of our ongoing experience. Ego does not exist in our experience as it is, it only exists as an illusion in our conceptualized experience, i. e., in our world as we know it. So the experience of absolute reality is the fruit of a state of mind that has realized the ego-less (anātman) mode of experiencing. This realization amounts to the total emptying or transparency of all egocentric concepts and attitudes. Having seen in one's own stream of experience the illusory nature of ego, relative reality or saṁsāra is extinguished and absolute reality, called nirvāṇa ('extinction'), is experienced.

We should, however, be careful not to think of saṁsāra and nirvāṇa as two separate realities. Both terms refer to one and the same reality experienced under two different modes — the egocentric mode of experience and the ego-less mode of experience, respectively.

7 The psychology of ego in Buddhism

As we saw above, our ordinary mode of experience not only creates a solipsistic world —the world as I know it— but also an egocentric one. Within this world, experience becomes experience-to-me. Out of this the psychology of ego develops, which has as its main theme how 'I' relates to the phenomenal world. The basic emotions in this psychology of ego-maintenance are passion (raga), aggression (dvesa) and delusion (moha). These three egocentric emotions are called poisons (klesa) because they poison our minds and lead to such action strategies as indulging oneself, fighting for oneself, and the egoism of ignoring what is not of interest to oneself. The world one sees through the veil of one's mistaken belief in ego and through the veil of egocentric emotionality is again the world of suffering, *saṁsāra*. Because we share this psychology, the poisons begin to look like a universal and inescapable aspect of human nature. Ösel Tendzin (p. 1) remarks: "As human beings, we spend most of our lives believing in a myth. We have heard that it is human nature to be bound by anger and fear, hatred and jealousy. We have heard all our lives that it is 'only human' to take care of ourselves first. Although it is extremely painful to think of ourselves in such a negative way, it is convenient to believe in that myth. At some point or other, most of us just shrug our shoulders and say, 'that's the way it is.' For although we often feel ashamed of ourselves and our fellow human beings, we feel helpless to change what seems to be inevitable."

According to the Buddhist, view the egocentric way of life transcends cultural and social boundaries. It characterizes the life experience of almost all human beings in all societies. This is so because human beings give their concept of ego some sense of reality by identifying certain aspects in their *actual* stream of experience as 'me' and 'mine'. Since our experience changes all the time we need to constantly shift around in order to reestablish our sense of 'I'. According to Buddhist psychology, our sense of 'I' is constantly shifting over five areas in our changing field of experience, called *skandhas* in Sanskrit. Loosely speaking, these five areas are physical form (in particular one's body), sensation, perception, mental formation (i. e., thought or what goes on in one's mind), and consciousness.

Let me give a few examples of this shifting sense of ego. For some of us our glasses or our car are part of 'me' when we use them, but not when we don't. A child bumps his knee against the door and says, "I am hurt, but I don't care." Are the two 'I's' in this sentence referring to the same 'I'? Does his knee not care or did the 'I' who turned out not to care bump against the door instead of the knee? Or when I say, "I was afraid my anger would overwhelm me," do I identify myself with the fear or with the anger? Do the labels 'I', 'my', and 'me' refer to the same entity in this sentence? If ego was a solid, permanent entity, this shifting would not take place. That is why Buddhism states that although we seem to experience something that we call 'I', there exists no solid entity 'I'. There is only an acquired mental activity which picks out certain aspects of the flow of experience one moment at a time as the reference for the concept of ego.

Having first anchored our sense of 'I' in aspects of our experience, we then begin to dress up this illusory entity with all kinds of ideas.

These ideas form what can be called our 'self-image.' This self-image is 'me as I (have come to) know it' that lives in the world as I know it. It is who I hold myself to be. The self-image is in turn a mental formation with which we can identify our 'I'. We then become our self-image. In that case, we feel that whoever praises or scorns our self-image praises or scorns us. When we identify with our body, our physical self-image comes along. If somebody belittles or glorifies our body at such a moment, we feel belittled or glorified. When we identify our ego with a particular emotion, our self-image of who we are emotionally follows in its wake. Then we will defend 'ourselves' when someone goes against our emotion or against the emotional self-image that we identify with.

I do not need to elucidate how much pain one's mental activity creates for oneself and others by maintaining the illusion of ego and its poisonous emotions. Also, it is clear how deeply one's belief in the reality of ego as defined above distorts one's experience of reality. Just as our mental activity can conceive of goblins, devils, angels, and gods as our permanent companions in life, which then become powerful rulers of our emotions and actions, so our mental activity creates ego and its psychology. Ego becomes our most intimate companion, and begins to rule our lives.

As we saw, it is easy —it seems even unavoidable to us— to share the egocentric experience of *saṁsāra* with each other, but can we share —even partly— the ego-less experience of *nirvāṇa* or ultimate reality? If so, how?

8   Meditation: the clarification of experience

As a famous sixteenth century meditation master once said, "The essence of Buddhist doctrine reveals that only by understanding the mind through meditation can one achieve insight into ultimate reality" (Takpo Tashi Namgyal, 6). The process of clarifying one's stream of experience through the practice of meditation refers to the clarification of one's experience of relative or dressed up reality, for that is the experience that we actually have on hand. The Buddhist contemplative practices provide a means by which to sort out our personal confusion of holding the world as we know it for the world as it is. As the quote above shows, this clarifying process is not merely an intellectual one but rather one which involves an intimate and immediate exploration of our ongoing stream of experience through the practice of meditation. In particular, it is an exploration of what our mental faculty does from moment by moment to the next to the products of the other sense faculties. Although this exploration is mainly carried out through the practice of meditation, it is usually supported by other contemplative disciplines that pertain to letting go of our self-interest in our conduct in life. I cannot elaborate on the techniques of meditation here, but I would like to point out its contemplative psychological function.

Buddhist meditation is a means of cultivating an awareness that can discriminate the contribution of our mental sense faculty from the contributions of our external sense faculties. This discriminating awareness, called *prajñā*, sees through any mentally fabricated illusion, imputation, or self-deception about reality. The issue is not so much one of *removing* our illusions, but seeing their true nature, that is seeing them *as they are*, that is, as illusions. In that way our experience of reality becomes purified. Thus the purifying process does not imply that our thoughts about experience need to be discarded or suspended. There is nothing wrong with thoughts or thinking as such. There is, however, something wrong with being taken in by them as a result of not seeing their true nature. Through the continuous practice of meditation we gradually begin to overcome our fixation on the content of our thoughts, which provides us with room to see them in a pure way; we begin to see our thoughts about our experienced reality *as they are*; they are not the experience they are about. Conversely, we begin to see the qualities of phenomenal reality as they are; they are not contained in the concepts we have about them. Our conceptual labels turn out not to hold 'water' or reality, so to speak.

Generally, through the practice of meditation, our discriminating awareness begins to expand and to cut through both our grasping of our thoughts as real, and therefore through our fixation on the world as we know it. That is, this awareness begins to cut through ego and its psychology.

Development in meditation has, of course, stages. Each stage has its particular realization in the form of a further clarification of one's egocentric and self-created experience of reality, which is concurrent with the gradual realization of egolessness. Through realizing complete egolessness, the illusion of ego and its psychology of passion, aggression, and delusion finally collapses. The tendency to see every experience as good, bad, or irrelevant to *me* drops away. *Saṁsāra*, the world that ego lives in, turns into *nirvāṇa*; the phenomenal world now appears in the space of egolessness.

Before we look into the question of whether the ego-less mode of experience, which makes us see the absolute reality of the phenomenal world, can be transmitted or 'shared' in some way, we need to discuss absolute reality in a little more detail.

9 Śūnyatā: the experience of absolute reality

For the contemplatives of the Mahāyāna schools of Buddhism, the notion of śūnyatā, which is often translated as 'emptiness,' is not so much a philosophical idea, but primarily a practice-related concept. The term śūnyatā refers to absolute reality from a particular perspective, that of relative reality. This perspective is useful as a pointer to how the practitioner, while living in the world as one knows it, can enter into the world as it is. The concept of śūnyatā is used as a means to speak about nirvāṇa in saṁsāra.

From the point of view of saṁsāra, absolute reality can only be defined negatively, as emptiness. From its own point of view, however, that is, from the point of view of nirvāṇa, absolute reality can be defined positively as tathatā — suchness, things as they are or luminosity. Absolute reality is not empty of itself but empty of relative reality, or as it is said in the Shentong school (e. g., Tsultrim Gyamtso) of the Mahāyāna: emptiness (i. e., absolute reality) is not empty of itself but empty of other (i. e., relative reality).

As a practice-related concept, śūnyatā indicates that something in our conventional mode of experience needs to be emptied or seen as empty. What is it? The notion of emptiness refers to the fact that our conceptual labels do not touch reality. We can both say that our concepts are empty of absolute reality and that absolute reality is empty of our concepts. Our conceptual labels are our own invention and when they are used to conceive of our experience they lead to conceptualized experience, that is, they lead to the world as one knows it, or rather to the world as one thinks it to be. Seeing the emptiness of one's conceptualized experience can be compared to seeing the terrifying view of a tiger turn into emptiness when it is seen to be a paper tiger. There is no tiger and our conceptualized experience of a tiger is empty of reality. There is no experience of 'no tiger' either, as one cannot experience something that is not there.

So 'emptiness' or 'things as they are' or 'absolute reality' refer to our moment to moment experience as it appears when we have completely cut through our ignorance and confusion, which stem from, and centres around, our holding on to the illusion of ego. Therefore, saṁsāra and nirvāṇa both refer to our experiential world. They both refer neither to a non-experiential or transcendental reality, like (a hidden) God, nor to a reality that is in some way separate from our experience. There is no such religious experience involved in travelling the Buddhist path towards enlightenment.

However, there is the experience of great clarity and joy when the mysterious nature of one's confusion is finally and totally unravelled. In the wake of such an experience, unconditional compassion for those who are drowning in the ocean of *saṁsāra* spontaneously arises. When one has cultivated the meditative discipline which leads to seeing the nature of one's mind through continuous effort, we can also see how our mind moves in the direction of either *saṁsāra* or *nirvāṇa* each moment. However, at this point, there is as little need to guard one's mind against going towards *saṁsāra* as there is a need to guard oneself against a paper tiger. Moreover, the guarding of *nirvāṇa* has become irrelevant as well. There is no longer a conflict or separation between *saṁsāra* and *nirvāṇa*. Painstakingly and at the same time effortlessly maintaining one's discipline of mindfulness and awareness is enough. Through such discipline the emotional and behavioral energy of one's conventional egocentric way of being turns into the compassionate qualities and actions of a Buddha. The desire and skill to liberate all beings who live in the confusing and painful world of *saṁsāra* becomes one's only lasting motivation, inspiration, and joy in life.

10 Some conclusions for interreligious dialogue

Our first conclusion is that, from a Buddhist point of view, there is no particular difficulty in sharing relative reality, since we all live in that reality. It is, in fact, more difficult not to share it, for it is the world as we know it —the world we talk about, hear about, gossip about, get excited about— the world that concerns 'me'. This world might be dressed up by all kinds of ideas: stupid ones and intelligent ones, materialistic ones and religious ones, philosophical ones and even Buddhist ones. All these ideas or concepts enter into our stream of experience and provide us with relative reality. These concepts might point towards or away from a more enlightened mode of experience. Although these concepts can to some extent be communicated in interreligious dialogue, they certainly do not contain the enlightened mode itself.

Secondly, the way to share or transmit the enlightened mode of experience is by actively engaging in the practice of meditation. Does that need to be Buddhist meditation? Not necessarily. Generally, it can be any contemplative practice as long as its aim is to clarify one's mind and one's moment to moment life experience. It can be any particular practice as long as it aims at seeing through the illusion of ego and at dismantling one's egocentric and solipsistic experience of reality. If we do not want to let go of our ego, there is no way to share even a glimpse of what Buddhists mean by absolute reality.

Interestingly, the need to let go of one's ego in some sense or other is a theme we find in almost all great religions (see De Wit 1987, 128; 1991). Holding on to ego, or to an egocentric mode of experience, appears to be a general religious concern. Therefore, we can safely say that inasmuch as a non-Buddhist realizes egolessness in his personal life and way of being, to that extent he shares his way of experiencing with the experience that Buddhists practitioners aim to develop. From the Buddhist point of view, any spiritual discipline that leads to the realization of egolessness makes it possible to share what Buddhists mean by *śūnyatā*. This kind of sharing is more than an intellectual matter. It needs to be based on actual contemplative practice by those involved in interreligious dialogue (e. g., Walker).

Finally, we should keep in mind that the Buddhist notions of absolute and relative reality *both* refer to our actual moment to moment experience of the phenomenal world as it appears under the ego-less and egocentric mode of experience respectively. Nether of these two notions refers to a transcendental principle. This is known as 'the indivisibility of the two truths' and it is central to the Buddhist understanding of the two truths. Obviously this has implications for interreligious dialogue, particularly when we explore the relationship between the concepts of a transcendental God and *śūnyatā*. Whatever concept of God or emptiness we might employ, in Buddhism there is no religious experience *of* God; there is, strictly speaking, not even an *experience of* emptiness or of *śūnyatā*. Ultimately there is only the *experience of reality*, void of or free from any belief in the reality of the fabrications of once's conceptual mind.

Bibliography

De Wit, H. F. *Contemplatieve Psychologie*. Kampen, 1987.
——. *Contemplative Psychology*. Pittsburgh, 1991. (forthcoming)
Kochumuttom, T. A., ed. *A Buddhist Doctrine of Experience*. Delhi, Patna, 1982.
Takpo Tashi Namgyal. *Mahamudra: The Quintessence of Mind and Meditation*. Boston, 1987.
Tendzin, Ösel. *Buddha in the Palm of your Hand*. Boston, 1982.
Trungpa, Chögyam. *Meditation in Action*. Boston, 1969.
Tsultrim Gyamtso Rimpoche. *Progressive Stages of Meditation on Emptiness*. Oxford, 1986.
Vasubandhu. In T. A. Kochumuttom, ed.
Walker, S. *Speaking of Silence*. New York, 1987.

CHAPTER 17

Can Śūnyatā Be Shared?
Religious Experience in Dialogue

H. Waldenfels

Can you share *śūnyatā*? My answer to this question is quite simply 'yes.'
Being a Western scholar, however, the simple answer 'yes' will most probably
not satisfy the Western intellect. We ask for further explanations, reasons,
and arguments. We seek first of all explanations of why and how such an
experience is possible, and, second, whether it can be a shared. At the
same time we realize that if we start by giving an argument, this threatens
not to lead to the immediate experience of sharing but rather to a discussion
about experiences: An experience I have undergone before, or an experience
I would like to have, or an experience someone else has had, or an experience I have heard or read about — there are a lot of possibilities. The sole
question is: Does a dialogue about sharing really lead to a sharing of
experience or rather to non-experience?

1 The Question of Approach

Engaging in dialogue means sharing with words. Yet standing before a
classic statue or image of the Buddha, we see him silent and smiling,
blissfully seated in the lotus position. Recall here the famous *Vimalakīrti
Sūtra*, which deals with the problem of how to meditate. Since meditation
seems to be the way to the experience we would like to deal with here,
teaching the way of meditation can be understood as teaching the experience. And since only an experienced person is able to introduce such an
experience, teaching is itself a way of sharing the experience.

In Chapter 3 of the *Sūtra* Śāriputra relates how Vimalakīrti elucidated
the proper way to meditate:

> As I was sitting in the forest under a tree in quiet meditation, Vimala-
> kirti approached me and said: "To sit is not necessarily to meditate.
> Not to reveal the body in the three worlds (of lust, form, and form-
> lessness), that is meditation. Not to rise up from concentration in which
> the inner functions are extinguished and yet to conduct oneself worthily,
> that is meditation. Not to abandon the way of the teaching and yet to
> go about one's business as usual in the world, that is meditation. Not

203

to allow oneself to be bothered about all sorts of possible bad intentions but rather to practice the thirty-seven aids to enlightenment, that is meditation. Not to cut (off) disturbances and yet to enter nirvāṇa, that is meditation. Anyone who sits thus in meditation receives the seal of the Buddha."

At the end, Śariputra is "speechless and unable to bring himself to answer" (cf. Dumoulin, *Zen* I, 50). In Chapter 9, Mañjuśrī, the *bodhisattva* of wisdom, asks the assembly of *bodhisattvas* what it means that a *bodhisattva* enters the realm of non-duality. After many attempts, Mañjuśrī himself finally replies:

In my view, there is nothing to say about all things, nothing to explain, nothing to show, nothing to know. Cut off from all questioning and answering — this is to enter into the doctrine of non-duality.

Here again Vimalakīrti is asked for his opinion. However —the text continues— "Vimalakīrti remained silent and spoke not a word." For this the *bodhisattva* of wisdom praised him saying:

"Well done, well done! No signs, no words — this is indeed to enter into the doctrine of non-duality." (Dumoulin, *Zen* I, 51)

Such spurning of words calls to mind another famous text in the Chinese Kōan collection *(Mumonkan 6)* where the Buddha holds a flower in his hands and shows it to the assembled monks:

At that time all were silent. Only the Venerable Kāśyapa changed his face into a smile. The Tathāgata said: "I have the true Dharma-eye, the wonderful spirit of Nirvāṇa, the formless true form, the mysterious Dharma-door which does not rely on words and letters, a special tradition outside of scriptures. This I entrust to the Mahākāśyapa." *(Mumonkan*, p. 52)

As a matter of fact, dealing with the innermost Buddhist experience means dealing with an experience beyond words. How, then, we might ask, can we share this experience in words?

2 *Śūnyatā*

The experience which we would like to share is called the experience of *śūnyatā*. In other words, the experience has a name which attempts to name that which —in view of the aforementioned stories— excludes a name. It calls to mind the opening of the *Tao te ching*:

The way that can be spoken of
Is not the constant way;
The name that can be named
Is not the constant name.

> The nameless was the beginning of heaven and earth;
> The named was the mother of the myriad creatures.
> (p. 101)

The problem is how we can avoid destroying the experience of the unnameable and unspeakable by naming it and speaking of it. For when we call an experience by a name, we seem to distinguish and separate this experience from other experiences. 'Non-duality' —using the key-word given by Vimalakīrti— is then destroyed.

We can find some aid through observation of the various interpretations and translations the term *śūnyatā* is subject to in various languages.

> Etymologically, the Sanskrit word derives from the root *śvi* meaning 'to swell.' The idea of swelling was then further tied to that of hollowness. "Something which is 'swollen' from the outside is 'hollow' inside." This relationship is made still clearer by the fact that the mathematical symbol for zero was originally none other than the symbol for *śūnyatā.* The root word can be shown to extend still further into the Indo-germanic realm in such Greek words as *kyō* (to become pregnant) and *koilia* (the body cavity, the inside of man), as well as in the Latin words *cumulus* (heap), *caulis* (stem), and *cavus* (cave). (Waldenfels, *Nothingness,* 19)

Turning to the Japanese translation of the term, which reached the Far Eastern islands via Chinese translations and characters, we encounter a different imagery. *Kū*, which is the Japanese rendering of *śūnya* and *Śūnyatā* respectively, stands for

> the vast and empty, to be empty, emptiness in the positive sense as radical openness; air, sky, heavens, space, void, emptiness, vacancy, vanity, vacuum, *śūnyatā.* (Waldenfels, *Nothingness,* 65)

Rather misleading is the European translation of *(absolute) nothingness,* although in first instance total negation, the radical *no* or *non-* appears to create the open and empty space which apparently is needed if *śūnyatā* is to be experienced. Nevertheless, two matters stand in the way of a positive evaluation of this European translation: (1) *Nothingness* is a negative term which excludes any positive content and meaning such as good and true, and (2) *absolute nothingness* in a Western context includes an abstract connotation and excludes any reference to anything concrete.

Nevertheless, some undercurrents of Western spiritual traditions and thought show a degree of affinity with a totally negative manner of speaking as a way of mediating an unnamed reality which cannot be spoken of: the ways of *negative philosophy* and *theology.* For this reason, Asian thinkers, Buddhists as well as Hindus, refer rather often to the Rhenanian mystics such as Master Eckhart and others, or to the famous Spanish mystics Teresa of Avila and John of the Cross. H. Dumoulin and H. M. Enomiya-Lassalle have gone even further, returning to the ascetic and spiritual teaching of the Church Fathers and medieval theology. (cf. Dumoulin, *Meditation*; Enomiya-Lassalle, 261-453)

Returning to the term *śūnyatā* we ought to add a few more remarks:

1. *Śūnyatā* meaning an *emptiness* like the womb of a mother or like an open sky or —in view of the 10th station of the famous Ox-herding Pictures— like open empty hands, does not describe a state of mind but a process and an attitude. For wherever *śūnyatā* becomes a new state or position, man is endangered with clinging to it as though to a new property which he can dominate and master.

2. True *śūnyatā* is realized where emptiness itself is emptied of emptiness, emptiness thus becoming non-emptiness, the word non-word, the (speaking) I non-I, etc. Moreover, in the Western understanding the process of emptying oneself basically implies ethical behaviour and attitude. It is therefore appropriate that the Sanskrit term *anātman*, translated in Japanese as *muga*, is rendered in English, on the one hand, as non-I or non-self, and on the other hand, as selflessness.

   That is to say, even if the concept seems a metaphysical term, at a more basic level it is practical and ethical.

3. Non-I is not limited to the interpretation of one's own ego or self, however; indeed, it simultaneously points rather to the other, Thou. The final example in the *Hekiganroku* 68 witnesses a remarkable exchange of names:

   > Kyōzan (Ejaku) asked Sanshō (Enen): "What is your name?" Sanshō replied, "My name is Ejaku." "Ejaku!" said Kyōzan, "that's me!" "Well then," replied Sanshō, "my name is Enen." Kyōzan roared with laughter. (cf. Waldenfels, *Nothingness*, 83ff.)

   Here the realization of non-I terminates in identity with Thou, and realization of one's true I or Self consists precisely in such non-egotistical identity with non-I = Thou.

4. Without entering into a detailed discussion, I would like to call attention to the fact that *śūnyatā*, 'emptiness,' has more recently also been related to the famous words of St. Paul:

   > In your minds you must be the same as Christ Jesus. His state was divine, yet he did not cling to his equality with God but *emptied himself* to assume the condition of a slave, and became as men are; and being as all men are, he was humbler yet, even to accepting death, death on the cross. (Phil. 2:5-8)

It was Keiji Nishitani who drew the attention to the New Testament words and was at least partly responsible for the comparison and discussion which has taken place in the last years (cf. Nishitani, 58ff.). In addition, interpretation of the divine *kenōsis* has a long history of its own in Christian theology (cf. Waldenfels, *Nothingness*, 155-162). Notwithstanding its age, it also forms a point of contact with modern Christian theology. (cf. St. Odin).

3 Sharing

'Sharing' as such is an experience which is not restricted to an exchange of ideas, reasons, and arguments. One who shares with others participates in good news and bad news, in hardships and joys, in darkness and brightness. 'Sharing,' therefore, cannot be reduced to pure knowledge. As the English term 'realization' indicates, both moments come together: the achievement of something as well as its full understanding and apprehension — in the German language we must use the two terms *Verwirklichung* and *Verstehen*. 'Sharing,' in like fashion, implies (a) a comprehensive interpersonal relatedness and (b) a cognitive connotation. The latter forms part of a comprehensive understanding of 'sharing.' At the same time, however, 'sharing,' taken in a comprehensive way, means that 'sharing' is never limited to words. We can share in the sorrows of someone in silence as well as with consoling words, tears, or cries, or indeed with any signs of sympathy. We can similarly share in the joy of someone else with words of rejoicing and congratulation, with a smile, with laughter, or indeed with anything which signifies taking part. Within the context of Buddhist thought, 'sharing' demands participation in *prajñā* 'wisdom,' and *karuṇā* 'sympathy and selfless love.' 'Sharing' in this sense calls for an exchange of arguments and ways of understanding, on the one hand, and for the practice of selfless love, on the other. (I will leave aside here the explanation of the various concepts of love such as *agape, caritas, maitrī, karuṇā,* etc.; however, what we call 'sympathy and selfless love' should by all means exclude any form of egotistical love.)

'Sharing' —continuing to another important matter to be considered— is never limited to receiving; it consists of giving and taking, in activity as well as passivity. One who shares with another person, is actively involved — in theory as well as in practice. He is changing himself. In a way, we might even say that any kind of true 'sharing' is itself a kind of self-emptying. 'Sharing' in general and the experience of *śūnyatā* are in this sense more thoroughly connected than we might have imagined.

I would like to comment further with regard to 'dialogue' that *dialogue* is only one way of sharing which —literally— occurs by means of words. However, since dialogue admits of various degrees of depth, the degrees of sharing are themselves also subject to discussion.

4 Sharing *śūnyatā*

We can now, at this juncture, deal more directly with the call for sharing *śūnyatā*, which —as we understand it— is a religious experience.[1] Summing up the results of our considerations so far we maintain that:

1. We can hardly deal with 'sharing' successfully as long as we restrict it ourselves to rational analyses and exchanges of arguments. This does not, however, mean that 'sharing' itself is something irrational. It includes rationalizing — but it does so in such a manner that rationalizing and understanding represent only one special moment in a more comprehensive process of participation, exchange, and encounter. (With good reason, G. Oberhammer chose *encounter*, German *'Begegnung,'* as a basic category of religious hermeneutics.)

2. 'Sharing' itself is understood as an existential form of participation in someone's possessions and needs, his/her life and fate, his/her merits and guilt. 'Sharing' can occur at both verbal and non-verbal levels, in words as well as deeds. It admits of various degrees of depth: partial sharing as well as total sharing, sharing of some belonging(s) as well as sharing of one's own self in total surrender and commitment.

3. *Śūnyatā* appears by origin to be less a concept and rather more a kind of imagery which provides a certain way of imagining the issue at hand, as well as furnishing an approach to it, yielding something which can at least to some degree can be communicated. *Emptiness* demands fulfilment. *Openness* implies readiness, expectation, time and space —again— room and time for something and someone. *Sky* symbolizes infinity but also cosmos and universe. It forms a way of overcoming a limited form of anthropocentrism in favour of a comprehensive form of cosmocentrism (cf. Waldenfels, *Gott*, 13-43). What appears at first glance to be abstract is actually very concrete.

Thus far, anyone might concur in our exposition. We nevertheless feel some uneasiness: Is it correct to talk about *śūnyatā* in such a universal way as though it were not an expression of the particular Buddhist experience? And is it justified to generalize the peculiar Buddhist experience in such a manner that it can in fact be shared by the whole world? Such objections must especially be taken seriously when directed

---

[1] We mention the term 'religious' without debating the question of its implications; I would merely like to recall the fact that without much reflection and previous discussion the Fathers of Vatican II considered Buddhism to be one of the most important world religions (see the *Nostra aetate* Declaration).

against Christians who seem to claim the Buddhist experience as belonging to their own heritage, or at least as being compatible with basic Christian insights, and who seem to be doing so in the conviction of their own superiority.

This leads us once more to the point at which we might ask whether it is possible for us to share *śūnyatā*. In reply to the issue at hand I would like to reiterate the answer I have given at the start: yes. However, having entered into the fray, I should like to proffer two additional considerations:

1. It is true that due to the influence Nāgārjuna and his school, the term *'śūnyatā'* served as a key for understanding his presentation of truth in both its dialectical and discursive functions (cf. Streng, 35; also Vroom, 169-174). Nāgārjuna undoubtedly lived in the tradition of Buddhism and himself influenced Mahāyāna Buddhism to a great extent. However, precisely because his thinking is grounded in a *religious* experience (cf. Streng, 171 *et passim*), F. J. Streng's assessment cannot be overvalued:

   > ... a religious statement is seen to express a situation rather than analyze and describe something. It includes (1) an awareness of the deficient character of human existence (often given in terms of pollution, blindness, or chaos) plus (2) the means to transform this deficiency. It is the exclamation that this transformation is necessary and possible for man to fully realize his true capacity. As we mentioned before, the religious man never admits that his expression is *simply* a feeling, an ideal, or a means of communal identification; he maintains that his religious vision expresses the way things are. But the situation expressed is not an objective description to be identified with practical work-a-day distinctions and definitions. A religious statement is always an expression of a *living* experience and meaning, whose validity is open to an internal judgment but not to an external one. A religious statement requires religious life as the context for establishing its meaning. (p. 175)

   That is to say, a merely philosophical or theological approach excludes any true apprehension of *śūnyatā* as long as the truth involved is not considered in terms of the religious perspective of salvation and liberation. It is precisely because *śūnyatā* as proposed by Nāgārjuna takes on a *soteriological* character that it is related (a) to the Buddha experience of enlightenment and liberation and (b) to religion as the way to man's radical salvation.

2. With the premise that —in order to reach some true understanding of the true meaning of *śūnyatā*— a purely scholarly reflection is bound to fail and that a "religious statement requires religious life as the context for establishing its meaning," the question arises whether

'sharing *śūnyatā*' in its religious substance presupposes from one's partner that he joins the Buddha way, becoming a Buddhist. In other words, is 'sharing *śūnyatā*' only possible inside the Buddhist community (Sanskrit *sangha*), or is it possible that the experience of *śūnyatā* can be achieved beyond the limits of the Buddhist community?

As a matter of fact, the Buddhism and Christianity of our own time have one thing in common. Both no longer exclude one another from the promise of final salvation or liberation. John B. Cobb even goes a step further in his book *Beyond Dialogue,* remarking upon the relation between God and Emptiness:

> If coming back from the passing over into Buddhism meant that the Christian would believe nothing that has been absent from traditional Buddhist belief, then it would entail abandonment of most what we have meant by God. But if it means, more reasonably, that Christians can appropriate central Buddhist insights and practices, then our results thus far are encouraging. We Christians can rethink our belief in God in light of the Buddhist insight that the ultimate reality of all things is Emptiness. Through this rethinking, our own heritage may be illumined in new ways. The result, far from being a compromise that waters down Christianity, may be a richer and purer grasp of the meaning of the God we have come to know through Jesus Christ.
>
> Our conceptualities about God, in the very service of glorifying, have often obscured the livingness and relatedness which is the basis of our knowledge of God. To think of God as the everlasting Empty One from whom all human Emptiness is derived may help us to break out of static and repressive categories. As we think of God differently the existential meaning of that belief will also change, but it will not be reduced or weakened. At the same time, the recognition that all is empty may allow Christian theocentrism to be complemented by the profound psychological and religious benefits attained through Buddhist methods of existential realization. Theoretical acknowledgment of the complementarity of God and Emptiness may provide a context in which faith in God and realization of Emptiness can mutually fructify one another in living human experience. (Cobb, 113ff.)

I fully agree with these statements by J. B. Cobb. By rethinking our belief in God, the result "may be a richer and purer grasp of the meaning of the God we have come to know through Jesus Christ." The problem of God is unfortunately handled by Cobb from a rather philosophical perspective and, consequently, in terms of Christian dogmatics; precisely the God "we have come to know *through Jesus Christ*" (i.e., the God whom we have come to know through the Jew, Jesus of Nazareth; the God he announced and 'represented' by his life and in his death)[2] — precisely this God is left rather beyond consideration. Yet the commemoration of his life and death is precisely what the Christian way of knowing God is. Moreover, death and dying is another *topos* intimately connected both with the experience of *śūnyatā* as well as the Christian God.

Before turning to the final *topos*, I think it helpful to quote once more K. Rahner's penetrating reflections on the kenotic passages in Holy Scripture which have thus far been seldom reflected upon within Buddhist-Christian dialogue:

> This man [Jesus Christ] is, precisely as man, the self-articulation *(Selbst-äußerung)* of God in his self-emptying *(Selbstentäußerung)*, because it is precisely when God empties *himself* that he expresses *himself,* it is when he conceals the majesty of his love and manifests *himself* as ordinarily human that he proclaims *himself* as love. (K. Rahner, *Schriften* IV, 149)

Accordingly, man

> comes into being when God's self-enunciation *(Selbstaussage)*, his Word, is lovingly uttered in the void *(Leere)* of god-less nothing. ... It is when God wills to be non-God that man comes to be; that, no more or less, is what we may say. (K. Rahner, *Schriften* IV, 150)

5 "Death was his Kōan"

In 1986 Winston L. King published a book about the Samurai-Zen of Suzuki Shōsan (1579–1655), a samurai who became a monk in the Sōtō Zen school and was very much concerned "that the followers of Sōtō Zen live the spirit of Buddhism and master the life that has been given them in the world" (Dumoulin, *Zen* II, 341). King gave his book the title *Death was his Kōan*. In the language of Zen Buddhism the Great Death is the most radical expression of the practice of Emptiness, because —as M. Abe puts it— "through the realization of the Great Death, the realization of the Great Life opens up" (Abe, 166). Yet it is hard to banish the suspicion that the Great Death sometimes invites us to overlook the death everyday people are dying and that everyone of us too is doomed to die. Precisely this fact seems to have become Shosan's life-kōan. A few quotes from his *Rōankyō* will serve to underscore this:

> One who makes no big issue out of death is no follower of the Way (of the Buddha) ... In that case one will never know one's own lord (within) who is free in the use of the six senses.

---

[2] For further details, consult Waldenfels, *Fundamentaltheologie* III, 225-228.

The word I must teach you is this: "Make the one (Chinese) character death lord within your bosom and, casting everything (else) aside, guard it!"

Truly by this 'death' (practice) I have penetrated into the very marrow (of practice). By no other method can one die (i.e., destroy one's self).

Two or three old women came and asked him about the essence of Buddhism. The Master said: "I do not know anything that I can teach you." After a while he said suddenly: "You will die, you will die. Never forget the fact of dying, and recite the *nembutsu.*" (Cited in King, 284f.)

How seriously Suzuki Shōsan took the question of death is attested by his astonishingly harsh criticism of the deterioration he discerns in the practice of *mu* (=no-, nothing)–Kōan (cf. *Mumonkan* 1, pp. 37-39). According to King, he admits that, it is true, the "mode of nothingness and no-self has represented the *monk's* way of attaining to selflessness, the dying of the Great Death about which so many Zen masters have written and spoken, Hakuin in particular. But by the same token, there have been many superficial and mistaken forms of this emptiness, no-self experience. Often it came to be equated with mere passivity, almost a kind of lethargic quietude or transient thoughtlessness in which a deliberate effort was made to make the mind blank." (King, 329) To give only one instance:

When a monk named Genshun told Shōsan that "in these days the meaning of the Dharma has been arrived at," Shōsan asked him what that meaning was, and Genshun replied with a verse:

> The nothing of nothing
> Which is the nothing of nothingness.
> On the pear tree bloom the flowers of nothingness
> That will soon fall.

But when Shōsan pressed him further and asked him whether he meant a very basic existential experience of "coming into being from the state in which Heaven and earth are not yet separate and again return to emptiness," Genshun admitted his mistake. His meaning had been somewhat less than that, maybe little more than semantic sport. He sees Genshun as typical of his day and age, and his understanding of nothingness as worthless, even harmful. (King, 331)

I do not mention this criticism in order to destroy at the very last my argument in favour of sharing *śūnyatā*. I would merely like to return to the point that the issue of an existential experience aimed at a decision about life and death —and sharing *śūnyatā*, directed as it is towards the Great Death and Great Life, does lead to a life and death decision— cannot be reduced to a matter of academic debate and —so-called— interreligious dialogues. It demands existential involvement.

Moreover, at least for Christians, *Death was his Kōan* might well serve as a description of the life of Jesus of Nazareth. For Christians his death has become a *kōan* which casts light on one's own death in the light of the Easter experience of God. Death as a daily *kōan,* on the other side, is nothing less than the continuous practice of emptying oneself by living a life of completely selfless love. Here I return the query: What else might then be signified by 'sharing *śūnyatā*?'

Bibliography

Abe, M. *Zen and Western Thought.* Honolulu: University of Hawaii, 1985.

Cobb, J. B., Jr. *Beyond Dialogue: Towards a Mutual Transformation of Christianity and Buddhism.* Philadelphia: Fortress, 1982.

Dumoulin, H. *Östliche Meditation and christliche Mystik.* Freiburg/ München: Alber, 1966.

——. *Zen Buddhism: A History.* New York: MacMillan; London: Collier MacMillan, vol I, 1988; vol II, 1990.

Enomiya-Lassalle, H. M. *Zen und christliche Mystik.* 3rd edn. Freiburg: Aurum, 1986.

King, W. L. "Death was his Kōan: The Samurai-Zen of Suzuki Shōsan." *Asian Humanities.* Berkeley, 1986.

Mumonkan. Die Schranke ohne Tor: Meister Wu-men's Sammlung der 48 Kōan. H. Dumoulin, tr. Mainz: Grünewald, 1975.

Nishitani, K. *Religion and Nothingness.* Berkeley: University of California, 1982.

Oberhammer, G. *'Begegnung' als Kategorie der Religionshermeneutik.* Wien, 1989.

Odin, St. "*Kenosis* as a Foundation for Buddhist-Christian Dialogue: The Kenotic Buddhology of Nishida and Nishitani of the Kyoto School in Relation to the Kenotic Christology." *The Eastern Buddhist,* N. S., vol. XX nr. 1 (1987): 34-61.

The Ox and His Herdsman: A Chinese Zen Text with Commentary and Pointers by Master D. R. Otsu and Japanese illustrations of the 15th century. M. H. Trevor, tr. Tokyo: Hokuseido, 1969.

Streng, F. J. *Emptiness: A Study in Religious Meaning.* Nashville/ New York: Abingdon, 1967.

Tao te ching. D. C. Lau, tr. Middlesex: Penguin, 1976.

Vroom, H. M. *Religions and the Truth: Philosophical Reflections and Perspectives.* Grand Rapids: W. B. Eerdmans; Amsterdam: Rodopi, 1989.

Waldenfels, H. *Absolute Nothingness: Foundations for a Buddhist-Christian Dialogue.* New York/Ramsey: Paulist, 1980.

——. *Gott – Mensch – Welt: Zum Angelpunkt des interreligiösen Gesprächs aus christlicher Sicht.* In W. Strolz/H. Waldenfels, eds. *Christliche Grundlagen des Dialogs mit den Weltreligionen.* Freiburg: Herder, 1983, pp. 13-43.

——. *Kontextuelle Fundamentaltheologie.* Paderborn: Schöningh. 2nd edn., 1988.

CHAPTER 18

Sharing in Japan's
New New Religions

Jacques H. Kamstra

The present volume's theme of sharing leads the author to distinguish
between two types of sharing: abstract impersonal sharing which perhaps
occurs among scholars of religion, missiologists, theologians, and the like
while securely seated at their desks; and truly personal sharing which may
occur among intellectuals as well as among ordinary folk. The urge to share
one's own religion and other daily needs with others has been so keen in
Japan since the second world war and particularly since the oil crisis of 1974
that it has given rise to a set of new religions, the *shin shin-shukyo*, the *new*
New Religions.

The problem of sharing between different religions first puzzled me many
years ago when the contours of my dissertation were becoming tangible.
For that reason, I entitled it *Encounter or Syncretism*. In its pages I
attempted to distinguish between a "real and an unreal 'encounter',"
considering such encounter at two levels — the personal level and the
impersonal, abstract one.

At the personal level, sharing means that one encounters the religion
of another person in such a way that his religion is experienced precisely
as something belonging to him, as something which adds definition to the
respective differences between people. Acceptance of his religion (conversion) would render me very dependent on him, since such religion belongs
to him in a very personal way. In such a process of personal exchange,
one will often only be able to discern the systematic characteristics of a
religion with difficulty. One can also theoretically imagine assenting to a
religion which does not appear concretely in the life of another person,
but which is an abstract structure or system which one might discover in
books. The question remains, however, whether such 'abstract' acceptance
is really a possibility at all at the level of inter-personal relationships,
which is also the level on which religion ultimately takes a place; we must,
in other words, ask ourselves whether acceptance or rejection of a religion
by a person is not ultimately something channelled by human relationships
and encounters. This line of questioning imposes itself all the more when

215

dealing with practically-minded East Asians such as the Japanese: abstract
assent proves to be an infrequent and unlikely occurrence among them.
Conversions are generally the result of encounter at the inter-personal
human level. One might extend this idea further and consider such
encounters as free of any particular tradition, as if two individual religions
were in confrontation with each other. It is goes without saying that to
label such an encounter as a confrontation between two different 'religions' is no more than an abstraction, since every mutual encounter
between religions can, initially, only come about within the context of
individual and communal human relationships. The question of abstract
encounter between religions can only arise after it has been established
phenomenologically how the religions concerned (seen as the mental
outlooks of individual persons) have 'appreciated' each other in the
concrete encounter of individual people. This could then occur in two
ways. Either the 'foreign element' of the new religion may be discovered
in its entirety even before it has been accepted or rejected, or the parties
concerned may become bogged down en route to such discovery. If the
latter occurs, little more is left of the new religion than a caricature
whose correspondence with the new religion is questionable. (Kamstra 1967, 6-7)

This statement, made more than two decades ago, points us down the
road to a distinction between two types of sharing when applied to the
conference theme: abstract impersonal sharing, which may or may not
occur during the desk labours of scholars of religion, and personal social
sharing. Both types can be discerned in the history of Japanese religion.

1 Abstract sharing

Abstract sharing is a matter for individuals who are well versed in the
systematic features of another religion such as scholars of religion and in
some cases theologians, particularly missiologists and specialists in dogmatic theology. Abstract sharing is very much a matter of desks, books,
academic congresses and workshops. Scholars of religion who discuss
problems with the phenomenon of 'syncretism' constitute a clear example
of an abstract approach to sharing. In personal sharing of religion the
problem of syncretism does not even exist. It crops only in the minds of
scholars of religion and theologians (Kamstra/Hoens/Mulder, 210-213). I
agree with Leertouwer in this regard, who points out that many definitions
of syncretism betray theological biases and represent a striking form of
intellectual ethnocentrism (Leertouwer, 9-10). Abstract sharing depends in
the minds of theologians on the degree of acceptance and tolerance with
regard to certain tenets of other religions. To many theologians sharing
with other religions is even prohibited by the Barthian dialectical opposi-

tion between religion and faith: religion is seen as being merely a human illusion leading mankind astray from God, whereas faith is the result of God's authentic and direct revelation to man. On the other side, there are many Catholic missiologists and theologians who consider sharing as one of the categorical imperatives of Catholicism. Other religions are viewed as culturally differentiated expressions of one and the same faith. Every non-Christian is believed to be endowed with the *'anima naturaliter christiana.'* On paper, even the dialectic of Nāgārjuna and the Buddhist doctrine of *nirvāṇa* and *śūnyatā* become useful Eastern means by which to explain the mystery of God's transpersonality (H. Küng, 557ff.). The results of such dialogue are rather dubious, however. On paper *nirvāṇa* may be compared with the *exinanitio* of Jesus Christ; both teachings refer to being "out with the self" (Fernando, 79; Kamstra 1985, 32). In this way, many theologians are ensconced behind their desks and computers, devising abstract schemes for sharing between various religions in books and articles.

In China and in Japan the same phenomenon can be observed. Abstract sharing with other religions may even be called a hallmark of East Asian Buddhism. Japanese religion consists essentially in mutual sharing between Buddhism, Shinto, and folk religion (Kamstra 1988b, 9-10). In a different context I have pointed out that the Japanese faithful live according to an undivided, unified religion which is Shinto during one's lifetime and Buddhist after one's death (Kamstra 1988b, 116ff.). Openness to other religions and an attitude of abstract as well as personal sharing thus strikes Japanese religious intuition as natural to a much greater degree than is the case in Christian countries.

In the systematic thought of Japanese Buddhism, relations with other Buddhist sects and even with non-Buddhist religions has very often been defined in terms of sharing. *Kyohan* is thus defined as a system for sharing Buddhism with other sects and religions. Other movements are considered to be pluriform ways of salvation which encompass all the developments within Buddhism from the time that Gautama Sakyamuni first preached right up to the present. It includes every historical stage and even describes 'outside' religions such as Shinto and Christianity which, though considered to be weak and imperfect ways to salvation, can sometimes nevertheless conduct one to *nirvāṇa*. The first *kyohan* arose in China during the Liang period (501–556) when a certain Pao Liang opposed three inferior Buddhist doctrines with a rather simple scheme, qualified by him as *upāya*, "skilful means, to the 'eternal and harmonious' teachings of the *Mahaparinirvāṇa sūtra*" (see Ito, 76-77). Since that time many *kyohan* have been devised in China and Japan. Every Buddhist sect in East Asia has become the proud custodian of a *kyohan* of its own: the Sanron sect has the *nizo samborin* (the two vehicles of the three wheels of the *dharma*), the Hosso sect has the *sanjikyo* (the teachings of the three periods), the Shingon sect, the *jujushinron* (discussion about the ten abodes of the human mind; see Kamstra 1988b, 69).

The two *kyohan* of the Tendai sect are quite famous. It would require more space than is presently available to describe these *kyohan* in detail. What is important to note in the present context is that all of them are based on the principle of sharing: not a single Buddhist sect is excluded from the difficult quest of reaching final *nirvāṇa*, for the existence of each of them is based on Buddha's own words (Kamstra 1989b). It is much easier for adherents of some sects to attain to their goal, however, because they have the most appropriate means at their disposal. These means are defined in superior sūtras such as the *Avataṃsaka*, the *Mahāprajñāpāramitā*, or the *Lotus sūtras*.[1] Such schemes are now current in the writings of the Soka Gakkai, which even approach Shinto and Christianity in an apologetic manner. All share the same word of Buddha[2], but believers conceptualize it in different ways, depending on their personal dispositions and intellectual qualities. Buddhist sects are thus classified according to abstract criteria which indicate the degree of perfection in these abstract modes of sharing.

2 Personal sharing

In 1985, I subdivided dialogue into two types, the one represented by the abstract and intellectual approach of specialists and theologians, the other by the entirely different brand sharing engaged in by ordinary people.

> What is called syncretism is to ordinary people what dialogue is for the scholar and intellectual. Dialogue is a matter for the upper class: it betrays the presence of an intellectual. Dialogue sounds aristocratic and dignified: dialogue is performed by intellectuals while standing astride of the world. Ordinary people do not speak in dialogues but just talk while crouching together in groups, close to the ground. Simple talk implies a feeling of togetherness and group consciousness; no one needs to be concerned about the loss of their identity. The fact that people in the Netherlands are increasingly in dialogue not only indicate the increasing number of intellectuals and university graduates but also the increasing obstruction of normal human channels of communication, a legacy of loneliness and isolation. Sociologists such as Elias and Aries

---

[1] For the Soka Gakkai *kyohan* see Kamstra 1989a, 33-36. The Tendai *kyohan* is described in detail in Ch'en, 305-310. In it, the hierarchical order of all Buddhist sects for the accomplishment of their goals depends on the classification of *sutras* and teachings.

[2] Concerning *kyohan* as deriving from the primæval voice of Buddha, see Kamstra 1988b, 57-66.

blame the increasing privatization and individualization in Western society for such impeded communication. Mutual aims such as family, work, and religion which ordinarily link common folk, chatting while squatting on their haunches, have fallen apart. (Kamstra/Hoens/Mulder 219-220)

In Japan, where people had to give up their old rural habitats in order to find jobs in the giant industries of large cities, this type of sharing among ordinary people has given rise to many new religions. Since World War II, the urge to share one's own religion and other daily needs with others has been so keen that it has given rise to the *shinkoshukyo,* the 'newly established religions.' It is widely accepted that the *hoza* — *dharma*-sessions, and the *zadankai* — the group-sessions of such new religions as the Soka Gakkai and the Rissho Koeikai, came about to foster mutual communication among the lonely, sick, and anxious, providing comfort and relief through the teachings, rituals, and many other activities of these new religions. The aims of the so-called *shinkoshukyo* have been defined by the post-war situation of poverty and sickness. The *shinkoshukyo* directed their efforts toward the material and physical welfare of the faithful. Wealth and good health were believed to be the main benefits accruing from the conversion to these new religions.

This situation came to an end in 1973 when Japan was struck by the oil crisis. Since then, completely new religions have arisen which have again brought people together in groups. The aims were entirely different, however, for they were faced with new challenges and with newly emergent dangers stemming from environmental pollution, supposedly one of the signs of the end of our world. These newly emerging religions have many common characteristics which distinguish them from the *shinkoshukyo* that flourished after the end of the War. In what follows our exposition will confine itself to sharing this new type of religion.

3 Sharing in the *shin shin-shukyo*

In an article published in April of 1990 I have pointed out that the *shin shin-shukyo* differ from the *shinkoshukyo* in many ways. In these religions, which are quite small in terms of numbers, there is strong belief in the end of the world, in magical power, and in miracles. There is a further characteristic boom in esoteric mysticism. They share a number of common characteristics, among them corporality, mutuality (communication with ancestors and spiritual beings in the universe), individualization (the care of the needs of the individual), and shamanistic features derived from their founders (Kamstra 1990). In the principal *shinkoshukyo* old Buddhist religions received a modern lay organization, if we were to put it in general terms. The tenets of these new religions, however, are fundamentally the same as those formulated by the medieval founders of the original Buddhist sects. The Buddhist doctrines of the Soka Gakkai and of the Rissho Koseikai are thus still the same as those of the Nichiren sect, founded by Nichiren himself (1222–1282). In the *kyohan* of the Soka Gakkai, that is, critical evaluation and classification of all Buddhist doctrines by means of comparison with its own doctrine, it is considered necessary to protect the nation against the influence of Christianity.[3] By contrast, some of the *shin shin-shukyo* movements rather conspicuously consider Christianity to be of almost equal significance to Shinto and Buddhism. Kiriyama Seiyu, the founder of the Agonshu, the largest of the *shin shin-shukyo,* said on the occasion of the foundation of the Agonshu in April of 1978:

> We are in need of great compassion *(mahakaruna)* and of love. For the realization of both we need the highest power and wisdom *(chie)* preached by Buddha himself. All this puts an end to the disorder of our times. It will build up a new future and will be the backbone of mankind. In order to achieve this aim Christianity and Buddhism alike will have to join in their efforts. (Yajima, 113)

According to Kiriyama, Buddhism and Christianity will have to share their virtues and benefits with one another. In another *shin shin-shukyo,* the Pyramido no kai or 'Pyramid-corporation,' respect is paid to the sun (Amaterasu), to Buddha, to Kobo Daishi (774–835), the founder of the Shingon sect, to the *mizuko* (the souls of aborted fetuses,   stillborn infants, and those who died shortly after birth),[4] and to ancestors who appear in the guise of the souls of UFOs. In 1982 its founder, Kamei, had a dream in which Jesus appeared to her dressed in an orange coloured garment, saying: "Save the souls." His voice came from the tip of the *torii* of a Shinto shrine. At the same time, she heard another voice coming from the darkness: "Save me, please." It was the voice of Jesus'

---

[3] For more details concerning the Soka Gakkai *kyohan* see Kamstra 1989a, 28-36. This *kyohan* not only contains heavy attacks on Christian doctrines, but also blames Christianity for the loss of World War II, since the translation of the Bible at the end of the Edo period (1603–1868) is believed to have had strong influence on Shinto, and to have given rise to its emperor cult. See also Kamstra 1989a, 49.

[4] The cult of *mizuko* (literally, 'water-child') has become, in recent decades increasing[4]ly popular due to the psychical stress and anxieties arising from the enormous numbers of yearly abortions. In order to overcome these problems, people very often adorn small stone images of the *bodhisattva* of rebirth, Jizo, with tiny, multicolored pieces of cloth. For some pictures of these tiny adorned Jizo see Kamstra 1988b, 87, and for the meaning of Jizo in modern Japan, see Kamstra 1988a, 80-88. A *mizuko-kuyo,* or a memorial service, conducted in most cases by Buddhist priests, is a widespread modern social and religious phenomenon; see Smith, 3-24. Hence the practice of *mizuko-kuyo* is widespread under the *shin shin-shukyo.* Some of these practices seem to have come into existence because of the abortion problem.

mother. Mrs. Kamei saved her soul (see Asahi Shimbunsha, 92-93). In the literature on the *shin shin-shukyo*, more of such information can be discovered, attesting the openness to sharing in a combination of Japanese and Buddhist beliefs with Christian views. In what follows below, the organization of the two larger *shin shin-shukyo* will be described — the *sekai mahikari unmei kyokai*, or 'The Cultural Brotherhood of the True Light of the World,' and the *sukyo mahikari*, or 'The Lofty Doctrine of the True Light.'[5] The latter sect arose shortly after the death of the founder of the original sect, the result of organizational disputes amongst the leaders. Minoo points out that there are no noticeable differences in doctrine and practice (Hirota, 237). I recently discovered a name in a folder issued by an office in Brussels which reminded me of the former sect: *Mahikari ni yoru shinbunmei kensetsu dantai*, meaning 'The Organization for the Realization of a New Civilization by means of the Light of the Truth.' In the folder, dated May 20, 1989, the organization bills itself as a promotional centre for the use of special Mahikari techniques for curing the sick. Nowhere in the brochure is there any indication of religious affiliation. It only mentions the Eastern art of curing and passing light to others, *okiyome*, which it describes as spiritual energy of an extremely high frequency, which is thought capable of purifying the spirit, the soul, and the mental and physical cells of every person. The name of the organization is used in order to conceal its religious aims and to stress its medical purposes.

4 The sekai mahikari bunmei kyodan

The *sekai mahikari bunmei kyodan*, numbering more than two hundred thousand believers, is the second largest *shin shin-shukyo*. The tenet of sharing is prominent in this sect, with its founders as well as in its doctrines and practices.

4.1 Sharing in the life of its founder

The roots of the *mahikari* movements are very old. In Shinto, the true light is a reminder of the light of the goddess Amaterasu, the shining sun. In Japanese folk religion, it harks back to old institution of *hijiri*, the sage, who, like the sun, let the light of his knowledge shine on others, who in

[5] By calling itself a *sukyo* (divine and lofty doctrine), this religion tries to distinguish itself from other religions which are called *shukyo*, the Japanese translation of religion, faith, creed or cult. The word *sukyo* is composed of *su*, (deify, honour) and *kyo* (doctrine); the word *shukyo* is composed of *shu* (sect, origin, and also honor) and of *kyo* (doctrine).

turn became the forerunners of the modern lay leaders of the new sects
(Kamstra 1987, 321-322). They derive their present sweep and spirit of
dialogue from the older *shinkoshukyo,* the Omotokyo, the tradition to
which they belong. It is widely accepted that the Omotokyo is a blend of
Buddhism, Shinto, and Christianity. Its co-founder, Onisaburgo Deguchi
(1871–1948), was a consistent advocate of religious dialogue. At one time
he wrote:

> We find that our surroundings are full of God, Buddha, or Maitreya.
> The Grace of Heaven, and the grace of Earth, is it not all the sub-
> stance of God, Buddha, and Maitreya? One drop of water, one gleam
> of light, a single act of kindness, the earth, the sun, moon, and stars all
> give us happiness. (Thomsen, 163)

'Omoto' means the great origin. It has been the source of many other
new religions which were also engaged in lively dialogue with other
religions in the world. Its colourful history has been a source of inspiration to many of its adherents. Religions which have sprouted from the
Omotokyo include the Ananaikyo founded by Nakano Katsutate, who broke
away from Omoto in 1949. Practically all of the Ananaikyo doctrines can
be traced back to those of the Omoto. The front of its worship hall is
slightly elevated, and there are three altars symbolizing heaven, earth, and
man. The five world religions —Buddhism, Christianity, Islam, Judaism,
and Shinto— are worshipped on these altars. This symbolism is expressed in the Japanese name of the religion: three and five *(ananai*;
Thomsen, 146; Kamstra 1988b, 39-41). Another sect connected to the
Omoto is the Seicho no Ie, the 'house of growth.' During the war, its
founder, Taniguchi, stressed that the emperor had to be identified with
the 'Only Existence,' and therefore, 'Ultimate Being': "the only thing that
really exists, and accordingly the centre of our loyalty and devotion"
(Thomsen, 155). Since the War the emphasis has been on the fatherland
and the national flag rather than on the emperor (Thomsen, 156). His
teaching is a mixture of poorly understood Christian and Buddhist doctrines. Nevertheless, he tries to unite these teachings in the superior
doctrine of the 'house of growth.' In his large forty-volume *seimei no
jisso* 'truth of reality of life,' he writes:

> Gautama is not the only incarnation of the Eternal Buddha in flesh.
> We are all the Eternal Buddha that is embodied in our flesh. Jesus
> alone is not the only son of God. We are all sons of God, and he is
> everyone's father, everyone has infinite power as they are God's children.
> (Thomsen, 161)

The Seicho no Ie has shares with the Mahikari movements their use of
biblical and Buddhist texts. More directly linked with the Mahikari sects
is the Sekai Kyuseikyo or 'World Messianity.' This religion was started

out 1934 as Kannonkyo, the religion of Avalokiteśvara. It thereafter first changed its name to Nippon Kannon Kyodan, 'the Japanese Brotherhood of Kannon,' and in 1950 to 'World Messianity.' The founder of this religion was Okada Mokichi (1882–1955). He was known as Jikan, the manifestation of Kannon, and later as Ohikarisama, the honourable Mr. Light. It is worth noticing that the word *hikari* (light) became his special title. His religion and the Mahikari movements have many common features, but its main contours resemble the *shinkoshukyo* more than the *shin shin-shukyo*, believing in the blessings of material and physical well being. According to Thomsen, Okada claimed in 1926 to have received a revelation from God, who appointed him as his messiah and prophet and who granted him the divine light, *jorei*, which he believed could cure diseases and to perform all kinds of miracles — securing easy births, protection from floods, and cures for blindness (Thomsen, 180). From that day on, Okada considered himself to be superior to all men. He claimed to be the greatest doctor in the world. He even aspired to a Nobel Prize, although he never received it (Thomsen, 175). Okado believed himself to be the reincarnation of Kannon, and to be the messiah the world was waiting for. He said that the *jorei* emanated from him and he claimed to be able to cure all kinds of diseases simply by applying pieces of paper on which he had written the Chinese character for *hikari* (light) to the part of the body affected. (Thomsen, 176)

When Okada died in 1955, the founder of the Mahikari *kyodan*, Okada Kotama, was still a member of the Sekai Kyuseikyo. He became the first leader of the new movement on February 27, 1959 when the Lord of Heaven and Earth supposedly appeared to him and ordered him to perform the *mahikari no waza* 'the performance of the true light,' saying: "The divine reason *(ri)* has entered your heart. Preach what you have heard from me. The time of Heaven has approached. Get up, call yourself *kotama*, pearl of light, and go into the world." Okada thus became the founder of the sect. At the same time *mitama*, the honourable pearl, origin of the *Mahikari*, gave him the strength to realize his task. His personal life destiny was also revealed to him. He was baptized on earth with the 'tip of the fire.' This baptism by fire gave him the strength to overcome the power of false souls. The future expectations maintained by this sect truly mark it as a *shin shin-shukyo*: great changes will occur in heaven and on earth; there will be many wars followed by the end of the world. This period of hardship will be followed by a new period in which the *tanebito*, the people of the seed, will secure peace and happiness. After these revelations Okada transferred the *mahikari no waza* to tens of thousands of people. Okada died in 1974. His sect, which until then was a branch of the Sekai Kyuseikyo, became independent in 1959 (Hirota, 243). His daughter became his successor, but dissent among the leaders of the sect gave rise to new factions and the independent Sukyo Mahikari movement. (Hirota, 247)

The sect takes great pride in its *suza-sekai-sohonsan-gohonden* 'the main seat of the world,' its primary temple and seat of the divinity on the Ito peninsula. It was constructed at a cost of more than thirty billion yen, about two hundred million dollars. Its completion was lavishly celebrated in November of 1987. The temple is about sixty meters high. Its interior surface is covered with twenty-seven hundred *tatami* which can seat more than five thousand *kumite,* the designation for its believers. In the centre of the platform at the front of the interior, a huge Shinto *mikoshi* commands attention. It is the seat of the great god 'Original Parent and Lord of the true Light.' The seat has been adorned with one hundred kilograms of pure gold (Hirota, 238, 247). On the fourth day of every month about three thousand *kumite* from all over the country assemble at this temple in order to celebrate the festival of the beginning of the month.

4.2 Sharing in the doctrine and practice of the Mahikari sects

This sect believes Light to be the most essential and important instrument of communication within many world religions. Light has the power to purify all kinds of souls and has the capacity to unite mankind into one great family. *Mahikari,* which is an abbreviation of *makoto no hikari,* means the True Light or the Light of Truth. The Mahikari movements refer to the saying by Jesus Christ: "I am the true Light." This appellation considered equivalent to the Buddhist designation for Amida: *muryōkō-butsu* 'the Buddha of Infinite Light' (Blyth, 204). The sect also points out that in Shinto, Amaterasu-omikami, the sun goddess, bestows her Light on all earthly beings (Hirota, 188, 243). Strangely enough, the sect does not appeal to Dainichi-nyorai 'the sun shining everywhere, the embodiment of the Truth.' (Dharmakaya; Soothill, 90)

The cult of light is also practised in other *shinkoshukyo* and *shin shin-shukyo.* In the Itto-en, the 'Garden of Light,' a relatively old *shinko-shukyo* (established in 1928), all these aspects of light have been united into a single teaching. The upper three, small vertical lines which constitute the upper part of the Chinese character for *hikari* ('light') represent Buddhism, Christianity, and Shinto (Hirota, 78ff.). These religions have thus become three aspects of one and the same Light. Hirota also classifies the *byakko shinkokai* 'the true and great congregation of the white light,' among the *shin shin-shukyo.* As the name indicates, the sect believes that God is pure white light. God is endless knowledge, love, and life. As light he is the god of the universe. The first light emitted by God was the first man, and hence the tutelary deity of mankind. This deity is invoked by the faithful of the sect in order to maintain peace in the world, the express aim of the sect. To that end, sixty thousand *piisuporu* 'poles of peace,' have been erected through 1986 in seventy-two countries. Its message of light and peace has been translated into twenty languages. Japan's task is to be the centre of the world, from where the world will be purified. The human soul is believed to be a partial soul *(waketama)* of God. This partial soul is the real form of man. Goi Mahikisa (1916–1980), the founder of the sect became a *kōtai* 'body of light' upon his death. In the daily life of the sect the most important practice is the prayer of *tōitsu*, which means: *kami no naka ni tokekomu* 'the merger with God.' This prayer must be recited with one's hands in the *nyorai-in*, the *mudra* of the *tathagata*, which consists in the folding of one's hands so that the thumbs and forefingers are united in the form of two rings. This union of fingers symbolizes the unity of God with men and women. *Tōitsu* thus leads to *makoto no tsukuware*, to 'real salvation.' (Hirota, 189-210)

This practice resembles the *tekazashi* practice of the Mahikari sects. They follow the same general thought, teaching a new and mystical meaning of the word *makoto*, which is in turn an abbreviation of *ma(koto)* 'true,' and *koto* 'god.' The true God consists in all the divine beings of the world religions united into one, just as the three upper lines of the character for *hikari* constitute one and the same light. The miracles performed in these religions thus originate from one and the same source.

How is this *mahikari* 'divine light' shared among human beings? Such sharing occurs by performing *tekazashi* 'shading,' or laying on of hands. The sect refers in this regard to Jesus Christ, who in laying on his hands cured the sick. Such laying of hands was *mahikari*, in their view. This act of *mahikari* (Japanese: *mahikari no waza*) has been passed on by Buddha to his followers, as well as by Jesus Christ to the twelve disciples. Since then, the power of *mahikari* in the laying on of hands, *tekazashi*, has been limited to these exceptional individuals; that is, until the eve of February 27, 1959, when "the preacher and lord of the first generation, Okada Kotama, who at that time was still a member of the Sekaikyusei-kyo, received a revelation from the Divine Lord, Creator of heaven and earth" (Hirota, 243). Okada is thus believed to be equal in his power to Jesus Christ and Gautama. *Tekazashi* has several meanings. Shading and laying on of hands have already been mentioned; it also implies touching the other. In essence, *tekazashi* means mutuality, sharing. The practice of *tekazashi* implies the other:

> For the practice of *tekazashi*, first two persons sit down facing each other. The recipient of *tekazashi* keeps his eyes closed and his hands folded. The bestower of *tekazashi* faces his partner and lays his hands on him or her. Hereupon, the true Light of God emits from his high

source, through the flat of the hand, the *mahikari,* and funnels all energies into the pineal body [*shokatai* — body of pine fruits is also possible=pituitary gland] of the chest (the seat of the soul). In this way the soul will be purified by the light of God. The purification of the partner's soul by *tekazashi* gradually produces the phenomenon of *reido,* the motion of the soul: as a result, the folded hands will shake up and down to the left and to the right, he will turn his head to the left and to the right, and will bend forward the upper part of his body. (p. 242)

Hence *tekazashi* is called *funrei* 'the floating of the soul' and *reiken* 'the investigation of the soul' (Hirota, 245). The *mahikari no waza* not only purifies the soul, but also spawns other miracles, such as the healing of diseases and wounds, success in business, and conversions.

The practice of *tekazashi* is not limited to the Mahikari sects alone. Hirota mentions quite a few sects which practise *tekazashi*: the Sekai Kyusei-kyo and the sects which sprang from it — Sekai Meishu-kyo 'religion of the light leader of the world,' Kyuseinushi-kyo 'religion of the lord of redemption,' Sekai-shin-kyo 'new religion of the world,' and the Tsukui No Hikari Kyodan 'the brotherhood of the light of redemption.' The practice seems to have been copied by Okada from his namesake and founder of the Sekai Kyusei-kyo. His practice is described by Thomsen:

Okada claimed that he could transfer this power from himself to the character for the word *hikari* (light). This was written by Okada himself and was to be carried as a charm *(omamorisama)* worn around the neck of a believer who had taken the Sekai Kyusei Kyo course of study. The bearer of this written character was then also able to cure others "... by raising his arm, whereupon the light will reach his hand and be emitted from his palm to the person to whom he is administering." (Thomsen, 180)

As is apparent in many *shinkoshukyo* and *shin shin-shukyo* the practice of abstract and personal sharing illustrates the growing tendency in Japan to share not only in one anothers' problems, but to do so in a manner of which it is believed that all religions take part.

Bibliography

Asahi Shimbunsha. *Gendai No Chisana Kamigami.* Tokyo, 1984.

Blyth, R. H. *Japanese-English Buddhist Dictionary.* Tokyo, 1965.

Ch'en, K. *Buddhism in China.* Princeton, 1964.

Fernando, A. *Buddhism and Christianity.* Colombo, 1981.

Hirota, M. *Shin Shin-shukyo.* Tokyo, 1988.

Ito, G. "Tendai Izen No Hankyosetsu Ni Tsuite." *Ryukokū Daigaku Ronso* 284 (1929): 46-77.

Kamstra, J. H. *Encounter or Syncretism.* Leiden, 1967.

——. "Kathina, een Boeddhistische Gemeenschapsviering van Boven en van Beneden Bekeken." In R. Bakker et al., eds. *Religies in nieuw perspectief.* Kampen, 1985, pp. 29-61.

——. "Hijiri." *The Encyclopedia of Religion,* VI. Ed. Mircea Eliade. New York/London, 1987, pp. 321-322.

——. "Jizo on the Verge of Life and Death." In J. H. Kamstra et al., eds. *Funerary symbols and Religion.* Kampen, 1988a, pp. 73-88.

——. *De Japanse Religie, een Fenomenale Godsdienst.* Hilversum, 1988b.

——. "Changes in Buddhist Attitudes towards Other Religions: The Case of the Soka Gakkai." *Zeitschrift für Missionswissenschaft und Religionswissenschaft* 73 (1989a): 28-61.

——. "De Oerklank en het Woord van de Verhevene als Beginsel van Eenheid." In Chowdury et al., eds. *Het kosmisch patroon.* Tilburg, 1989b, pp. 49-66.

——. "De Nieuwe Nieuwe Religies." *Nederlands Theologisch Tijdschrift.* 1990. (forthcoming)

——, Hoens, and Mulder, eds. *Inleiding tot de studie van godsdiensten.* Kampen, 1985.

Küng, H. et al. *Christentum und Weltreligionen.* Munich, 1984.

Leertouwer, L. "Syncretisme over de Dynamiek van Religieuze Verschijnselen." In Chowdury et al., eds. *Het kosmisch patroon.* Tilburg, 1989, pp. 5-20.

Smith, B. "Buddhism and Abortion in Contemporary Japan: *Mizuko Kuyo* and the Confrontation with Death." *Japanese Journal of Religious Studies* 15 (1988): 3-24.

Soothill, W. E. *A Dictionary of Chinese Buddhist Terms.* London, 1937.

Thomsen, H. *The New Religions of Japan.* Tokyo, 1963.

Yajima, T. *Agonshu to Kiriyama Seiyu.* Tokyo, 1985.

CHAPTER 19

The Experience of the Prophet Mohammed

Anton Wessels

This contribution examines (1) the relationship between revelation and experience the prophet Mohammed's case, and (2) tries to indicate to what extent the description of other prophets in the Koran is coloured by Mohammed's own experience, as well as to what extent the description remains specific for any single prophet. Finally (3) we will analyze the impact this experience has had on the description of Jesus as a prophet, and how Jewish and Christian positions are contested at certain points in the Koran. One should be careful —is the conclusion— not to use the so-called 'scheme,' which can undoubtedly be discerned in the tales of prophets who had come before Mohammed, as a straightjacket. One would thereby diminish the uniqueness of the stories regarding any individual prophet, including Jesus. The description of Mohammed's experience has avoided such constriction, leaving sufficient leeway for the unique significance of Jesus.

"Cultures interpenetrate and are more aware of doing so than earlier generations knew, with their geographical isolations and their spiritual *incommunicado.*" (Cragg, 7, 8)

Introduction

The presupposition of this contribution is that Muslims and Christians, in reality, can and must engage in dialogue concerning their respective deepest faith-convictions. Happily, that has indeed been the case. In this regard it is crucial that Christians take the Koran, and therefore implicitly, the prophet Mohammed, seriously, just as Muslims are asked to take the Bible and Jesus Christ seriously. By way of support, I quote Maḥmud Ayoub, who has said:

> If Muslim—Christian Dialogue is to be at all meaningful, it must go beyond the letter of scriptures, creed, and tradition. Men and women of faith in both communities must learn to listen to the divine voice speaking through revelation and history, and together seek to understand what God is saying to Muslims through Christianity and to Christians trough Islam. (p. 70)

Nevertheless, in this contribution, I would also like to address the 'letter' of the scriptures, which play such an important role in both traditions. The question which I would like to pose within the framework of reflection on the general theme of 'sharing religious experience' is as follows: How, according to the Koran, did the prophet Mohammed understand his prophetic function in relation to earlier prophets? Mohammed thought that he clearly shared in the experiences of the earlier prophets who were sent to their respective peoples. He above all believed that he had been sent as prophet, *al-nabi al-ummi* (7:157, 158 [156-158]), to the 'illiterate,' that is those who had not previously received a book. As prophet, Mohammed was inspired and encouraged by the experiences of the earlier prophets. He was convinced that he shared their experiences. As a result, the stories related in the Koran from the Bible and the Arab prophets are described in a way which, on the one hand, represents the features of the prophets themselves, but on the other hand, bear the *distinct colouring* of Mohammed's own experiences.

In the following, I would like (1) to reflect on the question concerning the relationship between revelation and experience in the case of Mohammed; (2) to examine to what extent we can speak of such a *colouring* in the interpretation and assimilation of the earlier prophets within Mohammed's own experiences, whereby certain 'lives of the prophets' will be used as examples of the degree to which they are marked by Mohammed's own life story; (3) to analyze to what extent this experience has had an effect on the way in which the Koran views Jesus as prophet, and the way in which Jewish and Christian positions are contested at certain points.

1 Revelation and Experience

The way in which revelation, as it descended *(tanzil)* upon Mohammed, is understood by perhaps most Muslims, is as a *mechanical* process. Consequently, it is actually taboo to speak of Mohammed's own experience in connection with this revelation. According to this explanation, Mohammed received the word of God *directly*, and the Koran contains the direct 'words of God,' dictated, as it were, by God himself (or the angel Gabriel). In certain orthodox (Islamic) circles, any mention of Mohammed's own *experience* in connection with the reception of divine revelation would be considered an attack on the nature of Koranic revelation as the direct word of God. For 'traditional' Muslims thinkers, the Koran is the word of God conveyed to Mohammed; God cannot be subject to cultural or literary influences. (Watt 1988, 9)

Nevertheless, consideration for the *human* factor in the revelation event, and therefore also for the contribution of Mohammed's own experience to it is, also present in Islamic circles, now as well as in the past. In tradition *(hadīth)* from the prophet Mohammed, quoted by Izutsu, it is related that al-Harit b. Hišam once asked the prophet:

> "O Apostle of God, how does the revelation come to you?", the latter replied, "Sometimes it comes to me like the ringing of a bell. ... And this is the most painful manner of revelation to me; then it leaves me and I have understood ... from that noise what He [God] meant to say." (Izutsu, 17)

Izutsu then goes on to explain what, in his opinion, Mohammed meant to say with "I have understood:"

> What Muhammad is trying to convey thereby seems to be that while he is actually receiving Revelation he does not have the consciousness of hearing any intelligible words spoken; all that he hears is something like a mysterious indistinct noise ..., but the moment it ceases and he himself returns to the level of normal human consciousness he realizes that the noise has already transformed itself into distinct meaningful words. *(Ibid)*

I would like to point out in this connection how the created or uncreated nature of the Koran was under discussion at that time. The view of the so-called 'Lafziya' was that while the Koran was uncreated, its *lafz,* or 'utterance,' resulting from recitation was created. This question "may have been suggested by the discussions of whether the words of God addressed to Moses were his eternal speech, or it may have arisen spontaneously" (Watt 1988, 82). In the circle of the Mu'tazilites, the opinion circulated that what is written, remembered, and heard is indeed the Koran, but that what is heard is the Koran in the sense of an *hikaya,* that is, an 'imitation,' or even better, a 'reproduction' of the Koran, and that a *mithl,* is perhaps "a likeness of it" (Watt 1973, 281). Ibn Kullab said that "the speech of God is a 'single meaning' *(ma'na wahid)* subsisting in him and that the sounds and letters are a 'copy' or 'trace' *(rasm)* of it and an 'expression' *(ibara)* of it" *(Ibid,* 283). He refers then to the so-called "Testament of Abū Hanīfa," which concedes that pen, paper, and writing is 'created,' but at the same time maintains that "the writing, letters, words, and verses are *dalāla,* an 'indication' or 'manifestation,' of the Qur'ān to meet human needs" *(Ibid,* 284). In a later document, the so-called 'Al-Fiqh al-Akbar II,' *hikaya* and *dalāla* are not mentioned, but rather that "our *lafz* of the Qur'ān is created, our writing of it is created, and our reciting of it is created, whereas the Qur'ān is not created." (Wensinck, 127)

The late Pakistani scholar Fazlur Rahman described how he viewed the process which took place upon Mohammed's reception of the revelation:

> Just as nature represents the inexhaustible 'words' or *logoi* of God, so does the Qur'ān (18:109ff.),[1] for, like nature, the Qur'ān flows through the mind of the Prophet with God's *permission*, and if God should so will, He could close down the flow of the revelation from the Prophet's heart. (42:24; etc.; Rahman 1980, 71)

Fazlur Rahman discusses Sūra 53 al-Nadjm ('The Star'), especially verses 5-18, where Mohammed's reception of revelation is dealt with. There is in this passage no description of anything which he *heard*, as is often the case in the Koran, but rather of what he *saw*.

> He was instructed by one great in strength, and wise. After which he stood on the highest horizon. Thereupon he came closer, and came down, to a distance of two spans or even closer. Then he revealed to his servant that which he revealed. His heart did not lie about what he saw. Can you then dispute what he saw? And he saw him when he came down another time, by the furthest lote-tree, where the garden of Abode is located. Then the lote-tree was veiled in that in which it is veiled. He did not avert his eyes, and he did not come down farther. Truly he had seen something of the great signs of his Lord. (53:5-18)

Fazlur Rahman comments as follows on this passage:

> It is obvious from this passage (1) that the reference is the experience at two different times; (2) that in one experience the Prophet 'saw' the Angel of revelation at the 'highest horizon,' and he possessed extraordinary, almost suppressive strength, while on an earlier occasion he had 'seen' him at the 'furthest lote-tree — where the garden of Abode is located'; (3) that instead of the Prophet 'going up' in Ascension, in both cases the agent of revelation 'came down'; (4) that the experience was spiritual and not physical-locomotive: 'his heart did not lie about what he saw'; (5) finally, that the revelatory experiences involved an expansion of the Prophet's self by which he enveloped all reality and which was total in its comprehensive sweep — the reference in both cases is to an ultimate, be it the 'highest horizon' or the 'furthest lote tree.' (1981, 92)

Fazlur Rahman characterizes Koranic revelation as, "a voice ... crying from the very depths of life and impinging forcefully on the Prophet's

---

[1] The comparison found in Sūra 18:109, which reads, "Say if the sea was turned into ink for the words of my Lord, then the sea would be exhausted before the words of his Lord were exhausted, even if we were to bring twice as much," goes back to a Jewish source (Paret, 395). Cf. 3:127 (126).

mind in order to make itself explicit at the level of consciousness."
(1979, 30)

He points out in his study how in the second and third centuries of
the Muslim calendar an acute disagreement arose among Muslims regarding the nature of the revelation. It was at that time 'orthodoxy' which
emphasized the externality of the revelation, "to safeguard its otherness,
objectivity, and verbal character" (1979, 31). Rahman then quotes a few
Koran texts in which, in his opinion, it is said that the revelation was
"brought down upon the heart of Muḥammad:"

> And lo! it is a revelation of the Lord of the Worlds which the
> true spirit has brought down upon thy heart, that thou mayest be one
> of the warners. (26:192-194)

> Say (Oh Mohammed to mankind): Who is an enemy to Gabriel!
> For he it is who has revealed (this scripture) to thy heart by Allah's
> leave, confirming that what was before it. (2:97)

According to Fazlur Rahman, 'orthodoxy' (indeed all Medieval thought)
lacked,

> ... the necessary intellectual tools to combine in its formulation of the
> dogma the otherness and verbal character of the Revelation on the one
> hand, and its intimate connection with the work and the religious
> personality of the Prophet on the other, i. e., it lacked the intellectual
> capacity to say both that the Qur'ān is entirely the word of God and, in
> an ordinary sense, also entirely the word of Muḥammad. (1979, 31;
> concerning the uproar which ensued upon this last statement, see the
> Pakistan Times, September 3 and 4, 1968.)

There are, as it were, moments when Mohammed,

> ... transcends himself and his moral cognitive perception becomes so
> acute and so keen that his consciousness becomes identical with the
> moral law itself (cf. Koran XLII, 52). But the moral law and religious
> values are God's commands, and although they are not identical with
> God entirely, they are part of Him. The Qur'ān is, therefore, purely
> divine. Further, even with regard to ordinary consciousness, it is a
> mistaken notion that ideas and feeling float about in it and can be
> mechanically 'clothed' in words. There exists, indeed, an organic relation-
> ship between feelings, ideas, and words. In inspiration, even in poetic
> inspiration, this relationship is so complete that feeling—idea—word is a
> total complex with a life of its own. When Muḥammad's moral intuitive
> perception rose to the highest point and became identified with the
> moral law itself ... the word was given with inspiration itself. The
> Qur'ān is thus pure Divine Word, but, of course it is equally intimately
> related to the inmost personality of the Prophet Muḥammad whose
> relationship to it cannot be mechanically conceived like that of a record.

The Divine Word flowed through the Prophet's heart   (1979, 32-33; italics ours).

Fazlur Rahman's interpretation illustrates that also in Muslim circles appeal has been made for what in Christian theology is known as an *organic,* as opposed to a *mechanical,* doctrine of inspiration (Bavinck, 400, 402, 409, 413f.). With *mechanical inspiration,* the divine factor is so emphasized that "... the human authors are reduced to stenographers, clerks, or secretaries of the Spirit who simply write down what is dictated to them" (Polman, 621). *Organic inspiration,* however, entails that

> the Holy Spirit employs active, living persons with their own personalities and gifts, thoughts and actions, experiences and memories, language and style, and uses them as his organs. *(Ibid)*

In a certain sense, the view of Fazlur Rahman could be placed in the latter category. M. Denny, who cited this same view of Fazlur Rahman, summarizes his position as follows: "He rejected any notion that Muhammad was simply God's appointed vehicle through which the message was communicated, in a *mechanical manner* to human kind." (Denny, 98; cf. Cragg, 36)

2 Mohammed and the other prophets

The Koran speaks at length about the prophets who preceded the coming of the prophet Mohammed. A number of their names are known from the Old and New Testament, even though they are not always called prophets there: Noah (Nut), Abraham (Ibrahim), Lot (Lut), Moses (Musa), David (Dawud) and Jesus (Isa). In addition, the Koran names the so-called 'Arab prophets,' such as Šu'ayb (perhaps to be equated with Jethro), who was sent to the inhabitants of Midian (Sūra 7:85-93 [83-91]); the prophet Hud, who was sent to the 'Adites (Sūra 7:65-72 [63-70]); and Salih, who was sent to the people of Thamud. (Sūra 7:73-79 [71-77])

The Koran relates many specifics regarding these prophets. In addition, however, these accounts have features which are very *similar* to Mohammed's own life as a prophet and the experiences which he underwent. For example, *specific* to Salih is the account that God sent a female camel to Thamud as a miraculous sign (7:59 [61]), to which they were to give food and drink (7:73 [71]; 26:155; 54:28). But the people severed the limbs of the camel and killed it (7:77 [75]; 11:65 [68]; 26:157). Salih asked them to take refuge in their houses for three days (11:65 [68]).

Then furious lightening began (51:44) which was followed by an earth-
quake, by which they were killed. (7:78 [76])[2]

Similar to Mohammed's own experience, however, is that Salih
summoned his people to serve no other God than God (7:73 [71]); 11:61
[64]). He called on them to remember the gifts of God (77:74 [72]). Salih
asked for no payment (26:145). But they rejected him, saying that he was
a under a spell (26:153), and that he was a man just like them (54:24).
They rejected the idea that they had to abandon the religion of their
ancestors (11:62 [65]) and scorned the idea of the day of judgment (69:4).
His appearance occasioned a rift among people (27:45 [46]); only the
oppressed believed in him, while the notables were arrogant and did not.
(7:75, 76 [73, 74])

A similar account is given of the prophet Hud, who appeared among
the people of 'Ad, according to the Koran. He belonged to this people,
and like Mohammed during his activity in Mecca, is described as a
warner, who had only met with rejection and arrogance and had only a
small number of followers. In the end he was rescued by God. (7:65-72
[70]; 11:50-60 [52-63])

Mohammed's own experiences are very clearly reflected in these
accounts. The same applies to the life and work of the prophet Noah
(who is not viewed as a prophet in the Bible). Specific to Noah in the
Koran is the account of the ark and the flood (10:73 [74]). But Noah, who
is called Muslim (10:72 [73]), is a "speaking warner" (11:25 [27]). It is said
concerning Noah that he asked forgiveness for his parents and for those
who visited his home (71:28 [29]) —the same is said of Abraham (14:41;
26:86)— which apparently has more to do with Mohammed's own experiences (Gibb and Kramers). "O my people, there is no error in me. For
I am a messenger of the Lord of the worlds. I bring you the message
from my Lord" (7:71, 52 [59, 60]). These words are placed in the mouth of
Noah, but could just as well be, or are (!) the words of Mohammed
himself. Noah heard from his opponents things which Mohammed too
had to endure, such as being declared a liar (10:73 [74]), and that he was
only a man like them, and that an angel should have been sent down
(23:24). Noah was, like Mohammed, considered to be in error (7:60 [58]),
possessed (54:9), only the most despicable followed him (11:27 [29]; 26:111).
The type of answer Noah gave to his opponents is reminiscent of the
reaction Mohammed himself displayed. (10:71-73 [72-74]; 11:29-31 [31-33])

When it is said that Noah rejected the demands of the powerful in
his community to break with the socially dispossessed, and when it is said
that the economically powerful did want to join forces with him, the story

---

[2] It is assumed that this story was based on an etiological saga by which an attempt was
made to explain a unique rock formation in the form of a lying camel. (Paret, 165)

describes a situation similar to what Mohammed confronted. Even the ancient gods of the Arabs are viewed as the gods of the generation of Noah (71:23)! The gods Wadd, Suwaʻ, Yaghuth, Yaʻuq and Nasr were worshipped primarily by the tribes of southern Arabia. (See Paret, 488, 489, and the literature cited there.)

The same *scheme* returns again and again in these tales of the prophets. To every people a messenger or warner is sent (13:7 [8]). Like Mohammed, so also Hud, Salih, Šuʼayb, as well as Noah (Nuh), Abraham (Ibrahim) and Moses (Musa) had to suffer from the sarcasm, insults, and threats expressed by their people. Their people declared them *liars,* mocking them, and refusing to accept their message. The majority of the people are punished as a result, while the messenger himself is saved. The salvation of the messenger is common to Noah (7:64 [62]), Lot (21:24), and Moses (2:50 [47]), as well as the Arab prophet Hud (11:58 [61]), Salih (11:66 [69]) and Šuʼayb (11:94 [97]). Each of them, in contrast to their own people, is saved.

Mohammed is named along with Noah, Abraham, and Jesus as one with whom God made a covenant (33:7). He was considered to be *bewitched,* like other prophets (17:47 [59]; 25:8 [9]). Moses before him was considered bewitched, and a sorcerer (40:24 [25]; 43; 49:49 [48]). The same is said of Salih (26:153) and Šuʼayb (26:185). Mohammed is accused of being 'possessed' (15:38; 37:36 [35]; 44:14 [13]; 68:5), which the Koran expressly denies (34:46 [45]; 52:29; 68:2; 81:22). Noah too was described as 'possessed' (23:25), as was Moses (26:27 [26]; 51:39). Even as Mohammed was called a *liar,* so also the former communities called their prophets liars (29:18 [17]). The *careers* of the other prophets, therefore, seem to follow practically the same course as that of Mohammed, according to the Koran. The Koran sketches, as it were, the repetition of the same drama of the experiences of Mohammed's appearance as prophet against a world backdrop. To a certain extent, then, one can in this way discern the life story of Mohammed by following the stories of the other prophets in the Koran. In a number of cases it is obvious, and in a number of other cases it may be assumed; one accordingly receives information concerning the life of Mohammed embedded in the stories of the other prophets. Thus, Šuʼayb is depicted as someone who warns his people against fraudulent business practices, which was precisely Mohammed's problem in Mecca. (11:84-95 [85-98]; 7:85-93 [83-91])

With regard to Salih it is said that his people initially put much hope in him, apparently before he began to alienate them with his preaching (11:62 [65]). If this too has a parallel in the life of Mohammed, it would shed an interesting indirect light on his life. (Gibb/Kramers)

There are, as noted, many specific features to be discovered in the descriptions of the lives of earlier prophets, but their image is at the same time one which has been filtered, so to speak, through the experience of the prophet Mohammed, so that through them we also gain insight into the way in which Mohammed understood his own prophetic function.

3 Mohammed and Jesus

How is the life of Jesus described in the Koran? There are, of course, in the ninety-five verses in the Koran dedicated to Isa ibn Maryam, several specifics mentioned, such as his miraculous birth (19:22-26 [22-27]), which is compared with that of Adam (3:59 [52]), his speaking from the cradle in order to silence the insults heaped on his mother (19:28-33 [28-34]). It also notes how he as child made birds of clay and blew life into them (3:49); how he preached the gospel, performed miracles, healed diseases, raised the dead with God's permission (3:49; 5:110 [109]); how he prophesied the coming of one after him whose name would be Aḥmed, or praise-worthy (61:6). Jesus ('Isa) is called 'spirit of God' and 'word of Him' in the Koran (4:171 [169]). His crucifixion was apparently denied and ultimately it is recorded that he was taken up to God. (4:157, 158 [156])

At the same time, however, many things are said about Jesus in the Koran which agree closely with what is said concerning earlier prophets as well as Mohammed. Thus, Jesus is called a prophet and God's envoy. The first words he speaks are already, as it were, the words of a Muslim: "He [Isa] said [while still in the cradle], 'I am a *servant* of God. He has given me a book and made me a prophet. And ... He has placed on me the *ṣalāt* and the *zakāt* for as long as I live' " (19:30, 31 [31, 32]). Jesus did not consider it beneath his dignity to be 'only a servant.' (4:172 [170]; 43:59)

If we are correct is assuming that Mohammed saw in the mission of the earlier prophets an analogy of his own mission (Bell, 330), then one can only wonder whether this might also be true with respect to the description of Jesus, and especially those facets of the image of Jesus in which the Koran expressly polemicizes against Jewish and Christian views.

This polemic is primarily directed at two points. The first point, which actually can be divided into two components which are interrelated, is the denial that Jesus is the 'son of God' or 'God,' and the denial that Jesus is 'one of three,' or 'three gods.' The Koran accused Christians of believing in three gods (5:116) Apparently the Koran understands the three as consisting of God, Jesus, and Maria (!). The second point is the denial that Jesus was crucified.

With respect to the first of these two points, Mohammed's message was for all intents and purposes from the very beginning strongly directed toward the oneness of God. Chapter 112 of the Koran (entitled *Ikhlās,* or 'sincere') best expresses it. "Say: God is one. God is eternal. He has never begotten nor been begotten. No one is like unto Him." In the time of Mohammed, in the surrounding regions, it was believed that God had *daughters* (Al-Lat, al-'Uzza and Manat).

A delicate question in this context is whether Mohammed himself had ever made a concession to the idea of polytheism. This question has been raised with respect to the fifty-third chapter of the Koran. In the Islamic tradition it is related that Mohammed was once rejected by the Qurayshites, his own people and neighbours. They caused him and his followers much harm. Mohammed is then reported to have said: "I wish that something were revealed to keep them away from me." When he once sat among their company in the vicinity of the Ka'ba, he recited Chapter 53 until he came to the question: "What do you think of the al-Lat and al'Uzza and Manat, the third?" (53:19, 20). In response, according to the tradition related by al-Tabari, he recited: "These are the exalted herons (*gharaniq*) and behold, in their mediation is hoped for" (At-Tabari, 1192-93; cf. Ibn Sa'd, 137-38). When Mohammed had brought up this passage together with the rest of the chapter, according to the same source, all the people bowed down behind him in prayer. In other words, this meant that as soon as Mohammed appeared prepared to make room for the goddesses worshipped by the Qurayshites, they were prepared to follow him.

However, as the story continues, as soon as Mohammed returned home, the angel Gabriel said to him: "Did I deliver these words to you?" Mohammed answered: "I have said about God what He has not said." The next day Mohammed recanted these so-called "satanic verses" and the following Koran verse was revealed to Mohammed: "They had almost led you into temptation to go astray from what We had revealed to you, so that they would fabricate against Us something other than that [Koran]. Then they would have certainly accepted you as friend. And if We had not made you firm, you would nearly have become dependent on them" (17:73, 74 [75, 76]). That the possibility of Satanic prompting was real is confirmed by another passage of the Koran: "And We have not sent a messenger or a prophet before your time that when personal inspiration arose in him Satan did not try to destroy that inspiration; yet God set at naught what Satan had achieved with his attempt and then He established His sign . . ." (22:52 [51]).

The authenticity of this tradition is often denied by Muslims. How sensitive this point is for Muslims can be seen from the reactions to the book by Salman Rushdie, *The Satanic Verses,* in which this tradition has been 'romantically' reworked. In light of the emphasis which was placed in Islam on the confession of the oneness of God, it was indeed a shocking episode. All the more reason, however, to believe, that this account which has been handed down by Islamic sources would not have been fabricated. Ultimately, in my opinion, this story is intended precisely to confirm the importance of Mohammed's preaching of the oneness of God and his faithfulness in conveying it.

Whatever the case may be, it is understandable, against the background of the emphasis on the preaching of the oneness of God, why the Koran so adamantly denies that Jesus is a son of god or God (5:116), that Christians make him Lord (9:31) or declare that the messiah is the son of God (9:30). Such a conviction is called *unbelief* (5:17 [19]; 72 [76]). Just as the Koran denies that God has daughters *(banat Allah)* in the phrase "God has not begotten and is not begotten," so also these texts reject the idea that God has a *son*. Here Mohammed's experiences with Arab heathens clearly has left their impress on his understanding of this facet of Christian faith, which is consequently regarded as like the faith of heathens.

With regard to the second point, it appears that the crucifixion of Jesus is denied by the Koran. That is the way, at least, in which the related passage from the Koran is usually interpreted by Muslims. It is frequently pointed out that the striking thing is that the passage in question stands in relation to a series of reproaches of the Jews, who have broken the covenant, have not believed in the signs of God, have unjustly killed their prophets, and have blasphemed Mary (4:155 [154]). The Koran continues:

> And concerning their [the Jews'] claim: "We have killed Jesus, the son of Mary, the messenger of God." They have not killed him and they have not crucified him, it only appeared that way to them. And those who disagree on that point are truly in doubt concerning him. And they have no knowledge concerning him except the pursuit of an assumption. And they have certainly not killed him. No, God has elevated him to himself, and God is mighty and wise. And there is no one of the people of the book who will not believe in him on account of his death. And on the day of resurrection he [Jesus] will be a witness against them. (4:157-159 [156-157])

This passage is often interpreted to mean that the Koran here denies the crucifixion, because according to the 'scheme' of the prophets, noted above, God does not ultimately allow his prophets to be destroyed. Just as Mohammed himself was ultimately victorious in spite of the resistance he met, so also Jesus was ultimately victorious.

This last expression indeed corresponds with what is repeated again and again with respect to the prophets. Divine help and ultimate victory belongs to the messengers of God and those who them (40:51 [54]). Concerning Noah it is said: "And We helped him escape the people, who had declared our signs lies" (21:77). Concerning Moses, Aaron, and their followers we hear: "We helped them so that they were victorious"

(37:116). Hud and Salih were saved (11:58, 66 [61, 69]) Noah was saved from the flood (7:64 [62]), Abraham from the fire (21:69; 29:24 [23]). Moses was saved from the hands of the Pharaoh and his hosts (2:50 [47]), and Jesus from the hands of the Jews. In the same way —that appears to be the point of the references to the stories of earlier prophets— Mohammed will be saved and his message will triumph. In light of the fact that Mohammed's own experiences was triumphal, Jesus too was saved, or such would seem to be the thought which lies behind it.

The question is whether this discretion is completely adequate and therefore whether it does *complete* justice to this passage. The question also is whether this apparent scheme does not here too forcefully determine the explanation of this passage concerning Jesus. Although it is true that there is something schematic expressed in the pattern to which the various prophets appear to conform, that does not diminish the fact that the stories also take into account *specifics,* a fact which also applies to in the story concerning Jesus.

In opposition to such explanation it may be noted that it would be untrue to assert that the Koran does not admit the thought that prophets cannot meet with 'failure.' Not all the prophets are ultimately triumphant in that sense. The Koran is, furthermore, aware of the suffering of the prophets. With respect to this latter statement Muḥammad al-Nuwayhi commented: "The Koran is nothing if it does not identify with the suffering creation and suffering mankind. This lies behind its vehemence, its suffering and sorrow over the disobedience and sins of humanity." He refers to the passage in the Koran "Oh how miserable for the servants. No messenger comes to them whom they do not mock" (36:30). Al-Nuwayhi then continues: "Note that God's misery (*hasra,* literally: 'yearning,' 'suffering,' 'sadness') not only occasioned Mohammed's reception by the Arabs, but also that all other messengers gained a like reception among their people." (p. 9)

But the Koran speaks not only of the suffering which the prophets had to undergo, but also expressly mentions the fact that they sometimes were *killed.* That prophets were killed by the Jews is mentioned directly before (4:155 [154]) the passage in which the crucifixion is purportedly denied (4:157 [156]). The Koran also elsewhere reproaches the Jews for having killed the prophets without justification or cause (2:61 [58]; 3:112 [108]; 3:21 [20]; 3:181 [177]; 2:91 [85]). A group of the prophets was declared liars by them, and another group was killed! (2:87 [81]; 5:70 [65]; cf. Acts 7:52)

There is another reason why one may question whether this passage (3:157-159 [156-157]) intends to maintain that the crucifixion never took place *historically.* For there are several other places where the Koran speaks openly about Jesus' death. "Happy is the day on which I was born, *on which I died,* and on which I was brought back to life " (19:33 [34]). "I [God] will collect the guilt of your death, and I will exalt you to myself, and I will free you from those who do not believe ..." *(mutawaffika wa rafi'uka ilāya* — 3:55 [48]). The word which is here translated as "collect the guilt of your death" means the return to God for the last judgment. This return is the work of God, the angels, or the angel of death (or death). In the Koran it is used twice with respect to Jesus.

It appears, therefore, that on the one hand the Koran says that Jesus died and that his death was collected by God, and on the other hand, that he was not crucified and killed, but was taken up to God. The usual Islamic explanation is that he was exalted *without having been crucified or having died.* The interpretations of other Islamic interpreters stand in opposition to this, although they usually have a particular slant. Over the years Muslims have also recognized that Jesus indeed died. This was taught, for example, by the Brothers of Purity *(Ikhwan al-Safa').* Another Ismaelite author, Abū Ḥātim al-Rāzī († 934) said that when explaining 4:156, the end of the verse should be noted: "They did not really kill him. God took him to himself." He maintains that Jesus died as a martyr, calling our attention to the passage in the Koran where it says: "Do not say to those who are killed on the path of God: 'you have died.' For they live, even though you do not take it into account." (3:169; cf. 2:154 — Massignon, 535; Hayek, 218, 230ff.)

It must be asked whether the aforementioned Koran passage (4:157-159 [156-157]) does not so much wish to deny that Jesus was killed, but above all wants to deny that people (in this case the Jews) were responsible for that act. Not the Jews, but God himself collected the guilt of his death, the Koran says (3:55 [48]). As has already been noted, it is striking that this apparent denial of the crucifixion stands not in relation to a dialogue with Christians, but with Jews. We should pause at the significance of the introductory words *"And on account of what they —the Jews— say" (wa qawlihim;* 4:157 [156]). The Koran elsewhere calls 'woe' on those who write the scriptures with their own hand thereby falsifying it (2:79 [73]), or remove the words from their place (5:13 [16], 41 [45]). They —the Jews— supposedly twist their tongues when they read the scriptures, so that the crucifixion is wrongly supposed to belong to the scriptures. (3:78 [72]; cf. 4:46 [48])

In the Koran, the Christians who maintain that the messiah is the son of God and the Jews who say that Ezra is the son of God are mentioned in one breath. Then follows: "that is what they say with their mouth" (9:30). The Koran therefore repeatedly emphasizes the negative things which the Jews and Christians are able to do *with their mouth:* "They [the possessors of scripture — Jews and Christians] began to dim the light of God with their mouth *(bi-afwahihim),* but want nothing other than to oppose it. He is the one who has sent his messenger with the right leading and the true religion, in order to help him overcome all religions, even though the polytheists are against it" (9:32 [33]; cf. 61:8, 9; 48:28). In this last text, therefore, mention is made of the dimming of the light by the words *from their mouth.*

Mahmud Ayoub once suggested that something similar could have been intended in the text in question: a denial of the killing of Jesus *with their mouth,* with their words! In this case, this text does not deny that the crucifixion and death of Jesus took place —other texts do say that he died— but that they did not succeed in killing him with their mouth, with their words, since God 'saved' him *(rafa'a).* The repeated Koranic perception is that it is God who is to be thanked for success and victory. That applies to the other prophets as well as Mohammed. That is also evident in the passage which deals with the well-known Muslim battle against its opponent at Badr. There a small group of Muslims gained victory over a great number of their 'heathen' Meccan opponents. This victory was thanks to God, according to the Koran (3:123 [119]). The Muslims did not kill their enemies; God killed them (8:17). Just as this latter statement does not intend to say that the Meccan opponents were not actually killed by the small band of Muslims —this did in fact occur; its historicity is not denied by the Koran text or otherwise— so also we can analogously conclude that the Koran does not deny that some of the prophets were killed in the past, or that Jesus was killed. "God collected the guilt for his death *([mu]tawafiqqa)."*

When viewed in this way, we see that there is a deeper 'theological' meaning lying behind this text. In spite of their *contention* that they killed and crucified him, God himself saved him through death *(rafa'a;* cf. Räisänen). God did not save him from death or crucifixion, but through death! God saved Jesus even as he saved the other prophets. Jesus was saved by God taking him to himself, he was 'raised up' *(rafa'a).*[3] In the Koran it is said that God granted to some of his messengers, among them Jesus, a higher position *(rafa'a ba'dahum daragatin* 2:253 [254]; cf. 6:165; 43:32 [31]; 6:83; 12:76; 4:158; 3:55). But in the case of Jesus, he will be specially 'raised up' in the end!

"I will take you to myself and I will exalt you to myself ..." (3:48 [55]); "... God has taken him to himself ..." (4:158). The Arabic word which is here employed, and is translated by "I will take you to myself," means the return to God for the last judgment (Michaud, 61). One could

---

[3] It is interesting to note in this connection that the Egyptian author Naguib Mahfuz, the nobel prize winner for literature in 1988, speaks of Jesus (and Mohammed) in a allegorical way in *Awlad Haritna.* The name which he gives to Jesus in this book is *Rifa'a* — the one raised up.

argue that the 'raising up' of Jesus to God (rafa'a) does not take the place of the crucifixion, but coheres with it in some way. Hasan Askari has commented that the different, apparently contradictory statements about Jesus' death in the Koran could perhaps be explained as different treatments of the same event. The statements "God let him die" and "God raised him up" would then refer to the same event.

It is noteworthy that the New Testament displays a similar coherence. The answer given by Jesus to the two men on the road to Emmaus is often translated: "Did the Messiah not have to suffer these things in order to enter his glory?" (Luke 24:26). The Greek word that is translated here as 'in order to' is simply the word 'and' (kai). Jesus' answer can also be rendered as "Did the Messiah not have to suffer these things and enter into his glory." That is, he was glorified in and through his suffering. John relates a similar coherence when he says: "And just as Moses lifted up the snake in the dessert, so must the son of man be lifted up" (John 3:14). John does not distinguish the raising up, this lifting up on the cross from the exaltation to heaven. (Zaehner, 213)

Conclusion

In the foregoing we have determined that at least some Muslim thinkers allow room for Mohammed's own personal experience in the reception of divine revelation. This does not, for such thinkers, diminish the divine character of the Koran which remains for them completely the word of God.

The account of the other prophets which we read in the Koran contain specific, unique features along with features which can be seen as containing an analogy with the experiences of Mohammed as prophet. Rather than speaking of the deficiencies, bias, and incompleteness of the 'information' found in the Koran with regard to the earlier prophets and Jesus in comparison with that found in the Old and New Testaments, as so often is done by Christians within Christian–Muslim dialogue, it seems of more importance to reassess the Koranic image of the prophets, in particular that of Jesus, to determine the extent to which the experience of Mohammed is reflected in them. In so doing, it is hoped that justice will be done to the specificity of Koranic insights. But at the same time we must be careful that the so-called scheme discovered in the tales of previous prophets not begin to function as a straightjacket, diminishing the uniqueness of stories of the individual prophets.

In Mohammed's experience, danger lurked in the thought and practice of polytheism. The oneness and uniqueness of God was threatened by polytheism, for example, by belief in al-Lat, al-'Uzza, and Manat. Mohammed also saw the oneness of God threatened in the form of

Christian belief which he encountered. Instead of speaking of the Koran's wrong or incomplete information in comparison with the Old and New Testament, the Christian reader should ask what the relevance is of the question explicitly or implicitly posed by the Koran of the Christian. Even apart from the Koranic accusation that Christians believe in more than one God, we would do well to note that the accusation of tritheism has not been taken seriously enough in the history of the Church (Berkouwer, 190). The Church can of course counter that it rejects the idea of a physical sonship as well as that of three Gods.

In the foregoing I wanted to demonstrate in particular that the schema which the Koran displays with regard to the lives of the prophets does not entail that Jesus was not crucified and killed. In addition to the similarities between the prophets, the Koran leaves room for the specific features of each prophet. The experience of Mohammed has left just such room for the unique significance of Jesus.

Bibliography

Ayoub, M. "Muslim Views of Christianity: Some Modern Examples." *Islamochristiana* 10 (1984).

Bavinck, H. *Gereformeerde Dogmatiek* I. Kampen, [4]1928.

Bell, R. "Muḥammad and Previous Messengers." *The Moslem World* 24 (1934).

Berkouwer, G. C. *De Verkiezing Gods.* Kampen, 1955.

Cragg, K. *The Christian and Other Religions.* London, 1977.

Denny, M. "Fazlur Rahman: Muslim Intellectual." *The Moslem World* 79 (April 1989).

Gibb, H. A. R. and J. H. Kramers, eds. *Shorter Encyclopædia of Islam.* Leiden/London, 1961. *sub voce* Nuh, Salih.

Ibn Sa'd. *Tabaqat* E. Sachau, ed. Leiden, 1905, I, 1.

Izutsu, Toshihiko. *God and Man in the Koran: Semantics of the Koranic Weltanschauung.* Tokyo, 1964.

Maḥfuz, N. *Awlad Haritna.* Beirut, 1967.

Massignon, L. "Le Christ dans les évangiles selon al-Ghazali." In *Opera Minora* II. Beirut, 1963.

Michaud, H. *Jésus selon le Coran.* Neuchâtel, 1960

Nuwayhi, Muḥammad al-. Address held in Cair , May 13, 1974. (stencil)

Paret, R. *Der Koran: Kommentar und Konkordanz.* Stuttgart, 1976

Polman, A. D. R. "Inspiratie." In *Christelijke Encyclopedie* III. F. W. Grosheide and G. P. van Itterzon, eds. Kampen, [2]1958.

Räisänen, H. *Das Koranische Jesusbild: Ein Beitrag zur Theologie des Korans.* Helsinki, 1971.

Rahman, F. *Islam.* Chicago, [2]1979

———. *Major Themes of the Qur'ān.* Chicago, 1981

Rushdie, S. *Satanic Verses.* London, 1989.

Tabari, At-. *Annals* I. Leiden, 1879

Watt, W. M. *The Formative Period of Islamic Thought.* Edinburgh, 1973.

———. *Islamic Fundamentalism and Modernity.* London/New York, 1988.

Wensinck, A. J. *The Muslim Creed: Its Genesis and Historical Development.* Cambridge, 1932.

Zaehner, R. C. *At Sundry Times: An Essay in the Comparison of Religions.* London, 1958.

CHAPTER 20

Sharing Religious Experience as a Problem in Early Islamic Mysticism

Hans Daiber

The problem of sharing religious experience played a dominant role in early Islamic mysticism. The Sufi, Djunayd († 908/910 A. D.), taking the Koranic conception of God's transcendence as his point of departure, developed Kharrāz' idea of 'indications.' These indications are the only manner in which one can articulate religious experience. The Sufi master's task as a teacher in relation to the novices is in fact the same as that of the prophet who is charged with explaining God's message to the people. It is not due to the Sufi's merit that he attains a higher plane of spiritual experience; God elects him; it His grace that bestows knowledge on him, enabling him to attain mystical experience of unification with God. Such experience is followed by a state of sobriety which enables the Sufi to convey his mystical experience to his fellow man. He cannot, however, inform them concerning the ultimate stage of mystical experience in which annihilation of the self yields to 'overwhelming' intoxication, since such experience is granted solely by the grace of God. He can only give them 'indications,' teaching them rules and preparing them for dialogue with God. In his calling, the Sufi resembles both the prophet who transmits God's wisdom and the teacher who prepares his students for receiving God's grace. All are charged with the quest of restoring people to their original divine existence.

It is widely accepted that the Koranic idea of God as invisible mystery *(ghayb)* plays a dominant role in the Islamic experience of God's transcendence (Sura 10:20-21; cf. MacDonald/Gardet). This experience of God's otherness finds its expression in the term *tawḥīd* — God's unity and unicity, which forms a central feature of the religion, theology, and especially the mysticism of Islam. Annemarie Schimmel, author of a standard work on Sufism (Schimmel 1985), correctly concludes, "Yet Islam has a large sphere of mystery of its own — the greatest one being the true confession of faith, the acknowledgment of God's Unity and Unicity, *tawḥīd"* (Schimmel 1987, 82). She has shown that mystical experience of God's transcendence cannot, according to Islamic mysticism, be fully described in words (1987). Kalābādhī († 995 A. D.) speaks of 'allusions' *(ishārāt)* to mystical experiences which "cannot be expressed literally" and he adds that "contemplation" and "revelations" "are learnt through actual experience of the mystical, and are only known to those who have experienced these mystical states and lived in these stations." (Arberry 1935, 84; cf. Schimmel 1987, 87)

According to Kalābādhī's explanation, the religious experience of a mystic or Sufi cannot truly be shared by those who hear him speaking of his experience; his words are only 'allusions' to something which can be learned only by direct experience. Examination of early Islamic mystical texts corroborate Kalābādhī's assessment; at the same time, however, these texts present us with a wealth of thought and ideas which portray a rather differentiated picture. This should come as no surprise. Islamic mystics have not remained silent —as one would expect— regarding their mystical experiences. On the contrary, they have intensively reflected on the theme of unification with God. Considerations of this theme on their part have been preserved either in oral utterances, transmitted by their adherents and subsequently preserved in written works, or in their own written treatises, sometimes in the form of letters to fellow mystics.

An impressive example from early Islamic Sufism is the Iranian, Djunayd, who later lived in Baghdad. He died between 908 and 910 A.D. (Schimmel 1985, 93-95). His letters and treatises, which have been preserved in later works (cf. Sezgin, 648f.),[1] primarily seek to tell the reader about unification with God and enable the reader to share his mystical experience, as it were. In reading the texts, however, we are puzzled by Djunayd's enigmatic style, terminology, and cryptic thoughts. Even then, these features of Djunayd's writing prompted a fellow mystic of Djunayd to remark:

"You talk far above my head and have left me in a whirl. Please be simpler and speak so that I can understand." (ed. Abdel-Kader, 37·14, trans. p. 158)

The difficulty of Djunayd's style is not without reason. Djunayd inserted the following remark in his treatise On Divinity:

This [i. e., what I have said] is the indication (ishāra) of what cannot be further explained. Moreover, one can only understand this through the category of indications, if one has received the state (kawn) which precedes my description. I have wrapped up what is in it and have not

---

[1] Most but not all of Djunayd's texts have been published with English translation and introduction by Ali Hassan Abdel-Kader, The Life, Personality, and Writings of Al-Junayd (London, 1962; rpt. 1976). All further references to this edition will be indicated as 'ed. Abdel-Kader.' A French translation of some of Djunayd's works has also been published by Roger Deladriere, Junayd, L'enseignement spirituel: Traités, lettres, croisons et sentences traduits de l'arabe presentés et annotés (Paris, 1983).

elaborated it. (Ed. Abdel-Kader, p. 45·8-10, trans. p. 166; cf. p. 57 — here, as elsewhere, my translation differs from that of Abdel-Kader.)

In this remark on 'indications' we are confronted by a type of symbolic and non-'esoteric' language which was perhaps inspired by Djunayd's older contemporary Kharrāz, who also uses *ishāra* several times in his texts in a manner that is not esoteric or cryptic (cf. as-Sāmarrā'ī, esp. 31ff.). Djunayd explicitly states that mystical experience can only be understood by someone who has had the same mystical experience. In a letter to a fellow mystic he writes:

> My brother — may God be pleased with you— I have received your letter which delighted me in its outward shape (*zāhir*) and in its inward meaning (*bāṭin*),[2] from its beginning to its end. I was happy at the peculiar knowledge ('*ilm gharib*), fine wisdom (*hikma*[3] '*azīza*) and clear, illuminating indications included [in your letter]. That which you hinted at and explained was not concealed from me. All this was known to me and I had previously comprehended your intentions. (ed. Abdel-Kader, 4·1-5, trans., slightly different, p. 125)

No one can comprehend what is totally unknown to him and what can thus be grasped only by personal experience. This fact prompted Djunayd to make the following recommendation to a fellow mystic, Abū Bakr al-Kisā'ī: "You must be careful with what you say and what your contemporaries know: say to the people only what they can recognize (*ya'rifūna*) and keep them away from what they cannot recognize" (ed. Nicholson, 241·1f.; trans., slightly different, in ed. Abdel-Kader, 57). These utterances by Djunayd should not be interpreted as an 'esoteric' attitude shared by Sufis implying that they 'somehow' shared the religious experience of each other as a group of like-minded companions, even though Abdel-Kader (p. 58) and Schimmel (1985, 95) do understand it in this way. Djunayd developed his mystical language not because he wished to conceal something from those who had no access to the knowledge of the Sufis; it was his awareness of the problems in transmitting religious experience to others which informed his use of language. Sufis were of course able to exchange thoughts regarding religious experiences with one another; yet it would be incorrect to speak of 'esoteric language' (as do Abdel-Kader and Schimmel) in such correspondence. Language is simply not capable of describing what can only penetrate human consciousness through personal religious experience.

This becomes evident in Djunayd's doctrine of 'unification' (*tawḥīd*), a central theme of Islamic mysticism. People, the *muwaḥḥidūn*, can be

---

[2] This follows Isma'īlī terminology, see Daiber 1989.
[3] Ed. Abdel-Kader (p. 42) has *ḥukm*.

divided into three classes according to the degree in which they have realized *tawḥīd*:

1. People who 'seek' *(ṭālib)* and 'search' *(qāṣid)* for God and are 'guided' by their knowledge of the 'outward shape' *(aẓ-ẓāhir),* that is, by rules (ed. Abdel-Kader, 55·11f., trans. p. 176). Their 'unification' consists of the 'assertion' *(iqrār)* of the unity of God *(al-waḥdāniyya),* including the negation of any other forces similar or opposite to God and in obedience to His commands and prohibitions (ed. Abdel-Kader, 56·1-10, trans. p. 176). Djunayd distinguishes them from 'common people' *(al-ʿawāmm)* who only assert the unity of God without any 'external' *(ẓāhir)* 'action' *(afʿāl;* ed. Abdel-Kader, 55·19f. trans. p. 176) and who have no 'true knowledge of the outward (rules)' *(ḥaqāʾiq ʿilm aẓ-ẓāhir;* ed. Abdel-Kader, p. 56·5, trans. p. 176).

2. The second class of people do not confine themselves to a knowledge of 'outward' rules and to observing these in their actions: they reach the door (of God; *wārid li-l-bāb),* stay there *(wāqif ʿalayhi)* and discover ways to get close to Him through the signs *(dalāʾil)* of inward purification *(taṣfiyat bāṭinihī;* ed. Abdel-Kader, 55·14-16, trans., not literal, p. 176). They have 'personal experience' *(shāhid)* of God *(al-ḥaqq)* through His call *(ad-daʿwa)* and by answering Him *(al-istidjāba;* ed. Abdel-Kader, 51·14, trans., not literal, p. 177). "He acts towards God *(muʿāmilun li-llāh)* in his interior *(fī bāṭinihī)"* (ed. Abdel-Kader, 55·15f.). Djunayd classifies their 'unification' as the first type of unification performed by 'distinguished' people *(al-khāṣṣ);* it is followed by the second and last stage which is ascribed to the third class of people. (ed. Abdel-Kader, 56·14ff., trans. p. 177)

3. The people of the third class 'come' *(dākhil)* to God, marshalling all their 'care' *(hamm)* for Him and 'staying before Him' *(qāʾim bayna yadayhi)*: they 'see' only (cf. *ruʾya)* God, 'notice' *(mulāḥiẓ)* 'what (God) is indicating to them' *(li-ishāratihī ilayhi)* and 'do without delay *(mubādiran)* what their Lord commands them' (ed. Abdel-Kader, 55·16-18, trans. p. 176). Djunayd characterizes the second type of unification by 'distinguished' people as the pure 'shape' *(shabaḥ/shabḥ)* of standing before Him, with no third (shape) intervening between them. There is no longer an overflow of regulations which He has disposed *(taṣārīf tadbīrī)* in (the form of) rules (determined) in His omnipotence *(aḥkām qudratihī;* ed. Abdel-Kader, 56·14-16).

The equation of *tawhīd-shabah* is remarkable: In his formulation Djunayd identifies the act of 'unification' as a 'shape' or a 'frame' standing before God. The term *shabah* 'shape' also means 'person,' 'figure,' and 'phantom' or 'ghost.' Evidently Djunayd intended to stress the evanescence of a mere apparition:

> Before God man is a mere phantom totally sunk in the flooding seas of [his] unification with God (*fī ludjadji bihāri tawhīdihī*), by annihilation (*fanā'*) of his self, of God's call to him and of his answer to God: by true realization of His oneness (*wahdāniyyatuhū*) in true proximity to Him and by the decrease of perception (*hiss*) and movements (*harakāt*) for God (*al-haqq*) performs for him what He wants from him. (ed. Abdel-Kader, 56·16-19)

This is an impressive description of the idea of man's fleetingness and nothingness before God, who totally determines man's thoughts, actions, and even his very being. Djunayd adds the following passage:

> Characteristic of it is [the result] that man in his final [state] returns to his first [state] and becomes just as he was because he existed before he [began] to exist. This can be proved by God's saying [Sura 7:172/171]:[4] "And when thy Lord took from the Children of Adam, from their loins, their seed, and made them testify touching themselves, 'Am I not your Lord?' They said, 'Yes' ... " (ed. Abdel-Kader, 56·ult.-57·3, trans., slightly different, p. 177)

In unification with God, man is restored to his divine home (cf. also ed. Abdel-Kader, 1·5, trans. p. 122), to their 'divine existence' (*al-wudjūd ar-rabbānī*) and 'God-like conception' (*al-idrāk al-ilāhī*) which only God 'knows' (ed. Abdel-Kader, 32·16, 13, trans. p. 153; cf. p. 77); they annihilate themselves "so that they take their stand (*fa-waqafū*)[5] together with what belongs to Him without turning to what belongs to themselves" (ed. Abdel-Kader, 57·11). Elsewhere, Djunayd describes this unification as "the separation of the Eternal from that which originated in time, and departure from familiar haunts and separation from brethren and forgetfulness of what is known and unknown, and God only in place of All." (-Qushayrī, p. 136; trans. in Abdel-Kader, 71; cf. comments, p. 70f.)

This separation may be compared with the Neo-platonic idea of the soul which, by practising the human virtues, seeks to return to its divine origin and become godlike (Abdel-Kader, 78f., compares it with Plotinus'

---

[4] The translation of this Sura, which describes the state of the primordial covenant (*mīthāq*) when God was yet alone follows Arberry 1955. On this Sura, cf. Speyer, 304f.; on its role in early Islamic mysticism, see Böwering, 153ff., and Gramlich.

[5] This terminology was adopted in the second half of the tenth century by Niffarī, who used *waqfa* to describe the personal relationship between man and God. See Niffarī, 14ff.

Enneads; cf. Dörrie, 433). There are indeed striking parallels. Yet we must bear in mind that Djunayd refers to the sura already mentioned (7:172/171) as his point of departure. In addition, Djunayd's classification of the highest stage of unification as an oscillation between ecstatic drunkenness and sobriety is quite distinct from the Neo-platonic conception. According to Djunayd the aim of man's unification with God is not the 'intoxication' *(sakra)* of God's 'overwhelming' *(ghalaba)*, but the return to the 'clarity' *(bayān)* of 'sobriety' *(ṣaḥw*; cf. ed. Abdel-Kader, 52·2, trans. p. 172). In this theory of man returning to self-control without a concomitant decrease of 'perception' and 'movement,' Djunayd differs from Abū Yazīd al-Bisṭāmī (Bāyezid) and his school (ed. Abdel-Kader, 93; cf. Schimmel 1985, 94). The true mystic is not the ecstatic who loses his sanity and self-control; he is a sane person, who regains his individual qualities *(ṣifāt* 'attributes') after annihilation *(fanā')* of the self and is thus able to stand as a model to be imitated *(iqtidā')* by his fellow men through his actions *(āthār/fiʿl)*. (ed. Abdel-Kader, 52·2-5, trans. p. 172; cf. pp. 90f.)

This represents a new element which is of decisive importance with regard to the problem of sharing religious experience. Djunayd rejected mysticism in the form of ecstasy. On the one hand he recognized that the ultimate consequence of unification with God was a restoration of man to his originally 'divine existence' (cf. above) and a simultaneous annihilation of individuality (ed. Abdel-Kader, 56·16-19). On the other hand, Djunayd is aware of the degradation of man to a 'phantom' *(sha-baḥ*; ed. Abdel-Kader, 56·14-16), to something with decreasing 'perception' and 'movement' in a state of ecstasy. One cannot let other people share in his mystical experiences while in this state. One must retain his sobriety and become a model for his fellow men to imitate. Djunayd further elaborates this idea in a letter addressed to Abū Yaʿqūb Yūsuf Ibn al-Ḥusayn ar-Rāzī (ed. Abdel-Kader, 29·10ff., trans. p. 150). According to this letter which makes reference to the Koran for corroboration on this point, God selects people and makes a covenant with them *(mīthāq*; cf. Abdel-Kader, 76ff.) obligating them to explain His revelation to the people at large. Djunayd supports his theory of sobriety with an appeal to the Koran (Sura 3:187/184, not noted in ed. Abdel-Kader): just as prophets are charged with conveying God's message, mystics are likewise elected to "impart his knowledge of God to his fellow men and not withhold it." (ed. Abdel-Kader, 29·12, trans. p. 150)

Djunayd adds several items of advice for the mystic in his capacity as a teacher to his disciples, an instructor of novices *(murīdūn)*:

So — may God have mercy on you— turn to your disciples and give them your full attention, face them and concentrate on them, give them of the knowledge which has been vouchsafed to you, grant them your kindness, and privilege them with your guidance, with that fine teaching which leads to God. Be generous to them with that in your knowledge which will help them, and show them the confidence of your understanding. Be with them both by night and by day and give them the special cognisance of your experience. (ed. Abdel-Kader, 29·15ff., trans. p. 150)

Shortly afterwards (ed. Abdel-Kader, 30·3-6) Djunayd cites Sura 18:28/27:

And restrain thyself with those who call upon their Lord at morning and evening, desiring His countenance, and let not thine eyes turn away from them, desiring the adornment of the present life, and obey not him whose heart We have made neglectful of Our remembrance so that he follows his own lust and his affair has become all excess. Say: 'The truth is from your Lord ... .' (Arberry 1955, 29)

The Koran appears as a guideline for the mystic who instructs the novices (murīdūn) in his own knowledge of God. His role appears to parallel that of the prophets mentioned in the Koran who are elected as intermediaries between God and the people at large. Those who are granted mystical experiences are similarly chosen by God who bestows knowledge (ma'rifa; cf. also ed. Abdel-Kader, 27·7f., trans. p. 147) of God on them. It is not the merit of the mystic that he attains a higher stage of spiritual development; on the contrary, God chooses him and it His grace that bestows such mystical knowledge on him; mans higher existence (wudjūdu-hum bi-l-ḥaqq; ed. Abdel-Kader, 33·10, trans. p. 154) comes into being through God's 'word' (qawl) and 'dominant power' (sulṭān ghālib) and is not what man 'claims' (ṭālaba), 'remembers' (adhkara), and 'imagines' (tawahhama) after being 'overwhelmed' by God (ba'da l-ghalaba; ed. Abdel-Kader, 33·11f.).

Referring to a prophetic tradition (Ibn Ḥanbal, p. 256·13; as cited ed. Abdel-Kader, 33·16f., trans. p. 155), the Ḥadīth an-nawāfil (on its use in Islamic mysticism, cf. Schimmel 1985, 393), Djunayd argues that man does not reach a higher stage on his own strength: "it is He who strengthens him, who gives him success (yuwaffiquhū), who guides him, who enables him to see what He wants and how He wants on (his way to) achieve rightness (aṣ-ṣawāb) and to accord with truth (al-ḥaqq)" (ed. Abdel-Kader, 34·3f., trans., slightly different, p. 155). The terminology shows, that Djunayd was able to base his theory of man's dependence upon God on the Koranic idea of tawfīq (Sura 11:88/90).[6]

---

[6] This term played a central role in early Islamic theology in discussions between determinists and advocates of the freedom of the human will; cf. Daiber 1988, 61f.

Just as God has chosen His prophets, He selects and enables others to receive the mystical experience of unification with God. Such experience is followed by a state of sobriety in which the mystic conveys to his fellow men *(murīdūn)* his mystical experiences. He cannot, however, inform others with regard to the ultimate stage of annihilation of the self, the 'overwhelming' intoxication which is granted only by God's grace. He can only give them 'indications' (ed. Abdel-Kader, 45·8-10, trans. p. 166), teaching them the 'outward' *(ẓāhir)* shape of religious rules, and of course their observance, and defending the assertion of God's unity (ed. Abdel-Kader, 56·1-10, trans. p. 176f.), thus preparing them for dialogue with God. (ed. Abdel-Kader, 51·14, trans. p. 177)

This is the mystic's peculiar contribution to society. The mystic is resembles the prophet who transmits God's wisdom to all the people as well as the teacher who prepares man for the reception of God's grace which restores him to his original divine existence.

As we have seen, the mystic is like a prophet who is dependent on divine inspiration. His ecstatic intoxication is followed by a state of sobriety enabling him to become a teacher and a model to his fellow man. Others can share his religious experience only with regard to the 'outward' rules and through instruction in 'indications.' The alternation between God's call and man's answer, the dialogue with God and the annihilation of individuality in God — these depend upon God's grace and cannot be achieved merely through action or through instruction by a mystic teacher.

Nevertheless, Djunayd's introduction of his theory of sobriety in elaborating the role of the mystic as a teacher in society for those who long for nearness to God —who yearn for restoration to their first godlike state— appear to be developed by Djunayd in a unique manner. Djunayd refers to traditional elements of Koranic theology as well as to contemporary discussions about authority and leadership (ed. Abdel-Kader, 22·19-21, trans. p. 143), and about the role of the prophet and his successors, the caliphs, in society at the same time that he discusses the role of the mystic. The philosopher Fārābī († 950 A.D.), who was influenced by Ismaili discussions, argued that the ruler-philosopher who leads and instructs society according to the rules of religion must be a leader inspired by God, like a prophet; he cannot afford to restrict himself to the limited insights of the human mind (Daiber 1986; 1989). In a similar vein, the true mystic receives his religious experience through God's grace, bringing him close to God, but this also carries the obligation to be a model and teacher to the rest of society.

An impressive combination of learning and religious experience emerges here: both facets need the other. We can share another's learning but not another's religious experience. Djunayd, though aware of this asymmetry, raised the hope of God's grace which enables man to receive religious experience and bring him close to God. This much we can, at any rate, learn from our study of Djunayd's texts; in spite of their often enigmatic style and singular terminology,[7] they nonetheless represent a goldmine of not yet fully explored ideas.

---

[7] The Abdel-Kader translation and study is unfortunately often disappointing and misleading as a result, underscoring the fact that we cannot rely on translations for our analysis.

Bibliography

Abdel-Kader, Ali Hassan. *The Life, Personality and Writings of Al-Junayd,* London, 1962; rpt. 1976.

Arberry, A. J. *The Doctrine of the Sufis.* London, 1935; rpt. Lahore, 1976.

———. *The Koran Interpreted.* Oxford, 1955; rpt. 1986.

Böwering, G. *The Mystical Vision of Existence in Classical Islam.* Berlin/ New York, 1980.

Daiber, H. *The Ruler As Philosopher.* Mededelingen der Koninklijke Nederlandse Akademie van Wetenschappen, Afd. Letterkunde, New Series 49, no. 4. Amsterdam/Oxford, 1986.

———. *Wāṣil Ibn 'Aṭā' als Prediger und Theologe.* Leiden, 1988.

———. "Abū Ḥātim ar-Rāzī (10th Century A. D.) on the Unity and Diversity of Religions." In J. D. Gort et al., eds. *Dialogue and Syncretism: An Interdisciplinary Approach.* Currents of Encounter 1. Grand Rapids/ Amsterdam, 1989, pp. 87-104.

Deladriere, R. *Junayd, l'enseignement spirituel: Traités, lettres, croisons et sentences traduits de l'arabe presentés et annotés.* Paris, 1983.

Dörrie, H. "Porphyrios als Mittler zwischen Plotin und Augustin." In W. Beierwaltes, ed. *Platonismus in der Philosophie des Mittelalters.* Wege der Forschung 197. Darmstadt, 1969, pp. 410-439.

Gramlich, R. "Der Urvertrag in der Koranauslegung (zu Sure 7:172-173)." *Der Islam* 60 (1983): 205-230.

Ibn Ḥanbal. *Musnad,* VI. Rpt. Beirut, n. d.

MacDonald, D. B., and Gardet, L. "Al-ghayb." *Encyclopedia of Islam²* II. Leiden/London, 1965, pp. 1025-26.

Nicholson, R. A., ed. *Kitāb al-Luma' fī t-taṣauwuf.* Leiden, 1914; rpt. London, 1963.

Niffarī. *Kitāb al-Mawāqif.* Trans. and ed. A. J. Arberry. London, 1935.

-Qushayrī, ar-Risāla. Cairo, 1346/1927.

Sāmarrā'ī, Qāsim, ed. *Rasā'il al-Kharrāz.* Madjallat al-Madjma al-'ilmī al-'Iraqī 15. Baghdad, 1387/1967, pp. 1-67.

Schimmel, A. *Mystische Dimensionen des Islam.* Cologne, 1985 (revised version of *Mystical Dimensions of Islam,* Chapel Hill, 1975).

———. "Secrecy in Sufism." In K. W. Bolle, ed. *Secrecy in Religions: Studies in the History of Religions.* Supplements to Numen 49. Leiden (1987): 81-102.

Sezgin, F. *Geschichte des arabischen Schrifttums,* I. Leiden, 1967.

Speyer, H. *Die biblischen Erzählungen im Qoran.* Hildesheim, 1971.

CHAPTER 21

The Prayers for Peace at Assisi, October 27, 1986: What was Shared?

Arnulf Camps, O.F.M.

In this contribution the author gives a survey of what actually occurred on October 27, 1986 when Pope John Paul II convened religious leaders from around the world to pray for peace at the city of Saint Francis of Assisi, the universal brother. He then deals with the reactions and discussions arising subsequent to that day. The discussions are theological in nature and pertain to the theology of religions: Is it permissable —from a Christian point of view— to pray in such a setting? The author tries to legitimate the historic event at Assisi by referring to developments within Asian theology concerning the encounter between religions, pointing out that in Asia today a deeper sharing of the common *homo religiosus* is practised than elsewhere. The Day of Prayer at Assisi is a challenging contribution to the theology of dialogue and to the *praxis* of interreligious cooperation.

One may wonder whether Pope John Paul II foresaw all the consequences of the day of prayer which he announced was to be held at Assisi on October 27, 1986. He announced the event in the Church of St. Paul, outside of the walls of the city of Rome on January 25, 1986, and it had been precisely that date in the same church when Pope John XXIII told his audience in 1959 that he was preparing an ecumenical council, subsequently known as Vatican II. Both announcements came rather unexpectedly and both introduced important changes. At such moments even popes may be unaware of what the Spirit intends and accomplishes through the intermediation of human beings! On April 6, 1986 the actual date of the day of prayer was set by Pope John Paul II, and on June 27, 1986 Cardinal Etchegaray revealed further details in a press conference (Paix aux Hommes de Bonne Volonté, 15-21). During an ecumenical meeting at Lyons in France on October 4, 1986, the day of the liturgical celebration of Saint Francis of Assisi, Pope John Paul II called for a cease-fire in all parts of the world; the design was that not only prayers for peace would be offered on October 27, but also actions for peace and signs of true humanity (Paix aux Hommes de Bonne Volonté, 22-23). In all of these exhortations the strong conviction is noticeably present that the ecumenical and interreligious gathering at Assisi would be something quite new in the history of the religions of the world. Never before had a religious leader called together as many religious leaders as possible —Christian as well as non-Christian— for a day of prayer.

This call to prayer was, however, also new to the development of the theology of religions. After the Assisi meeting, a theological discussion on the implications of the day of prayer for peace was begun both in newspapers and in books and articles, and this discussion is still being continued (Dörmann, Beyerhaus, Seckler, Ries). Just as Vatican II continues to influence history, so does Assisi, October 27, 1986. Francis of Assisi, whom we call the 'universal brother,' would have been receptive to such a situation. Did he not greet everyone he met with the words: 'Peace and All Good!'? And had he not, for the first time in the history of the church, written a rule containing a special chapter on how friars should live *among* (and not in opposition to) Muslims and people of other faiths? Did he not cross the lines of the Christian crusaders and Muslim armies at Damietta in Egypt in 1219 in order to speak with the sultan personally (Camps 1983a, 95-98)? The *Wirkungsgeschichte* ('history — effective and effectuating') of what Francis did, of Vatican II, and of the event at Assisi on October 27, 1986 is not yet merely a matter of past history.

This contribution does not intend to recount all the events of that memorable day nor to give a summary of all the positive and negative reactions aroused by that unexpected papal act. These two topics will be dealt with only briefly. My main purpose is to answer the question facing us: What was shared that day at Assisi? The present article hopes to be able to put the event at Assisi in a broader perspective so that we are better able to understand the event itself.

1 What actually occurred on October 27, 1986

In 1986 the United Nations celebrated its fortieth anniversary and called for a World Year for Peace. This was the context in which the pope issued his invitation for the day of prayer. Since the closing of the Second Vatican Council in 1965 the relation between religion and peace had become an important theme all over the world. Pope Paul VI started what is now known as the Council for Interreligious Dialogue in 1964 in the Vatican and the Commission Justitia et Pax in 1967. In his encyclical letter *Populorum Progressio,* he declared in 1967 that development was the new name for peace. On the wider stage, a number of religious organizations had come into existence which were fighting for common goals, one of them directly concerning itself with peace: The World Conference on Religion and Peace, which held world assemblies in Kyoto (1970), Louvain (1974), Princeton (1979), Nairobi (1984), and Melbourne (1989) (Waldenfels, 63-66, Camps 1983b, 11-21; 1988, 20-26). It is well known that the World Council of Churches is quite active in this area (Arai/Ariarajah). The meeting in Seoul at the beginning of 1990 was originally intended by Carl Friedrich von Weisacker as a Council for Peace. All this indicates that there is a strong awareness today of the contribution that religions should make towards peace and it is against this backdrop that Pope John Paul's initiative undertaken in 1986 needs to be understood.

The invitation to come to Assisi was answered by the chief of the Crow Indians from North America, by chiefs and witch doctors from Kenya, Ghana, and Togo in Africa, by Shintoists from Japan, by Hindus from India, by Parsees, Jains, and Sikhs from India, and from many other quarters. It was answered by Buddhists from Thailand, Japan, and Tibet, by members of the Rissho-kosei-kai in Japan, by Muslims from Asia, Africa, Turkey, Arabia and Italy, by Jews sent by the synagogue in Rome as official representatives and by twenty-seven Christian churches and communions. *(Bulletin,* 100-104)

The day itself was divided into three parts, each held at a different place. The day began in the Basilica of Our Lady of the Angels, in which the Portiuncula chapel has been preserved, the place where Francis had died. The pope received his guests on the steps in front of the church and accompanied them inside. An official introduction was followed by a short address by the pope. He pointed out that the intention of the meeting was not to be a peace council, to engage in discussions, to plan for action, nor to strive for a religious consensus. He clearly indicated that the real purpose of the meeting was to display to the entire world a commitment to peace and to do so in a religious way — through silence, pilgrimage, and fasting, to pray in a multiform way in view of the plurality of religions, and to gather in the city of Francis, who is loved by many in the world as a symbol of peace, reconciliation, and fraternity.

The second part of the day consisted of a pilgrimage into Assisi, which lies some distance from Portiuncula. Each religion was appointed a specific place in the town where the adherents of that religion could pray or practise their religious customs. Hindus and Sikhs prayed on the same large ecclesiastical property; Buddhists and Shintoists could hear their prayers and music in the vast abbey of Saint Peter; the representatives of the traditional religions gathered in the council chambers of Assisi, and the Christians came together in the Cathedral of San Rufino. No complete record exists of all that happened during these meetings. We only know that during the meeting of the Buddhists a statue of the Buddha was placed on the altar, shocking some Christians but not others. We have also been informed concerning the address which the pope gave during the assemblies of the Christians. He professed that peace is a gift

of God in Jesus Christ and that the church is meant to be an effective
sign and means of reconciliation and peace for the family of humankind.
But the pope also realistically confessed that all Christians stand in need
of conversion and penance since all too often they are unfaithful to their
vocation. He called for Christians to continue their pilgrimage in a
prayerful way, in silence (to listen — not argue) and in fasting (to do
away with greed and egoism). No other records exist. This second part
of the day was purposely left undocumented in order to avoid folkloric or
religious studies.

In the afternoon, the third part of the day took place. In silence, the
religious leaders from the various parts of the town gathered at the
compound of the Basilica of San Francesco, where Francis is buried. This
meeting was held in the open space in front of the church; a possible
visit to the tomb of Saint Francis remained a discretionary matter of
personal devotion. This meeting was called: 'being together in order to
pray for peace.' Cardinal Etchegaray opened the ceremony by stating
clearly that the sole purpose was to pray for peace in accordance with the
way in which each religion cherishes peace —both in the heart of human
beings as well as in the relations between peoples— though in various
different and original ways. There was no intention to obscure lines of
difference since no common prayers were held but there was, rather, a
community of the praying faithful. The world situation being such that it
is a matter of life and death to commit oneself to peace, it was appropriate to show the world that in their finest and deepest inspiration all
religions seek peace. The religious leaders, in consequence, prayed in
turn to show to the world and to one another the earnestness of their
intention to foster peace. We possess full records of all the prayers
(Waldenfels, 19-60; *Bulletin*, 105-24; Paix aux Hommes de Bonne Volonté,
pp. 51-83). Prayers or meditations were offered by Buddhists, Hindus,
Jains, Muslims, Shintoists, Sikhs, Africans, Indians, Zoroastrians, Jews, and
Christians. At the end young people distributed olive branches, and
pigeons were set free to spread the message of peace from Assisi to the
entire world.

In conclusion, the pope addressed all present and called himself "a
brother and friend, but also a believer in Jesus Christ, and in the Catholic
Church, the first witness of the faith in Him." He added, "I profess here
anew my conviction, shared by all Christians, that in Jesus Christ, as
Saviour of all, true peace is to be found" *(Bulletin,* 39). But he also
stated that all women and men in this world have a common nature, a
common origin, and a common destiny. If there are many and important
differences between them, there is also a common ground upon which to
operate together in the solution of this dramatic challenge of the age:
"true peace or catastrophic war?" *(Bulletin,* 40). He stressed the import-

ance of the moral conscience which enjoins people to respect, protect, and promote human life as well as the common conviction that peace goes far beyond human efforts. The source of peace is a Reality beyond all people. Even though the situation is such that all think differently about the relation between that Reality and the gift of peace, all affirm that such a relation exists. He added, "This is what we express by praying for it. I humbly repeat here my own conviction: peace bears the name of Jesus Christ. But at the same time and in the same breath, I am ready to acknowledge that Catholics have not always been faithful to this affirmation of faith. We have not always been 'peacemakers.' For ourselves, therefore, but also perhaps, in a sense, for all, this encounter at Assisi is an act of penance. We have prayed, each in his own way, we have fasted, we have marched together. In this way we have opened our hearts to the divine reality beyond us and to our fellow men and women." *(Bulletin,* 40-41)

The day ended in the refectory of the Franciscans now living in Saint Francis's proto-monastery. There, all the religious leaders took 'break-fast' for the first time that day, although it was already evening: some bread, pizza, vegetables, tea, and water. Although the pope was very tired he did no leave before he had prayed in silence and in privacy for ten minutes, kneeling in front of the tomb of Saint Francis in the basilica's crypt.

2   Reactions to Assisi, 1986

The events which occurred at Assisi on October 27, 1986 were received in a positive way by many people, in the first place by all who attended. Not only the leaders of the world's religions but also the staff of the Papal Council for Interreligious Dialogue (who together with members of various organizations specialized in interreligious dialogue, such as the World Conference on Religion and Peace, had prepared the meeting in a very conscientious way) stated that they had experienced a miracle. One religious leader said, "Our relationships have now entered a decisive turning-point," and another confessed, "I now see other believers with new eyes, a gift I have received here at Assisi" *(Bulletin,* 146). The press and various communications media remarked upon its importance. 800 accredited journalists were present, whereas only some 500 attended the Second Vatican Council. The documentation on this event is enormous. The novelty of the event and the level at which it took place (Christians and other believers praying together for peace, the social role of prayer, and the social and religious value of peace) were the main topics stressed in the press.

The morning after the Day of Prayer in Assisi on October 28, 1986, a meeting was held between the invited guests of the pope together with

their companions and followers (108 people in all) and the staff of the
Pontifical Council for Interreligious Dialogue under the chairmanship of
Cardinal Francis Arinze. It was an attempt at evaluation and also provided occasion to present proposals for peace. Mr. Okomfo Kodwo Akon,
a leader of a traditional religion in Ghana, expressed what had been
underscored in one way or another by all: "Peace does not mean uniform-
ity but rather pluralism, or humanity in its diversity. This is shown by the
diversity of human language. It is important that the leaders of the
various religions know how to respect religious tolerance for the mainten-
ance of peaceful and harmonious life together" *(Bulletin,* 129; for the
entire meeting see pp. 125-30). It is also important to mention that the
Venerable Etai Yamada, a Buddhist leader from Japan, invited, in the
name of all the Japanese representatives, all the religions to continue this
initiative by coming together on Mount Hiei, near Kyoto, in August of
1987. This meeting was, in fact, held on August 3-4, 1987 and was well
attended (Michel, 84-88). On September 1, 1989 a third Day of Prayer was
held at Varsavia, Poland, the fiftieth anniversary of the beginning of
World War II (Trouw, 1-9-1989: 5). Christians, Buddhists, Hindus, Shintoists,
and Muslims attended. It was unfortunate that a Jewish delegation could
not attend the meeting since they objected to some remarks made some
time before the meeting by Cardinal Joseph Glemp, primate of Poland.

One should not, however, conclude that everyone was pleased with
Assisi. There were also statements in the press accusing the Assisi
meeting of not addressing in plain language those in power, responsible
for politics and economics. Others took offence at the interreligious
character of the prayers (Glüer, 4). The first objection is easily
countered: Assisi was intended to be a Day of Prayer, stressing the
relationship between the Reality beyond and the gift of peace, confessing
that peace can only be realized by politicians and economists when they
become conscious of these relationships. The second objection is more
serious and needs to be dealt with in more detail.

The discussion concerning the interreligious character of the Assisi
meeting is theological in nature. An attempt shall be made here to
summarize the arguments of some Catholic theologians who do not agree
with the *'modell Assisi 1986,'* adding some observations made by other
Christians. On the Catholic side, an example is Johannes Dörmann, who
was professor of missiology and history of religions at the Catholic
theological faculty of Münster in the Federal Republic of Germany, and
who wrote several articles on this topic in the conservative review *Theologisches.* These articles were later re-edited for a book published in 1988.
Dörmann has completed the first volume of a two-volume work published
in 1990 on the theological journey of Pope John Paul II which lead to the
World Day of Prayer at Assisi. In 1989 a Dutch Dominican professor of

Old Testament exegesis, J. P. M. van der Ploeg, who was professor at the Catholic University of Nijmegen in the Netherlands, published his comments in the review *Theologisches*. We shall be brief regarding the objections put forward by Peter Beyerhaus, professor of missiology at the Protestant theological faculty of the university of Tübingen in the Federal Republic of Germany.

On the Catholic side the main objections are:

1. False religions have been invited to pray in Catholic churches and chapels. That prayers were offered in various churches by each religion is not considered grave. Rather, the purported mistake is that prayers were offered to false gods in the houses of the true God in violation of the first commandment. (Van der Ploeg, 383; Dörmann 1988, 152)

2. The prayers were in fact not directed to a Reality beyond, as the pope claimed, and as Horst Bürkle has written (Bürkle, 123, 126), but were concretely raised to Krishna, Vishnu, Allah, and others. According to Holy Scripture, however, one must confess that all heathen gods are demons. (Van der Ploeg, 383; Dörmann 1988, 153)

3. Some of the religious leaders present at Assisi were atheists. In this connection mention is made of the Dalai Lama, Therevada Buddhists, and the Jains. Mahayana Buddhists also do not believe in a higher being who created the world and humankind. If one does not believe in God, how can one pray? In the opinion of the critics, these atheists should not have accepted the Assisi invitation. (Van der Ploeg, 383; Dörmann 1988, 160-162)

4. The Jews and the Muslims were honest enough not to pray in a church; the former prayed in the open air while the latter prayed in a neutral place. It should be mentioned that as far as Muslims are concerned, peace is a prerogative of only one exclusively true religion, Islam. All other religions are wrong and need to convert to Islam. The concept of holy war is still very much a reality; the scope of this idea can be seen in the current situation in Lebanon and Iran. For Muslims, there is no common ground for peace. The Jews were right in praying that all nations should come to Jerusalem and do away with their false gods. But the words of the prophet Micah (4:1-4) obtain their true meaning from the interpretation given to them by the New Testament: the Son of God hanging on the cross at Golgotha is the historical revelation of God before all the nations, and the mission of the church is to bring all nations to Him. (Van der Ploeg, 384; Dörmann 1988, 164-67)

5. Co-operation in matters important for peace in the world is a good thing. All religions are endangered by communism and secularism. But common prayer and the invitation addressed to each religion to

be radically true to its own deepest inspiration are impossible for a
Christian. (Van der Ploeg, 384)

6. Dörmann is very much disturbed by the theology of religion which
was developed by theologians such as Karl Rahner and others since
Vatican II (Nostra Aetate), and by the Pontifical Council for Interreligious Dialogue in a statement of 1984 (1988, *passim*). In his
opinion it is impossible to claim that other religions are ways of
salvation, that the God of Jesus Christ is the same as other gods, that
conversion can never be attained through human activity but comes
only from God, that dialogue is the new name for mission, and that
the aim of dialogue is not conversion but awareness of a deeper unity
and understanding. Allow me to quote from p. 181: "The new peaceful world must now be built upon the safe foundation of the prayer-
pluralism of the religions. Assisi has provided a cornerstone for this.
The new economy of salvation realizes itself as a fraternal pilgrimage
of all religions, accompanying one another in peace and harmony
towards a transcendent goal or towards their historical eschatological
point of convergence. The new motto is: instead of conversion —
interreligious worship and dialogue. The theological foundation of
this new vision by Rome was already given in 1984 by the Secretariat
for non-Christians in the document, *Dialogue and Mission*. Is this
also the theological position of the pope?"

No corrections to wrong interpretations of the events at Assisi such as
these authors give will be made; there are too many and they are too
self-evidently wrong. My main concern is with the charge that a wrong
development of the theology of religion in the Catholic theological world
has taken place during and after Vatican II. It is here that the battle has
to be fought. I will attempt to answer this charge in the concluding part
of this article.

Not much remains to be added to this summation from the arguments
of Peter Beyerhaus. I want to clearly express my admiration for him for
having written to the pope as soon as he heard about the coming Assisi
meeting as well as after the meeting. This was an act of Christian
fraternity. It should also be stated that Beyerhaus was answered in a very
kind but firm way. The Vatican assured him that there was no intention
to move toward syncretism, no intention to pray together, no intention to
offend anyone. This exchange of letters resulted in several public Vatican
statements indicating what the real intentions were before the meeting in
Assisi took place. However, Beyerhaus was not convinced of the good
theological intentions of the pope. In his view there is only one true
religion, the Christian faith, and all other religions are ways of self-
redemption which are for that reason false. The Assisi meeting was

based on a wrong theology of religion and opens the door to syncretism.
(Beyerhaus, 92-93)

3 The real theology of religion of Assisi 1986: What was shared?

The only theologian I know who furnishes us a clue to an answer is
Marcello Zago. He was the secretary of the Council for Interreligious
Dialogue at the Vatican during the preparations for the historic event at
Assisi. "The day at Assisi, however, would have remained impossible
without the remote preparation provided by Vatican Council II which had
sowed the premises that gave direction to the Churches in Asia. In fact,
it is in Asia that the pioneers of dialogue opened the way even before the
Council. Next came a collective awareness on the part of the Asian
episcopacy, particularly from 1974 onwards, after the first plenary meeting
of the Federation of Asian Bishops' Conferences (FABC). Gradually the
forms and participants of dialogue increased in number, especially in
certain more significant areas such as Japan, India, and Indochina."
(Bulletin, 151)

Upon reading this, I fully agreed with Zago. Asian theologians met
with their bishops in workshops organized during the course of more than
two decades by departments of the FABC. They were able to help the
bishops to find a way to liberate the local churches from their ghetto
situation. Catholics in most Asian countries form a minority. After
independence they had to find ways and means to get in touch with the
realities of Asia. They discovered that Asia is a poor, extremely religious,
and pluralist continent. These facts called for a threefold dialogue: with
the poor, with the religions, and with the various cultures^U They also
discovered that there is a common religion at the heart of the religions,
or, in other words, that *homo religiosus* lies at the root of the religions.
From the very beginning God has been revealing himself to all nations
and all nations have responded to God's call in communities. This
common answer to God's call has brought forth religion in the form of
many religions. The plurality of religions, therefore, is quite natural, since
such answers are given by a community that is situated in a specific
culture. Since there are many cultures, there are many responses or
religions. This does not imply that everything in every religion is as good
as in another religion. The implication of all this is that religions have
their own place in human history and also in the history of salvation.
Each religion has its own soteriology, and Christianity exists among the
religions of the world.

The question is: What is the exact relationship between Christianity
and the other religions, or vice versa? The Asian theologians and bishops

begin by accepting the fact that they live in a culture and in a religious culture which offers people salvation. Christianity should not attempt to ignore or abolish this. Rather, Christianity ought to be baptized in the Jordan of these soteriologies in order to ascend from the Jordan with a new vision. Christians should practise a double loyalty; they should ignore neither their cultural and religious surroundings nor their own Christian identity. In Asia this is the normal attitude toward life. The Asian way of thought is quite different from the Western. Western people are inclined to make choices; we tend to be people of the either/or principle. Asians are inclined to look for harmony rather than putting things over against one another in opposition; they are people of the both/and way of thought (yin/yang). They seek holism, aware of the fact that the whole truth is found only by harmonizing the partial truths. This leads to a spirituality of double loyalty. Such spirituality must be distinguished from relativism or fundamentalism, attitudes which are not helpful to human beings in their spiritual endeavours; relativism resolves the problem before it is even raised and fundamentalism ignores the riches God has given to each nation and people. Asian theologians accept this way of thought, which is, after all, really their own. Thus, they do not oppose mission to dialogue nor do they oppose sacred scriptures or founders of religions and seers to Jesus Christ. They seek a new concept of theological and Christian activity within their own cultural and religious surroundings and within their local churches. This results in a different way of life. For them a Christian —in accord with this double loyalty— must live in a basic human community together with the faithful of other religions as well as in a basic Christian community — and must do so in full harmony. Faithful to his or her Lord, the Christian must find an identity in the basic Christian community which forms the leaven at work in the basic human community. Together with people of other faiths, Christians should strive for full humanity and for the coming of the kingdom. Humanity and Kingdom are not exclusively Christian possessions. God has spread his riches among all nations. All of these riches must be brought together in a fuller unity in diversity. After all, neither the length, nor the depth, nor the height, nor the breadth of the mystery of Christ is yet known to us, and they will be revealed only in the future. The Word and the Spirit of God, at work since the very beginning among human beings and in this world, did not stop calling people after the Word became flesh. The historical person of Jesus is not merely pre-existent, but the Word of God and his Spirit are pre-, in-, and post-existent.

This new theology that has developed in Asia is a rich theology. I have recently made an attempt to describe the harmonious coherence within this theology (Camps 1990). I hereby make reference to all the authors quoted in that publication. To return now to the real question:

What did they share? They shared the *homo religiosus* who exists in plurality. They shared the common striving for the fullness of life and for the values of the kingdom (and especially for peace); they shared that ultimate Reality which is not an abstraction but a reality in plurality. This was not a *communicatio in sacris*. From January 19 to 25 in 1988 a meeting of fifty-two bishops and theologians was held at Bangalore, India, on "Sharing Worship," resulting in a report of 820 pages. Allow me to offer some good advice. Study all these contributions and see how filled with prejudices we are towards other religions. This forms the main obstacle standing in the way of working, living, and worshipping together — yes, together. In India there is now already more togetherness than there was at Assisi! After all, in the eyes of Asians, Assisi was a very humble beginning. Asians know that the *homo religiosus* in all of us is capable of more than "be[ing] together to pray:" he can pray together with other companions on the pilgrimage to full humanity and towards the kingdom. This was not yet possible at Assisi, but upon reading the exhortations by Pope John Paul II, the statements by Cardinal Etchegaray, and the articles by various members of the Pontifical Council for Interreligious Dialogue, one can sense the theology of Asia and whence the historic Assisi initiative came. Surely the future will bring more and deeper sharing. Allow me to close with a line from Tagore:

> The leaf becomes flower when it loves.
> The flower becomes fruit when it worships.

Bibliography

Arai, T. and Ariarajah, W., eds. *Spirituality in Interfaith Dialogue.* Geneva, 1989.

Beyerhaus, P. *Diakrisis* 4 (1986): 92-94.

Bulletin Secretariatus pro Non Christianis 22 (Città del Vaticano 1987): pp. 11-160.

Bürkle, H. "Das Modell 'Assisi 1986' und der interreligiöse Dialog." *Forum Katholische Theologie* 5 (1989): 117-27.

Camps, A. "Franziskanischer Dialog mit anderen Religionen." In *Baue meine Kirche auf: Franziskanische Inspirationen aus der Dritten Welt.* L. Boff and W. Bühlmann, eds. Düsseldorf, 1983a, pp. 88-105.

——. *Partners in Dialogue: Christianity and other World Religions.* New York/Maryknoll, 1983b.

——. "WCRP in context: Historisch en Actueel." In *Geloven in Vrede.* H. E. Schouten, ed. Amersfoort/Leuven, 1988, pp. 20-26.

——. *Het Derde Oog: Van een Theologie in Azië naar een Aziatische Theologie.* Nijmegen, 1990.

Demeerseman, G. "Journée de prière pour la Paix à Assise." In *Islamo-christiana*. 13 (1987): 200-204; see also pp. 217-21.

Dörmann, J. *Die eine Wahrheit und die vielen Religionen. Assisi: Anfang einder neuen Zeit*. Abensberg, 1988.

——. *Der theologische Weg Johannes Pauls II: Zum Weltgebetstag der Religionen in Assisi*. Vol. I. Vom Zweiten Vatikanischen Konzil bis zur Papstwahl. Senden, 1990.

Glüer, W. *A letter* dated Stuttgart, November, 1986.

Hoeres, W. "Der Weg nach Assisi." *Theologisches* 20 (1990): 219-22.

Michel, Th. "Mount Hiei Day of Prayer for Peace." *The Japan Missionary Bulletin* 42 (1986): 84-88.

Paix aux Hommes de Bonne Volonté: Les Grandes Religions au Rendez-vous d'Assise, 27 octobre 1986. Paris, 1986

Ploeg, J. P. M. van der. " 'Gebete' zu falschen Göttern in Kirchen des wahren Gottes?" *Theologisches* 19 (1989): 383-84.

Puthanangady, P., ed. *Sharing Worship: Communicatio in Sacris*. Bangalore, 1988.

Ratzinger, J. "Congregatie voor de Geloofsleer: Enige aspecten van de Christelijke Meditatie." *Kerkelijke Documentatie 121* 18 (1990): 10-23.

Ries, J. *Les Chrétiens parmi les Religions. Des Actes des Apôtres à Vatican II*. Tournai, 1987, pp. 408-409.

Seckler, M. "Synodos der Religionen: 'Das Ereignis von Assisi' und seine Perpektiven für eine Theologie der Religionen." *Theologisches Quartalschrift* 169 (1989): 5-24.

Waldenfels, H., ed. *Die Friedensgebete von Assisi*. Introduction by Franz Kardinal König, Commentary by Hans Waldenfels. Freiburg/Basel/Vienna, 1987.

Part 3

Common Themes
and Problems

Sharing Religious Experience: Recapitulation, Comments, and Questions

Hendrik M. Vroom

In the following essay an attempt will be made to recapitulate and link together some of the main theoretical argumentation put forward in the workshop papers and discussions on the issue of the sharing of religious experience. The *first* and by far longer part of the paper comprises descriptive summarization of and commentary on the various contributions to the congress. The *second*, final section consists of an inventory of a number of systematic points of agreement that seem to have emerged from the symposium, a corpus of more or less collectively held views that may quite fairly be termed the 'harvest' of the workshop and simultaneously characterized as generative of questions needing further investigation and reflection.

The concept *sharing* can connote 'sameness' or 'likeness,' but it can also very definitely imply 'difference,' 'discreteness,' 'partiality.' None of the workshop participants gives a completely unqualified reply to the question as to whether interreligious sharing is possible. Some authors answer the question with a more or less cautious 'yes'; others lean toward the opposite position, though they, too, modify their 'no' to a greater or lesser degree.

Summary and Comments

1.   Gerhard Oberhammer, like others, distinguishes types of sharing. The basic mystical core of religious experience, which consists in unreserved, affirming human surrender to the Transcendent, may well be susceptible to interreligious sharing. Such experience, however, is always mediated by a given religious tradition, which is 'appropriated' when a believer, faced by the immediacy of existence and death, 'realizes' or relives the traditional myths by virtue of actual surrender to transcendence and in so doing finds *Heil* (wholeness, salvation). Religious experience in this sense belongs to the very stuff of human nature, Oberhammer argues. Religious traditions structure and facilitate concrete incidents of the experience of transcendence. Since one is enabled to encounter transcendence by a

specific religious tradition and thereby comes to place profound trust in that tradition, one cannot arbitrarily exchange it for another or regard all religious traditions as equally valid. Religious experience in its *concrete* form, therefore, cannot be shared by a believer steeped in another tradition. At another level, though, sharing between believers of differing religions is eminently possible according to Oberhammer.

Since, as argued, religious traditions open up the possibility for their adherents to experience transcendence through surrender to It, I as a religious believer standing outside these traditions can do nothing other than take them very seriously: they and the experiences of transcendence they engender take on the character of plausibility and those enabled by them to have such experiences can become dear to me. I do not share the myths of other traditions existentially, nor is it possible for me to apprehend them as concrete instances of encounter with the Absolute in the same way as do believers standing within those traditions. Nevertheless, I *can* share such myths *intellectually*, seeking fuller understanding of them through a process of hermeneutical exploration. It is in this way that Oberhammer answers the question implicit in the theme of the symposium.

2. Willem Dupré locates the basis for religion in human existence. Human beings *experience* the fact that they experience things and demand an interpretation of reality. Since all humans share the same nature, they are all related to the transcendent wholeness and end of being. Moments of the Divine are experienced by all humankind in togetherness, acceptance, goodness, trust, solidarity, justice, forgiveness, and peace, in meaningfulness, grace, happiness, beauty, holiness, and truth. Hence, religion is as universal as the human condition. The various traditions, with their concern for the whole of existence and the totality of reality, invite people to join them and learn to experience things through their symbols. While such traditions, thus, are universal and inclusive as to meaning and end, at the same time they are local and exclusive since all human knowledge and experience is mediated and shaped within specific and thus limited religio-cultural contexts. Plainly, Dupré does not consider it possible for adherents of different traditions to share each other's religious experiences: it is incumbent upon all believers to respect the otherness of the other.

Dupré offers an alternative, however, which he considers to be a promising approach to greater interreligious understanding and growth in religious perception. He feels that encounter between people of various faiths can over time lead them to grow closer together: such positive encounter could engender the formation of a new community of religious people who would learn gradually to reinterpret their several traditions in a common search for meaning and truth.

One might wish to question Dupré's interpretation of what constitutes a religious tradition: are they really as closed and integrally exclusive as he seems to argue? Do they indeed represent totality-of-meaning systems? Such a contention would appear to have little support in empirical reality. To cite but one example: as was pointed out by Wilfred Smith during the course of the workshop discussions, the so-called 'Christian community' is in point of actual fact not a community at all; in some places Christians are even at fierce odds with one another. Can religious traditions not be better understood as configurations of basic human experiences that have made an enduring impression — experiences of the transcendent expressed in a variety of ways in the form of religious beliefs? Clearly, this latter concept of religion would provide far more allowance for the possibility of interreligious overlapping and sharing.

3. André Droogers distinguishes between two forms of sharing: the act of communication on the one hand and common experience as an act of existential communion on the other. In cultural anthropology 'sharing' has always had reference to the notion of understanding other people's religious life. Understanding, here, presupposes mutual, two-way communication between the people being studied and the anthropologist. The participant observer tries to enter the experience of others. The path to this kind of sharing is marked out by the religious symbols of a culture and the meaning they lend to experience. Symbols are subject to continual reinterpretation; any given symbol, therefore, could point to experiences which differ quite markedly from each other. The quest for such understanding is made possible by the commonality of the human condition: all people experience themselves as being simultaneously part of and separate from a social and natural totality and all are in search of wholeness in a confusingly plural world. Droogers views the basic human problem as consisting in this longing for wholeness. Meaning-making answers to the questions evoked by this longing are provided by culture, and therefore religion, in the form of symbols.

Drooger's distinction between sharing as communication and sharing as communion might well be viewed as synonymous to that between initial and more advanced sharing. Though from a hermeneutical point of view sharing and understanding can never fully transcend the state of partiality, they do remain a distinct possibility on the condition that a certain degree of commonality exists among human beings. In Drooger's position this commonality is found in the anthropological basis or human substratum of all religious life.

4. Wilfred Cantwell Smith, a scholar who has considerable personal experience in interreligious sharing, relates some of the background history of the Center for the Study of World Religions at Harvard Divinity

School. Under his direction the Center chapel, originally constructed as a place for common worship, was transformed into a library and common hall for use as the venue for numerous lectures delivered throughout the years by representatives of the world's various religious traditions.

Smith tells with great sincerity of the religious experience effected in his own life by a word from the Koran "He is sufficient." In his view it is possible that he may have had the same experience of trust felt by Muslims to whom this Koranic word has spoken. Wilfred Smith, it would seem, can not be characterized only as a liberal theologian; he clearly also represents a type of pietism. In a vein similar to that of Oberhammer, with his accentuation of personal relationship with the Transcendent, Smith regards religion not so much as a cultural or historical system but first and foremost as lived experience. All who are struck by the affirming nearness of God, all who realize life in God's grace share the same faith, even though the beliefs, symbols, and rituals of their various traditions differ. The question Smith holds up to believers is whether they are willing to share with one another on a permanent basis, whether they are prepared to seek for mutual enrichment and purification. Because faith is both personal and generic human beings are capable of understanding each other. No two believers will be able to understand each other perfectly or fully, but it is possible for them to achieve partial mutual understanding and sharing.

5. Rein Fernhout's approach to the question of sharing and holy scriptures differs markedly from that of Smith. Fernhout observes that sacred texts are ascribed absolute authority by many adherents of religious traditions. It can be argued, therefore, that in a formal sense believers of various religions share the idea of the inspiration, i. e., the supernatural origin of the scriptures to which they give assent. Furthermore, even in a material sense it is possible for believers to have *faith* in the inspiration of holy writings stemming from a tradition or traditions other than their own. In Christianity the inspiration that gave rise to the New Testament is also attributed to the Jewish Bible, which Christians interpret as the Old Testament. Similarly, taking its departure from the inspiration of the Koran, Islam considers the Jewish and Christian scriptures to be supernaturally inspired. Fernhout examines the Hindu and Buddhist traditions in this regard as well and discovers in them analogies to the Christian and Muslim views of scriptures belonging to other traditions. In all of the cases dealt with, attribution of inspiration to traditional scriptures entails an *intra*-traditional interpretation of this inspiration. Moreover, the evidence examined indicates that all such 'foreign' interpretation of inspiration is viewed as unacceptable by the adherents of the scriptures involved. It can be concluded, therefore, that *sharing* in this connection does not extend beyond the *idea* of inspiration.

Fernhout emphasizes the incompatibility of various claims regarding the absolute authority of scriptures. From the point of view of systematic theology, however, the question could be put whether this notion of incompatibility ought not to be somewhat qualified. No religious tradition can escape confrontation with the hermeneutical problem in the broadest sense of the term. Each of them must wrestle with certain basic questions regarding sacred writings. What was the original intention of the authors of scripture (what did the text mean then and there)? How should these texts from another time and context be applied to a new situation (what does the text mean here and now)? And even the central insights of a tradition are subject to reinterpretation in one form or another. Would this not seem to allow sufficient hermeneutical freedom, certainly for Christian theologians, to acknowledge the possibility of the existence of areas of faith overlap with other traditions?

6. Lamin Sanneh contends that in mainstream Islam religious experiences such as dreams and visions do not lead to deviation from the common forms of religious life. Matters are in fact the other way around: supernatural experiences reinforce the authority of the code, provide the stimulus for the correction of dubious practices, effectuate dramatic changes from unauthentic to authentic existence. In Islam religious experience is, in the final analysis, the 'affirmation' of the Creator by the creature. Sanneh follows a middle course with regard to the question of interreligious sharing. He seeks to wend his way between the extreme of an overly tight interpretation of the uniqueness of religious experience, which renders such experience strictly private and thus non-sharable, and that of a view of sharing so loose that it becomes superficial and merely 'user-friendly.' In genuine human encounter sharing helps to deepen religious experience.

7. Jerald Gort raises the question as to why we should attempt to share religious experience with people of other faiths. A number of grounds are adduced for the pursuit of interfaith understanding and cooperation. The main answer to the question, though, is quite simply that the future of human history on earth depends on the nurture of such encounter. The urgent necessity for interreligious sharing today, Gort argues, derives from the situation of the modern, pluralistic world, with its problems of ever-increasing division, injustice, poverty, and abuse of nature. There are several interrelated kinds or levels of religious sharing, including that of mutual participation. If human dividedness is to be overcome, people must learn to appreciate the insights and try to take empathetic part in the convictions of those who adhere to a faith other than their own. There is, Gort contends, a promising gateway to such sharing. Areas of interreligious overlap may well materialize in consequence of cooperative

action by people of differing faiths on behalf of and in solidarity with the poor. From a missiological point of view Gort pleads the cause of a 'liberative ecumenism' which entails the 'risk' of mutual influence. In principle such sharing is possible at the level of beliefs, of religious practice, and of worship. Christians should explore the possibilities of sharing on the basis of the belief in the presence of God among the poor.

One of the questions to be raised relative to this Christian view on social action has to do with its acceptability within other religious traditions. To what extent do people of other faiths share this starting point? Nevertheless, this 'option for the poor' is surely a very important issue and ought to play an important role in dialogue and the search for interreligious understanding.

8. Walter Strolz approaches the matter of interfaith sharing in terms of the innermost core of biblical teaching: the prophetic word of salvation and its concomitant critique of idolatry. God is incomparable and as a consequence the biblical message witnesses to the unity of all aspects of being *and at the same time* critically unmasks all idolatrous regard for that which is finite. Can this biblical experience of faith in the incomparable God be shared with others? According to Strolz this biblical faith is in fact shared by Christians, Jews, and Muslims. And Christians share with Zen Buddhists a portion of the path to enlightenment. Strolz examines the question whether the Zen realization of *nothingness* is comparable to the Christian meditative experience and whether the buddha-nature is analogous to God's sustenance of creation. The possibility of such interreligious sharing finds its theological undergirding in God's universal salvific will which has been revealed in Israel's history and is at work everywhere in the world where people experience *Heil*. The history of Israel, though particularist, reveals that which is universal.

The method Strolz employs to determine whether interreligious sharing is possible seems to be comparison of what people say about their ultimate experiences. If they make similar statements and use cognate symbols, e. g.: God is One and Incomparable, they may be said to share a belief. One could give many similar examples of the overlapping of religious traditions. Though terms such as *sharing* and *overlapping* have a certain indistinctness about them, they are nevertheless suitable for use as tools to give expression to the possibility that people from various traditions may have some significant things in common despite the real differences between them.

9. Hasan Askari deals, in his highly personal presentation, with the relationship between the inward and outward dimensions of religion, which, he argues, is and must needs be one of mutuality. Human beings can never experience the transcendent as it is in and of itself. The

transcendent can be 'seen,' 'felt,' 'experienced' only when it is clothed with human garments, garments which simultaneously serve to reveal and conceal. In fact, it may be said that the garments which render the transcendent 'visible' are the very humans to whom it presents itself. Since the transcendent is inexhaustible, an unending variety of 'clothes' is needed to 'disclose' its presence. Though it is ultimately impossible to know what the other garments of the transcendent really feel like, it is eminently possible to enter into contact with other believers with whom the transcendent clothes itself. The achievement of such encounter requires the kenotic emptying of oneself with a view to becoming a mirror through which the other may come to see more clearly. Religiously speaking, Askari feels that people are related to one another at the deepest level, united to each other by the innermost 'part' of their being, their Soul: "... upon meeting a so-called other, though he belongs to a different religious tradition, I recognize in him my inward companion." In the depths of their existence human beings are related to transcendence; by emptying themselves they can attain this ground of existence, which fills them to repletion.

Askari offers no facile equation of varying outward forms of religion nor does he seek to diminish the significance of their differences. He is concerned to stress the relatedness of all human beings. His is an earnest and compassionate view of sharing, one that is inspired by the faith experience associated with the more inwardly directed, mystical religious tradition. This tradition is an irenic one, and in his person and words Askari evinces possession of that same charisma.

10. James Fernandez' study of the Bwiti religious movement of the African Banzie led him to articulate a number of methodological considerations that he says need to be taken into account by anyone seeking to understand people from a different cultural and religious tradition. Experiences are never completely identical and therefore can not be fully shared. The word *sharing* itself implies partiality. The question here, therefore, is not what it *is* to be a Banzie but what it is *like* to be one. In cultural anthropology experience is approximated through description of the context and external indicators involved: sounds, sights, smells — clues that might help the observer or reader understand the culture being studied. Note is taken of images employed by the older generation to convey their cultural heritage to the young. Narrative is of crucial importance for achieving understanding of things unseen, such as religion. No matter how carefully such methods are applied, however, a certain gap will continue to exist between the culture being examined and that of the anthropologist's audience. If this gap is to be bridged, it will be necessary to employ a certain amount of analogy. Fernandez provides a fasci-

nating account of how he tried to understand the Bwiti and convey this understanding to his fellow anthropologists.

This methodological movement from external description to attentive reception of stories which evoke meaning and structure the world-view of a religious tradition seems very important. What can be described 'objectively' should be so described, and that as precisely as possible. When it comes to faith, religion, and life as a whole, however, understanding will have to be gained through that which can not be said or expressed directly. How are we to understand this indirect use of language? Fernandez provides a methodology which opens up the possibility of engaging in such ventures of understanding. The philosophical question that continues to hover in the background, however, is that concerning the conditions for understanding. Is it possible for people genuinely to understand one another on any basis other than that of their common *human condition*, the shared unseen aspects of human life with which religion deals: fear, wonder, sorrow, guilt, happiness, and the awareness of that which transcends finite existence?

11. Michael von Brück defines religious experience as participation in any event creative of the wholeness whereby individuals or groups are provided with identity and orientation in their search for meaning. He distinguishes three layers of identity and correspondingly three levels of interreligious sharing: social, emotional, and personal. He highlights Hindu folk religion as a social event in which the community participates in the cosmic order *(dharma)* through rituals and festivals. In religious experiences of a more mystical nature social and emotional identity is not as important as in 'ordinary' religious life. Even in mystical experience, however, the *manner* in which one experiences is structured by the religious tradition to which one belongs. Religious encounter is always determined by the hermeneutical framework of the specific religion within which it takes place. Every event of religious encounter represents a new experience; religious life is an ongoing hermeneutical process, which makes it impossible to separate the sharers from that which is shared.

Von Brück's answer to the general question of whether interreligious encounter and sharing is possible is wholeheartedly affirmative. This process of sharing has been going and continues to go on all the time in many places and on many occasions in the world. But this affirmation also needs qualification. To the extent that religious experience is related to group identity sharing becomes increasingly *im*possible: it is impossible to be both a Western Christian *and* a caste-Hindu whose forebears have lived for centuries in the same village community. Mystical experience presents greater opportunities for interreligious sharing, though it must be borne in mind that such experience is exceptional rather than usual. Rites, festivals and holy places also provide room for interfaith participation. As a rule Hindus are more open to participation in Christian rituals and festivals than are Christians —whose attitude is determined by their understanding of the exclusivity of Christ— in Hindu celebrations. Since the group identity of Hindus and Christians remains substantially different, actual sharing in one another's living traditions has up till now been marginal. Dialogue is carried on largely by a small number of intellectuals; *communicatio in sacris* between Hinduism and Christianity has not yet been achieved.

Von Brück argues convincingly that religious traditions can also be characterized as *social* and *cultural* phenomena; this emphasis on the social dimension of religious life is a very important one. In terms of the topic of the workshop, however, it is not the possibility of social and cultural but rather *religious* sharing which is at issue. In participating in a Hindu festival a Christian might well be able to share in the social event but quite unable to appropriate the related religious experience. In a religiously pluralistic culture it would appear that personal faith and relationship to the Transcendent constitute the most essential part of religion, though of course it must also be said that such personal faith is always embedded in the whole of a religious tradition.

12. Reender Kranenborg is concerned to show that the theosophic tradition represents a combination of Western and Eastern beliefs. He analyzes a number of fragments from the Western esoteric tradition which evidence both Christian and Hindu influences. Such religiously 'mixed' messages or revelations were entrusted to certain individuals, who thus may be said to have had extraordinary experiences. Messages from the masters were passed on to Mrs. Zohra. Mrs. Blavatsky and others received special revelations while in the state of trance or through the gift of clairvoyance. Can their extraordinary experiences be shared by others? Kranenborg argues that this is possible only for those who possess the gifts of such extraordinary people. People capable of going into trance or who have clairvoyant vision do in fact share in the experiences of their predecessors, though this sharing can only be partial since later revelatory experiences always take precedence over and in some sense supersede earlier ones. It is possible for 'ordinary' people to share in the experiences of these 'extraordinary' figures only in the sense of acceptance of or assent to what has been related by the latter. Generally speaking, this kind of extraordinary religious experience, being of an intensely personal nature, is incapable of being wholly shared. The degree to which sharing is possible depends on the range of a person's receptive gifts and experience. The fact that such partial sharing does indeed take place assures the continuation of the cumulative Western esoteric tradition with all its elitist social aspects.

13. Corstiaan van der Burg describes a conflict within the Madhva community in Bangalore caused by one of its Swamis who tried to break through preestablished lines of social demarcation by establishing a devotionalist Madhva movement outside the boundaries of his own traditional group. His efforts included the teaching of Sanskrit and clerical training even among outcaste youths. His aim was to share his beliefs with people belonging to other social groups. The background to his concern was formed by the cultural changes taking place in urban society and the social and legal pressures being exerted with an eye to the revision of traditional relations between social groups. The Swami believed that adherence to the caste system could be overcome and that accusations of discrimination levelled at the Madhva community should be countered by means of a renewal of Madhva tradition. His initiative nearly split the community in half, though in the end it did hold together. This paper, thus, relates the story of an inspired local religious leader, some of whose people were unable or unwilling to share his vision due to their strong adherence to traditional Brahmanic doctrine.

14. Tilmann Vetter describes Father Lassalle's contribution to the fascinating ongoing story of the Buddhist–Christian encounter. Vetter approaches his subject particularly in terms of the notions of *satori* and *theologia negativa*. Lassalle used Buddhist meditation, in which he actively participated with Zen Buddhists, as a means of freeing the mind from thinking and not-thinking in order to reach the point of non-thinking and in this way came to share in the experience of enlightenment. Lassalle maintains, on the basis of his own experience, that Zen provides a means by which it is possible to achieve encounter with God. Once naive Christian concepts of God have been relinquished, the Buddhist path to full freedom of the mind assumes Christian content by virtue of the Christian's experience of the nearness of God. Vetter questions whether it is really possible to share in Zen meditation while at the same time maintaining traditional Christian doctrines. To Vetter sharing means passing over to another tradition and coming back enriched to one's own, which explains why he has more reservations than does Lassalle concerning the ability of a Christian or other non-Buddhist to share fully in *satori*. He does leave room, however, for the emergence of mutual transformation as a result of a genuine passing over.

15. Han de Wit, a practising Buddhist, describes the process of the transmission of religious insight. Such insight is not religious truth but an analysis of the seemingly normal way of experiencing things. Buddhist teachings are directed toward the goal of freeing human beings for real experience and, subsequently, helping them to cultivate their minds through meditation. 'Sharing' in a Buddhist sense implies personal

involvement. It constitutes a way of escaping the 'normal' confused mode of experience in the ordinary life that human beings in fact 'share' with one another. Attainment of this freedom requires a total self-emptying of all ego-centred concepts and attitudes and even the renunciation of the 'I' since it is the source of passion, aggression, and delusion. From the Buddhist point of view there is no problem involved in sharing the 'normal' experience of reality. But anyone who desires to attain the enlightened mode of experience must be prepared to engage in a process whereby his or her personality and the world are subjected to total reinterpretation through the medium of meditation. This view bears implications for dialogue between Buddhists and monotheists: Buddhism has no concept of God; transcendence is, in a sense, synonymous with this world (the real world, absolute reality). Consequently, Buddhism has no special religious experience to share.

In light of this we might well ask whether the blend of Christian belief and Zen meditation proposed by Father Lassalle is really viable. De Wit's argumentation lends support to Vetter's criticism of Lassalle's position. But John Cobb's notions of 'passing over' and 'mutual transformation' would seem to be equally doubtful in terms of De Wit's perception of Buddhism. This raises a question for further discussion: Does De Wit's interpretation really preclude any kind of passing over in the Christian–Buddhist encounter?

16. Hans Waldenfels offers an interesting interpretation of *śūnyatā*. On the basis of Western translations it is often thought that this notion has the negative meaning of *void*. In reality, however, it connotes a kind of fullness: emptiness is transformed into non-emptiness. Self-emptying is creative of space or non-space for a very special experience. Can a singular experience such as this, an experience so insusceptible of verbal articulation, be shared? Sharing, according to Waldenfels, means participation in the experience of others. Sharing is encounter, which involves the active giving of oneself and the passive assumption of a listening attitude. Thus, engagement in sharing is engagement in self-alteration. This, too, seems reminiscent of Cobb's idea of passing over and coming back changed. Waldenfels argues that there are various degrees of sharing, ranging from partial to total. Can the sharing of *śūnyatā* be anything other that partial? Can it be shared at all? Though many would respond negatively to the latter question, Waldenfels does not. Taking his departure from the biblical witness to God's kenotic self-emptying in Jesus' life, love, and crucifixion, he strongly maintains that it is possible to share *śūnyatā*. Sharing is more than an academic enterprise, however. It requires deep existential involvement.

17. Jacques Kamstra offers an analysis of the new New Religions of Japan. In them elements of traditional Japanese Buddhism have become mingled with ideas and practices originating in Shinto and Christianity. Thus, these religions are themselves characterized by extensive internal sharing (a marriage of East and West). There is also the sharing that takes place between the founders and followers of the new New Religions. Kamstra makes a rather sharp distinction between abstract, academic, impersonal sharing on the one hand and the personal, free, existential sharing practised by ordinary believers and groups of believers in practical, everyday religious life on the other. It is intellectuals who engage in the first type of sharing: they read books and contribute to discussions in workshops and the like. In this environment sharing is often viewed as a problem and warnings are sometimes raised against the danger of syncretism. The second, more personal type of sharing is common practice in Japan. There Buddhist sects freely borrow and employ elements deriving from other religious traditions.

This distinction is very important, though the issue is a very complicated one. People may well make religious blends of their own choosing and liking. But just as in a kitchen not all combinations are savory, so, too, not all mixtures of religion are palatable or agreeable. One may equate the Buddha to Jesus Christ on the grounds that they both represent Transcendental Light, but honesty demands the admission that any such a comparison entails a procrustean approach to either the Buddha or Jesus Christ or both. The 'logic' of religious belief can not be neglected at will: any tradition that evidences a high degree of internal inconsistency will not endure long.

18. Anton Wessels explores the boundaries of Islamic–Christian sharing. He compares the Koranic and biblical accounts of the prophets who were sent out to address the people. It seems evident that Mohammed shared the fortunes of his predecessors. Though God was their strength, it was ordained that they endure suffering at the hands of their fellow human beings. Some were even put to death. The story of Mohammed runs parallel to the stories of the prophets who went before him. Muslim–Christian dialogue is most often burdened by the alleged contradiction between the Koranic and biblical accounts of the death of Jesus. Wessels suggests the possibility of creating a new opening in this dialogue by pointing out that the traditional exegesis of the Koranic texts having to do with Jesus' death is not entirely without ambiguity. He calls Muslims and Christians to mutual reverence for the lives and deaths of both Jesus and Mohammed. Although genuine differences remain between the message of Mohammed and that of the life and death of Jesus, Muslims and Christians, Wessels argues, have more in common than is often realized.

For Wessels sharing seems to mean having things in common: destiny, createdness, finitude, belief in One God. This approach provides room for free dialogical exchange regarding areas of overlap and remaining differences between Islam and Christianity. Wessels advocates exploration of the boundary areas with an eye to the expansion of the area held in common by the two traditions.

19. Hans Daiber cites Djunayd's recommendation to a fellow mystic: Tell people only what they are capable of perceiving. By virtue of its unique nature the mystical experience of unification with the Most High is not susceptible of description. Only those who have had a mystical experience of this kind can fully understand it. Nevertheless, mystics attempt to transmit their experience to others through the written word and instruction. The mystical tradition has delineated the path that needs to be followed in order to reach the ultimate goal, a path consisting of a series of progressively advancing levels. In Daiber's account the path is divided into three stages, each of which is classified according to the degree and intensity of unification it affords. According to Djunayd mystics are like prophets, elected through divine grace to seek unity with God and to practice sobriety in this worldly life with a view to leading the masses nearer to God. Mystics can not gift others with the mystical experience, but they can offer counsel regarding the life that God wants people to lead, they can teach people the outward forms of religious life so that the latter can prepare themselves for inward dialogue with God. Thus, whereas the mystical experience itself is intensely personal and therefore does not lend itself to description, the more earthly and external aspects of this experience are communicable and can be shared by those eager to learn.

20. Arnulf Camps elaborates the idea of *double loyalty,* a notion he introduced in his farewell address at the University of Nijmegen in March 1990. It is argued in much of Asian Christian theology that Christians should live "in a basic human community together with the faithful of other traditions as well as in a basic Christian community." People should strive cooperatively for peace and full humanity for all. Because God, in whom Christians place their trust, is the God of all humankind, He reaches out to all human beings, granting them salvation in one way or another. From a Christian point of view all humans are religious. In the interreligious gathering that met in Assisi to pray for peace, Camps writes, it was precisely this deep human religiosity that was shared by and among the participants. Those who took part in these prayers shared the experience that Ultimate Reality is not an abstraction but a reality in plurality. This does not mean that all religious traditions ought to be considered to be the same, nor does it imply that mission should be

neglected for the sake of dialogue. The concept of *double loyalty* entails profound faithfulness both to God and to one's neighbour. It would be very interesting to have a more detailed elaboration of this view of *homo religiosus/a* with a view to its implications for the theme of this symposium.

Concluding Philosophical Notes and Theoretical Comments

1. Since religious experiences are related to the whole of human existence, concrete religious experience is always personal and can not, therefore, be fully shared (cf. Oberhammer). If the idea of interreligious sharing is conceived not in terms of 'sameness' but rather of partiality and thus of the 'overlapping' of distinct personal religious experiences, it may be said to be possible.

2. Interreligious sharing would also be impossible if religious experience were fully woven into the fabric of the whole of a religious tradition (Dupré). Moreover, if all aspects of religious experience were related to each other unequivocally, this, too, would constitute an insurmountable barrier to sharing. If, however, religious traditions represent ongoing hermeneutical processes and if religious experience consists of a variety of concrete experiences, then interreligious overlapping and change within the several religious traditions can take place.

3. Sharing religious experience consists, thus, in 'having things in common' (Smith, Wessels), i. e., religious practice, rites, symbols, beliefs, or religiously motivated social involvement such as action on behalf of the poor (Gort). It is precisely through acquaintance with their religious rites and symbolic objects and language that it becomes possible to come to an understanding of other people's faith (Droogers).

4. Such understanding and sharing will remain partial (Fernandez). The confines of the particular context in which a religious tradition is articulated will prohibit full passing over and sharing (cf. Von Brück). The Western secularized and individualistic culture allows people to believe what they wish, compels them to make up their own minds in this regard. In religiously pluralist cultures faith is a highly personal matter (even though people remain social beings).

5. If people have enough in common, they may rightly conclude that they share a number of beliefs and experiences (cf. Strolz). From a Christian point of view all humans have religiosity or relatedness to God in common (Camps). According to Buddhism all people share the same nature, although they may not realize it (cf. De Wit).

6. The need for sharing and the willingness to encounter people from other religious traditions are determined to a large extent by the relative social and economic power possessed by the various religious groups within a culture (Droogers).

7. Ways of sharing can differ significantly. In one society people may share mainly through personal acquaintance (Von Brück). An anthropologist, orientalist or student of religion can achieve sharing through concentrated study. Any real sharing requires personal involvement and carries with it the 'risk' of personal change (Vetter, Gort). Most authors in the present volume consider encounter to be superficial if it does not lead to change of some kind (e. g., Dupré, Sanneh, Waldenfels).

8. Such modifications of faith are occasioned by constant reinterpretation of beliefs and adaptation of currents practices. The history of religions constitutes a continual process of interreligious encounter and evinces an ever present impingement of contextual influences (including non-religious ones) on religious life (cf. Camps' 'double loyalty').

9. The problem of sharing religious experience can also arise *within* a given religious tradition. In fact, the possibilities and impossibilities of sharing within the Christian tradition have been broadly explored in ecumenical theology (cf. Gort). One important form of intra-confessional sharing is that of the transmission of tradition by an older to a new generation. Other cases of sharing within a tradition are: (a) the transmission of the insights of those who have undergone special experiences such as mystical union (Daiber), dreams, and visions (Sanneh) or trance (Kranenborg), and (b) proposed renewal (Van der Burg). While extraordinary experiences can not be shared by the ordinary believer, they do have a bolstering effect on his or her faith.

10. Partial sharing of religious experience is possible on the basis of shared humanity and (at least among religious people) the common search for wholeness, meaning, peace, rest, a worthy life, etc. Areas of overlap between religious traditions is made possible by the *human condition*.

11. The quest in some religions for trustworthy ground in which to anchor beliefs has led to the recognition of holy scriptures. Even in the more orthodox quarters of religious traditions sharing in the idea of scriptural inspiration is possible in a formal sense (Fernhout).

12. It is possible to share in experiences specific to other religious traditions (cf. Smith). When people are struck by a hymn, a rite, a text or an idea from another religion, they construe and appropriate this 'symbol' through a process of reinterpretation whereby it is rendered more or less compatible with their own faith. This implies that even when a

Christian, e. g., is moved by a 'Muslim word,' the experience he or she undergoes will remain a personal one. Or again, the irreducible personal core of religious experience implies that one's encounter with emptiness/non-emptiness need not necessarily be identical to that of another believer (cf. Waldenfels).

13. If a believer's own tradition is lacking in any way, he or she can reach out to another religious community to try to fill the gap (Askari). At the personal, practical level sharing seems to be easier to achieve than at the level of official dialogue and academic discussion (Kamstra).

14. A question which requires further reflection and discussion is whether and to what extent one's religion needs to be consistent, both from a psychological and a systematic point of view. Another important point in this connection is the need to establish right priorities in interreligious encounter: should people be encouraged to attain *śūnyatā*, e. g., or to become involved in cooperative liberative action on behalf of the poor and oppressed?

The present volume, while furnishing a number of important answers, leaves many questions open. The editors hope that these unsolved problems will stimulate broader reflection and discussion.

Index of Names and Authors

Abdel-Kader, Ali Hassan 246-253
Abe, M. 211
Abraham 233-235, 239
Abraham, K. C. 101, 102
Abū Bakr al-Ṣiddīq 79
Abū Ḥātim al-Rāzī 240
Adler, P. S. 137
Agni 67
Akon, Okomfo Kodwo 260
Alcyone 156
'Alī 79
Allah 66, 67, 69, 261
Ananaikyo 222
Anantha Murthy, U. R. 163
al-'Arabī, Ibn 82
Arai, T. 257
Arberry, A. J. 246, 249, 251
Ariarajah, W. 257
Arinze, Cardinal Francis 260
Arockiadoss, P. 148
Arrupe, Pedro 179, 180
Asahi Shimbunsha 221
al-Ash'arī 77
Askari, Hasan 242, 274, 275
Ayoub, M. 228, 241
Ayyapan 148
Baal, J. van 49
Badhwar, Inderjit 89
Bailey, Alice 151, 157, 158, 161
Balasuriya, Tissa 90
Balthasar, H. U. von 111
Batchelor, John 83
Baṭṭūṭa, Ibn 80

Bavinck, H. 233
Begrich, J. 106
Bell, R. 236
Berkouwer, G. C. 243
Bernstein, Richard J. 46, 47
Besant, A. 154
Beyerhaus, P. 256, 261-263
Bhattacharya, K. 70, 72
al-Bisṭāmī, Abū Yazīd (Bāyezid) 250
Blavatsky, Madame H. P. 151-155, 157, 158, 160, 161
Bloch, L. 114
Blyth, R. H. 224
Bochner, S. 139
Bonino, José Míguez 94
Bosch, David 101
Böwering, G. 249
Bragt, Jan van 186, 187
Brahmā 21
Brandson, S. G. F. 91
Brocke, M. 110
Brück, Michael von 139, 143, 144, 149, 276, 282, 283
Buddha 8, 25, 68, 69, 71, 113, 190-192, 201, 218, 220, 222, 224, 225, 257
   Gautama 152
Bukhārī, Muḥammad b. Ismā'īl al- 66
Burg, Corstiaan J. G. van der 170, 171, 177, 278, 283
Bürkle, H. 261
Calvin, John 56

Camps, Arnulf O. F. M. 256, 257, 264, 265, 281-283
Carman, J. B. 142
Ch'en, K. 218
Chao-chou 181
Chethimattam, J. B. 141, 143
Christ 65, 66, 69, 70, 73, 206, 207, 209-211, 213
  Maitreya 152, 155-158
Clement of Alexandria 181
Cobb, J. B., jr. 210
Cohen, Anthony P. 47
Coleridge 134
Cragg, Kenneth 94, 228, 233
Crick, Malcom 46
Cyrus 109
Daiber, Hans 247, 251, 252, 254, 281, 283
Dalai Lama 261
Dasgupta, S. 71
David 233
De Silva, Lily 68
Deladriere, R. 246
Denny, M. 233
Devātideva 71
Dilthey, Wilhelm 4
Dionysius the Areopagite 111, 144
Djibrīl 66
Djunayd 245-253
Djwal Khul 153, 158
Dōgen, Zenji 112, 113, 185
Dörmann, J. 256, 260-262
Dornberg, Ulrich 95
Dörrie, H. 250
Droogers, André 271, 282, 283
Drummond, Richard H. 90
Duchrow, Ulrich 89
Dumont, L. 164-167, 174-176
Dumoulin, H. 204-206, 211
Dupré, Willem 270, 271, 282, 283
EATWOT 90, 95, 101, 102

Eckhart, Meister 111, 184, 205
Etchegaray, Cardinal 255, 258
Evans-Pritchard, E. E. 46
Fabella, Virginia 90
Fahd, Toufic 80
Falaturi, A. 109
Falwell, Jerry 61
Fārābī 252
Fernandez, James W. 47, 49, 50, 54, 125, 132, 135, 275, 276, 282
Fernando, A. 217
Fernhout, Rein 54, 70, 135, 273, 283
Fischer, A. 66
Forward, Martin 94
Francis, St. Francis of Assissi 255-259
Freud 80
Gabriel 66, 67, 229, 232, 237
Gadamer, H. -G. 4, 5
Gandhi, Rajiv 81
Gardet, L. 245
Gautama 152
Geertz, C. 138
Genshun 212
Gibb, H. A. R. 234, 235
Giddens, Anthony 47
Gidado, Malam 77
Glasenapp, H von 167
Glemp, Cardinal Joseph 260
Glüer, W. 260
Goi Mahikisa 225
Gonda, J. 67, 70
Gort, Jerald D. 48, 54, 88, 99, 105, 273, 274, 282, 283
Gotama 68
Gramlich, R. 249
Harada, Sogaku 180-182,
Heidegger, Martin 4, 9
Hikari Kyodan 226
Hirota, M. 221, 223-226
Hiskett, Mervyn 76, 77, 79, 80

Holmström, M. N. 165, , 165, 166, 168, 169, 173-175, , 176
Holy Spirit 65, 103, 255, 264
Houtepen, Anton 94
Hud 233-235, 239
Hui-neng 178, 185, 186
Hunwick, John 79
Ibn Ḥanbal 251
Ibn Sa'd 237
Ignatius 69
Indra 67
'Īsā 70
Isaiah 106, , 106, 107, 109-111
Ismaili 252
Ito, G. 217, 224
Izutsu, Toshihiko 230
James, William 5, 32, 84, 90, 193
Jantzen, Grace 11
Jayatilleke, K. N. 68
Jesus Christ 5-11, 25, 82-85, 89, 90, 92-95, 97, 99-103, 136-138, 140, 141, 143-148, 152-158, 161, 217, 218, 220-222, 224, 225, 228, 229, 233, 235, 236, 238-243, 255-260, 262-264
Jesus 65, 69, 70, 73
Jesus of Nazareth 103
Master 152, 155, 161
Jizo 220
John, St. John 65, 66, 69, 242
John, St. John of the Cross 57, 205
John, T. K. 143
John Paul II 255, 257, 260
John XXIII 255
Jongeneel, J. A. B. 97
Kadushin, M. 11
Kalābādhī 245, 246
Kamei 220, 221
Kamstra, Jacques 216-220, 222, 227, 280
Kannon 223

Kant, Immanuel 10
Kaspers, W. 186
Katz, St. T. 8, 143, 144, 146
Kern, H. 71, 72
Khadija 118
Khaldūn, Ibn 80
Kharrāz 245, 247
Khumayni, Ayatollah 61
King, W. L. 211, 212
Kiriyama Seiyu 220
Kitagawa, Joseph 83
Kobo Daishi 220
Kramers, J. H. 234, 235
Kranenborg, R. 162, 277, 283
Krishnamurti 151, 156, 157, 161
Krṣna 142, 261
Kuitert, H. M. 9
Kümmel, W. G. 65
Küng, Hans 217
Kuthumi 153-158
Lanczkowski, G. 31
Lassalle, H. M. Enomiya- 178-187, 205, 206
Leadbeater, C. W. 151, 154-158, 161
Leertouwer, L. 216
Levinas, Emmanuel 5, 107
Light, Mr. Light 223
Lot 233, 235
Luke 65
Luther, Martin 56
MacDonald, D. B. 245
Mahadevan, T. M. P. 140
Maḥfuz, N. 241
Maitreya 152, 155-158, 222
Malcolm X 84-86
Manu 71
Mañjuśrī 204
Massignon, L. 240
Micah 261
Michaud, H. 241
Michel, Th. 260
Miers, H. 157

Minoo   221
Mitra   67
Morgan, R.   31
Master Morya   152-155, 158, 161
Moses   9, 230, 233, 235, 238,
    239, 242
Mu'īn al-Dīn Chishtī   145
Mudaliar, A. Shanmugha   70, 71
Muhammad   8, 9, 25, 66, 67, 69,
    70, 77, 78, 80, 117, 228-239,
    241, 242, 243
Munson, T.   29, 39
Nāgārjuna   209
Nagel, Thomas.   127-129, 131
Nakano Katsutate   222
Nanjio, B.   71, 72
Nichiren   220
Nicholson, R. A.   247
Niffarī   249
Nishitani, Keiji   112, 206
Noah   233-235, 238, 239
Nuwayhi, Muḥammad al-   239
O'Brien, Donal Cruise   78
Oberhammer, Gerhard   8, 13-15,
    17, 19, 20, 24, 113, 115, 208,
    214, 269, 270, 272, 282
Odin, St.   207
Ohikarisama   223
Okada Kotama   223
Okada Mokichi   223, 225, 226
Olcott, H. S.   153, 154
Onisaburgo Deguchi   222
Origen   72
Panduranga   170
Panikkar, R.   141, 148
Pao Liang   217
Paret, R.   231, 234, 235
Parmenides   111
Paul, Pope Paul VI   256
Paul, St. Paul   58, 65, 85
    Damascus   92
    Saul   92
    Peniel   92

Pharaoh   109
Pieris, Aloysius   101
Plato   111
Ploeg, J. P. M. van der.   261, 262
Polman, A. D. R.   233
Prabhushankara, S.   173
Puthanangady, P.   145
Pye, M.   31
al-Qādir, Shaikh 'Abd   77-79
Qushayrī, ar-Risāla   249
Raalte, J. van   88-90, 101
Raguin, Yves   92
Rahman, Fazlur   231-233
Rahner, Karl   7, 8, 11, 211
Räisänen, H.   241
Rao, C. R.   170
Rao, S. N.   142
Renou, L.   68, 70, 71
Ricoeur, Paul   4
Ries, J.   256
Rilke, R. M.   19
Rissho Koeikai   219
Rūmī   82
Rushdie, Salman   80, 81, 237
Ruth   94
Sadāśiva   70
Sahi, J.   142
Salih   233-235, 239
Ṣāliḥ, Subḥi al-   66, 69
Sāmarrā'ī, Qāsim   247
Samartha, Stanley J.   90, 100,
    102, 103
Sanneh, Lamin   100, 273, 283
Santa Ana, J. de   90
Satan   95, 237
Saul   92
Schimmel, A.   245-247, 250, 251
Schmidt, W. H.   114
Schuré, E.   157
Seckler, M.   256
Sezgin, F.   246
Shakyamuni   113
Sharma, B. N. K.   167, 169

Shaykh 'Uthmān b. Fūdī 76-81
Shehu Usuman dan Fodio
  Shaykh 'Uthman b. Fudi 76-81
Sinnett, A. P. 154
Śiva 21, 70, 71, 146
Smart, N. 137
Smith, B. 220
Smith, Wilfred Cantwell 3, 12,
  38, 44, 90, 271, 272, 281
Soka Gakkai 218-220
Soma 67
Soothill, W. E. 224
Spae, Joseph J. 96
Speyer, H. 249
Spindler, Marc 97
Stachel, Günter 179, 184
Steere, Douglas V. 179, 180
Steiner, Rudolf 151, 156, 157,
  161
Sting 96
Streng, F. J. 209
Strolz, Walter 109, 113, 115,
  214, 274, 282
Šu'ayb 233, 235
Suzuki Shosan 211, 212
Svami V. 164, 165, 167-169,
  171-176
Tabari, At-. 237
Tajfel, H. 137, 138
Takpo Tashi Namgyal 198
Taniguchi 222
Tendzin, Ösel 197
Teresa, St. Teresa of Avila 205
Thoma, C. 108
Thomsen, H. 222, 223, 226
Tillich, Paul 5, 90
Torres, Sergio 90
Trimingham, J. Spencer 80
Trungpa, Chögyam 191
Tsultrim Gyamtso Rimpoche 200
Ueda, S. 112
Ulin, Robert C. 46
Vaidya, P. L. 71, 72

Vaidyanathan, K. R. 148
Van Elderen, Marlin 98
Vandana, Mataji 142
Varuna 67
Vasubandhu 192
Veer, Peter van der 164, 170,
  173, 174
Vergote, A. 5, 6
Vetter, Tilmann 8, 68, 278, 279,
  283
Vimalakīrti 203-205
Viṣṇu 21, 70, 261
Vitthala of Pandharpur 169, 170
Voetius, Gijbertus 97
Vroom, Hendrik M. 6, 12, 31,
  38, 44, 49, 54, 59, 105, 140,
  150, 209, 214
Waldenfels, H. 13, 24, 185-188,
  205, 206, 208, 211, 214, 257,
  258, 266, 279, 283
Walker, S. 192
Watt, W. M. 66, 229, 230
Webb, J. 161
Weisacker, Carl Friedrich von
  257
Wensinck, A. J. 66, 230
Wessels, Anton 54, 59, 280-282
Wilson, Bryan R. 46
Wit, Han F. de 10, 12, 201, 202,
  278, 279, 283
Wittgenstein, Ludwig 4, 83
Wyschogrod, M. 108, 109
Yahweh 106-109, 146
Yajima, T. 220
Yāska 67
Yūsūf 79
Yuvaka 168
Zaehner, R. C. 242
Zago, Marcello 263
Zeid, Hamzah 98
Zwingli 56

General Index of Subjects

abhidharma 193
abhisamaya 185
abnegation
  self-abnegation 82, 83
absurdity 33, 42
activity 29, 42
Acts
  book of 65, 69, 239
adhaesio intellect 91
adhikāra 142
Advaita Vedānta 7, 140
Africa 100, 257, 258
āgamas 70, 71, 145
Ainu 83
Ajita Āgama 70
allegorical interpretation 72
allusion 245, 246
Amaterasu 220, 221, 224
Amerinds 57
amorphous feelings 96
analogy 65-68, 73, 128, 129,
  131, 133
anima naturaliter christiana 217
annihilation 245, 249, 250, 252
anthropologist 45-48, 51
anthropology 45, 46, 49, 271,
  276, 283
anubhāva 142
Apauruṣeya 68
apocalyptic 65
apostle 78, 79
  Apostolic Fathers 69
apperception 31

appropriation/subjection/annexati
68-73
Arab 229, 233, 235, 238, 239,
  241
arahat 68
arcana 145
Aristotle
  Aristotelian science 82
Ashram 146
Asia 100, 255, 257, 263, 264
Asian theology 255, 263, 264
Assisi 255-263, 281
āthār/fī'l 250
atheism 261
ātman 196
attribution/extension/ascription
  64, 66, 67, 69-73
authenticity 92, 95, 101
  religious faith 95
authority 252
  absolute 64-66, 68, 72, 73
Avalokiteśvara 223
Avataṃsaka 218
'awāmm 248
awareness 28, 29, 32
  discriminating 189, 199
  self-awareness 28, 29, 32
Babylon 106, 107, 109
Bangalore 163, 164, 167, 168,
  171, 172
Banzie 129, 131-134
bāṭin 247, 248
bayān 250
beyond-being 13, 15-17, 113

encounter with 16, 17
openness 17
openness of 15, 16
Bhagavad Gītā 62, 142, 143
bhakti 4, 140, 142, 163, 164,
    167, 170, 175, 176
bhāvanā 185
Bible 55-62, 64, 80, 81, 85,
    106-114, 228, 229, 234
bibliocentrism 58, 61
Black Muslims 84
Black Untouchables 95
bodhisattva 155, 158, 220
    Jizo 220
Brahman 7
Brahmanism 64, 169, 170
Brahmans   163, 165, 167,
    169-171, 173-175
brahmavidyā 142, 143
brokenness 99, 100
Buddhavacana 68
Buddhism 6, 8, 9, 11, 64, 68,
    71, 73, 106, 111-114, 116-118,
    140, 142, 147, 189-201, 257,
    258, 260, 261
    Buddhahood 112, 113
    Buddhahood of nature 112,
    113
    Hīnayāna 190
    Mahāyāna 71, 190, 195, 200,
    261
    meditation 191, 199, 201
    Samurai-Zen 211
    Shentong school 200
    Sōtō 211
    Tendai 218
    Theravāda 64, 68, 190
    three *yana* 190
    Tipiṭaka 64, 68, 71
    Vajrayāna 190
    Zen 4, 8, 92, 106, 111-114,
    147, 178-187, 204, 211, 212,
    274, 278, 279

Buddhist path 191, 192, 200
*Bulletin Secretariatus pro Non
    Christianis* 257-260, 263
Bwiti 125, 129-134, 275, 276
Canadian Indians 57
canon 64-73, 78
case method 130
caste   140-142, 145, 148, 276,
    278
Catholic 258-263
charismatic 78
    leadership 78
charlatanry 78
child 41
Christian 55-62, 136-138, 140,
    141, 143-148, 228, 229, 233,
    236, 238, 240, 242, 243,
    255-260, 262-264
    church 95
    mission 97
Christianity 6, 8, 11, 83, 85, 92,
    93, 99, 103, 106, 108, 109, 111,
    117, 140, 144, 146, 217, 218,
    220, 222, 224, 263, 264
Christians 93, 97, 99, 100, 103
Christocentrism 58
church
    early church 69
clarity 250
Cloud of Unknowing 181, 182
coherence 94
Colombo 99
Commission Justitia et Pax 256
common ground 258, 261
communicatio in sacris 136, 148
communication 26-30, 37
communio 14, 17, 18, 21-23,
    144-146, 148
    human *communio* 22
communism 261
community 5, 25, 26, 30, 38-40,
    119, 120, 137, 141, 142, 145,
    146, 258, 263, 264

with others 22
Comparative Religion 137
complementary 142, 147
concrete universality 42
concreteness
    repeatable 21
confession 91, 93, 96, 97
    of faith 77
confusion 189-196, 198, 200, 201
conscience 26, 41
consciousness 26, 41, 193, 197
Constitution of the Church of South India 97
contemplation 142-144, 146, 189-193, 195, 198-201
    path 189, 192
    psychology 190, 193
contingency 28
conversion 48, 72, 73, 88, 92-94, 102
    horizontal 88, 94, 96
    mutuality 102
convert 41
cosmotheandric 141
covenant 249, 250
creation 106-114
    creatio continua 114
    creatio ex nihilo 106, 114
    integrity of 98
    respect for 98
Creator 76, 82, 86, 107, 109-112
crucifixion 236, 238-243
cultic
    word 67
culture 27, 30, 32, 33, 35-38, 46-50
    cultural specificity 93
Dalit
    Dalit Voice 95
Dalits 95
Damascus 92
Damietta 256
darśanas 140

Dasakuta 167, 169, 175
Dasas 167, 169, 170, 175
Day of Prayer in Assisi 255, 259, 260
death 108, 112, 113, 134
deficiency 33
delirium 78
deluding Scriptures 71
dependency 89, 90
detachment 36, 112
determinants 96
    particularizing 96
dhamma 68
dharma 67, 68, 71, 137, 140-142, 145, 168, 170-172
Dharmaparyāyas 71
dhyāna 145
diakonia 101
dialectic 178, 186, 187
dialogue 3, 5-7, 25, 27, 46, 48, 50, 51, 53, 99-103, 106, 107, 111, 113, 120, 144, 148, 175, 178, 185-187, 189, 190, 192, 201, 203, 207, 210, 211, 213, 217, 218, 222, 228, 240, 242, 245, 252, 255, 256, 259, 260, 262-264, 274, 277, 279-282
    interreligious 189, 190, 201
difference 30, 39
discriminating awareness 189, 199
distinctiveness 94, 96
distinctives 94, 97, 103
disunity 90
diversity 26, 27, 29, 30, 36, 91, 94, 98
dividedness 98-100
divine 8, 32-35, 37-40, 42, 43, 55, 58, 60-62, 67, 68, 73, 83, 90-93, 97, 103, 117, 144, 147, 148, 151, 169, 206, 221, 223-225, 228, 229, 232, 233,

238, 242, 245, 246, 249, 250,
252, 259, 270, 271, 281
  divine character of reality　39
  experience of　90, 97
  grace of　35
  idea of　33
  moments of　32, 33, 42
  Other　91, 99
  presence of　37
  recognition of　34
  revelation　91, 92
  Will　90, 91
docetic　93
double loyalty　264
dream　76, 78-81
dualistic　106, 109, 112
Dvaita　167, 169
East–West　107, 108, 110-112,
114
eboga　130
ecstasy　250, 252
  ecstatic drunkenness　250
ecumenism　88, 102
egalitarianism　163-165, 169-172,
174-77
ego　189, 192, 196-201
  ātman　196
egolessness　199
elliptical　82, 84
emancipation　16, 20
emptiness　189, 195, 200, 205,
206, 208, 210-212
  śūnyatā　200, 203-213
encounter　3-5, 7, 13-19, 23, 25,
41, 46-49, 51, 83, 86, 89, 90,
91, 95, 99, 112, 113, 117, 118,
120, 127, 136, 137, 138-145,
151, 153-157, 160, 161, 178,
184, 205, 208, 215, 216, 243,
255, 259, 269, 270, 273, 275,
276, 278, 279, 283
enculturation　180

enlightenment　8, 67, 68, 71, 91,
92, 111, 113, 154, 180, 181,
183-185, 190-193, 196, 200,
201, 204, 209, 274, 278, 279
epistemology　101
  religious　137, 139, 144
equality　163, 165, 169, 170, 175,
176
esoteric　151-161, 247
Essenes　155
ethical
  transformation　85
Eucharist　56, 141, 145, 147
evanescence　249
evangelism　99, 102
  Commision on World Mission
  and Evangelism　102
  media evangelists　83
  mission　91, 96, 97, 99-102
exclusive
  exclusivity　19
  validity　18
exclusivity　30, 39, 43
  exclusivist　84, 85
  exclusivist position　93
exinanitio　217
existentials　49
Exodus　57
experience　25-33, 36-43, 47,
189-201
  articulated　88, 95-97, 102
  experience of experiences
  28-32
  human interior　90, 91
  mystic　139, 143-146
  of non-being and death　95
  of the Divine　90, 97
  of Transcendence　13-15,
  17-19, 21, 22
  outward articulation　91, 96,
  97
  salvific　96
  sharing　14

exploitation 89, 98, 99
extrapolation 64, 65, 72, 73
faith 3, 4, 11, 38, 42, 43, 106-112, 114
faith and order 91
false gods 261
fanā' 249, 250
Federation of Asian Bishop's Conferences (FABC) 263
fidelitas Dei 91
fides
depositum fidei 91
qua 91, 97, 103
quae 91, 97, 103
fiducia cordis 91
figure of identity 83, 84
finitude 90, 95, 96, 98, 100
finitum non capax infiniti 98
finitum non capax infiniti 98
frame of reference 29, 137
framework 137-139, 141, 144
freedom 30, 35, 36
freedom of religious movement 94
fundamentalism 264
Gāyatrī 146
ghalaba 250, 251
ghayb 245
ghetto 263
glossolalia 81
gnosis 181
God 7, 140-146
God's 245-253
nearness to 252
unicity 245
unification with 245, 246, 249, 250, 252
unity 245, 248, 249, 252
Golgotha 261
gospel
Gospel of John 65, 66, 69
gospel for the poor 99
grace 32, 35, 245, 251-253

event 16
grass roots 53
group
projection 83
guilt 82, 84, 85, 95, 240, 241
guṇas 140
ḥadīth 230, 251
halachah 11
Harijans 163-165, 168-176
Harvard University 55, 57
Hebrews
epistle to the Hebrews 69
Heil 13-18, 21-23, 269, 274
actualization of 15, 22
heretical tendencies 179
hermeneutic 4, 5, 13-21, 23, 31, 47, 72, 99, 101, 102, 120, 125, 137-139, 168, 208, 270, 271, 273, 276, 282.
circle 125
community 137
comparative 31
epistemology 101
faulty 99
new common 101
of religious experience 13
process 137
Hiei, Mt. Hiei (Kyoto) 260
hijrah 79
hikari 223, 224
ḥikma 247
Hīnayāna 190
Hindu 64, 68, 73, 89, 95, 100, 118, 136-138, 140-148, 257, 258, 260
caste system 100
Hindu–Christian 136, 140, 143, 144
revivalism 89
history 106-114
holism 264
holy 33, 37, 38, 42, 43, 90, 91, 96, 103, 109

Holy Scriptures 64, 72, 73
Holy Spirit 65, 103, 255, 264
holy war 261
homa 145
human 107-109, 112-114
  being human 26, 27, 29-37, 42
  completion 29, 32, 33, 37-39
  human division 89
  human nature 197
  nature 28, 30-32, 37, 42
  person 30, 37
  situation 31, 33, 36, 39, 42
humanity 26, 33, 35, 41, 42,
  255, 260, 264
  function fellow-humanity 17
Hymn of Wisdom 67
idea 25-33, 35-37, 39, 40, 43
ideal type 26, 39
identity 117, 136, 138-148
  emotional 136, 140, 142, 143,
    145-147
ideology 53
ignorance 189, 192-194, 200
images 7, 48, 132, 134, 142,
  143, 145, 148
  temple 20
imitation 250
immanence 29, 43
immediacy 117, 118
incarnation 21, 111
inclusivity 39, 43
  inclusivist view 93
  normative inclusiveness 84
incomparable
  Yahweh 108-112, 114
India 4, 5, 89, 95, 97, 145-148,
  163-168, 170, 173, 257, 258,
  263
Indians 57
indication 245-247, 252
individuality 250, 252
Indochina 263
inhumanity 33

injustice 90, 98, 99
inspiration 64-73, 232, 233, 237
integrality 37
integrity 37
inter-canonical application 65,
  69
internodal analogies 129
interreligious
  dialogue 189, 190, 201
  discussion concerning inter-
    religious character of Assisi
    260
  division 89
  overlap 94
  phenomenon 65
intoxication 245, 250, 252
intuitive thrust of the heart 96
iqtidā' 250
ishāra 245-248
Islam 4, 8, 56, 60, 61, 76, 77,
  79-81, 83-86, 106, 111, 117,
  118, 261
  Black Muslims 76, 77, 79-81,
    83-86
Isma'īlī 247
Israel 106-111, 114
iṣṭadevatā 145
Īśvara Saṃhitā 70
Itto-en 224
Jains 257, 258, 261
Japan 215-217, 219-223, 225,
  226, 257, 260, 263
Jeddah 85
Jerusalem 106, 261
Jesuit order 179
Jew 69, 70, 257, 258, 260, 261
Jewish 8, 11, 60, 62
Jews 106, 109, 110, 112
jīvanmuktiḥ 16
jñāna 142, 143
John
  gospel 242
Jordan 264

jorei 223
Judaism 8, 106, 109, 111, 117
justice 89, 90, 98-103, 270, 273
Ka'ba 8, 86
kāhin 66
karma 142, 172
kensho 92
Khalwah 80
khāṣṣ 248
kill 233, 234, 238-241, 243
kingdom 264
knowledge 245, 247, 248, 250, 251
kōan 181, 204, 211-213
Kūrma Purāṇa 71
kyohan 217, 218, 220
language 27, 137, 138, 144, 147
  religious language 82-84
leadership 252
levels 138, 140-143, 145
liberation 9, 16, 20, 68, 88, 99, 101-103, 107, 109, 112, 143, 146, 166, 170, 173, 180, 201, 209, 210, 212, 263, 274
liberative 88, 99, 101-103
  ecumenism 88, 102
  elements 102
  movement of innovation 102, 103
life and work 91, 98
liminal 134
liturgy 145-147
Lord of Creation 77
Lotus of the True Law 71, 73
Lotus sūtra 71, 73, 218
Luke
  gospel 242
Madagascan Confession of Faith 97
Madhvas 163-176
madi 168, 172
Madras 70
magic 52

Mahāprajñāpāramitā 218
mahikari 221-226
  mahikari no waza 223, 225, 226
  Sukyo Mahikari 224
Mahāyāna 71, 190, 195, 200, 261
makoto 224, 225
mantra 146
mantra 67
maṣlaḥah 82
Masters 151-158, 160, 161
meaning
  total 39, 43
  universe of 25, 31
  meaning-making 45, 49
Mecca 85, 86, 234, 235, 241
Medāthiti 71
media evangelists 83
mediation 19, 29, 30, 34, 36, 38, 40, 109, 111, 113
  speaking 17
meditation 48, 141, 144, 145, 191, 192, 198, 199, 201
metaphor 7, 47, 50, 53
metaphysics 108, 112
method 65
mind
  nature of 189
mission 91, 96, 97, 99-102, 256, 261, 262, 264
  Commision on World Mission and Evangelism 102
  evangelism 99, 102
  missiology 88, 97, 100, 101, 274
  World Missionary Conference 101
misunderstanding 47
mitama 223
mīthāq 249, 250
modell Assisi 1986 260
mokṣa 143, 166

monotheism 106, 107, 109-111
Mourides 77, 78
mu 181, 182, 212
muktih 16
Multi-Lateral Dialogue 99
munen muso 181
murīdūn 250-252
mūrtih 20
music 30
Muslim 4, 8, 11, 55-62, 110,
　117, 118, 120, 143, 145, 228,
　229, 232-234, 236-238, 240-242,
　256-258, 260, 261
　Black Muslims 84
　Muslim–Christian 228, 242
mutual
　accountability 88, 94
　conversional mutuality 102
　critical witness 94
　leavening 94
　mutual responsibility 101
　participation 88, 93-96
　seasoning 94
　sharing of guilt 95
muwahhidūn 247
mystery 106, 109, 111-113
mystical 6-8, 11, 111
mysticism 245-247, 249-252
mythical 13, 16-23
　mediation 19
　mythically present 17
　pattern 18
　presence 20
　presence of transcendence 22,
　　23
　mythologization of Transcen-
　　dence 18, 20, 21
narrative 125, 132-134
nature
　nature of things 28
an-nawāfil 251
necessity 27-29
negative 205

philosophy 205
　theology 7, 106, 111
Negro 86
Neo-Platonism 144, 249, 250
Nigeria 76
Nippon Kannon Kyodan 223
nirukta 67
nirvāna 16, 21, 196, 198-201,
　217, 218
non-dual 112
nothingness 205, 206, 212
　absolute 112, 114
　before God 249
novices 245, 250, 251
nyorai-in 224, 225
okiyome 221
omniscience 68
one specimen-centered method
　65
openness 14-17, 22, 205, 208
order 136, 137, 139, 141, 144,
　148
orthodoxy 163, 165, 167, 169,
　170, 229, 232
otherness 39, 40
　God's 245
overlap
　areas of 88, 89, 94, 102, 103
　initial 96
　interreligious 94
　of meaning 94
overwhelming 245, 250-252
Paccekabuddha 68
Paix aux Hommes de Bonne
　Volonté 255, 258
paleo-anthropologist 128
paleo-anthropologists 134
paleolithic 126
Palestine 57
Pañcaratra 70, 72
paradigm 25
paramārtha-satya 195
paramasamhitā 18, 20

participation 136-141, 145-148
    participant observation 46
passivity 29, 42
path
    Buddhist 191, 192, 200
    contemplative 189, 192
peace 89, 98, 100, 103
Pen of Power 76
perception
    of religious phenomena 32
perspective 10, 43
Peter, St. Peter
    epistle 69
phantom 249, 250
phenomenology 48, 127-129
phenomenon
    tradition 13-18, 20, 22
philosophy 26, 38, 40, 41, 142, 145
    of religion 6, 8, 9
piacular intention 83
pilgrimage 85, 86, 142, 145, 148
planetary life 89
pluralization 88-90, 94, 98
pollution 50
polytheism 237, 241, 242
Pontifical Council for Inter-religious Dialogue 256, 259, 260, 262, 263
poor 5, 11, 50, 88-90, 99-103, 273, 274, 282
    religiosity of 100, 101
Pope 255-257, 260
Populorum Progressio 256
possibility
    recovery of 40
possibility of becoming 36
power 45, 46, 51-53
    powerless 89, 100
pragmatism 98
praxis 91, 101-103, 113
    caritatis 91
    common 103

cultus 91
    interreligious 102, 103
    meditationis 91
    pietatis 91
pray together 255-262
prejudice 137, 138
presence 34, 35, 37, 42
projection
    group 83
prophet 69, 70, 73, 77, 78, 80, 245, 250-252
prophetic 106-111, 114, 117, 118, 228-239, 241-243
proximity 249
Psalms 69
psychology 189, 190, 192-194, 196-199
    contemplative 190, 193
    ego 196
pūjā 141, 142, 145
Purāṇas 71
purity 168, 172, 173, 176
Pūrvamīmāṃsā 68, 71
Qādiriyya 77
Qaṣīda al-sudāniyya 77
qawl 251
Qur'ān 55-60, 62, 64, 66, 69, 70, 73, 79, 80, 83, 110, 111, 117, 228, 229, 230-243, 245, 250-252
Qurayshites 237
Rajastan 145
rationalism 98
rationality debate 46
reaching-out 14, 15, 17, 21
    trancendental 21
reality
    absolute 189, 195, 196, 199-201
    cosmotheandric 141
    crisis of social reality 148
    personal 193
    Reality beyond 259-261

relative 189, 194-196, 200, 201
realization
  God-realization 142
  transpersonal 143
reasoning 65, 70, 73
recognition 34, 41
reconciliation 82, 98
reflection 119
  contemplative 92
  missiological 101
  reflective distinctions 28
reincarnation 155, 157, 223
reinterpretation 270, 271, 273, 279, 283
relations
  interpersonal 33, 38, 39
  self-relations 35
relative
  reality 189, 194-196, 200, 201
  relativism 264
  truth 194
religion 13, 15-19, 23, 30-38, 43, 90, 137, 138, 140-147
  Comparative 137
  one 31
  plurality of 257, 263
  popular 52
  theology of 53
  tribal 140
religious
  beliefs 38
  language 82-84
  religious belief 103
  religiously other 90
  tradition 13, 14, 16, 18, 25-27, 30-32, 36-43
religious experience 3-7, 9, 11, 12, 13-18, 20-23, 25, 26, 31, 38, 40, 43, 45, 46, 48-53, 56, 58, 76-86, 88-97, 102, 103, 106, 107, 110, 112-114, 116-119, 125, 129, 130, 133, 136-143, 145-148, 151-153, 156, 158, 160, 163, 164, 166, 178, 189, 192, 200, 208, 209, 229, 245-247, 250, 252, 253, 269, 270, 272, 273, 276, 277, 279, 282, 283
religious specialists 51, 52
repentance 95
representation 35, 42, 43
revelation 8, 9, 17, 19, 65-68, 70, 81, 91-93, 95, 108-112, 118, 130, 131, 133, 151-153, 157-160, 186, 217, 223, 225, 228-232, 242, 246, 250, 261, 277
  bipolar 92
  divine 91, 92
  docetic 93
  essence 92
  final aim and purpose of 95
  particularity 93
  revelatory incident 130, 131, 133
  revelatory event 92
  self-revelation 68
  supernatural disclosure 91
Ṛgveda 67, 68, 70, 141
rite 10, 11, 72, 145, 148, 172, 276, 282, 283
rites
  initiation 145
  Vesak ritual 147
ritual 3, 129, 132-134, 141, 145-148, 167, 168, 172, 180, 219, 272, 276, 277
Rōankyō 211
Rome 255, 257, 262
root
  root of the universe 70
  root of the Veda-tree 70
ṛsi 67, 68
ṛta 67, 68
ru'yā al-ṣāliḥah 79
ruler-philosopher 252

saṁsāra 16, 196-201
saṁskāras 145, 163
sacrifice 139, 141, 143, 145, 147
  yajña 141, 145
saga 234
ṣaḥw 250
Śaivism 70, 140, 145, 148
sakra 250
ṣalāt al-istikhārah 80
salvation 7, 13, 48, 92, 93, 95,
  96, 103, 106-110, 113, 114, 141,
  187, 209, 210, 217, 225, 235,
  262-264, 269, 274, 281
  salvific experience 96
  salvific help 96
  self-redemption 262
  soteriologies 263, 264
  ways of salvation 262
saṁhitās 70, 71
Sammāsambuddha 68
sampradayas 167
saṁvṛti-satya 194
Saṁyutta Nikāya 68
Samyaksambodhi 71
San Antonio 101
sane 250
sangha 165, 168-170, 172-176,
  210
sannyasin 166, 174, 176
Śāriputra 203, 204
satori 92, 178, 181, 183, 184
science 26
scripture 64, 65, 69-71, 73, 144,
  146, 204, 211, 228, 229, 232,
  240
  deluding scriptures 71
seal of the prophets 70
Secretariate for non-Christians
  262
sect 49, 52
secularism 50, 98, 261
  state 176
Sekai Kyuseikyo 222, 223, 226

sekai mahikari unmei kyokai 221
self 25-32, 34-37, 39, 41-43,
  107-109, 112, 113
  self-control 250
  self-image 198
  self-mediating 15, 16
  openness 15
Senegal 77
senses 125-131, 134
  auditory 127-131
  gustator 129, 130
  olfactory 126, 130
  sense apparatus 126-128
  sense world 127
  sensorium 125, 127-130, 134
  six sense faculties 193, 195
  visual 128, 129
Seoul 257
shabaḥ/shabh 248-250
shahādah 77
Shaker 79
shape 247-249, 252
sharing 45-50, 52, 53, 90, 99,
  101, 103, 203, 207, 208, 210,
  212, 213
  authentic 92, 95, 101
  communicate 116
  communication 26-30, 37
  complementary apprehensions
    of Truth 98
  essential conditions 93
  granting a share 18
  heart to heart 97
  limits to 94
  mind to mind 97
  mutual participat 88, 93-96
  mutuality 225
  of guilt 95
  possibility of 50, 51
  religious experience 14, 22,
    23
  soul to soul 95
  spirit to spirit 97

Shentong school 200
shin shin-shukyo 215, 219-221, 223, 224, 226
shinkoshukyo 219, 222-224, 226
Shinto 217, 218, 220-222, 224, 257, 258, 260
shukyo 215, 219-224, 226
ṣifāt 250
signification 46, 48, 51-53
signs 28, 35
Sikh 257, 258
skandha 197
sobriety 245, 250, 252
social 3, 4, 11
  social bifurcation 89
social change 163
soteriological
  auto- 91, 92
  deo- 91
soul 29, 116
spirit 65, 66, 69, 70, 73
  Holy Spirit 65, 103, 255, 264
spirituality 264
Ṣri Kapaleeswarar Temple 70
subhaniyya 117
subject 13-16, 21, 22, 90, 92
  specific receptive capacities 92
  subjectivity 90
suchness 200
suffering 191, 193, 196, 197
  saṁsāra 196-201
ṣufī 8, 145, 245-247
sukyo 221, 224
śūnyatā 6, 8, 195, 203-213, 217
Sura 7:172/171 249, 250
surrender
  to transcendence 22
sūtra 62, 203, 217, 218
Sword of Truth 79
symbol 9, 11, 35, 38, 39, 41, 43, 45-52, 55, 56, 82-84, 113, 137, 138, 141-148, 172, 176, 205,

208, 222, 225, 247, 257, 270-272, 274, 282, 283
symbolical 83, 84
Vedāntic 147
syncretism 45, 48, 52, 99, 215, 216, 218, 262, 263
synesthetic 128, 131
synthesis 32, 33, 36-38, 42
tactics 71
Taḥrīf 70
ṭarīqah 79
task
  religious 25, 26, 34-39, 41-43
tathatā 195, 200
tawfīq 251
tawḥīd 245, 247-249
teacher 245, 250, 252
tekazashi 225, 226
Testament 64, 65, 69, 70, 72, 73, 108, 109, 206, 230, 233, 242, 243, 261, 272
testimony 13, 17, 18, 22, 88
  fellow-human 17
Theologisches 260, 261
theologoumena 94
theology
  negative 106, 111
  of religion 93, 255, 256, 262, 263
theonomous
  character of reality 96
theosophic 84, 151, 153, 155-158, 161
Theravāda 64, 68, 190
things as they are 189, 195, 200
Tipiṭaka 64, 68, 71
tradition 66, 67
  communio 14, 17, 18, 21-23
  cumulative 151, 153, 155-159
  phenomenon of 13-18, 20, 22
  principle of 18
  religious 13, 14, 16, 18, 25-27, 30-32, 36-43

trance 151-154, 156-161
transcendence 3, 6-8, 11, 13-23, 25, 37-39, 43, 109, 116, 117, 118-120, 245
  mythologization of 18, 20, 21
  surrender to 16, 18, 22, 23
  the Transcendent 67, 73
  transcendental principle 39
  transcendental Wherefore 17
transcendent 90, 91
transformation 90, 95
  ethical 85
transition 34, 35
transitoriness 107-109, 112
translation 27, 32
transmission 189-192, 199, 201
transmit 96
tribalized deity 93
trinity 111
tropes 131
trust
  confident trust 18
truth 25-28, 33, 36-38, 40-43, 191
  monopoly of 84
  relative 194
  truth-claims 97
TV evangelism 61
ʽulamā 78
ultimate concern 5
unbelief 238
understanding 35
  abstract 43
unification with God 245, 246, 249, 250, 252
unique 107-109, 111, 112, 114
uniqueness 94
United Nations 256
unity 25-27, 29-31, 36-40, 42, 43
universality 28, 31, 37, 39, 41-43, 120
universalized idol 93
upāya 142, 217

Vāc 67, 68
Vaiṣṇavism 70, 140, 145, 148, 167, 169, 174
Varsavia, Poland 260
Vāsudeva 70
Vatican II 179, 255, 256, 259, 262, 263
  Commission Justitia et Pax 256
  Council for Interreligious Dialogue 256, 259, 260, 262, 263
  Paix aux Hommes de Bonne Volonté 255, 258
Vedāntic 140, 142, 147
Vedic religion 64, 67, 68, 70-72, 141
Victorines 181
vijñāna 193
vision 76-81, 86
Vyasakuta 167, 172
waḥdāniyya 248, 249
waḥy 66, 67, 69
waqfa 249
wāridāt 76
WCC 5, 100-102, 257
  Commision on World Mission and Evangelism 102
  Sub-Unit on Dialogue 100, 102
  World Conference on Religion and Peace 256, 259
wholeness 37, 42, 43, 269-271, 276, 283
witness 65, 66, 69, 73, 88, 91, 93, 94, 100-102
word 27, 28, 38
  word of God 229, 230, 232, 242, 264
world
  world disorder 89
  world problems 53
  world structure of apartheid 89

World Conference on Religion
   and Peace 256, 259
World Missionary Conference
   101
World Year for Peace 256
yajña 141, 145
yatra 148
yearn 98
   for transcendence 96
yin/yang 264
ẓāhir 247, 248, 252
Zen 4, 8, 92, 106, 111-114, 147,
   178-187, 204, 211, 212, 274,
   278, 279
   Bompu 182
   Daijō 182
   Gedō 182
   kensho 92
   Saijōjō 182
   satori 92
   Shōjō 182
Zoroastrian 258

Contributors

HASAN ASKARI, Islamic Thought, Ilkley, West Yorkshire.

MICHAEL von BRÜCK, Comparative Religion, University of Regensburg.

CORSTIAAN J. G. van der BURG, Indology and Comparative Religion, Faculty of Theology, Free University: Amsterdam.

ARNULF CAMPS, O. F. M., Missiology, Faculty of Theology, University of Nijmegen. Wijchen.

HANS DAIBER, Arabic Studies, Faculty of Semitic Languages, Free University: Amsterdam.

ANDRÉ DROOGERS, Cultural Anthroplogy, Faculty of Social-Cultural Studies, Free University: Amsterdam.

WILLEM DUPRÉ, Philosophy of Religion, Faculty of Theology, University of Nijmegen: Nijmegen.

JAMES W. FERNANDEZ, Cultural Anthropology, Princeton University: Princeton.

REIN FERNHOUT, Comparative Religion, Faculty of Theology, Free University: Amsterdam.

JERALD D. GORT, Missiology and Evangelism, Faculty of Theology, Free University: Amsterdam.

JACQUES KAMSTRA, Comparative Religion and the History and Phenomenology of non-Christian Religions, Faculty of Theology, University of Amsterdam.

R. KRANENBORG, New Religious Movements, Faculty of Theology, Free University: Amsterdam.

GERHARD OBERHAMMER, Indology, Institute for Indology, University of Vienna.

LAMIN SANNEH, Missiology, Yale Divinity School: New Haven, Connecticut.

WILFRED CANTWELL SMITH, Center for the Study of World Religions, Harvard University. Toronto.

WALTER STROLZ, Philosophy of Religion, Former Moderator of the Publications Program on Interreligious Encounter for the Herder Verlag: Innsbruck.

TILMANN VETTER, Buddhist Studies and Indology, Faculty of Letters, Rijksuniversiteit of Leiden.

HENDRIK M. VROOM, Philosophy of Religion, Faculty of Theology, Free University: Amsterdam.

H. WALDENFELS, Philosophy of Religion, Faculty of Theology, University of Bonn: Bonn.

ANTON WESSELS, History of Religions and Missiology, Faculty of Theology, Free University: Amsterdam.

HAN F. de WIT, Theoretical Psychology, Faculty of Psychology and Education, Free University: Amsterdam.